PENGUIN CLASSICS

# FIVE ITALIAN RENAISSANCE COMEDIES

NICCOLÒ MACHIAVELLI (1469–1527) was first and foremost a politician and political theorist. He held office under the Florentine Republic from 1498 to 1512, but was disgraced and lost his employment. His fame chiefly rests on *The Prince* and the *Discourses*, but he was also a formidable historian and, as this volume shows, playwright.

LUDOVICO ARIOSTO (1474–1533) was born in Reggio Emilia, but spent most of his life at the court of Ferrara, where he served the ducal family of Este loyally as courtier, administrator and court poet. His masterpiece is the *Orlando Furioso*, an epic of chivalry in which he displayed unsurpassed narrative gifts and poetic mastery.

PIETRO ARETINO (1492–1556) was born in Arezzo, made his literary reputation in Rome under the Medici Popes, and eventually settled in Venice after a stay at the court of Mantua in 1526–7. His most important work was the *Letters*, which provide a shrewd and witty insight into the character of the Italian Renaissance; but he also wrote some religious works and the scandalous *Sei Giornate*, which is a series of dialogues about the seamier side of sexual life in the Italian cities.

GL'INTRONATI of Siena were a literary and dramatic circle who flourished in that city in the sixteenth century. Whether *The Deceived* is really the product of a collaboration is not known; the first edition (1538) is claimed on the title page to be the collective responsibility of the whole group.

GIAMBATTISTA GUARINI (1538–1612), like Ariosto, was a courtier who served his prince in a number of different capacities – diplomatic and administrative as well as literary. Ferrara was both his birthplace and the scene of the greater part of his adult career, though he also served in the courts of Florence and Urbino.

# FIVE ITALIAN
# RENAISSANCE COMEDIES

*Machiavelli:* The Mandragola
*Ariosto:* Lena
*Aretino:* The Stablemaster
*Gl'Intronati:* The Deceived
*Guarini:* The Faithful Shepherd

*edited by*
**BRUCE PENMAN**

PENGUIN BOOKS

PENGUIN BOOKS

Published by the Penguin Group
27 Wrights Lane, London W8 5TZ, England
Viking Penguin Inc., 40 West 23rd Street, New York, New York 10010, USA
Penguin Books Australia Ltd, Ringwood, Victoria, Australia
Penguin Books Canada Ltd, 2801 John Street, Markham, Ontario, Canada L3R 1B4
Penguin Books (NZ) Ltd, 182–190 Wairau Road, Auckland 10, New Zealand

Penguin Books Ltd, Registered Offices: Harmondsworth, Middlesex, England

This selection first published 1978
3 5 7 9 10 8 6 4 2

Printed and bound in Great Britain by
Cox & Wyman Ltd, Reading
Set in Bembo

To Jennifer

# CONTENTS

# EDITOR'S FOREWORD

The academic definition of a comedy requires that it should have a happy ending, while the popular definition merely insists that it should be funny. All the five plays in this selection satisfy both these criteria, but they show great variety in other respects. They have been chosen to illustrate as many different strands as possible in the varied fabric of Italian Renaissance life and thought.

Three of the plays do indeed derive much of their humour from the common theme of the vices of private society. But *The Mandragola* also satirizes the corruption of the clergy; the *Lena* criticizes with surprising freedom the shortcomings of the administration of the dukedom where the author was the court poet; and *The Stablemaster* exemplifies the extraordinary Renaissance passion for prolonged, elaborate and often heartless practical jokes.

*The Deceived* illustrates the Italian genius for light-weight comedy, bordering on farce. It tells a good story primarily in order to amuse, without satirical intention. It is also of special interest as an earlier treatment of the theme of *Twelfth Night*.

*The Faithful Shepherd* reminds us that the Renaissance was a time of supreme artistic achievement as well as one of amusing intrigue and interesting depravity. It takes us into a world of pure beauty, remote from this life and full of wonders, like the great allegorical pictures of Renaissance art; yet it is a world peopled with real human beings, and full of action, wit and humour.

Each of the five comedies has a prologue, written by the author for a specific individual performance, and these are generally printed with the plays in Italian editions. They have however been omitted in the present volume, because they have little connection with the action of the plays, and tend to generate a disproportionate number of explanatory footnotes. *The Mandragola* has a second set of accompanying verses, also written for a specific performance, and these too have been omitted – with some regret, for they are among Machiavelli's best poems.

Further information on the authors and their work is contained in the introductory notes which precede the individual plays.

Stage directions are very scanty in the printed texts of these early plays, and we feel we should make it clear that most of the stage directions in the present volume have been contributed by the translators or the editor.

# ACKNOWLEDGEMENTS

The editor and translators would like to express their thanks for advice on the selection of texts and on specific points of interpretation to Professor J. H. Whitfield, Professor G. Aquilecchia, Professor John Scott and Mr Wilfred Cameron-Curry.

The editor's special thanks are also due to Mr William E. Simeone, who, together with the late Mr Walter F. Staton, Jr, edited the admirable critical edition of Fanshawe's translation of *The Faithful Shepherd* which was published by the Oxford University Press in 1964. Mr Simeone has kindly given us permission to make any use we wished of his work, and his introduction, text and notes have been of the greatest value to us.

We should also like to thank Mr Richard Andrews for some extremely valuable suggestions.

None of those mentioned above bear any responsibility for any mistakes in this volume.

# THE MANDRAGOLA

*(La Mandragola)*

*by*

NICCOLÒ MACHIAVELLI
*(1469–1527)*

# NICCOLÒ MACHIAVELLI

NICCOLÒ MACHIAVELLI (1469–1527) was first and foremost a politician and political theorist. He held fairly high office under the Florentine Republic from 1498 to 1512, but was disgraced and lost his employment after the return of the Medici in the latter year. His international fame is based primarily on his main political writings – *The Prince* (completed 1513; published 1532) and the *Discourses* (1519). He was also a distinguished historian (*Florentine History*, 1525) and the author of what is generally considered to be the best comedy in the Italian language – *The Mandragola*. (The other two plays to be found in his collected works are translations or adaptations from Terence and Plautus.)

There are many English translations of Machiavelli's main political and historical works, among which we may mention *The Prince*, translated by George Bull, Penguin Classics, 1961. *The Mandragola* has also been translated several times before – by Stark Young in 1927, by Anne and Henry Paolucci in 1957, by Frederick May and E. R. Bentley in 1958 and by J. R. Hale in 1961. There is also a very free adaptation by Ashley Dukes.

The text on which the present translation of *The Mandragola* is based is that edited by Roberto Ridolfi from a recently discovered manuscript and published by Leo S. Olschki in 1965.

# CHARACTERS

in order of appearance

CALLIMACO, in love with Lucrezia
SIRO, Callimaco's servant
MESSER NICIA, Lucrezia's husband
LIGURIO, a parasite
SOSTRATA, Lucrezia's mother
FRATE TIMOTEO, a friar
WOMAN, a parishioner of Frate Timoteo
LUCREZIA, Messer Nicia's wife

# ACT ONE

*A row of houses bordering a square in Florence.* CALLIMACO's *house to the Left,* MESSER NICIA's *to the Right, with one or two buildings in between, including a church, Centre. To the Right of* MESSER NICIA's *house is a street corner.*

[CALLIMACO *is standing outside his own front door with his servant* SIRO, *who is on the point of going.* CALLIMACO *calls him back.*]

CALLIMACO: Don't go, Siro; I want you.

SIRO: Here I am, sir.

CALLIMACO: I expect you were surprised by my sudden departure from Paris; and now you must be wondering why I've been here in Florence for a whole month without doing anything.

SIRO: You're right there, sir.

CALLIMACO: If I haven't told you the whole story before, it doesn't mean I don't trust you. But if a man doesn't want something generally known, I think it's best for him not to say a word about it till he has to. Now I can see I may need your help, so I'm going to tell you everything.

SIRO: I'm your servant, sir, and servants should never ask their masters any questions, or pry into what they do. But if our masters want to tell us something, it's up to us to serve them faithfully, as I always have, and always shall.

CALLIMACO: I know you have.

Well, you must have heard this bit ninety-nine times already, but it won't hurt you if we make it up to the round hundred. My parents were both dead by the time I was ten years old, and my guardians sent me to Paris, where I stayed for twenty years in all. I'd been there for ten of them, when King Charles VIII invaded Italy, which was the beginning of the wars that have ruined the country, and I decided to stay in Paris and never come home to Florence, because I judged that I could live more safely in France than here.

SIRO: Yes, sir.

CALLIMACO: So I had all my property in Florence sold up, except for my house, and settled down in Paris, where I lived very happily for a further ten years.

SIRO: I know, sir.

CALLIMACO: I devoted part of my time to study, part to pleasure, and part to business; and I took care not to let one of these occupations get in the way of another. In this way, as you know, I led a very quiet life, doing my best for everybody, and trying not to harm anyone, so that I got on well with gentlemen and tradesmen, with Parisians and foreigners, and with rich and poor.

SIRO: Yes, sir.

CALLIMACO: But the fates must have thought I was having too easy a life, and the next thing that happened was that Cammillo Calfucci turned up in Paris.

SIRO: I can almost guess what the trouble is, now.

CALLIMACO: Like the other Florentines in Paris, he was often my guest. One day there was an argument whether the most beautiful girls were to be found in Italy or in France. I couldn't say much about the Italian girls, having been so young when I last saw them. So Cammillo took the Italian side, and one of the other Florentines who was there argued for the French ladies. There was a lot said on both sides, but finally Cammillo got quite heated about it, and claimed that even if all the other Italian women were Gorgons, there was a girl in his family who'd win the competition for them all by herself.

SIRO: Now I know what's coming next.

CALLIMACO: And he named Madonna Lucrezia, the wife of Messer Nicia Calfucci. He praised her beauty and her goodness so highly that we were all amazed. He made me want to see her so badly that I forgot everything else, stopped worrying about whether Italy were in peace or at war, and came here as fast as I could. And now I'm here, I can see that the reality is far above the rumour – which doesn't often happen. And I long for her company so much that I don't know where to put myself.

SIRO: If you'd spoken to me in Paris, I'd have known what to say; but now I don't know how to advise you.

CALLIMACO: It's not so much that I need your advice, as that I had to get the story off my chest, and that you must be making up your mind to help me when I need it.

SIRO: It's made up already, sir. But what hope of success do you see in this?

CALLIMACO: None at all.

SIRO: Why d'you say that, sir?

CALLIMACO: I'll tell you.

First of all because of her character. She's very honest, and not at all given to thoughts of romance.

Then her husband's very rich, and lets her have her own way in everything; and though he's not young, he's not really old either, it seems.

And she never joins in with relations or neighbours on the eve of a feast-day, or on the feast-day itself, or any other kind of pleasant occasion when young women generally enjoy themselves.

No work-people of any kind enter her house, and she's got no servants who aren't right under her thumb. I can't see who I can bribe.

SIRO: What do you think you can do, then, sir?

CALLIMACO: You won't find many cases so desperate that there's no loophole for hope. That hope may well be a weak and useless sort of thing, but if a man has the will and the desire to make it come true, it won't seem like that to him.

SIRO: So what gives you hope in this case?

CALLIMACO: Two things.

First, the simple nature of Messer Nicia, who is the silliest and most foolish man in Florence, though he's a doctor of law.

The second thing is that they're both longing to have children. They've been married six years now, and there's no sign of a baby. They've got plenty of money and they're desperate to start a family.

And a third point – there's her mother, who wasn't too fussy herself when she was younger. But she's got plenty of money too, so I don't see how to make use of that.

SIRO: But have you tried to do anything yet?

CALLIMACO: Yes, I have. But it doesn't amount to much.

SIRO: What was it, then?

CALLIMACO: You know Ligurio, who's always coming to dinner

with us. He used to be a marriage broker, but now he lives mainly by cadging meals where he can. And because he's an amusing fellow, Nicia keeps on quite close terms with him, and gets cheated for his pains. Ligurio doesn't get asked to Nicia's house for dinner, but he does manage to borrow money from him from time to time. I've made friends with Ligurio, and told him about my love for Lucrezia.

He's promised to help me in every way he can.

SIRO: Mind he doesn't fool *you*, then! You can't trust these spongers very far.

CALLIMACO: That's quite true. But once you've given a man a job to do, and he knows there's something in it for him, it's best to assume that he'll carry it out faithfully. I've promised him a good sum of money if it comes off; and if it doesn't, he's to get a couple of free meals anyway. At least I shan't have to eat by myself.

SIRO: What's he promised to do so far?

CALLIMACO: To persuade Messer Nicia to take his wife to the baths some time in May.

SIRO: How would that help you, sir?

CALLIMACO: Help me? Why, the change of scene may alter her outlook, for life's one long series of festivities in a place like that. And I'll go there too, bringing with me everything imaginable that may give her pleasure, and showing all the generosity I can. I'll become an intimate friend of Madonna Lucrezia and her husband. How do I know what'll happen? One thing leads to another, and time turns them the way it will.

SIRO: That sounds all right.

CALLIMACO: When Ligurio went off this morning, he promised to speak to Messer Nicia about it, and let me know what he said.

SIRO: I can see them coming along the street now.

CALLIMACO: I think I'll step aside for a minute, so that I can get hold of Ligurio when he takes leave of the lawyer. You go back indoors and get on with your work. If I want you for anything I'll tell you.

SIRO: Yes, sir.

[*Exeunt separately* CALLIMACO *and* SIRO. *Enter* NICIA *and* LIGURIO, *from round street corner, Right.*]

NICIA: I know your advice is very good, very good indeed, and I spoke to the wife about it last night. She said she'd give me her answer today; but to tell you the truth I don't take to the idea very much myself.

LIGURIO: Why's that?

NICIA: Because I don't fancy all this to-ing and fro-ing. And having to drag wives, maids, and kitchen utensils all over the place doesn't suit me. And then there's another thing – I had a chat about all this last night with several doctors. One tells me to go to San Filippo, another to Porretta, and another somewhere else. They looked like a lot of boobies to me; and to tell you the truth, I don't believe some of these doctors of medicine know what they're talking about.

LIGURIO: But I expect the main point is the one you mentioned first – that you aren't used to being out of sight of the great dome of Florence Cathedral.

NICIA: You're quite wrong there. When I was young, I was a great wanderer. Why, I never missed the Prato Fair, and there isn't a castle round here that I haven't visited, and that's not all – I've been to Pisa and Leghorn – so there!

LIGURIO: At Pisa, you must have seen the famous Leaning Spire?

NICIA [puzzled for a moment; then triumphantly]: Leaning Tower, you mean!

LIGURIO: Ah yes, the Leaning Tower, of course. And while you were at Leghorn, did you see the sea?

NICIA: Of course I did – what d'you think?

LIGURIO: How much bigger would you say it was than the Arno?

NICIA: Arno, indeed! Why, it's four times as big – six times as big – more than seven times as big, since you ask – and wherever you look it's all water . . . water . . . water . . . !

LIGURIO: One thing that puzzles me, since you've lifted your leg against so many signposts, is why you make such a fuss about going a few miles to take the waters.

NICIA: Good heavens, you are green! Haven't you any idea what it's like to uproot a whole household? But I'm so anxious to start a family, that I'm ready to do anything. But you go and have a word with those learned gentlemen yourself, and see which baths they really think would be best for me to visit. I'll just go in and see the wife, and you and I can have another talk later on.

LIGURIO: Good!

[*Exit* NICIA.]

I don't believe there's a sillier man than that alive in the world today; and yet how fortune has heaped her favours on him! All that money, *and* a lovely wife, wise, virtuous and fit in every way to be a queen. The old proverb about birds of a feather doesn't seem to apply very well to marriages, for we often find that an able fellow gets a fool for a wife, or a sensible woman is paired off with an idiot. But the idiocy of Messer Nicia has this much good in it, that it gives Callimaco some grounds for hope.

But here he is.

[*Enter* CALLIMACO, *furtively*.]

LIGURIO: Lying in wait for someone, Callimaco?

CALLIMACO: No, I saw you with the lawyer, and I was waiting for you to finish with him, so that I could ask you what you'd done.

LIGURIO: Well, you know what he's like – not very sensible, not very brave. He doesn't want to leave Florence, but I encouraged him a bit, and in the end he agreed to everything. I'm pretty sure that if we still want him to go to the baths, he'll go; but I don't know if that'll really serve our turn.

CALLIMACO: Why not?

LIGURIO: Well . . . People of every sort go to these watering-places. Someone else might turn up who liked Madonna Lucrezia as much as you do – someone with more money than you, or more charm. So you'd run the risk of taking all that trouble for another man's benefit.

Or having a great flock of admirers round her might make her more on her guard than ever. And if she does take kindly to it in the end, she may pick someone else instead of you.

CALLIMACO: That's all perfectly true, I know. But what am I to do? What decision can I take? Which way shall I turn? I must try something, even if it's a strange or dangerous thing that I do, or wicked, or dishonourable. I'd rather die than live like this. If I could sleep at night, or eat my food, or talk to people, or find pleasure in anything in the world, I'd be more patient about waiting till the right moment comes. But there's no way out. If I can't find a plan that'll give me some degree of hope, I shall die anyway; and with death before my eyes I'm not going to stop at anything –

I shall grasp at any course of action, no matter how crazy, cruel or infamous it may be.

LIGURIO: Don't talk like that, Callimaco. Try to banish these violent thoughts.

CALLIMACO: You can see well enough that if I banish them it's only to make room for more of the same kind … We must either get on with the plan of sending that fellow to the baths, or start something else that'll give me some hope. If it isn't real hope, never mind – I'll settle for false hopes as long as they keep me in a train of thought that will do something to lessen my agony.

LIGURIO: You're right. I will do something for you at once.

CALLIMACO: And I believe you, though I know that your sort live by cheating other men. I don't think that arises between us, though, because if you did cheat me and I found out about it, I'd have my own back on you, and you'd lose both the present advantage of having the run of my house and the future reward I've promised you.

LIGURIO: You needn't have any doubts about me, for even if it weren't for your present kindness and future promises, I feel a sort of natural kinship with you, and I want you to get your heart's desire almost as much as you do yourself. But no more of that. The lawyer has given me the task of finding a doctor who'll decide which are the best baths for him to visit. Now I want you to do exactly what I say. Pretend that you've studied medicine, and practised it in Paris. He'll believe everything you say, both because he's a fool and because you're a well-read man who can speak to him in Latin.

CALLIMACO: What use is that to us?

LIGURIO: It could help us to pack him off to whichever baths we choose, and it could help towards another plan I've got in my head, which is quicker, safer and more likely to work than any baths in the world.

CALLIMACO: What do you mean?

LIGURIO: I mean that if you show a bit of spirit, and if you trust in me, I'll fix the whole thing up for you by this time tomorrow. And if Messer Nicia had enough sense in his head to think of checking whether you're a doctor or not, which I'm sure he hasn't, there's so little time and the plan's of such a kind that he probably won't think of it, and it won't do us any harm if he does.

CALLIMACO: You've given me new life. This is a promise I can hardly believe, a hope I can scarcely grasp. But how will you do it?

LIGURIO: I'll tell you my plan later – not now, because we've barely time to carry it out, let alone talk about it. Go indoors and wait for me there; I'll go and find the lawyer. If I bring him round to see you later on, just follow my line of talk and adapt yourself to what I say.

CALLIMACO: Very well – though I'm afraid the hope you've given me is only a will o' the wisp.

[CALLIMACO *goes into his house. Exit* LIGURIO, *Left.*]

# ACT TWO

*Scene as in* ACT ONE.

[NICIA, LIGURIO *enter from Right. They walk slowly across stage towards* CALLIMACO's *house during following conversation.*]

LIGURIO: As I was saying, sir, I think God must have sent this man here specially to grant your wishes. He's done wonders in Paris; and you needn't be surprised that he hasn't been practising here in Florence. For one thing, he doesn't need the money, and for another, he's going back to Paris any time now.

NICIA: *Is* he, indeed? – I wouldn't like it if he got me in the soup and then went off and left me stranded.

LIGURIO: Don't worry about that, sir; the only fear is that he won't take your case on. If he does, he won't let go till he sees the end of it.

NICIA: Well, I'll take your word as far as that part of it goes. But as for him being a man of learning, that's something I'll tell you myself when I've met him. He won't pull the wool over *my* eyes!

LIGURIO: I know that, sir, and that's why I'm taking you to see him, so that you can talk to him yourself. And if his presence, his learning, and his way of speech don't convince you that you can trust him like a child trusts its mother, never believe me again.

NICIA: So be it, in the sweet name of Jesus! Let's go at once! But where is he staying?

LIGURIO: In this square – that's his front door.

NICIA: Good, good. Give him a knock.

LIGURIO [*knocking*]: There you are, then.

SIRO [*from inside*]: Who's there?

LIGURIO: Is Callimaco at home?

SIRO: Yes, sir.

NICIA: Why don't you call him *Dr* Callimaco?

LIGURIO: He doesn't care for all that nonsense.

NICIA: Don't talk like that! Give him his proper title, and if he doesn't like it he can do the other thing!

[*Enter* CALLIMACO.]

CALLIMACO: Who wants me?

NICIA: *Bona dies, domine magister.*

CALLIMACO: *Et vobis bona, domine praeclarissime!*

LIGURIO: What do you think of that?

NICIA: My goodness! Tremendous!

LIGURIO: If you want me to stay here with you, you must talk in a way I can understand. Otherwise I'll leave you to it.

CALLIMACO: What do you wish to discuss?

NICIA: I don't know, really . . . I'm trying to do two things which another man might want to avoid – to make trouble for myself and for other people, you might say. I've no child, and I want one. I'm giving you a headache so that I can have a headache myself.

CALLIMACO: It will always give me great pleasure to help you, or any other worthy and honourable man like yourself. I spent many years studying in Paris, and what would the use of that be if I didn't do all I could for people like you?

NICIA: Thank you very much; and if you ever need my professional services, I'll help you most gladly. But let's return *ad rem nostram.* Have you considered which of these watering-places is most likely to help my wife to conceive? Ligurio has told you about my problem, I know.

CALLIMACO: Yes, indeed; but if we are to satisfy your wishes, we must know the reason for your wife's barrenness – and there is more than one possibility. *Nam causae sterilitatis sunt: aut in semine, aut in matrice, aut in instrumentis seminariis, aut in virga, aut in causa extrinseca.*

NICIA: This is the finest fellow you could ever wish to meet!

CALLIMACO: Then again, the cause could lie in impotence on your own side; and in that case there would be no hope of a cure at all.

NICIA: Impotent? Me? I can't help laughing at that! I don't believe there's a harder case or a better performer in Florence than I am!

CALLIMACO: Well, if we can exclude that possibility, you may rest assured that a cure will be found.

NICIA: Isn't there anything else but going to the baths that will do the trick? I don't fancy all that upheaval, and the wife doesn't like leaving Florence.

LIGURIO: Yes, there is another way – I can answer for that. Callimaco overdoes the caution sometimes. [*Turning to* CALLIMACO.] Didn't you tell me that you knew how to prepare a certain potion that's sure to make a woman conceive?

CALLIMACO: Yes, I did. But I go a bit carefully with strangers, because I don't want them to think I'm a charlatan.

NICIA: You needn't worry about me. You've already impressed me so much with your talents that I'd believe anything you say and do anything you advise.

LIGURIO: You'll have to see a specimen, I suppose.

CALLIMACO: Oh, yes; we can't do anything without that.

LIGURIO: It'd be best to call Siro, then. Messer Nicia can take him home and give him the specimen, and he can bring it back here. We'll wait for him indoors.

CALLIMACO: Siro! [*Enter* SIRO.] Go with this gentleman. Messer Nicia – if you'd like to come back with Siro straight away, we can begin to plan for better things at once.

NICIA: 'If I'd *like* to', did you say? I'll be back in a couple of seconds, for I've more faith in you than a Hungarian has in his sword.

[CALLIMACO *and* LIGURIO *go into* CALLIMACO's *house.* NICIA *and* SIRO *walk slowly across the stage towards* NICIA's *front door.*]

NICIA: That master of yours is a very able fellow.

SIRO: Even abler than you say, sir.

NICIA: The King of France must think a lot of him.

SIRO: He does indeed.

NICIA: And that's why your master's so fond of living in France.

SIRO: Very true, sir.

NICIA: And it shows his sense. They're a miserable lot here in Florence. Ability counts for nothing. If he settled here, there'd be no one of his calibre to keep him company. I know what I'm talking about, for I had the devil of a job to learn the bit of Latin I know; and if I'd had to earn my living by what I've learnt, I'd be in trouble, I can tell you!

SIRO: I wonder if you earn a hundred ducats a year?

NICIA: A hundred ducats, indeed! I don't earn a hundred lire! The reason is that if you haven't got the powers that be on your side,

in Florence among people of my profession, you can't get even a
dog to notice you as you walk past, and we're fit for nothing but
to go to funerals and weddings, or to waste the whole day twiddl-
ing our thumbs on a bench in the Proconsul's office.[1] But I don't
give a damn for them, I don't need anyone's help; I only wish everyone was as well off as I am. But don't go quoting me, or I'll get a
swingeing fine, or a touch of the whip [*rubbing his posterior*] that'll
make me caper properly.

SIRO: You can trust me, sir.

NICIA: But here we are; this is my house. Wait for me here; I'll be
back in a minute.

SIRO: Very well.

[*Exit* NICIA.]

SIRO: If all lawyers were like this one, they'd have the rest of us
banging our heads against brick walls in no time.

There's no doubt about it, that blackguard Ligurio and my
lunatic of a master are going to lead him by the nose into some very
dishonourable situation. And I'd be glad to see it happen, if I could
be sure it wouldn't come out; but if it does, I risk my life, and my
master risks both life and property. He's already turned himself into
a doctor . . . I don't know what their plan is, nor what the object
of all these lies can be.

But here's the lawyer, back again with a piss-pot in his hand.
Who could help laughing at the sight of this booby?

[*Enter* NICIA, *carrying a chamber pot.*]

NICIA [*speaking over his shoulder to his wife offstage*]: I do what you
want nine times out of ten, so it's right that you should do what I
want for once. If I'd known there'd be all this trouble over starting
a family, I'd rather have married a peasant girl in the first place . . .
[*to* SIRO] Is that you over there, Siro? Come along . . . You'd never
believe what trouble I had with Madame Ignorance in there before
she'd give me this specimen. [*Giving* SIRO *the pot.*] Yet it's not that
she doesn't want to have children; she's even keener on the idea
than I am; but when I try to get her to do anything, it's always the
same story.

SIRO: You must be patient, sir. Most ladies can be persuaded to do
what you want with a few sweet words.

1. The Proconsul was a senior legal officer in the Florentine Republic.

NICIA: Sweet words indeed! I've just had an earful, I can tell you! But be off with you now, and tell the doctor and Ligurio that I'm ready for them.

SIRO: They're coming now, sir.

[*Enter* LIGURIO *and* CALLIMACO.]

LIGURIO [*to* CALLIMACO]: It'll be easy enough to talk the lawyer into it; the difficulty's going to be to persuade the lady, but we'll find a way of doing that too.

CALLIMACO [*to* NICIA]: Where's the specimen?

NICIA: Siro's got it, under his cloak.

CALLIMACO: Let me see ... Oh! This specimen plainly shows a weakness of the kidneys.

NICIA: It looks a bit cloudy to me; and yet she only did it a moment ago.

CALLIMACO: There's no reason to be surprised at that. *Nam mulieris urinae sunt semper maioris grossitei et albedinis, et minoris pulchritudinis, quam virorum. Huius autem, inter caetera, causa est amplitudo canalium, mixtio eorum quae ex matrice exeunt cum urina.*

NICIA: Oh! Oh! Goodness me! He gets better and better while you listen to him! See how well he speaks about these things!

CALLIMACO: I fear the patient may not be well covered at night, and perhaps that may cause the poor quality of her urine.

NICIA: She always has a good quilt over her; but then she'll spend three or four hours on her knees stringing paternosters together before she comes to bed, and she's as strong as a horse when it comes to standing the cold.

CALLIMACO: Well now, sir, the question is, have you faith in me, or haven't you; and do you want me to tell you a certain remedy or don't you? I'm quite ready to give it to you, for my part. If you have faith in me, you shall have the remedy, and if your wife doesn't have a baby in her arms by this time next year ... why then I wouldn't mind if I had to give you two thousand ducats.

NICIA: Go on then, sir – I'm ready to give you credit for everything, and ready to believe you more than my own confessor.

CALLIMACO: Then first of all you must understand that there is no more certain way to get a woman pregnant than to give her an infusion of mandragora to drink. This is something I've prescribed myself several times, and I've always found that it works. And if it weren't for this, the Queen of France would be barren, and several other princesses of that noble state besides.

NICIA: It's almost incredible!

CALLIMACO: And fortune has been kind to you indeed, for I've got everything here with me that's needed to make the infusion, so that you can have it whenever you like.

NICIA: When should she take it then?

CALLIMACO: This evening after supper, for the moon's in the right quarter and the time couldn't be more suitable.

NICIA: So there's nothing much to it, really ... prepare the draught by all means, sir, and I'll give it to her.

CALLIMACO: Now there's just one point that we ought to consider. The first man who has anything to do with her after she's taken the draught will die within eight days, and there's nothing in the world can save him.

NICIA: Ugh! I don't want to have anything to do with the nasty stuff! You won't catch me like that! What sort of mess do you want to get me into?

CALLIMACO: Cheer up, sir, there's a way round this difficulty.

NICIA: What do you mean?

CALLIMACO: Why, you get someone else to sleep with her. He stays one whole night with her, and draws all the poison of the mandragora out of her into his own body. After that you can sleep with her yourself without any danger.

NICIA: But I won't do that.

CALLIMACO: Why not?

NICIA: Because I don't want to make my wife a whore, nor myself a cuckold.

CALLIMACO: Whatever do you mean, sir? I can see now that you're not the intelligent fellow I took you for. Can you really have doubts about doing something that the King of France and half the great lords of his court have done before you?

NICIA: But who d'you think I'll ever find to do such a crazy thing for me? If I tell him the truth, he won't want to do it; and if I don't tell him, it's treachery and murder, and I'll be up before the Eight,[2] and that's the last thing I want.

2. The magistrates who tried criminal cases.

CALLIMACO: If that's all that's worrying you, leave it to me to find the answer.

NICIA: What shall we do, then?

CALLIMACO: I'll tell you. I'll give you the draught this evening after supper. Get her to drink it and put her straight to bed. This will be about ten o'clock. Then we'll disguise ourselves, you and I, Ligurio and Siro, and we'll go and have a look round the Old Market and the New Market and that neighbourhood. The first idle lout we come across, we'll get hold of him and gag him, and drag him along to your house, giving him a bit of a thrashing on the way. We'll shove him into your bedroom, in the dark, and put him in your bed. We'll tell him what he's got to do, and there won't be any trouble at all. In the morning you send him away before it gets light, make sure your wife has a good wash, and you can go to bed with her yourself without any danger.

NICIA: Well, I'll be quite happy about it then, especially as you say that these kings and princes and nobles have done the same; but we must keep it dark, because of the Eight, you know!

CALLIMACO: But who's likely to tell them about it?

NICIA: There's still one difficulty, though, and it's a big one.

CALLIMACO: What's that?

NICIA: Getting my wife to agree to it, and I don't think she ever will.

CALLIMACO: There's that, of course. But I personally wouldn't want to be married at all if I weren't master in my own house.

LIGURIO: I know how we can persuade her!

NICIA: How?

LIGURIO: Through her confessor.

CALLIMACO [aside to LIGURIO]: Who'll convince him?

LIGURIO [aside to CALLIMACO]: You and I will. Money will. Our wickedness and the wickedness of the clergy will.

NICIA: But apart from anything else, I don't think she'll even go to see her confessor, if I suggest it.

LIGURIO: There's an answer to that too.

CALLIMACO: Tell me then!

LIGURIO: Get her mother to take her.

NICIA: Yes, the wife's got great faith in her.

LIGURIO [aside to CALLIMACO]: And I know the old lady will agree with us.

[*Addressing everybody*] Come on, then, let's make the most of our time, for the day's wearing on. Callimaco, you'd better take a walk now, but be ready with the potion as prescribed when we come along to your house an hour before sunset. Messer Nicia will go and see his mother-in-law, to get her agreement, and I'll go with him, for I know her too. Then we'll visit the friar, and we'll tell you what we've done when we get back.

[NICIA *walks slowly off, Right.*]

CALLIMACO [*aside to* LIGURIO]: For God's sake don't leave me alone!

LIGURIO: You seem to be in a pretty bad way!

CALLIMACO: Where do you want me to go?

LIGURIO [*pointing*]: This way ... that way ... down that street ... up this one ... Florence is a big place, you know!

CALLIMACO: I'm half dead.

[LIGURIO *walks off rapidly after* NICIA.]

# ACT THREE

*Scene as before.*

[SOSTRATA, NICIA, LIGURIO *are talking in front of* NICIA's *door.*]

SOSTRATA: I've always heard that a clever man ought to be able to make up his mind to accept the lesser of two evils. If this is the only way you can start a family, you'd better take it – as long as there's no objection to it in the matter of conscience.

NICIA: Yes, yes – quite right.

LIGURIO: Well, madam, you go and talk to your daughter, and Messer Nicia and I will go and talk to her confessor. We'll tell him the whole story, so that you won't have to go over it again when you visit him. Then you'll have to see what he says to you.

SOSTRATA: Yes, we'll do it like that. You go that way; and I'll go and find Lucrezia. I'll take her to see the friar, whatever happens.

[SOSTRATA *goes into* NICIA's *house.* NICIA, LIGURIO *move off towards the church.*]

NICIA: You may be surprised, Ligurio, that it should be such a business to get my wife to do anything; but if you knew more about it, it wouldn't surprise you at all.

LIGURIO: Aren't all women suspicious by nature?

NICIA: No, it's not that. She's the gentlest girl in the world and the easiest to persuade. But my neighbour's wife told her that if she'd vow to go to early mass at the Servites forty days running, she'd be sure to get pregnant. So she made the vow – and stuck to it for about twenty days. You can guess what happened – one of those damned friars started sniffing around her, so she wouldr't go back there at any price. Isn't it a sad thing that those who ought to set us an example should behave like that? Aren't I right?

LIGURIO: Of course you're right!

NICIA: From that time on she's had her ears pricked up like a frightened hare, and whatever you say to her, she finds a thousand objections.

LIGURIO: Well, I'm not surprised any more; but what did she do about fulfilling her vow?

NICIA: She got a dispensation.

LIGURIO: Good – But if you happen to have twenty-five ducats with you, give them to me. These things cost money; we've got to get the friar on our side straight away, *and* give him hope of better things to come.

NICIA: Take the money, then. It doesn't worry me; I can get it back another way.

LIGURIO: These friars are cunning devils, and you can see why. They know all our sins, and their own as well. If you don't know how to handle them, it's easy to make a mistake, and then they won't do what you want. Now I don't want you to say something that might spoil the whole business; because a man like yourself, who spends all day in his study, may know all about his books, but he isn't so good at discussing the things of this world. [*Aside*] (This fellow's such an idiot that I'm really afraid he may ruin everything.)

NICIA: Tell me what you want me to do.

LIGURIO: Just leave all the talking to me, and don't speak unless I give you a special sign.

NICIA: Very well. But what sign will you give me?

LIGURIO: I'll tip you a wink . . . I'll bite my lip . . . no, dammit, let's do it another way. How long is it since you spoke to this friar?

NICIA: More than ten years.

LIGURIO: Good . . . I'll tell him you've gone deaf; then you can leave his questions unanswered, and stay out of the conversation unless we begin to talk very loudly.

NICIA: I'll do that, then.

LIGURIO: And another thing – don't worry if I say something that doesn't seem to fit in with our plan – it'll all come right in the end.

NICIA: Good.

LIGURIO: There is the friar – but he's talking to a woman. We'd better wait till he's finished with her.

[NICIA *and* LIGURIO *move aside. Enter* FRA TIMOTEO *and* A WOMAN.]

FRA TIMOTEO: If you'd rather make a confession now, I will do what you wish.

WOMAN: No, not today; they're waiting for me. All I needed was to get some things off my chest, just talking ordinarily, like this. Have you said those masses of Our Lady?

FRA TIMOTEO: Yes, madam.

WOMAN: Then take this florin, and say the mass for the dead every Monday for the next two months for my husband's soul. And though he was a brute, blood's thicker than water, and I can't help feeling something inside me whenever I remember him ... But do you really think he's in Purgatory?

FRA TIMOTEO: No doubt of that whatever![3]

WOMAN: I'm not so sure, myself. You know what he used to do to me, sometimes ... How I used to weep when I told you about it! I kept him off as long as I could, but he would have it. Ugh!

FRA TIMOTEO: Never fear, the mercy of God is boundless. So long as a man has the will to repent, he will always have the time.

WOMAN: Do you think that the Turks will invade Italy this year?

FRA TIMOTEO: Yes – if you don't say your prayers.

WOMAN: My word! Heaven help us, then, with those devils! I'm terrified of that impaling. But I can see a woman inside the church there who's got some wool that belongs to me; I must go and talk to her. Good-bye!

FRA TIMOTEO: Good fortune go with you!

[Exit WOMAN.]

FRA TIMOTEO: There's nothing like women for giving generously to charity, and nothing like women for being a nuisance. If you chase them away, you say good-bye to both the benefit and the nuisance; if you put up with them you have to accept the nuisance with the benefit ... Ah, well – where there's honey there's flies, as the proverb says. [NICIA, LIGURIO come forward.] – But what brings you here, gentlemen? And isn't that Messer Nicia?

LIGURIO: Speak up, please – he's so deaf he can hardly hear a word.

FRA TIMOTEO [loudly]: Welcome, Messer Nicia!

LIGURIO: Louder, please!

FRA TIMOTEO [shouting]: Welcome!

NICIA: Glad to see you, father!

FRA TIMOTEO: And what brings you here?

3. Souls in Purgatory are the only ones that can benefit from masses for the dead. Souls in Hell are past help and souls in Heaven do not need it. (Translator's note.)

NICIA: Yes, yes – you're quite right.

LIGURIO: You'd do better to speak to me, father, because if you try to get him to understand you, you'll have this whole square in an uproar.

FRA TIMOTEO: And what can I do for you?

LIGURIO: Messer Nicia here, and another worthy gentleman – I'll tell you about him later – have several hundred ducats to distribute in alms.

NICIA: The devil we have!

LIGURIO [aside to NICIA]: (Be quiet, sir; it won't cost you a lot.) – Now, father, you mustn't be surprised at anything he says. He can't really hear at all; but sometimes he imagines he can hear, and then he says things that don't make sense.

FRA TIMOTEO: Go on, then, and we won't take any notice of him.

LIGURIO: I've got some of the money here, and the gentlemen have decided that it's to be you that distributes it.

FRA TIMOTEO: I'll be very glad to.

LIGURIO: But before this act of charity can be done, you must help us. Messer Nicia is in a strange situation, where only you can assist him; and it touches the honour of his family.

FRA TIMOTEO: What is the problem?

LIGURIO: I'm not sure whether you know Cammillo Calfucci, the nephew of Messer Nicia here?

FRA TIMOTEO: Yes, I do.

LIGURIO: He went off to France on business, a year ago; and as his wife was dead, he left his daughter, who's of marriageable age, in the care of a nunnery – I can't tell you which one for the present.

FRA TIMOTEO: And what happened?

LIGURIO: Well, I don't know whether the nuns were unusually care-less, or the girl was unusually silly, but the fact is that she's four months pregnant; and if the right steps aren't taken, Messer Nicia, and the nuns, and the girl, and his nephew, and the whole family of the Calfucci will be disgraced. Messer Nicia's so upset about it that he's sworn to give three hundred ducats to a good cause if it can be hushed up.

NICIA: What a lot of rubbish!

LIGURIO [aside to NICIA]: (Be quiet, sir!) – And you shall have the distribution of it. For it's only yourself and the abbess that can save us.

FRA TIMOTEO: What can I do?

LIGURIO: Persuade the abbess to give the girl a potion to make her miscarry.

FRA TIMOTEO: This requires very careful thought.

LIGURIO: Careful thought? Why? Only consider, father, how many good consequences your action will bring. You'll be maintaining the honour of the convent, the girl and her whole family. You give a daughter back to her father, you bring contentment to Messer Nicia here, and all his relations; and think of all the good you can do with those three hundred ducats. On the other hand, you harm nobody – except a bit of flesh that hasn't yet come into the world and has no feelings, and might easily miscarry in a dozen other ways. I consider that it's right to do what will benefit the greatest number, and make the greatest number happy.

FRA TIMOTEO: So be it, then, in heaven's name. What you wish shall be done – done for the sake of heaven and the love of charity. Tell me the name of the convent, and give me the potion. And you can give me the money now as well, if you like, so that I can make a start with the good works straight away.

LIGURIO: I can see now that you're the man of religion I took you for. Here's part of the money. [*Handing it over.*] The name of the nunnery is ... But just wait a moment; there's a woman in the church there who's beckoning to me. I'll be back in a minute – you stay with Messer Nicia. I must have a couple of words with her.

[*Exit* LIGURIO.]

FRA TIMOTEO: How old is this girl?

NICIA: My god, I'm furious about this.

FRA TIMOTEO [*louder*]: I said, How old is the girl?

NICIA: Damn him!

FRA TIMOTEO [*shouting*]: Why damn him?

NICIA: Because I want him to be damned!

FRA TIMOTEO: This is like a monkey house! Here I am, dealing with one man who's mad and one man who's deaf. The first keeps running off, and the other can't hear what I say. But if this is real money, and not gaming counters [*pulling it out anxiously to check. Relieved, he puts it away again*], I'll do better out of it than they will. But here's Ligurio, back again.

[*Enter* LIGURIO.]

LIGURIO [*to* NICIA]: Don't say anything, sir! [*To* FRA TIMOTEO] Great news, father!

FRA TIMOTEO: What is it, then?

LIGURIO: The woman I spoke to just now tells me the girl's had a miscarriage without any help.

FRA TIMOTEO: Good. Then the alms can go into the central fund.

LIGURIO: What did you say, father?

FRA TIMOTEO: I said that there's all the more reason to carry out this act of charity.

LIGURIO: The act of charity will be carried out whenever you please; but first of all you must do something else for Messer Nicia here.

FRA TIMOTEO: What is it?

LIGURIO: Something less onerous, less scandalous ... more welcome to us, and more useful to you.

FRA TIMOTEO: Tell me what it is, for I've reached a stage with you, and feel I know you so well, that I'd do anything for you.

LIGURIO: I'll tell you in the church, just the two of us, then, and Messer Nicia won't mind waiting for us while I do the talking for him. [*Loudly*] Wait here, sir; we'll be back in a minute.

NICIA: As the toad said to the harrow, you needn't hurry back!

FRA TIMOTEO: Let's go.

[*Exeunt* FRA TIMOTEO, LIGURIO.]

NICIA: Is it day, or night? Am I really here, or am I dreaming? I must be drunk – I haven't had a drink all day, but I must be drunk, or I couldn't have got involved in all this chatter and nonsense. We agree to tell the friar one thing, and he tells him another; then he wants me to pretend to be deaf – and God knows I'd have done well to stuff my ears with wax like the famous Dane to avoid hearing the rubbish he was talking! God knows what it's all for, anyway! I've said good-bye to twenty-five ducats, and not a word's been uttered about my problem. And now they've left me here like a stuffed dummy ... But here they are, coming back; and if they still haven't spoken about my affairs, I hope they trip over something and break their necks!

[*Enter* FRA TIMOTEO, LIGURIO.]

FRA TIMOTEO: Send the women to me. I know very well what to say to them, and if my authority's worth anything, this match will be concluded this evening.

LIGURIO: Well, sir, Fra Timoteo has agreed to everything. It's just a matter of getting the women here.

NICIA: You give me new life. Will it be a boy?

LIGURIO: It will.

NICIA: The tears are coming into my eyes.

FRA TIMOTEO: You can go into the church, while I wait here for the ladies. Keep on one side so that they won't see you, and when they've gone, I'll tell you what they said.

[*Exeunt* NICIA, LIGURIO.]

FRA TIMOTEO: I don't know who's having the wool pulled over his eyes and who's doing the pulling. The scoundrel came and told me that first story to try me out. 'If the friar agrees to the first little scheme,' he must have said to himself, 'it'll be all the easier to talk him into the second; while if he doesn't agree to the first, we won't tell him about the second at all. There'll be no risk of his blabbing out our real plans, and if he blabs the imaginary ones it won't matter.' He had me there, I admit; but there's some good in it for me as well.

Messer Nicia and Callimaco are both rich, and I should be able to get quite a lot out of both of them, in one way and another. The whole thing is sure to be kept very quiet; they don't want it known, and nor do I. Whatever happens, I shan't be sorry. True enough, there may be difficulties, for the lawyer's wife is a good, discreet sort of woman. Well, her goodness is the side I'll catch her by. After all, no women have much in the way of brains. If you find a female that can string two words of sense together, it's a wonder that'll do as the text for a sermon, for in the country of the blind the one-eyed man is king. – But here she is, with her mother, who's a silly woman and will be a great help to me in getting her to do what I want.

[FRA TIMOTEO *goes into the church.* SOSTRATA, LUCREZIA *come out of* NICIA's *house.*]

SOSTRATA: My dearest daughter, I'm sure that you believe that I put as high a value on your honour and well-being as anyone in the world, and that I'd never advise you to do anything that wasn't right. Now I've told you, and I tell you again – if Fra Timoteo tells you that there's nothing in this to burden your conscience – why, then, you'd better do it without worrying about it any longer.

LUCREZIA: I've always been afraid that my husband's longing for children would lead us into doing something wrong, and that's why I've been so worried and anxious about all his suggestions – especially since that thing happened to me through going to the Servites. But of all the suggestions I've heard, this seems to me to be the strangest – that I should have to subject my body to this shame and disgrace, and to be the death of the man who shames me and disgraces me. If I were the only woman left in the world, and the human race had to start again through me, I still wouldn't think I had any right to carry out a plan like that.

SOSTRATA: I can't tell you about all that, my daughter. You're going to talk to the father; you'll see what he says, and then you'll take his advice, and our advice – the advice of everyone that cares for you.

LUCREZIA: I'm so distressed, I'm all in a sweat.

[*Enter* FRA TIMOTEO.]

FRA TIMOTEO: Welcome to you both! I know what you want to ask me, because Messer Nicia has spoken to me about it. You know, I've been at my books for over two hours; and after a great deal of research, I can see a lot of points, both general and particular, which tell heavily on our side.

LUCREZIA: Do you mean it, or are you joking?

FRA TIMOTEO: Why, now, madam, is this a joking matter? Don't you know me better than that?

LUCREZIA: Yes, of course I do, father. But this seems to me the strangest thing that ever was heard.

FRA TIMOTEO: I'm sure it does, madam; but don't continue with those thoughts. There are many things in life which, seen from a distance, appear terrible, unbearable, unheard of; but when you come closer to them, they turn out to be gentle, endurable and familiar. Their bark's worse than their bite, as the saying goes; and you'll find this is one of them.

LUCREZIA: May heaven prove you right!

FRA TIMOTEO: Now I'll go back to what I was saying before. In matters of conscience, you must accept this general truth, that where there is a prospect of certain good and uncertain evil, we should never let the good slip for fear of the bad. Here you have a certain benefit – that you will conceive, and create a new soul to

38

praise God. The uncertain evil is that the man who lies with you, after you take the potion, may die – but in fact they don't always die and some do survive. But since the point is uncertain, it is better that your husband should not take the risk. As for there being anything sinful in the act itself, that's all nonsense. It's the will that sins, not the body. If you were to offend your husband, that would be a sin; but in this case you are doing what he wants. If you took pleasure in the act, that would be a sin; but you hate the thought of it. Besides, we must always look to the intention in these things; and your intention is to fill a place in heaven and make your husband happy. We read in the Bible that the daughters of Lot, when they thought that they were left alone in the world, lay with their father; and because their intention was good, their act was without sin.

LUCREZIA: Oh, father, what are you persuading me to do?

SOSTRATA: Let yourself be persuaded, Lucrezia. Don't you know that a woman without children can't call her home her own? If her husband dies, she's left like a brute beast, abandoned by everyone.

FRA TIMOTEO: I swear to you, madam, by this holy robe that I wear, that obeying your husband in this case need weigh on your conscience no more than eating meat on Wednesday.[4] It's a sin that a few drops of holy water will wash away.

LUCREZIA: Where are you leading me, father?

FRA TIMOTEO: To something which will always give you cause to bless my name, and will give you more pleasure a year hence than it does now.

SOSTRATA: Oh, she'll do what you want all right. I'm going to put her to bed myself this evening. What are you frightened of, you silly girl? There are plenty of women in Florence who'd thank heaven if they were in your place.

LUCREZIA: Very well, then – but I'm sure you won't find me alive tomorrow morning.

FRA TIMOTEO: Have no fear, my daughter. I'll pray to God for you; I'll say the Archangel Raphael's special prayer for you, so that he will have you in his keeping. Go with my blessing then, and make yourself ready to receive this mystery, for evening approaches.

4. Wednesday was formerly a day of abstinence, although not such a strict one as Friday.

SOSTRATA: Peace be with you, father!

LUCREZIA: God be with me, Our Lady help me, or I shall come to a bad end tonight.

[*Exeunt* SOSTRATA, LUCREZIA.]

FRA TIMOTEO: Come on out then, Ligurio!

[*Enter* LIGURIO, NICIA.]

LIGURIO: What's the news?

FRA TIMOTEO: Good news. They've gone home fully resolved to do all that we want. There won't be any difficulty now, because her mother's going to stay with her, and she's going to put her to bed with her own hands.

NICIA: Is that really true?

FRA TIMOTEO: Why, your deafness is cured, I see!

LIGURIO: St Clement has had mercy on him.

FRA TIMOTEO: You should put up a votive offering in gratitude to the good saint then, so that the thing won't pass unnoticed; and that'll be another reason for me to be glad of your kindness.

NICIA: Let's stick to the point. Will the wife make a lot of difficulty about doing what I want?

FRA TIMOTEO: No, I'm sure she won't, as I said before.

NICIA: Then I'm the happiest man in the world.

FRA TIMOTEO: I believe you. You'll get a little son out of this, and you'll be laughing at those that haven't got one.

LIGURIO: Go to your prayers, then, father; and if we need anything else we'll come to you. You, sir, go to your lady and make sure she doesn't change her mind, and I'll go to Dr Callimaco and get him to send you the potion. Make sure we meet again an hour after sunset, to arrange what we are going to do later in the evening.

NICIA: Well said, Ligurio! Good-bye!

FRA TIMOTEO: Go in peace!

[NICIA *goes into his house. Exit* LIGURIO, *Right.* FRA TIMOTEO *goes into the church.*]

# ACT FOUR

*Scene as before.*

[*Enter* CALLIMACO *Left. He gazes wildly round the stage, back the way he came in, and round the stage again.*]

CALLIMACO: I must know what those fellows have done! Why isn't Ligurio back yet? He said an hour before sunset – and the sun's setting now! They've left me in such agony of mind! It must be true that fortune and nature keep their books balanced with everyone of us – if they give you something good, something bad always crops up to go in the opposite column. As my hopes have grown, so have my fears. What misery! How can I go on living among these agonizing uncertainties, tormented by these fears and hopes? I'm like a ship harried by two contrary winds, which put her in ever greater danger as she comes nearer to port. The folly of Messer Nicia arouses my hopes, while Lucrezia's obstinate virtue arouses my fears. Alas, there's no more peace for me anywhere! Sometimes I try to conquer my own folly and reprove my own passions. What do you think you are doing? – I say to myself – Are you out of your mind? If you get her, what comes next? You'll realize the error into which you've fallen, you'll regret the time and trouble you've spent on it. Don't you know that the pleasure of getting what you want never comes up to the expectation? On the other hand, the worst that can happen is that you'll die and go to hell. But then think how many other men have died! How many good fellows there are in hell! Why should you be ashamed to go there too? – Look your fate in the eye! Avoid the evil that may come of it, if you can do so; if not, bear it like a man. Don't prostrate yourself before it, don't grovel like a woman.

– And that's how I get my spirits up again; but not for long, because I'm so hard hit from every side by the desire to be with Lucrezia, just one single time, that my whole body's affected by it, from head to toe. My legs tremble, my bowels turn over, I feel my heart uprooted from my breast, my arms dangle uselessly, my tongue loses the power of speech, my eyes dazzle, my head swims. Still, if only I could find Ligurio, I could get some of this off my chest. But here he comes – in a hurry, too. The message he brings will either give me a few hours' life or kill me outright.

[CALLIMACO *goes into his house for a moment or two. While he is out of sight,* LIGURIO *enters Right, crosses Centre, looks wildly round, and turns towards the audience. Re-enter* CALLIMACO.]

LIGURIO: I've never needed to see Callimaco so badly before, and never had so much trouble in finding him. If it'd been bad news, I'd have run into him straight away. I've been to his house, I've been to the Piazza, to the Market, to the Spini, to the Tornaquinci Loggia, and I haven't found him anywhere. These lovers seem to have quicksilver under their feet, so that you can't make them stay still.

CALLIMACO: Why don't I call out to him, and get it over? He looks quite cheerful, in point of fact . . . Ligurio! Ligurio!

LIGURIO: Oh, Callimaco, where have you been?

CALLIMACO [*impatiently*]: What's the news?

LIGURIO: It's good news!

CALLIMACO: Really good?

LIGURIO: It couldn't be better.

CALLIMACO: Has Lucrezia agreed?

LIGURIO: She has.

CALLIMACO: The friar fixed it up, did he?

LIGURIO: He did.

CALLIMACO: O most blessed of all friars! I'll pray to God for his soul every day of my life!

LIGURIO: Well said, indeed! – if God rewarded bad deeds as well as good ones. But this friar will want more than just your prayers.

CALLIMACO: What do you mean?

LIGURIO: Money!

CALLIMACO: Why, then, we'll give him some. How much have you promised him?

LIGURIO: Three hundred ducats.

CALLIMACO: That sounds about right.

LIGURIO: And the lawyer's contributed twenty-five of them.

CALLIMACO: But how on earth . . . ?

LIGURIO: Never mind – be content with the fact that he has.

CALLIMACO: What did Lucrezia's mother do?

LIGURIO: She practically did the whole job for us. When she heard that her daughter could have a night's pleasure without it being a sin, she encouraged her, wheedled her and used her maternal authority on her until she persuaded Lucrezia to go and see the friar, and when she'd got her there she managed to make her agree to the whole thing.

CALLIMACO: Dear God, what have I done to deserve so many blessings? I'm ready to die of happiness!

LIGURIO: What extraordinary fellows these are! One moment it's for sorrow, one moment it's for joy, but Callimaco seems bent on dying one way or the other – Have you got the potion ready?

CALLIMACO: Yes, of course.

LIGURIO: What's really in it?

CALLIMACO: Just a glass of hippocras, which is recommended to settle the stomach, cheer the mind, and . . . oh God! oh God! I'm done for!

LIGURIO: What is it? What are you worried about?

CALLIMACO: There's no way out of it!

LIGURIO: What the devil do you mean?

CALLIMACO: It's no good, no good at all. I've done nothing but paint myself into a corner.

LIGURIO: What are you talking about? Spit it out, man! Take your hands away from your face!

CALLIMACO: You know very well that I told Messer Nicia that you and he and Siro and I would kidnap someone and put him to bed with Lucrezia?

LIGURIO: And what's wrong with that?

CALLIMACO: What's wrong with that, do you ask? If I'm with the rest of you from the beginning, how can I be the one that's kidnapped; and if I don't come with you, he'll smell a rat.

LIGURIO: That's true; but can't we find a way round it?

CALLIMACO: I don't think so.

LIGURIO: Yes, there is a way.

CALLIMACO: What is it?

LIGURIO: I'll have to think about it for a bit.

CALLIMACO: A fine load you've taken off my mind! I'm really on velvet, if you've got to start thinking now!

LIGURIO: I've got it!

CALLIMACO: Got what?

LIGURIO: Why, the friar, who's helped us so much already, will take care of this as well.

CALLIMACO: How?

LIGURIO: We'll all have to go in disguise. I'll disguise the friar myself; he'll alter his voice, his appearance, his dress. I'll tell the lawyer that he's Callimaco, and the lawyer will believe it.

CALLIMACO: I like your plan; but what do you want me to do?

LIGURIO: You'd better put on a short cloak, and come along the street from the corner of his house over there, with a lute in your hand, singing a little song.

CALLIMACO: With my face uncovered?

LIGURIO: Yes – he'd suspect something if you wore a mask.

CALLIMACO: But he'll recognize me.

LIGURIO: No, he won't, because you'll disguise your face. Hang your mouth open – purse your lips up – twist your jaw sideways – shut one eye.

Try and do it now.

CALLIMACO: Like this?

LIGURIO: No.

CALLIMACO: Or this?

LIGURIO: That's not enough.

CALLIMACO: How about this, then?

LIGURIO: Yes! Yes! Try to remember that one. And I've got a false nose at home – you'd better have that as well.

CALLIMACO: Very well then – and what comes next?

LIGURIO: When you come round the corner, we'll be there. We'll whip your lute off you, we'll grab hold of you, blindfold you and twirl you round a few times. Then we'll drag you into the house and put you to bed. After that you'll have to fend for yourself.

CALLIMACO: The main thing is to get in there in the first place.

LIGURIO: You'll do that, I assure you; but getting an invitation to come back another time is your job, not ours.

CALLIMACO: What do you mean?

LIGURIO: Why, win her to yourself tonight, so that before you leave you can tell her who you are, explain the whole trick to her, show her how you love her. Say how you adore her; and tell her that her reputation can't suffer from being your friend, and might suffer greatly from being your enemy. She can't help coming to terms with you – she can't possibly want tonight to be the only night she has with you.

CALLIMACO: Do you really believe that?

LIGURIO: I'm sure of it. But don't let's waste any more time – it's getting very late. Call Siro, send the potion to Messer Nicia, and wait for me at your place. I'll go and fetch the friar. I'll disguise him and bring him here, and we'll get the lawyer, and do whatever else needs to be done.

CALLIMACO: Good. Be off with you, then!

[*Exit* LIGURIO.]

CALLIMACO: Siro!

[*Enter* SIRO.]

SIRO: Yes, sir?

CALLIMACO: Come here.

SIRO: Here I am.

CALLIMACO: There's a silver cup in the cupboard in my room. Put a cloth over it and bring it here. Mind you don't spill it on the way.

SIRO: Very good, sir. [*Exit.*]

CALLIMACO: He's been with me for ten years, and always served me faithfully. I expect he'll be as loyal as ever this time too. Although I haven't told him what we're doing, he's guessed, because it's right up his street, and I can see he's entering into the spirit of the thing.

[*Re-enter* SIRO.]

SIRO: Here it is, sir.

CALLIMACO: Good. Be off with you to Messer Nicia's house, and tell him this is the medicine his wife is to take immediately after supper; and the sooner she has supper the better it'll be. And say we'll be at the corner as arranged, at the time we said, and that he must manage to be there too. Be as quick as you can.

SIRO: I'm going now, sir.

CALLIMACO: One more thing. If he wants you to wait, wait for him, and go on to the meeting-place with him. Otherwise, come back here as soon as you've given him the potion and the message. Have you got all that?

SIRO: Yes, sir. [*Exit.*]

CALLIMACO: Now I've got to wait for Ligurio to come back with the friar. It's a true saying that waiting's hard work. I must be losing about ten pounds weight every hour, as I stand thinking where I am now and where I may be in a couple of hours' time, always terrified that something may crop up which'll spoil the whole plan. If it does, this'll be the last night of my life. I'll drown myself in the river, or hang myself, or throw myself out of one of those windows, or stab myself on her doorstep. I'll do something to put an end to my misery.

But isn't that Ligurio? It is! and he's got someone with him who seems to be hunch-backed and lame – it must be the friar in his disguise. What fellows these friars are! When you know one of them, you know the lot. And who's the other man that's just joined them? It looks like Siro, back from taking the message to the lawyer – yes, it is Siro! I'll wait for them here.

[*Enter* SIRO, LIGURIO, FRA TIMOTEO – *the friar being in disguise.*]

SIRO: Who's that with you, Ligurio?

LIGURIO: An honest fellow.

SIRO: Is he really lame, or pretending?

LIGURIO: Stop staring at him.

SIRO: He's got a really villainous look about him.

LIGURIO: Be quiet, will you? We've had enough of your nonsense. Where's Callimaco?

CALLIMACO: I'm here. Welcome to all of you!

LIGURIO: Callimaco, you'd better take this idiot Siro in hand. He's said a whole lot of silly things already.

CALLIMACO: Listen to me, Siro – for this evening, you're to do whatever Ligurio says. If he tells you to do anything, it's to be as if I'd told you myself. And anything you see or hear tonight has got to be kept absolutely secret, if you care about my honour, my life and my property – or about your own skin.

SIRO: Very good, sir.

CALLIMACO: Have you given the cup to Messer Nicia?

SIRO: Yes, sir.

CALLIMACO: What did he say?

SIRO: That he'll make the necessary arrangements.

FRA TIMOTEO: Is that Callimaco?

CALLIMACO: Yes, at your service, father. Let's take our agreement as read: you can rely on me and on all I possess as you rely on yourself.

FRA TIMOTEO: So I hear, and I believe it. I've taken something in hand for you that I wouldn't have touched for anyone else in the world.

CALLIMACO: I'll make it worth your while.

FRA TIMOTEO: Your friendship is all that counts with me.

LIGURIO: That's enough of compliments for now. Siro and I will go and disguise ourselves. You come with us, Callimaco, so that you'll be ready to go on and play your part in the plan. The friar can wait here for us; we'll be back in a moment, and then we can go and get Messer Nicia.

CALLIMACO: Good. Let's go, then.

FRA TIMOTEO: I'll wait here for you.

[*Exeunt* LIGURIO, SIRO, CALLIMACO.]

FRA TIMOTEO: It's a true saying that bad company leads a man to the gallows. It's just as easy to come to grief by being too kind and obliging as by being wicked. God knows I had no thought of doing harm to anyone. I lived in my cell, said my prayers, looked after the good people who asked my help. Then this devil Ligurio turned up, and persuaded me to dip one toe in a quicksand of error; and now I'm in it up to my middle, if not over my head, and I don't know what's to become of me ... But there is this to be said, that when a thing concerns a lot of people, there'll be a lot of people trying to make a success of it. But here's Ligurio and the servant back again.

[*Enter* LIGURIO, SIRO, *disguised.*]

FRA TIMOTEO: I'm glad to see you back again!

LIGURIO: Do we look all right?

FRA TIMOTEO: Fine, fine!

LIGURIO: There's only Messer Nicia to come then. Let's go on to his place. It's getting late – we'd better be on our way.

[*They move across toward the lawyer's front door.*]

SIRO: His door's opening ... Is that his servant?

LIGURIO: No, it's the lawyer himself. Ha! ha! ha!

SIRO: What are you laughing at?

LIGURIO: He's got a funny short jacket on, that doesn't cover his arse. And what's that on his head? It looks like one of those hoods that the canons wear. And he's got a funny little apology for a sword. Ha! ha! And he's mumbling something to himself. Let's stand on one side, and I'm sure we'll hear something to the disadvantage of his wife.

[*Enter* NICIA, *disguised.*]

NICIA: What a lot of silly fuss from my fool of a wife! She's sent the maids to her mother's house, and the manservant down to the country ... that wasn't a bad idea, in fact, and I don't blame her for it at all; but I do blame her for all that squeamish nonsense before she'd make up her mind to go to bed. [*Puts on a falsetto voice.*] 'I won't! I won't! How could I ever do such a thing? What are you making me do? God help me! Mother! Mother!' [*Reverting to his normal voice*] And if her mother hadn't talked to her like a Dutch uncle, we'd never have got her to bed at all! A plague on her! I'm all in favour of feminine modesty, but not to this extent! She drove us half mad, the featherbrained creature! And yet, if she heard anyone say: 'Down with the wisest woman in Florence!', she'd say: 'Why, what have I done to you?'

Well, Israel's going to enter into Egypt tonight, and no mistake, and before I leave the scene of action I intend to be able to say, like the silly woman in the story, 'I saw it with my own hands!'

This outfit suits me all right! No one would know me! It makes me taller, younger, slimmer ... No woman would charge me anything for you know what tonight! – But I can't see the other fellows anywhere.

LIGURIO [*coming forward*]: Good evening, Messer Nicia!

NICIA [*terrified*]: Oh! Oh! Oh!

LIGURIO: Don't be afraid, it's only us.

NICIA: Oh, you're all here! If I hadn't recognized you straight away, I'd have been at your throats with this sword! So you're Ligurio? And you're Siro? And the other fellow? Ah, the doctor, of course!

LIGURIO: That's right, sir.

NICIA: My word! He's certainly disguised himself well. The famous head jailer of Florence prison wouldn't know him.

LIGURIO: I made him put a couple of nuts in his mouth so that no one would know his voice.

NICIA: You *are* a fool!

LIGURIO: Why?

NICIA: Why didn't you tell me that before? I'd have put a couple of nuts in *my* mouth – it matters just as much to me not to be known by my voice.

LIGURIO: Here – put this in your mouth now.

NICIA: What is it?

LIGURIO: A ball of wax.

NICIA: Give it to me ... [*He coughs, splutters and spits.*] I hope you break your neck, you wretched fellow!

LIGURIO: I'm sorry, sir; I gave you something else by mistake, without noticing it.

NICIA [*coughs and spits again*]: What was it?

LIGURIO: Aloes.

NICIA: Damn all aloes, then! ... But doctor, haven't you anything to say?

FRA TIMOTEO [*heavily disguised so that* NICIA *can take him for* CALLI-MACO; *in a strange voice*]: I'm very angry with Ligurio.

NICIA: Oh! You do disguise your voice well!

LIGURIO: Well, we mustn't waste any more time here. I'll be the general, and set out the army in order of battle. The right wing, or shall we say horn, of our formation, will be commanded by Calli-maco. I shall take charge of the left horn. Messer Nicia will stand here between the two horns, and Siro will be the rearguard, and lend his support to any contingent that gives ground. Our watch-word will be 'St Coucou'.

NICIA: St Coucou? Who was he?

LIGURIO: The most highly honoured saint in the Kingdom of France.[5] But let's get on; we must lay an ambush at this corner. Listen! I can hear a lute.

NICIA: That'll be the man for us! What shall we do?

LIGURIO: We'd better send forward a scout to find out what sort of fellow he is. We'll make our plans according to his report.

NICIA: Who – who's to go?

LIGURIO: You go, Siro; you know what you have to do. Look

---

5. Compare Montaigne, *Essays*, I, 40: 'I know some who consentingly have acquired both profit and advancement from cuckoldom, of which the bare name only affrights so many people.' (*Translator's note.*)

closely, think carefully, come back quickly, and let us have your report.

SIRO: Very well. [*Exit Right, round street corner.*]

NICIA: I'd be sorry if we got off on the wrong foot, and picked some feeble, sickly old fellow, so that we'd have to start off again with the same game tomorrow.

LIGURIO: Don't worry; Siro knows what he's about. Here he is, back again. What's your news, Siro?

SIRO: He's a fine, strong young lout – the finest you'll ever see. He's hardly twenty-five, and he's coming this way now, all alone, dressed in a short cloak and playing a lute.

NICIA: Just the fellow we want, if you're telling the truth – otherwise, it'll be you that'll be in the soup.

SIRO: You'll find it's just as I have said, sir.

LIGURIO: Wait till he comes round the corner, and then we'll grab him.

NICIA [*tries to tug friar over in front of him*]: A little more over this way, please, doctor. [*Friar resists.*] It's like trying to shift a man of lead! – But here he comes!

[*Enter* CALLIMACO, *from round street corner, disguised and pretending to be drunk.*]

CALLIMACO [*sings*]:

'And since you won't let me come to your bed,
    I hope that the devil may lie there instead!'

LIGURIO: Stop where you are. Give me that lute.

CALLIMACO: Oh, God! What have I done?

NICIA: You'll soon find out! Blindfold him, gag him!

LIGURIO: Turn him round!

NICIA: Spin him round again! And once more! Now take him indoors!

[LIGURIO, SIRO, *drag Callimaco to* NICIA's *front door and force him inside.*]

FRA TIMOTEO: Messer Nicia, I'm going home to bed now, for I've a terrible headache. And I don't think I'll be coming to help you tomorrow morning, unless it's specially necessary.

NICIA: That's all right, doctor; you needn't come back first thing. We'll be able to manage by ourselves.

[*Exit* FRA TIMOTEO *round the street corner.* NICIA *goes into his house. Re-enter* FRA TIMOTEO *a moment later.*]

FRA TIMOTEO: Well, they're all kennelled up, now, and I'm off to my monastery. [*Addressing the audience*] But you, kind listeners, don't accuse us of infringing the unity of time.[6] No one's going to sleep tonight, so there won't be any break between the acts.

I shall be saying my office. Ligurio and Siro will be busy with their supper, for they've had nothing to eat all day. The lawyer will be trotting to and fro between his bedroom and his parlour, keeping an eye on everything.

Callimaco and Madame Lucrezia certainly won't get any sleep – and I know that if I were in his shoes and you were in hers, we wouldn't get any either.

6. The classical rules of comedy demand that the action should be confined to a period of twenty-four hours, and not be interrupted by a night. As the friar points out, the night does not cause any break in the action of the present play.

# ACT FIVE

*Scene as before. Time: early the following morning.*

[FRA TIMOTEO, *in his normal ecclesiastical dress, comes out of the church.*]

FRA TIMOTEO: I couldn't sleep at all last night for wondering how Callimaco and the others were getting on. I did what I could to pass the time. I said matins, I read one of the lives of the saints, I went into the church and relit a lamp that had gone out, and I put a new veil on a statue of Our Lady that's done several miracles. I don't know how many times I've told those friars, to keep her looking tidy! And then they wonder why people aren't as devout as they used to be! I can remember when there were five hundred votive images around her; and now there aren't twenty. And it's our fault, because we don't know how to keep up her reputation. We used to go there in procession every evening after compline, and have lauds sung there every Saturday. We always made our own vows there, so that there were always fresh votive images on view; and when men or women came to confession we used to encourage them to do the same. Now none of these things are done at all, and we're surprised at the general coolness toward religion. They haven't much sense, those colleagues of mine!

But now I can hear a lot of noise coming from the lawyer's house. Here they are, as I wish to be saved! They're bringing out the prisoner. So I'm in plenty of time. They must have gone on till there wasn't a drop left in the bottle, for day's already breaking. I'll stand here and listen to what they have to say, without letting them see me. [*He goes round the street corner.*]

[*Enter* NICIA, CALLIMACO *in disguise*, LIGURIO, SIRO *from* NICIA's *house.*]

NICIA: You grab him by that side, and I'll hold on to him from here: and you, Siro, hang on to his cloak at the back.

CALLIMACO: Don't hurt me!

LIGURIO: Don't be afraid, just get moving!

[*They drag him towards the street corner.*]

NICIA: We needn't go any further than this.

LIGURIO: You're right, we'll turn him loose here. Spin him round a couple of times, so that he won't know where he's been. Turn him round, Siro!

SIRO: That's done, sir.

NICIA: And again!

SIRO: That's done too.

CALLIMACO: What about my lute?

LIGURIO: Be off, you blackguard, be off with you! If there's another word out of you, I'll cut your throat!

[*Exit* CALLIMACO, *round street corner.*]

NICIA: He's running for it! Let's go and take off our disguises. And we'd better all be out and about fairly early, so that it won't look as if we've been up all night.

LIGURIO: You're right, sir.

NICIA: Now, then, Ligurio and Siro, you'd better go and find Dr Callimaco and tell him that everything went off all right.

LIGURIO: And what can we tell him, sir? We don't know anything. As soon as we got indoors, we went off to the cellar for a drink, as you know. You and Madame Sostrata took him over, and we haven't seen you since, except just now, when you called us to help you get rid of him.

NICIA: You're right, of course. Oh, I've a fine story to tell you! My wife was in bed, with the lights out. My mother-in-law was waiting for me by the fireside. I brought the lout upstairs, and to be on the safe side, I took him into a little room that I've got next door to the parlour, where there's a faint sort of lamp, that gave a poor sort of light, so that he couldn't see my face properly.

LIGURIO: Very wise of you.

NICIA: I made him strip off. He protested, but I showed my teeth at him, so that in the end he was glad enough to strip stark naked. He's got an ugly face, with a great clumsy nose and a crooked mouth; but you never saw such skin and flesh as he's got on him – white . . . soft . . . firm . . . – and other things that you needn't ask me about!

53

LIGURIO: It's best not to discuss those matters. Why did you have to examine him all over like that?

NICIA: It's clear enough, isn't it? Once I'd got a finger in the pie, I wanted to see what was under the crust. And then I wanted to see if he was healthy. Where would I have been if he'd had the pox? You tell me!

LIGURIO: You're quite right.

NICIA: When I was sure he wasn't diseased, I made him follow me, and led him by the hand into my room, all in the dark, and put him to bed. And before I left them, I felt round to see how things were going, for I'm not one to buy a pig in a poke.

LIGURIO: How carefully and wisely you've attended to everything, Messer Nicia!

NICIA: When I'd touched and felt everything, I left the room, and locked the door, and went off to join my mother-in-law by the fireside, and we sat and talked all through the night.

LIGURIO: What did you talk about?

NICIA: About Lucrezia's stupidity, and how much better it would have been if she'd agreed to the whole thing straight away, without all this to-ing and fro-ing. And then we spoke about the baby; I feel as if I'd got him in my arms already, dear little thing! We went on talking until I heard the clock strike six. Then I was afraid we'd be overtaken by daylight, and I went back to my room. Do you know, I couldn't get the blackguard out of bed!

LIGURIO: I can believe that!

NICIA: The greedy fellow – he'd found the joint to his taste, all right! But he got up in the end, and so I called you, and we pushed him out of doors.

LIGURIO: The whole thing's turned out very well.

NICIA: There's just one thing I'm sorry about . . .

LIGURIO: What's that?

NICIA: It's that poor young fellow – to think he's going to die so soon, and that last night's going to cost him so dear!

LIGURIO: Why, sir, you can't have much else to worry about! Leave that problem to him!

NICIA: You're right, of course. You know, I can't wait to see Dr Callimaco, and share the good news with him.

LIGURIO: He'll be up and about in an hour or so. But it's broad daylight now – we're going off to get changed. What will you do?

NICIA: I'll go home now, and put on my best clothes. I'll make my wife get up and have a wash, and then I'll bring her along to be churched. I'd like you and Callimaco to be there; and then we can talk to Fra Timoteo. We ought to thank him, and reward him for the good he's done us.

LIGURIO: You're right, sir; we'll do that. Good-bye!

[*Exeunt* LIGURIO, SIRO, *Left.* NICIA *goes into his house.* FRA TIMOTEO *comes forward.*]

FRA TIMOTEO: I heard what they said, and it all made good hearing, because of the great folly of the lawyer; but the last bit was what really delighted me. If they're going to talk to me, it had better be on my own ground, so I won't stay here; I'll go and wait for them at the church, which is the place where my wares command the best price. But who's this coming out of the house over there? It looks like Ligurio, and that must be Callimaco with him. I don't want them to see me, for the reason I mentioned just now ... And if by any chance they don't come looking for me this morning, there'll still be plenty of time for me to go and look for them.

[*Exit* FRA TIMOTEO, *round the street corner.*]

[*Enter* CALLIMACO, LIGURIO, *left.*]

CALLIMACO: As I was saying, Ligurio, I wasn't very happy about the whole thing until after midnight. I had my pleasure, all right, and plenty of it, but it didn't seem right. But after I'd told her who I was, and how much I loved her, and how easy it would be for us to be happy together without any scandal, in view of her husband's simple nature; and after I'd promised to marry her if ever Heaven had other plans for him; and after, besides all those other good reasons, she'd found out how much difference there was between sleeping with me and sleeping with Messer Nicia, and tasted the difference between the kisses of a young lover and those of an old husband – why, she sighed a few times, and said:

'Well, your cunning, the folly of my husband, the simplicity of my mother, and the wickedness of my confessor have led me to do something I'd never have done by myself, so that I can only think that it must be the will of Heaven; and I'm not bold enough to refuse anything that Heaven wishes me to accept. So I take you as my lord, my master and my guide, my father and my natural defender. I want you to be the whole world to me; and I want my husband to have the label he meant to wear for a single evening hung round his neck for ever. You'll get him to accept you as a friend of the family. You can meet us today at the church, and come to dinner with us afterwards. And after that you'll be able to come and go as you please, and we can be together any time you like without suspicion.'

When I heard her say that, I thought I was going to die of joy. I couldn't find the words to tell her the hundredth part of what I felt. So now I'm the happiest and most contented man that ever drew breath, and if death or time doesn't put an end to my happiness, I'll be more blessed than the blest, more sainted than the saints.

LIGURIO: I'm always glad of any good thing that happens to you; and you can see it's turned out just as I said. But what shall we do next?

CALLIMACO: We'll go towards the church, because that's where I promised her I'd be. She's going there with her mother and her husband.

LIGURIO: What's that at the lawyer's door? – It's Lucrezia and her mother coming out, and there's Messer Nicia following them.

CALLIMACO: Let's go into the church and wait for them there.

[CALLIMACO, LIGURIO *go into the church. Enter* LUCREZIA, SOSTRATA, *followed by* NICIA, *who tries to catch* LUCREZIA *up and attract her attention. She ignores him to begin with.*

NICIA: Lucrezia! . . . In my view, Lucrezia, we ought to do everything in the fear of God, and not rashly or unthinkingly . . .

LUCREZIA: What do you want me to do now?

NICIA: Look at the way she answers me! She's got her hackles up like a gamecock!

SOSTRATA: You mustn't be surprised at anything she says today; she's still a bit upset.

LUCREZIA [*to* NICIA]: What are you trying to say?

NICIA: I'm saying that I'd better go on ahead to talk to the friar, and tell him to come and meet you at the church door, so that he can take you in for the churching ceremony, because today, you know, it's just as if you were being reborn.

LUCREZIA: Why don't you go and do that, then?

NICIA: You're very full of yourself this morning! And to think that last night she seemed to be at death's door!

LUCREZIA: Well, it's all thanks to you!

SOSTRATA [*soothingly, to* NICIA]: Yes, go and fetch the friar.

[FRA TIMOTEO *appears at the church door.*]

But you needn't bother now, in fact, for there he is, in front of the church.

NICIA: So he is!

[LUCREZIA, SOSTRATA, NICIA *move over towards the church.*]

FRA TIMOTEO: I must look out for the lawyer and the two ladies; Callimaco and Ligurio tell me that they're on their way to the church – and here they are!

NICIA: *Bona dies*, father!

FRA TIMOTEO: Welcome, ladies, welcome! [*To* LUCREZIA] I wish you all happiness, madam, and may Heaven bestow on you the blessing of a fine son!

LUCREZIA: God grant it!

FRA TIMOTEO: He will, He will.

NICIA: Isn't that Ligurio and Callimaco over there inside the church?

FRA TIMOTEO: Yes, sir.

NICIA: Then beckon them to come and join us!

FRA TIMOTEO [*beckoning*]: Over here, please, gentlemen!

[*Enter* CALLIMACO, LIGURIO.]

CALLIMACO: God's blessing on all of you!

NICIA: Dr Callimaco, I'd like you to take my wife's hand.

CALLIMACO: Most gladly.

NICIA: Lucrezia, it's thanks to the doctor that we shall have a staff to support our old age.

LUCREZIA: He's made me very happy, and I think we should have him as a friend of the family.

NICIA: Bless you for those words! And I want him to come and have dinner with us today – and Ligurio too.

LUCREZIA: Of course.

NICIA: And I'll give them the key of the ground floor room which opens on to the loggia, so that they can use it as they please, for they've no women to look after them and they're living like animals.

CALLIMACO: I'm very glad to accept your offer, and I'll make use of the room as occasion arises.

FRA TIMOTEO: And the money for my charities?

NICIA: Why, *domine*, I'll send it off today.

LIGURIO: Has no one a thought for Siro?

NICIA: Siro can ask what he likes – what's mine is his. – Listen, Lucrezia, how much do you have to give the friar for the churching?

LUCREZIA: I can't remember.

NICIA: But how much is it?

LUCREZIA: Oh, give him ten *grossi*!

NICIA: Ruination!

FRA TIMOTEO: And you, madame Sostrata, seem to have blossomed out again like a young girl.

SOSTRATA: And who wouldn't be happy on a day like this?

FRA TIMOTEO: Let's all go into the church. We'll say the usual prayers, and then, after the service, you can all go home to dinner.

[LUCREZIA, SOSTRATA, NICIA, CALLIMACO, LIGURIO, SIRO *begin to file into the church.* FRA TIMOTEO *turns to address the audience.*]

But you, listeners, don't wait for us to come out again. The service is a long one, and when it's over I shall stay in the church, and the others will go home by the side door.

So farewell to you all!

[FRA TIMOTEO *follows the others into the church.*]

# LENA

*(La Lena)*

*by*

LUDOVICO ARIOSTO
*(1474–1533)*

# LUDOVICO ARIOSTO

LUDOVICO ARIOSTO (1474–1533) was born in Reggio Emilia. He spent most of his life at the court of Ferrara, where he served the ducal family of Este loyally and well as courtier, court poet and administrator, for a less than generous reward.

His masterpiece is the *Orlando Furioso*, an epic of chivalry in which he displays unsurpassed narrative gifts and a poetic style as musical as that of Spenser and as rapid and polished as that of Pope. Gibbon rightly speaks of 'the boundless variety of the incomparable Ariosto'. His four comedies were written for the stage, and he supervised their production himself. All are witty and well constructed, though some of them owe too much to Terence and Plautus. The 'Lena' (1528) stands out by the subtlety of the characterization and the remarkable realism of the background. The general picture of inefficient bureaucracy and petty corruption in ducal Ferrara commands instant belief, and prompts the reflection that few absolute governments, ancient or modern, have been enlightened enough to allow themselves to be satirized in such a manner.

The *Orlando Furioso* has been translated into English many times, most recently by Barbara Reynolds, Penguin Classics, 1975. The only previous translation of a play by Ariosto is George Gascoigne's version of *I Suppositi*, which was acted at the Inns of Court in 1566.

# CHARACTERS

in order of appearance

CORBOLO, Flavio's servant
FLAVIO, Ilario's son, in love with Licinia
LENA, Pacifico's wife, Fazio's mistress
FAZIO, Licinia's father
ILARIO, Flavio's father
EGANO, an old friend of Ilario
PACIFICO, Lena's husband, a man ruined by debts
CREMONINO, Giulio's servant
GIULIO, a moneylender
TORBIDO, a surveyor
GEMIGNANO, apprentice to Torbido
BARTOLO, one of Pacifico's creditors
MAGAGNINO
SPAGNUOLO }bailiffs
FALCIONE
MENICA, Fazio's maidservant
GROOMS
MENGHINO, Fazio's serving lad

[LICINIA, Fazio's daughter, plays an important part in the story, but does not appear on stage.]

# ACT ONE

*A street in Ferrara. In the centre of the stage is the frontage of* LENA's *modest dwelling. To the left of it stands a larger house belonging to* FAZIO; *to the right another belonging to* ILARIO. *A side-turning leads offstage at Left Centre.*

*The time is shortly before sunrise.*
[ILARIO's *son* FLAVIO *comes furtively out of his father's front door and looks around.* CORBOLO, *his servant, follows him a few moments later.*]

CORBOLO: Master Flavio, if you don't mind my asking, where are you going at this time of day? The bell is only just ringing for matins. And there must be some special reason for you to be so carefully dressed, so elaborately got up, and smelling so sweet – like a box of perfumes.

FLAVIO: Led on by love, I go to feast my eyes on an incomparable beauty.

CORBOLO: And what beauty do you think you're going to see in the pitch dark? I believe Martin d'Amelia fell in love with a star – is that the beauty you want to see? But even she, as it happens, doesn't rise till nearer dawn.

FLAVIO: Not Martin's star, Corbolo, nor any other of the lights of heaven – not even the sun himself – can shine as brightly as the fair eyes of Licinia.

CORBOLO: Nor the eyes of our cat, you might have added – it's a better comparison, too, because they really are eyes and really do shine.

FLAVIO: Heaven send you ill-fortune for comparing the eyes of a brute beast to those angelic orbs.

CORBOLO: What about the eyes of Cucchiulino, then, or Sabbatino, or Mariano, or any other of their boon companions, when they come rolling out of the inn?

FLAVIO: Be off, and my curse go with you!

CORBOLO: It's a blessing that I'm going to have – the blessing of stretching out in my bed and finishing off the sweet sleep I was having until you woke me up.

FLAVIO: No, no, Corbolo – come back here and listen to me, without any more of your silly jokes. I've always had great faith in you, as you must have noticed from many clear signs. But now I'm going to give a bigger proof of my trust than ever before – I'm going to tell you a secret of such vital importance that I'd rather lose my property, my honour and my very soul than have it become public knowledge. I need your help in this matter, but I must tell you that I can't even ask you for it until you promise me your silence.

CORBOLO: There's no need for all these preliminaries with me. You know from experience that I can keep my mouth shut when necessary.

FLAVIO: Well, I needn't repeat one thing, which you know already – I'm in love with Licinia, our neighbour Fazio's daughter, and she loves me. You've been there several times when we've had a chance to speak to each other, and witnessed our words, our sighs, our tears – Licinia standing at that little window, and myself down here in the street. From the very beginning, the only thing that's stopped us from satisfying our longing for each other is lack of a place to meet. But in the end Licinia found the answer – she told me to make friends with Lena, Pacifico's wife, who lives next door. You see, when Licinia was a little girl, Lena taught her to read and to sew, and she's still giving her lessons in embroidery, fancy work and so on. Licinia spends the whole day in Lena's house, right up to sunset; so Lena can quite easily let me come to her, without anyone knowing about it. And she's said she will – and today's the first day – but she doesn't want the neighbours to see me going in, in case they suspect anything, so she wants me to arrive while it's still dark.

CORBOLO: A very suitable arrangement.

FLAVIO: Licinia can come and go as she likes, just as she does every day. But I can't come out again until it's dark. I shall steal out, very quietly, late tonight.

CORBOLO: But how were you able to get Lena to be the procuress of her own pupil?

FLAVIO: How have better people than Lena been persuaded to betray their princes' castles, cities and armies – and sometimes their princes themselves – into the hands of their enemies? With money, which is the simplest persuader of all. I've promised Lena twenty-five florins, and I meant to take the money with me now; I was hoping to get it from Giulio, who promised to let me have it yesterday. But he kept me waiting and kept me waiting; and then late yesterday evening he told me that he wasn't lending me the money himself, but a friend of his would let me have it and I needn't pay any interest for the first four months. But if his friend provided the money, he'd want me to deposit something of value with him as security, and I couldn't lay my hand on anything at such short notice; but as I'd made this arrangement to go to Lena's to-day, I didn't want to break it, and here I am. I know it's pretty doubtful whether Lena will trust me for the money; but I'm going to do my best. I'll tell her exactly what's happened, and hope she'll agree to wait until tomorrow.

CORBOLO: If she does trust you, it'd be a real good deed on your part to let her down! What a swine she is! She deserves to be burnt at the stake! Betraying the daughter of a man who trusts her!

FLAVIO: And how do you know that she isn't in the right? To understand all this, you need to know that the miserable old man used to fancy Lena himself, and he's had what he wanted from her lots of times.

CORBOLO [laughing sarcastically]: I can scarcely believe it! And I suppose he was the first to spoil her record?

FLAVIO: He may have been, at that. Her husband puts up with it, or pretends not to notice, because old Fazio has repeatedly promised to pay all his debts. The poor fellow's reached the stage where he daren't set foot outside his door, for fear of being seized by his creditors and left to rot in prison. But instead of helping him, the treacherous old man denies ever having promised to do so, and says: 'You ought to be well enough pleased with the house I let you have rent-free!' As if Lena didn't deserve something for the lessons she gives to Licinia!

CORBOLO: Well, even if she hadn't deserved anything for past instruction, she's going to deserve something now, when she teaches the girl to set her hand to the most delightful form of fancy work in the world – double blanket-stitch, with insertions. That'll put Lena in the right, and no mistake!

FLAVIO: Right or wrong, what do I care? As long as she helps me, I'm under an obligation to her. Now what I want you to do for me is to buy two or three brace of quails or turtle-doves, or failing that two brace of pigeons, and have them roasted; and get me a fine fat capon, and have that boiled; and bring the lot along at dinner time. And we shall want some good bread, and some even better wine. Above all, make sure there's plenty for us to drink. Here's a florin for you, and I'm not expecting to see any change out of it.

CORBOLO: No need to tell me that, sir.

FLAVIO: And now I must give Lena a knock.

CORBOLO: Give her a proper knock, and black her eye for her! That's what she certainly deserves!

FLAVIO: And why should I want to harm her, when she's helping me?

CORBOLO: She sticks you up for twenty-five florins, and you call that helping you? But tell me this – if you do manage to borrow them, how are you going to pay them back?

FLAVIO: Oh, I shall have four months to think about that; and who knows what may happen in that length of time? Why, isn't it quite possible that my father may die long before then?

CORBOLO: Yes, but it's also possible that he'll stay alive. And if he does, which is more likely after all, how are you going to pay your debt?

FLAVIO: And won't you always be ready to help me if I want to fiddle something from the old man?

CORBOLO: As often as you like!

FLAVIO: Listen! Someone's opening the door.

CORBOLO: Then you be ready to open your purse.

[LENA *appears in the doorway of her house.*]

FLAVIO: Good day to you, Lena.

LENA: 'Good night' would be more like it. You *are* in a hurry.

CORBOLO: You might be more polite, though, and return his greeting.

LENA: Actions speak louder than words; and that's how I intend to return his 'good day'.

66

FLAVIO: My hopes of a good day rest in your hands; I know that, Lena.

LENA: And mine in yours.

CORBOLO [to LENA]: And I'd like to put mine in yours, too.

LENA: A fine idea! But tell me, Flavio – have you brought the ... you know what?

CORBOLO: Why, he'd never come without *that*! He's brought it all right – *and* it's in the pink of condition!

LENA: I don't mean *that*, you fool! I mean the money.

FLAVIO: I thought I'd be able to bring it today ...

LENA: You *thought*? That's a bad beginning!

FLAVIO: You see, a friend of mine was going to oblige me with the money yesterday; but then last night he told me that he'd let me have it today or tomorrow without fail. Believe me, Lena, you'll have it by two o'clock tomorrow.

LENA: If you can get the money tomorrow, I'll let you come in here this time the following morning. Till then you'll have to stay outside.

FLAVIO: But, Lena, you can reckon the money's as good as in your purse now.

LENA: This is just talk, Flavio. *You* can reckon that I won't trust you till I see the cash.

FLAVIO: I give you my solemn word ...

LENA: It's a bad bargain to take a man's solemn word instead of his money. You can't buy anything with a solemn word; and the tax office has banned it as counterfeit coin.

CORBOLO: You're joking, now, aren't you, Lena?

LENA: No, I'm not; I'm talking the best sense I know.

CORBOLO: But how can one so beautiful be so cruel?

LENA: Whether I'm beautiful or ugly, there's one thing I do know – any kicks or halfpence that come out of this will come my way. And there's one thing I won't be – and that's a fool, to be joked out of my rights.

FLAVIO: God be my witness ...

LENA: I've no use for a witness who can't be called into court.

CORBOLO: And do you put so little trust in us?

LENA: There's no point in your master staying here and wasting his time. I tell him this: he's not going to set foot inside this house until twenty-five florins come and open the door for him.

FLAVIO: Are you afraid I'll try to put something across you?

CORBOLO: You put something across her, sir! [*Lifting one leg expressively*] See if that doesn't make her more agreeable.

LENA: I don't need anything put across me, thank you: I haven't got a cold.

CORBOLO [*aside*]: What you need is a good thick ash-plant put across your back, like the she-ass you are!

LENA: Once and for all, it's money I want, not chatter. He knows that's the bargain, and he can't complain about it.

FLAVIO: That's the truth, Lena; but can you really be so cruel that you won't let me into your house?

LENA: Can you really think that I'm such a fool as to believe that, with all the time that's passed since we first discussed the matter, you couldn't have laid your hands on twenty-five florins if you'd really wanted to? Fellows like you are never short of money. If your friends won't help you, try the middlemen who can put you in touch with the money-lenders. Take off that velvet gown and that expensive cap and send them to the Jews. You've got plenty of other stuff to wear.

FLAVIO: Then let's do it like this, Lena. You take the things you mentioned and keep them locked up until tomorrow. Then you can pawn them if I don't give you the money, or send it to you by Corbolo, before two o'clock in the afternoon.

LENA: No, no. You take those things off and send them to be pawned yourself.

FLAVIO: Very well; I'll do as you say, and prove that I'm not trying to cheat you. Here, Corbolo, you'd better take my cap and my gown – help me off with it, so that it doesn't get in the mud.

CORBOLO: Are you really going to do it?

FLAVIO: I must satisfy her somehow. What the devil does it matter?

CORBOLO: Well, all the butchers in town might as well go and hang themselves, because none of them will ever be able to handle a skinning-knife half as well as Lena.

FLAVIO: Go along to Giulio's this morning between nine and ten, and ask him if he can find anyone to let me have the cash I need straight away on the security of these clothes. And if he puts you off, try at the Sabbioni, and pawn the things there for twenty-five florins. And as soon as you've got the money from one or other of them, bring it here.

CORBOLO: And leave you here half naked?

FLAVIO: Don't fuss! Fetch me a plain cloth gown and cap.

LENA: And be quick about it! I'm letting him come in now; but he needn't think that the girl will be coming to visit me until he's counted the money into my hand.

FLAVIO: Well, I'll go indoors, then.

LENA: Yes, come in – on my conditions, mind!

[LENA, FLAVIO *go into* LENA's *house and shut the door.*]

CORBOLO: Pox on it! I nearly gave her something to make conditions about then! I've had to deal with plenty of bawds and whores and so on in my time, and they all lived from the same rotten business; but this one takes the prize for the sheer shamelessness and greed that she puts into her dirty trade. – But it's getting light. That can't have been the bell for matins I heard just now; it must have been for the Ave Maria or for the sermon – unless the priests drank too much wine last night so that this morning '*erant oculi gravati eorum*'.[1] I don't think I shall be able to see Giulio yet; he generally sleeps till nine or ten in the morning. In the meantime, I'd better go to the piazza and see if I can find any quails or turtledoves to buy.

[*Exit* CORBOLO, *Right.*]

1. 'Their eyes were heavy.' *Matthew*, XXVI, 43.

# ACT TWO

*Scene: the same.*

[FAZIO *comes out of the front door of his house, followed by* MEN-
GHINO, *his servant.*]

FAZIO: A man who doesn't get up early, and get on with important
business in the morning, loses the day; and after that his affairs
can't go well. Menghino, I want you to go to Dugentola, and tell
the bailiff that the carts must be loaded this evening, and the wood
must be sent off tomorrow. And there'd better not be any mistake
about it, because I've got no fuel left. So don't come back until
you've seen that everything is in hand. And put yourself in a
position to tell me how the sheep are, and how many male and
female lambs have been born. And make them show you what
ditches they've dug, and account to you for the green timber
they've used; and make sure you count what's left over.

[LENA *opens her door and comes out.* FAZIO *does not see her, but
she hears what follows.*]

FAZIO: And now be off with you! Don't waste time! – But wait a
moment. If they've got a specially good lamb . . . But no, it would
be better to sell it anyway . . . Be off with you, then, Menghino . . .
It's a pity, but better not . . .

LENA: I should think not, indeed! I thought a miracle was going to
happen, when that spendthrift idea crossed your mind.

FAZIO: Good morning, Lena.

LENA: Good morning and much good luck to follow, Fazio.

FAZIO: You're up very early, Lena! It looks bad . . . looks bad.

LENA: Yes, of course, it would be much more fitting, since you
clothe me so splendidly and maintain me in such lavish style, if I
were to lie in bed until noon, and spend the whole day in idleness.

FAZIO: I do what I can, Lena. It would take a bigger income than
mine to set you up like that; but I do make a point of giving you
all the help that lies within my means.

LENA: *What* help?

FAZIO: You're always like that – always forgetting what I do for you. You show gratitude only at the moment when I'm giving you something. As soon as you've got it, it's a very different story.

LENA: And what have you ever given me? Are you going to bring up the rent-free house again?

FAZIO: And is that so little in your eyes? It's worth twelve *lire* a year in actual money, without counting the convenience of having me for a neighbour. But I won't say too much about that, because I don't want to throw it in your face.

LENA: Throw *what* in my face? The odd plate of soup or broth which you send me sometimes, when you've got more than you need?

FAZIO: No, something else, Lena.

LENA: Or the gift of two or three loaves of bread a month? or a small bottle of sour wine? or letting me take a couple of sticks when a cart-load of firewood arrives for you?

FAZIO: That's not all you have!

LENA: What else do I have from you? Come on, tell me! Robes of satin? Gowns of velvet?

FAZIO: You wouldn't be allowed to wear them, and I wouldn't be able to give them to you.

LENA: Show me an ordinary dress that you ever gave me.

FAZIO: I prefer not to answer.

LENA: You do give me the odd pair of clumsy old shoes or slippers for Pacifico, when they're well down at heel and full of holes.

FAZIO: And I give you new shoes for yourself!

LENA: Yes, but I'm lucky if I get three pairs in four years. And what about the accomplishments your daughter is learning from me, and has been for years past? Aren't they worth anything?

FAZIO: They're worth a lot, I won't deny it.

LENA: And when I came here, she couldn't spell out the Our Father in her first reader, and she didn't know how to hold a needle.

FAZIO: That's true.

LENA: And she couldn't handle a spindle. Now she can say the office, and sew and embroider as well as any girl in Ferrara. What's more, she can copy any stitch at sight, no matter how difficult it may be.

FAZIO: I admit all this. I don't want to be like you, denying my obligations. But I will say this: if you hadn't taught her, someone else would have done it, and only charged ten *giulii* a year. That's a lot less than the twelve *lire* you cost me!

LENA: And haven't I ever done anything else for you, to make up the difference? Why, devil take it, if you gave me twelve *lire* twelve times a year, it wouldn't make up for the disgrace you've brought upon me; for the neighbours say openly that I'm your whore. God curse you for a scabby old miser for putting me in a hovel like that! But I won't stay there any longer – you can give it to someone else.

FAZIO: Be careful what you say.

LENA: Go on, give it to someone else! I'm tired of having it rammed down my throat that I live in your house and don't pay you any rent. Even if I have to take a place in the Gambaro or the Paradiso,[2] I'm moving out of here!

FAZIO: Think it over, and let me know what you decide.

LENA: I've thought it over. Give the place to whoever you like!

FAZIO: I'd rather sell it . . . that's what I'll do.

LENA: Do what you like with it! Sell it, give it away, set fire to it! I'll find somewhere else.

FAZIO [*aside*]: The kinder I am to her and the more I humble myself before her, the more arrogant and inflexible she becomes. Everything I give her might as well be thrown away, for all the gratitude she shows. She'd like to have the very soul out of my body.

LENA: As if I couldn't live without him!

FAZIO [*aside*]: And it's God's own truth that quite apart from the rent she and her husband cost me at least another twelve lire per year.

LENA: Thank God, I'm still young enough to do myself some good.

FAZIO [*aside*]: I want to humble that overbearing pride of hers. I don't really want to sell the house; I just want her to think I will.

LENA: It's not as if I were cross-eyed, or crippled!

FAZIO [*aside*]: I'll bring Biagiolo along, or that surveyor fellow, to measure the place up, and I'll discuss the price with them while Lena's there; and I'll pretend I've got a buyer. These people haven't the money or the credit to find themselves another house – they'd

2. Two ill-reputed parts of Ferrara.

die of hunger anywhere else. I'm going to goad the brute from every possible angle till I get her properly broken in to bridle and saddle!

[FAZIO *goes indoors.*]

LENA [*soliloquizing*]: My god, he does want things all his own way! He thinks he can poison me with his stinking breath, ride me to exhaustion like a damned donkey, and then reward me with a 'Thank you very much!' A fine young gallant he is, to make a girl want to give him something for nothing! Oh! I was a silly woman to listen to his stories and his promises in the first place. But my useless brute of a husband kept on at me about it, till I thought he'd never stop. 'My dear, you'd better do what he wants. It'll make our fortune! If you know how to handle him, he'll pay all our debts.' And anyone would have believed it to begin with. He promised us the earth and all that therein is, as these scholars say. Well, he laid a trap for us, and I hope to see him break his own neck in it. Since he won't keep all those promises, I'm going to behave like servants do when their wages aren't paid – they get their own back on their masters by cheating them, robbing them and murdering them. And I'm going to get paid somehow, too, and I'll do anything, whether it's right or wrong. And no one can blame me for it – neither god nor man. If Fazio had a wife, I'd put all my efforts into making him a . . . . . . ., a . . . . . . . – what he's made Pacifico. But that's impossible, because his wife's dead; so I'll make him a . . . . . . . – what I said before – through his daughter.

[*Enter* CORBOLO, *Right.*]

CORBOLO [*aside*]: One helper's better than twenty, they say; and I've seen the truth of that proverb this morning.

LENA: That looks like Corbolo over there. Yes, it's Corbolo, and he's coming this way.

[CORBOLO *crosses stage slowly, repeatedly stopping to continue his story.* LENA *shows interest but cannot catch what he is saying.*]

CORBOLO [*as before*]: When I went off to get the things Flavio wanted, I went to the piazza and searched every inch of it; and then I went along the portico and looked in all the stalls. Then I went on towards the Castle, asking at every shop if they had any quails or doves.

LENA: He's coming very slowly; you'd think he was counting every step.

CORBOLO [*as before*]: I couldn't find a thing – only a few pigeons which were so thin and undernourished that you'd think they'd been suffering from a quartan fever for a year at least.

LENA: I hope he's got the money!

CORBOLO [*as before*]: Another fellow might have bought them, and thought to himself: 'Well, there's nothing better to be had; what does it matter to me whether they are thin or fat? They aren't for me anyway.'

LENA: He's all weighed down on the left-hand side.

CORBOLO [*as before*]: But I wouldn't do that. 'Orders is orders, but sense is sense,' as the proverb says. So I went and stood by the courtyard gate, and waited to see if any peasant would appear, or anyone else who might have something better than what I'd seen. Some of the duke's gamekeepers were standing there in a group; I think they must have been hoping that some of these noblemen who love hawks and dogs would come along and offer them a drink at the Gorgadello. Then one of them, who's a friend of mine, said: 'Corbolo, what are you looking for?' So I told him, and went on to say what a pity it was that for some time there's been no game on sale here, like there is in every other city, and how there's no decent food at all to be had, but only tough old meat, which you can't cook through no matter how long you try, and which costs the earth anyway. And everybody said I was right.

LENA: I'll wait here for him, and find out what he's done.

CORBOLO [*as before*]: So I walked on; and one of them follows me and catches me up just at the beginning of Goldsmiths Row. 'If you like,' he whispers to me, 'you can have a pair of fat pheasants for fifteen *bolognini*.' – 'Yes, yes, I'd be delighted,' says I, and he says: 'Wait for me by the bishop's palace, then; and mum's the word!' – 'I'll be as silent as Duke Borso's statue over there,' says I. And in the meantime there was a fine fat capon that I'd had my eye on, and I bought him, and half a dozen bitter oranges, and then I went on to the bishop's palace. And here comes my friend with the pheasants under his gown. They weighed as much as a pair of geese! I grabbed them, and paid down fifteen *bolognini* on the nail. Then he said: 'Any time you want four brace . . . or six, seven, up to ten brace, just let me know, provided it's kept secret between the two of us.' – 'Thank you very much,' says I.

LENA: What a lot of chat, all by himself! What a state he's in!

CORBOLO [*as before*]: So I promised him on my honour not to breathe a word – but I couldn't help laughing to think how the Duke guards his game with such care, and protects it with such ferocious proclamations and penalties, and all the time it's the gamekeepers who do the poaching!

LENA: He'll be late for his own funeral – and the sooner that happens the better.

CORBOLO [*as before*]: You never see pheasants at wedding breakfasts or public festivities, because of the proclamations. But rakes and their whores, dining discreetly in back rooms, have them all the time. Well, I've had my brace of birds roasted, and I've had the capon boiled, and here they are, all hot in this basket – But here's Lena.

LENA: Have you got the money, Corbolo?

CORBOLO: No, but I'll be giving it to you before long.

LENA: 'Giving' is a word I like the sound of; but I don't like 'before' and I don't like 'long'.

CORBOLO: You're different from other women; things can't be long enough for most of them.

LENA: I just like things here and now.

CORBOLO: Very well! Here and now I'm giving you a capon, two pheasants, bread, wine, and cheese, for you to take straight indoors. There wouldn't be any point in bringing you any pigeons, as you seem to have a fine big bouncing pair there already! [*Looking at her bosom.*]

LENA: Oh, get away with you!

CORBOLO: Let me just touch them, to see how tender they are!

LENA: You'll get my fist in your teeth. Where's that money?

CORBOLO: Every psalm ends with an 'Amen', they say. I know you're not likely to forget the money, and I'll bring it within half an hour. Giulio was still in bed when I got to his place. I gave him the message, and he told me to leave the clothes on his cash-desk and come back at midday. Meanwhile I've had the dinner cooked and seen to everything – But tell me, Lena, what reward shall I have for all my labours, since it's all because of me that you're going to get your twenty-five florins?

LENA: What do you want?

CORBOLO: You're asking me to tell you? I want something that you could give to me, or to a hundred other fellows, without being a penny the poorer for it.

LENA: I don't understand you.

CORBOLO: I'll tell you straight out then.

LENA: Bring me the money first; I can't understand anything without that.

CORBOLO: Does money help the understanding, then?

LENA: It does with me, and I reckon it does with most people.

CORBOLO: Would it make the deaf hear, too, do you think?

LENA: There's a lot of difference between hearing and understanding, idiot!

CORBOLO: Will you explain the difference to me, please? .

LENA: When donkeys bray to each other in the mill, we can hear them, but we can't understand them.

CORBOLO: I can, though! It means they want the very thing I want from you.

LENA: You're a cunning devil. Well, as the meal's ready, let's go and eat it.

CORBOLO: I'm coming. But where's the girl?

LENA: Where's the money?

CORBOLO: I'm sure I shall be able to let you have it within an hour.

LENA: And I'm sure I shall be able to persuade the girl to come here once the money's arrived. But let's go in; the food will be getting cold.

CORBOLO: You go in, I'll follow you in a minute.

[LENA *goes into her house.*]

CORBOLO: May this be the last meal you ever eat! May it choke you! To think I went to all the trouble of buying those birds and getting them cooked, just so that a sow and a billy-goat should have the pleasure of eating them! But they won't have quite the feast they think, because I intend to get my feet in the trough too.

# ACT THREE

*Scene: the same.*

[*Enter* CORBOLO.]

CORBOLO: Well, that's one of my two jobs finished successfully, and I feel quite pleased about it. The capon and the pheasants were plump and tender, the bread was good, and the wine was excellent; now Flavio keeps on saying how good I am at getting him value for money. I'll do the other job too, but I shan't enjoy it so much as this one. I don't like the idea of my master spending twenty-five florins, or rather chucking them away, without my doing anything to stop him. Borrowing's easy enough – it's paying back that's the difficulty. I don't see what he can do in the end, except sell his clothes; but if he does that, his father will find out sooner or later, and then we shall have shouting and uproar and turmoil all over the place, and Flavio will run a risk of being turned out of the house. What's needed here is the sort of cunning servant I've sometimes seen on the stage, who'd know how to tap the old boy's purse for a sum like that with a few well-thought-out tricks. Ah well, I may not be Davus or Sosia[3] – I may not have been born among the Getae or the Syrians – but oughtn't I still to have a bit of cunning in this ugly old head of mine? Can't I set up some audacious plot, in which Fortune will take a hand as well, since she's supposed to favour the brave? The trouble is, my old master isn't a credulous old fool like Chremes and Simon in the plays of Terence and Plautus. But never mind – the more cautious he is, the more glory it'll be for me if I can catch him out. He went off to Sabioncello yesterday by boat, and he's expected back this morning. So I'd better start thinking what I'm going to say to him. [*Looks off-stage, Left.*] But here he is now! This really is like a stage

3. Davus and Sosia were the names of cunning slaves in the old Latin comedy. They came from the countries indicated.

comedy, to have him turning up from the country just after I've mentioned him. But I don't want him to see me till I've got my trap ready for him.

[CORBOLO *withdraws to wings, Right. Enter* ILARIO, EGANO, *Left.*]

ILARIO: It's best to avoid getting so attached to things that you can't bring yourself to sell them even if the price is right . . . except for wives, of course, eh?

EGANO: I wouldn't make an exception for them either, if our laws and customs permitted it.

ILARIO: You're right – we ought to be able to sell them, exchange them, or give them away for nothing.

EGANO: You mean wives who don't happen to suit you, of course.

ILARIO: That's it. It's against the custom to sell them, but lending them out seems to be quite an accepted practice nowadays. But I'm really talking about a pair of bullocks. I got thirty ducats, and gold ducats at that . . .

CORBOLO [*aside*]: Just what we need!

ILARIO: . . . when I sold them yesterday to a peasant from Sandalo.

EGANO: They must be a fine pair of beasts.

ILARIO: My dear fellow . . .

CORBOLO [*aside*]: I must have that money – I will have that money!

ILARIO: They're magnificent.

CORBOLO [*aside*]: It's as good as in my pocket.

ILARIO: Very fine beasts in their own way; but I'd rather have the money.

CORBOLO [*aside*]: He'll cough up – I know he will.

ILARIO: At least I shan't have to worry any more about the authorities commandeering them to work on the moat and returning them to me half foundered.

EGANO: You've done the wisest thing. But here's my turning. If I can do anything for you, let me know.

ILARIO: Good-bye, Egano.

[*Exit* EGANO, *Left Centre.*]

CORBOLO [*aside*]: The bird's half under the net – now to drive it right inside, get it properly entangled and put it in the bag. [*Aloud*] What shall I do? Where can I turn, as my master's not at home?

ILARIO [*aside*]: Oh god! What's this?

CORBOLO: But why did Flavio have to go himself?

ILARIO [*aside*]: This sounds like bad news.

CORBOLO: It would have been much more sensible to write a letter to his father and send it off at once by messenger ...

ILARIO [*aside*]: There must have been an accident!

CORBOLO: ... rather than go there himself.

ILARIO [*aside*]: What can have happened?

CORBOLO: He'd have done better to tell the whole story to the duke himself.

ILARIO [*aside*]: Heaven help us!

CORBOLO: As soon as Ilario hears about it, he'll come flying back.

ILARIO [*aloud*]: Corbolo!

CORBOLO [*pretending not to hear*]: He won't stand for it – he'll play hell when he hears ...

ILARIO: Corbolo!

CORBOLO [*as before*]: ... but what can even he do now?

ILARIO: Corbolo!

CORBOLO: Who's that calling? Oh, master!

ILARIO: What's happened?

CORBOLO: Have you seen Flavio?

ILARIO: Why do you ask?

CORBOLO: The sun was hardly up when he left town, saying he was going to see you.

ILARIO: What was the emergency?

CORBOLO: You don't know what danger he's been in!

ILARIO: Danger? Tell me about it – what happened to him?

CORBOLO: My young master can reckon his life starts again from today. He was nearly killed by some ruffians, but, thank god, the harm they did him ...

ILARIO: He was injured, then?

CORBOLO: Not very badly.

ILARIO: But if he's been injured, whether seriously or not, whatever possessed him to make the journey out to the farm?

CORBOLO: It isn't the sort of injury that can be made worse by travel.

ILARIO: What? Why not?

CORBOLO: I assure you it can't – in fact it's made him lighter on his feet than before.

ILARIO: But tell me – is he wounded?

CORBOLO: Yes – it's a wound that's very difficult to heal. Not that it's bleeding, exactly ...

ILARIO: Oh! This'll be the end of me!

CORBOLO: But let me tell you where it is.

ILARIO: Go on.

CORBOLO: Not in the head, not in the shoulders. Not in the chest, and not in the side.

ILARIO: Where was it, then? Get on with it! He *is* hurt, you say?

CORBOLO: Oh yes, he is, and very unpleasantly too.

ILARIO: He'll have a heavy affliction to bear, then.

CORBOLO: And yet it's made him lighter!

ILARIO: Don't torture me! Is he injured or isn't he? No one could understand you, the way you're carrying on!

CORBOLO: I'll tell you.

ILARIO: Tell me then, curse you!

CORBOLO: Listen!

ILARIO: *Go on!*

CORBOLO: It's not a bodily injury.

ILARIO: Is he hurt in the soul, then?

CORBOLO: Something of the sort ... Last night he went out to supper with a group of young fellows. As he went off, he told me to go and fetch him with a torch at eleven o'clock. But then, I don't know why, he left the others some time before ten, and set out for home alone and without a light. When he got to the portico opposite San Stefano,[4] he was surrounded by four armed men, who seemed to come out of one of the shops there, and they gave him a very rough time of it.

ILARIO: And yet they didn't wound him? What terrible danger he was in!

CORBOLO: It was the will of heaven that he should escape bodily harm.

ILARIO: I thank god for that!

CORBOLO: So he took to his heels and ran for it as fast as he could. One of them struck at his head ...

ILARIO: My god!

4. The shops in the portico opposite the church of San Stefano were pawn-brokers. Corbolo is amusing himself by veiled hints at the truth.

CORBOLO: But he hit that gold badge that he used to wear, so that his cap fell off.

ILARIO: And did he lose it?

CORBOLO: No; those villains took it.

ILARIO: Well, they didn't give it back to him did they?

CORBOLO: Not likely!

ILARIO: It cost me more than twelve ducats, with the gold embroidery it had on it. But thank god they didn't do worse than that!

CORBOLO: And his gown came half off on one side, and got tangled up between his legs, so that it nearly had him over two or three times. Finally he gave it a tug with both hands, and got free of it.

ILARIO: So he lost that too?

CORBOLO: No, the thieves got it.

ILARIO: And if the thieves got it, doesn't that mean that Flavio lost it?

CORBOLO: I didn't think you could call a thing lost if someone else had found it.

ILARIO: Oh, you're an idiot! That gown cost eighty *scudi*, with the lining! But at the end of it all, the boy's not wounded?

CORBOLO: Not in the body.

ILARIO: And where the devil else could they wound him?

CORBOLO: In the mind. He was very disturbed, because of his loss and also because of the distress that he knew it would cause you when you heard about it.

ILARIO: And did he see who his attackers were?

CORBOLO: No – the night was too dark, and he was too frightened.

ILARIO: Well, I might as well write those things off.

CORBOLO: I'm afraid you're right, sir.

ILARIO: The young fool! Why didn't he wait for you, when you were going to fetch him?

CORBOLO: Well, sir ...

ILARIO: But you're an idiot too, not to have fetched him earlier.

CORBOLO: That's what you always do, sir – blame me for his mistakes. He ought to have waited for me; or if he didn't want to do that, he should have come back with his friends, for I'm sure they'd all have come with him if he'd asked them. But don't let's waste any more time, sir – you must do something about it while the scent is still warm.

ILARIO: Do something? But what can I do that's worth anything?

CORBOLO: Report the matter to the mayor,[5] to the secretaries, and if need be to the duke himself.

ILARIO: And what do you think any of them will do for me?

CORBOLO: They can put out proclamations.

ILARIO: That'll only add loss of reputation to loss of goods. The common people are sure to spread the story that it wasn't really a case of four ruffians attacking a single unarmed man, but a fair fight between equals, and that he agreed to surrender his arms and the other things to save his skin. And suppose I do go to the duke and tell him the story, what do you think he'll do but refer me to the mayor? And the mayor will just glance up to see if I've got a present for him, and when he sees I haven't, he'll say he has more urgent matters to attend to. And anyway, if I haven't got any evidence or witnesses, he'll think I'm a fool. Besides, who do you think commits half these crimes but the very people who are paid to catch the criminals? Then the mayor goes shares with one or other of their officers – they're all in it together.

CORBOLO: What can we do, then?

ILARIO: Possess our souls in patience.

CORBOLO: Flavio will never be able to do that.

ILARIO: He'll have to, whether he likes it or not. If he's escaped unhurt, he should reckon that heaven's been very kind to him. He's been badly frightened and in real danger, I know; but that's over now, and he's none the worse. I wish I could say the same about myself, but I've got a very nasty wound in the purse. What harm has been done has been done to me, and I'm the one that should be complaining, not Flavio. I'll get him another cap like the old one straight away, and a gown suitable to his station; but no one's likely to come along and reimburse me for the money I'm going to spend on replacing the things Flavio's lost.

CORBOLO: Do you think we should notify the second-hand shops and the Jews, so that if those villains try to sell the things, or pawn them, they can be kept waiting till you've been informed about it? Then you could go and get the goods back and have them arrested.

ILARIO: Now there's an idea that might do more good than harm.

5. The mayor was also chief of police, and had certain judicial functions as well.

But I don't base any great hopes on it. There's no doubt about usurers being villains; and those other fellows, who buy stuff and sell it again, are a crooked lot too and never tell you the truth. And stolen property is what they like best, because it's cheap to buy; and if they lend money on it they can be sure it'll never be redeemed.

CORBOLO: Let's tell them, anyway; it's no more than doing our duty.

ILARIO: Very well, tell them if you want to.

[ILARIO *goes into his house.*]

CORBOLO: The job's going all right; in fact I can regard it as finished. All I've got to do now is to get the things back from Giulio, and send them off again with someone whose face isn't known, to pawn them for whatever they'll fetch. I'm sure the old boy will redeem them as soon as he knows where they are. But I must tell Flavio about this scheme, so that he'll know what line to take with Ilario and won't contradict anything I've been saying.

[PACIFICO *comes out of his house.*]

CORBOLO: Here comes Pacifico.

PACIFICO: Flavio wants you.

CORBOLO: I was just coming to see him – I've got good news for him.

PACIFICO: He knows all about it. We heard everything you said from beginning to end. We were both listening behind the door, and we didn't miss a word.

CORBOLO: And what did you think of it?

PACIFICO: We give you full credit for being a better liar than any poet in the world. But wait a moment, and don't let Fazio see you come in here. Wait till he's safely indoors again, and then you can come in.

[CORBOLO *retires to wings, Right.* FAZIO *comes out of his house.*]

FAZIO: I don't want to turn you out from one day to the next, Pacifico, so I'm telling you now that you must find somewhere else to live within a month. I'm going to sell this house.

PACIFICO: It's yours, sir, to do what you like with it.

FAZIO: The buyer and I have agreed to get Torbido to survey it for us, and he's gone to fetch his measuring rod. I think the buyer wants to conclude the deal straight away.

PACIFICO: I wish I'd known about this yesterday, and I'd have tidied things up. You've caught me in a bit of a mess.

FAZIO: Well, go in now and try to get things in order quickly, as best you can. They'll be here in a minute.

PACIFICO: Please tell them to come tomorrow.

FAZIO: The buyer can't come tomorrow; he's got to go to Modena.

[FAZIO *goes into his house.* CORBOLO *returns from wings.*]

PACIFICO: Where are we going to put your young master, Corbolo, so that they don't find him? If Fazio sees him, he'll guess what's happening, and the fat *will* be in the fire.

CORBOLO: Isn't there anywhere in your house where you can hide him safely?

PACIFICO: If they're going to measure the whole place, how can any part of it be safe?

CORBOLO: Haven't you got a chest or a wardrobe where you could put him?

PACIFICO: There are only two little chests – so small that you couldn't get the duke's dwarf into either of them, even if you stripped him first.

CORBOLO: Well then, let's get him out of the house before they arrive.

PACIFICO: With his clothes at the pawnbrokers?

CORBOLO: I'll go home, and get him something else to wear.

PACIFICO: Very well – but come straight back. I'll wait here for you.

CORBOLO: Here comes Ilario.

[PACIFICO *goes indoors.* ILARIO *comes out of his house.*]

ILARIO [*aside*]: It can't do any harm if I go and attend to that matter myself, even if I have told Corbolo to do it. I'm too old a hand to think that anyone else will put as much diligence into looking after my affairs as I do myself. But here he is – What have you done so far?

[*Enter* CREMONINO, *Right, carrying* FLAVIO's *gown and cap. He goes up to* ILARIO's *house during the next speech, and prepares to knock on the front door.*]

CORBOLO: I've told Isaac and Benjamin at the Sabbioni; now I'm going to the Carri; and the Riva lot will be last of all.

ILARIO: What does that fellow want who's just going to bang on our door?

CORBOLO: Why, it's Cremonino! [*Aside*] To hell with it! The cat's out of the bag now!

ILARIO [*to* CREMONINO]: What do you want, my boy?

CREMONINO: I'm looking for Flavio.

ILARIO: Why, I believe that's Flavio's gown.

CORBOLO: I believe it is; and look, there's his cap, too. [*Aside*] Help me now, O father of lies, or we're done for!

ILARIO: Corbolo, what's going on here?

CORBOLO: It looks to me as if it was his friends all the time – pulling his leg for the fun of seeing him run away.

ILARIO: A silly sort of joke, I call it.

CREMONINO: My master Giulio sends back the things Flavio wanted to pawn, and says that his friend . . .

CORBOLO [*interrupting*]: Friend, indeed! A likely story!

CREMONINO: . . . his friend who was going to lend him the money on the security of these . . .

CORBOLO: Nonsense!

CREMONINO: . . . of these clothes, owed him the money which you, Corbolo . . .

CORBOLO: What a tissue of lies!

CREMONINO: . . . yes, you, Corbolo, came to ask him for today.

CORBOLO: Who, me?

CREMONINO: Yes, you!

CORBOLO: Just look at his face! What an accomplished liar he is!

ILARIO: Well, take the things back, Corbolo, and put them away. And you, my boy, go and tell Giulio that this isn't the sort of trick to play on a friend . . .

CREMONINO: Trick? What trick do you mean?

ILARIO: . . . nor the sort of thing I'd expect from a man in his position.

CREMONINO: But I don't think my master has been playing any . . . [*To* CORBOLO] What are you making those signs at me for, you fool? I'm going to tell the whole story, just as it . . .

CORBOLO: Making signs? Me?

CREMONINO: . . . just as it happened, and stick up for my master, because you're not being fair to him. If he'd had the money, he'd have gladly lent it to you.

CORBOLO: What money do you mean? Have a heart! Are you in a dream? Or do you think we're drunk, or raving mad?

CREMONINO: But didn't you bring this gown to Giulio, yourself, this very morning?

CORBOLO: Me and who else? We've got your measure all right!

CREMONINO: There you go making signs at me again!

CORBOLO: Who, me?

ILARIO: To hell with it, Corbolo! I saw you doing it myself that time!

CORBOLO: Well, of course, I did make a little sign, just to show him that we can see through his tricks, and aren't going to be taken in by them.

CREMONINO: The trickery's all on your side.

ILARIO: I want to hear this story. Where did you get these clothes from, my lad?

CORBOLO: Giulio was in his shop yesterday . . .

ILARIO: I want to hear him, not you!

CORBOLO: He'll try to get you to believe some ridiculous story. He's a great leg-puller.

CREMONINO: It's you who's doing all these things, not me.

CORBOLO: Now look me in the eye and take that smile off your face.

CREMONINO: What smile? Why should I look at you?

CORBOLO: Now go! – go quickly, and tell Giulio that Flavio will be in a position to pay him out for this one day.

ILARIO: No, my boy, don't go . . . you go away, Corbolo; I want to talk to him, not to you.

CORBOLO: Never let it be said that I allowed him to lead you by the nose!

ILARIO: What are you afraid of? Do you think he's going to put a spell on me with his words? Now tell me, my lad, how was it that these clothes . . . but be off with you, Corbolo! Get away from here!

CORBOLO: Are you really going to give him a hearing? You could put him through a crushing-mill and you'd never squeeze a word of truth out of him.

CREMONINO: I'm going to tell the whole truth.

CORBOLO: I'll believe that when I hear a donkey say the 'Our Father'.

ILARIO: Let him speak, I say!

CREMONINO: I'll tell the gospel truth.

CORBOLO: Let's bare our heads then, for it isn't right to listen to the gospel with your hat on.

ILARIO: There you go again, trying to interrupt everything he says. If you say another word, I'll . . . Oh, never mind, my lad, come indoors with me, and we'll leave Corbolo out here. I'm determined to find out about this silly trick – because that's what it must be, there's no doubt about it. We'll lock this tiresome fellow out of doors.

[ILARIO *goes into his house, taking* CREMONINO *with him.* PACIFICO *comes out of his front door.*]

CORBOLO: We're done for now. Those twenty-five florins are on their way all right, but they're travelling so fast that we'll never catch up with them. Giulio's done us a real good turn, I must say! I'll remember this as long as I live. He says, 'Come back in an hour's time and we'll see what can be done' – and then he does the opposite of what we'd agreed, and sends this idiot after me to break the threads of the web I'd woven and ruin my plans for the future.

PACIFICO: Why did you waste all that time out there arguing with him? Where are the clothes you're supposed to be getting for Flavio? We must get him out of the house at once, dammit! Do you want to wait until Fazio comes and finds him here?

CORBOLO: But I can't get into his room! Can't you see that Ilario's locked me out?

PACIFICO: What are we to do?

CORBOLO: You'll have to hide him in the house.

PACIFICO: There's nowhere to put him.

CORBOLO: Then send him out in his shift. Those are the only two things you can do, and you'll have to choose one of them.

PACIFICO: I won't do either.

CORBOLO: What will you do, then?

PACIFICO: I've just remembered I've got a big barrel in there, which a relation of mine lent me at harvest time. He wanted me to use it as a fermenting-tub for my wine, to get rid of a sort of dry woody smell it had; and he's never taken it back. I'll put Flavio in it until those fellows who're coming with Fazio have seen everything they want to see.

CORBOLO: Will there be enough room for him?

PACIFICO: Yes, room and to spare – and I cleaned it out thoroughly the other day. There's an end I can take out and put back quite easily, too.

CORBOLO: Let's go in, then, and talk to him about it.

PACIFICO: But these must be our visitors coming now! Yes, it is, for sure – I can see Torbido. We must get on with what we've got to do.

CORBOLO: We must!

PACIFICO: Come on inside then.

CORBOLO: Lead the way, and I'll follow you.

[PACIFICO, CORBOLO *go into* PACIFICO's *house. Enter* TORBIDO, GEMIGNANO, *Right.*]

TORBIDO: Once I've done my job, this rod of mine will tell me what the house is worth, to within a small margin of error.

GEMIGNANO: So your rod can talk, can it?

TORBIDO: Yes, it can; and it's also useful for making people sing [*brandishing rod*] if I lay it across their backs.

[FAZIO *comes out of his house.*]

TORBIDO: But here's Fazio – What do you want us to do, sir?

FAZIO: What I said before. You can start taking your measurements as soon as you like. This is the beginning of the frontage, and it ends here.

TORBIDO: We'll start from here, then.

FAZIO: Yes, that's right.

TORBIDO [*measuring*]: One rod, then – mark the end of it with your knife, boy!

GEMIGNANO: Done, sir!

TORBIDO: And that makes two – two rods, and something over. In all, three rods less two sixths of an ell. And now let's go indoors.

FAZIO: Hadn't you better make a note of what you've done so far?

TORBIDO: Very well, sir ... there it is!

[FAZIO, TORBIDO, GEMIGNANO *go into* PACIFICO's *house. Enter* GIULIANO, *Right, followed by* PORTER.]

GIULIO: I was up at the palace just now, and I saw the magistrate issue an order that Pacifico should furnish goods to serve as a security to cover a debt of forty-three lire which he owes to Bartolo Bindello. Now I know very well that Pacifico hasn't got enough to cover half that sum, or even a third of it. That makes me wonder if they won't confiscate a barrel which I lent him at harvest time to make his wine in. I'd do better to get it back now, rather than let the bailiffs take it away, and then have to sue for recovery, and argue, and prove that it belongs to me. The door seems to be open, so I'll go straight in, like one of the family – Come on, porter, follow me!

[GIULIO, PORTER *go into Pacifico's house.*]

# ACT FOUR

*Scene: the same.*

[*Enter* CREMONINO.]

CREMONINO: I can see now that I've put my foot in it properly. My
master will certainly have something pretty harsh to say when he
hears that it's through me that Ilario has found out about the tricks
Corbolo was playing to get some money out of him for Flavio.
But I didn't mean to do anything wrong – it was just a mistake.
And anyway, how could I know about it, when nobody told me
anything? If they want to complain about it, they ought to complain to my master, who should have let me know what was going
on. Where I slipped up was in not noticing that something was
wrong until it was too late to do anything about it. [*Enter three
bailiffs* – MAGAGNINO, SPAGNUOLO, *and* FALCIONE, *Right.*] – But
where are those bailiffs going? Some poor citizen's going to get a
nasty shock in a minute! The swine! Bastards!

[*Exit* CREMONINO, *Right.* BAILIFFS *lounge across stage, glancing
at front doors as if half-heartedly trying to identify an address, and end
up leaning against a wall, Left Centre. Enter* BARTOLO, *Right.*]

BARTOLO: I've sent the men off to Pacifico's house a dozen times at
least to collect the goods to serve as security against his debt. But
provided they get paid for their time, those blackguards don't
care about doing their duty. The original debt was forty lire fifteen
soldi, and he's spun out the legal proceedings for four years.
Judgement has been given in my favour on two separate occasions.
I've spent twice the sum involved in lawyer's fees, issue of summons, and copies of documents and rulings. And then it's involved
an intolerable amount of extra work for me personally, and I've
had to pay the cost of examinations in court and transcripts of
proceedings and judgements. Why, forty lire wouldn't even cover
the caps I've worn out taking them off to every Tom, Dick and

Harry, and the shoes I've worn out chasing attorneys (who're always in a hurry) round the corridors of the palace! And after all that labour and expense, the judgement against him is still only for forty lire, and the poor plaintiff can go and scratch his behind for all anyone cares! That's the way the law works in Ferrara! I wouldn't mind so much if I could *get* the forty lire I've had judgement for! And if I start thinking about some little ways of economizing in the home to make up for part of what I've lost, up pops my wife to remind me how much dowry she brought me, and that's the end of that! And I can't and won't believe that Pacifico is really half as poverty-stricken as he's supposed to be. [*Catches sight of head bailiff.*] Ah, Magagnino, come along and do your duty. Give that door a bang!

MAGAGNINO: Why should I hit it, when it hasn't done me any harm?

BARTOLO: It's doing me some harm, though! It's preventing me from getting my rights from the man who lives on the other side of it.

MAGAGNINO: Then take your own revenge! If you can't get any other satisfaction, take it out on the door! You can hit it, and kick it as well!

BARTOLO: But I'm hoping to get more than that out of it. Come on, we've got to make an entry – But the door's opening now, anyway.

MAGAGNINO: It shows the door's sense, for it to obey your orders, and not wait to be beaten.

BARTOLO: There seem to be a lot of people coming out. Come over here out of the way for a minute and let's see ... It looks as if they're bringing out the furniture and clearing the house right out.

[GIULIO, PACIFICO *come out of the house as* BARTOLO, MAGA-GNINO *move to one side.* GIULIO *dragging out barrel,* PACIFICO *trying to stop him.*]

GIULIO: But as the barrel belongs to me, why don't you want to let me have it?

PACIFICO: And why, when you've left it with me for six months, do you suddenly want it back in such a hurry?

GIULIO: Because if I don't get it today, I run the risk of losing it altogether, as I explained to you.

BARTOLO [*aside*]: They must have heard about my judgement; we didn't get here a moment too soon!

GIULIO: And until you explain to me what good or harm it can possibly do you whether I take it back or not, I can't for the life of me see why it should make any difference to you at all.

PACIFICO: If you take it now, you do me a great disservice!

GIULIO: And you do me one if you keep it!

PACIFICO: Well, please leave it with me for just half an hour longer.

GIULIO: But suppose the bailiffs come in the meantime and clear you right out? – And here they are now! Here they come! I shan't get it without an argument even now, so it's just as well I didn't leave it with you any longer.

[PACIFICO *goes indoors.* BARTOLO, MAGAGNINO *return to centre of stage, accompanied by the other two* BAILIFFS.]

BARTOLO: I'll take that barrel as part of Pacifico's debt to me. Falcione and Magagnino, lift it up on your shoulders, and you help too, Spagnuolo.

MAGAGNINO: I don't do porter's work.

SPAGNUOLO: Nor do I.

BARTOLO: A lot of use you are, I must say!

GIULIO: No one's to dare to touch that barrel, unless he wants to find himself . . .

BARTOLO: And are you going to try to stop me executing a court order to attach his goods as security for a debt?

GIULIO: I'm not stopping you taking anything that belongs to him, but that barrel, let me tell you, belongs to me!

BARTOLO: How can it be yours?

GIULIO: It's mine, all right – I lent it to him at harvest-time.

BARTOLO: What a cock-and-bull story! As I found it here in his doorway, I shall certainly take possession of it as belonging to him!

[BARTOLO *seizes the barrel.*]

GIULIO: Would you, by god! You would if I'd let you, no doubt of that! You just let go of it, or I'll . . .

BARTOLO: I call all you good people to witness that he's placing obstructions . . .

GIULIO: Obstructions be damned! Let go of it, I say!

[PACIFICO *comes out of his house, followed by* CORBOLO. *The* BAILIFFS *slip in through the open door.* FAZIO *comes out of his house.*]

FAZIO: What's all this noise? Why all the disturbance?

GIULIO: This is my barrel, and I want to take it home with me. This fellow's trying to stop me doing so.

PACIFICO: Giulio's telling the truth. It is his barrel.

BARTOLO: They're not telling the truth at all!

GIULIO: It's you that's lying!

FAZIO: Just tell me what's happened, without insulting each other.

BARTOLO [to GIULIANO]: You're lying!

GIULIO [to BARTOLO]: If you say that I'm lying, you're a liar yourself!

BARTOLO: Listen, Fazio – if I see the barrel on the way out of Pacifico's house, do you think I should let anyone tell me that it belongs to someone else?

GIULIO: If it belongs to Pacifico, why should it be on its way out into the street?

BARTOLO: Because you were taking it away to hide it somewhere.

PACIFICO: Not a bit of it – I was bringing it out to give it back to Giulio, who lent it to me at harvest-time.

FAZIO: Shall I say what I think?

BARTOLO: Yes, please do – I'll accept your opinion.

GIULIO: And so will I.

FAZIO: Let me take the barrel into safe keeping, Bartolo. If Giulio can prove to me within two days that it belongs to him, he can have it. If he can't prove it to my satisfaction, he must resign himself to its loss.

GIULIO: I agree to that.

BARTOLO: So do I.

GIULIO: I can easily prove my ownership.

BARTOLO: If you can produce fair and honest proof of that, you must have the barrel, and you can take it away whenever and wherever you like.

PACIFICO [to GIULIO]: I don't think you're very wise to agree to arbitration, and confuse an issue where your rights are as clear as daylight.

CORBOLO: That's true enough. Why not leave it where it is, in Pacifico's house?

BARTOLO: That wouldn't help me much, would it?

FAZIO [to CORBOLO]: And what's it got to do with you? Why are you putting in your oar? It's not your barrel, is it?

93

CORBOLO: I have got something to say about it, though – maybe
I've got a part interest in it after all.

GIULIO: That's something I'm not prepared to concede!

CORBOLO: Maybe I've got more interest in it than you think.

FAZIO: If you say so.

GIULIO: What do you mean, 'if he says so'? He's got no interest in
it at all!

FAZIO: Let him say what he likes. Don't you think the barrel will be
safe enough in my house? Aren't I just as much your friend as
Bartolo's?

GIULIO: Very well. We've agreed that Fazio should arbitrate, so let
him be the judge, and let him guard the goods in the meantime.

BARTOLO: And that's my view too.

FAZIO: Then let's take it over into my house here; and you can rest
assured that I won't allow it to be moved until I'm fully convinced whose property it is.

[*The barrel is moved over to* FAZIO'*s house and taken inside.*]

PACIFICO [*aside*]: Flavio's inside the barrel! See how every misfortune, every calamity falls on my head!

FAZIO: Pacifico, you'd better go indoors, and make sure the bailiffs
don't take a lot of other things that matter more to you than this.

PACIFICO: What can they take? There's little enough there, and
what there is belongs to my wife, as they know very well. They've
been here before. Still, perhaps I'd better ... but here they are,
coming out again.

[BAILIFFS *come out of* PACIFICO'*s house.* PACIFICO *goes indoors.*]

MAGAGNINO: Well, there's nothing there, except for the bits and
pieces we've found there before, and got on our list.

[TORBIDO *comes out of* PACIFICO'*s house.*]

TORBIDO: Why, you thieves, you ruffians! You've stolen my cloak!

MAGAGNINO: It's very wrong of you to make these false accusations
and insult us like that.

TORBIDO: You wretched jailbird, I hope you break your neck!
What have you got hidden away there?

MAGAGNINO: Oh, that? I took it to cover my expenses, not to steal
it from you.

TORBIDO: I'll give you expenses, all right, if this measuring-rod of
mine doesn't let me down!

GEMIGNANO: And I'll give you a hand, sir.

GIULIO: And I won't stand idly by either.

TORBIDO: See that stone, Gemignano? Pick it up, and break his head with it. Show what a lad from Modena[6] can do.

MAGAGNINO: Is this the way to treat the duke's officers?

TORBIDO: The duke doesn't have thieves in his service! [*He recovers his cloak.*] And now be off with you, you cowardly robbers. Go to the devil! [*Exeunt* BAILIFFS.] – If I hadn't noticed what was happening when I did, I'd have been done for! I'd have had to go home in my doublet and precious little else! This rod of mine would have come in useful in another way then – I'd have shouldered it like a pike, and people would have thought I was a German soldier, or a Swiss.

FAZIO: Have you got anything else to measure?

TORBIDO: No, I've measured everything down to the last brick and the last beam; I've got it all written down and I'll take it with me. Then I'll do my calculations, and I'll notify both parties about the correct price.

GEMIGNANO: When will you be finished, sir?

TORBIDO: Today. Is there anything else I can do for you, Fazio?

FAZIO: Not for the present.

TORBIDO: Good day to you, then, sir.

FAZIO: Thank you very much. Licinia! [*Calling to his daughter inside his house.*] If anyone asks for me, send him on to Onofrio's. I'll be there till supper time.

[*Exeunt omnes, Right.* LENA *comes out of her house.*]

LENA: We've had one bit of good luck among all the bad, and that is that Fazio's decided to go out. Otherwise we'd never have got Flavio out of the barrel. When I saw the barrel with him inside it being taken into Fazio's house, I had such a fright, such a flutter round my heart, that I don't know how it was I didn't die then and there. If he'd moved a finger, they'd have spotted him – a sigh, a sneeze, a cough would have been enough to ruin us. Now that this crisis has gone by without doing us any harm, we must make sure that something else doesn't happen. All we've got to think about now is getting Flavio out of there without anyone seeing him. Corbolo will have to go and get him some clothes;

6. The Modenese were proverbially ferocious.

LENA

but first of all we'll have to get Fazio's maidservant out of the way.
If she stays in the house, there's every chance that she'll see the
young fellow, or hear him. [*Goes over to* FAZIO's *front door.*]
Menica! ... Menica! ... I'm wasting my breath. Licinia! Ask
Menica to get her veil and come over to my place – But here
she comes.

[MENICA, *an elderly maidservant, comes out of* FAZIO's *house.*]

MENICA: Yes, Lena; what is it?

LENA: Will you do me a great favour, Menica dear – something I
shall never forget?

MENICA: What is it?

LENA: Will you do it for me?

MENICA: Yes, I will if I can.

LENA: Dearest Menica, will you go to Santa Maria degli Angeli for
me?

MENICA: What, now, d'you mean?

LENA: Yes, now.

MENICA: Just let me put the supper on to cook first.

LENA: No, no – please go now! I can put a pot on the fire without
your being there. And when you're opposite the church, turn off
between the Mosti orchard and the convent. Then go straight on
up till you turn left for a place called Mirasol,[7] I think. And please
hurry!

MENICA: Yes – but what do you want me to do when I get there?

LENA: I *am* a scatterbrain! Ask for Pasquino's wife – I think it's the
third door on the right – her name's Dorotea, and she teaches the
girls to read. Go to her, and say: 'Lena has sent me for her spindle
irons – the ones she uses for silk', and ask her to let you have them,
because I need them badly.

Go now, dear Menica; and when you get back, I'll give you
enough cloth to make a bonnet.

MENICA: The meat has been washed, and it's in the basin – all ready
and waiting to be put in the pot.

[*Exit* MENICA, *Left.*]

LENA [*glancing through* FAZIO's *front door*]: Ready and waiting the
meat may be; but one particular joint isn't going to get put in
the pot until I've had those twenty-five florins. I know these

7. Ariosto himself lived at Mirasol.

young lovers! The grand passion lasts just as long as they're at the stage of trying to get what they want. While they're in that condition, they'd gladly sacrifice the last penny in their pockets, the last drop of blood in their veins. But see what happens when they get it! It's like pouring water on a fire – the flames go out in a moment. And once the flames have gone, they won't give you a twentieth part of what they promised you before. So I'm going in to put a stop to any little games that Flavio and the girl may be getting up to.

[CORBOLO *comes out of* PACIFICO's *house.*]

Ah, Corbolo, hurry up and fetch Flavio something to wear. Then we'll get him out of the house, while the opportunity's there.

CORBOLO: No, no, Lena! While the opportunity's there, give him a chance to get it in. All you and Pacifico have to do is to keep out of the way.

LENA: Certainly not! Don't you think I'd ever let him get what he wants, unless he pays up first. I'll be watching over the girl, you can be sure of that!

[LENA *goes into* FAZIO's *house.*]

CORBOLO: You can watch her until the eyes pop out of your head, for all I care! – But can I really stand by and let Flavio be dragged away from Licinia without having a bit of what he fancies, after getting up in the small hours, being locked up in Pacifico's house like a prisoner, and then this unpleasant and dangerous business of being carted around packed into a barrel like a load of mullet, or eels from Comacchio? But what can I do, now that I've got that dirty whore and her cuckold against me? They take no notice of entreaties, and there's no scope for threats. It's out of the question to use force, because we're in enough danger already without stirring up more trouble. Well, we've got to get hold of those twenty-five florins that we've been condemned to pay – there's no hope of a pardon, nor even of extra time to find the money! But where am I going to find a sum like that? I've tried to borrow it on credit, and that was a waste of time; and we can't pawn the clothes, because Ilario has put a stop to that. And it would be very risky to try to devise a new trap for him – he won't let himself be caught again ... and yet it *is* sometimes possible to catch a bird a second time though it's been in the net before!

97

It might even be easier to fool him this time, because he won't think I'd ever have the nerve to try again so soon after my first failure. But what shall I do? What can I do, after all? I'd better think quickly; there isn't much time. I'll try . . . What? I'll say . . . Yes, that'll do! – but will he believe me? – he'll have to! – But here comes Pacifico.

[PACIFICO *opens his front door and looks out.*]

PACIFICO: Where are the clothes?

CORBOLO: Clothes? What clothes? Are you trying to make a tailor out of me? You don't seem to know my real profession, which is minting money. I'm just going to strike twenty-five florins now, and they're all for you!

PACIFICO: I wish you could!

CORBOLO: Then just do what I say. What arms have you got in the house?

PACIFICO: Well, there's Fazio's coat of arms, painted over the fire-place.

CORBOLO: Not that kind of arms – things to hurt you with!

PACIFICO: I've got plenty of them. There's poverty, there's despair, there's my wife's filthy temper, and the insults she heaps on my head all the time.

CORBOLO: Yes, but have you got a sword, or a bill-hook, or a spit, or anything like that?

PACIFICO: There is an old spit, eaten away with rust. You can tell what a wretched state it must be in from the fact that the bailiffs have never bothered to take it away.

CORBOLO: Very well – come out and show it to me. [PACIFICO *fetches spit.*] Won't you agree that I'm a great alchemist if I can transmute that mass of old rust into twenty-five golden florins?

[PACIFICO, CORBOLO *go into* PACIFICO's *house.*]

# ACT FIVE

*Scene: the same.*

[*The front door of* PACIFICO's *house opens, and* CORBOLO *comes out, trying to persuade* PACIFICO *to follow him.* PACIFICO *is armed with the spit, and looks very frightened.*]

CORBOLO: Come on out! Further than that! Further still! Try to put a little space between yourself and the house! You look more timid with the handle of a weapon in your hand than you'd have any right to be if the point of it was stuck up against your chest. What are you so frightened of?

PACIFICO: Of the captain of police, who might find me here armed with this spit, and put me in prison.

CORBOLO: No fear of that! I'll tell him you're a bailiff, or the hangman; he'll believe it, because you could easily be either one or the other, by the look of you. Hold your head up! You look as if you're going to burst into tears. Stand up straight! Stand up boldly! Be fierce! Be a bravo!

PACIFICO: What do I have to do to be a bravo?

CORBOLO: Be free with the names of God and his saints! Hold your spit like this! Turn towards me, and put on a dark, threatening countenance! [*Aside*] – I must be mad, to think I can make a lion out of a sheep! – But here come two of Don Ercole's[8] grooms; they'll help me if Pacifico can't! [*Enter* GROOMS, *Right.*] I'll go and speak to them. [*To* GROOMS] Good day to you, brothers!

GROOMS: And a very good day to you, Corbolo! How are you? Are you going to buy us a drink?

CORBOLO: Yes, I'd like to; but I was thinking of doing you a better turn than that.

GROOMS: What is it?

8. Don Ercole was the heir apparent to the Dukedom of Ferrara at the period in which this play is set.

99

CORBOLO: If you'll stay here with me for half an hour, I'll put you in the way of detecting a contraband which will be worth at least two scudi for each of you.

GROOMS: We shan't forget your kindness to us.

CORBOLO: Listen, then. The Jews who run the money-lending business at Riva bought a big consignment of cheese yesterday. They've got it loaded on to two carts, well covered over with straw. You'd never spot it unless you happened to know it was there, as I do. It was the supplier who told me about it. They haven't got a permit and they haven't paid any tax on it, and they're going to bring it right past here. Well, I didn't want it known that I was behind this scheme of detecting the contraband, so I told my neighbour here about it, and stationed him here armed with that spit, so that he could search under the straw when the carts arrive, and find the cheese. I was going to be here myself so that I could step in and arrange a settlement, so that the Jews wouldn't actually be taken to court. But he's such a coward that I'd rather not get involved in anything with him. If you'd like to come in with me, I'd be very glad to have you as partners.

GROOMS: We'd like that very much, and we'll promise to split the takings with you like honest companions.

CORBOLO: Then take up your stations! [To FIRST GROOM] You stay here, and watch out carefully; if the carts go past that way, you can run over to them in a moment. [To SECOND GROOM] And you watch the other road over there. [Aside] Well, that's the artillery properly posted on the flanks! Just now my lies were in full retreat, defeated and broken; but now they can make a stand, launch a counterattack, and put their main pursuer, Ilario, to flight! But here he comes. My lies are going to have a hard struggle to begin with, but if they survive that, victory is certain!

[ILARIO comes out of his house. CORBOLO retires to wings, Left, during the following speech.]

ILARIO: What a tangle that thieving blackguard would have got me into, if heaven hadn't sent young Cremonino to me at just the right moment! I was so near to falling into the trap – and it was pure chance that the boy let the cat out of the bag – he didn't mean to do anything of the kind. I think Corbolo wanted to persuade Flavio to sell the clothes secretly, and then get him to waste the money on women – though no doubt he'd have managed to get his hands on most of it himself. I believed his story, and I was all ready to get Flavio another gown and another cap to cheer him up. I thought he'd be sad, because I believed he'd really lost those things. But what I can't understand is why my son should behave like that with me. You won't find a father anywhere who's so indulgent, so anxious to gratify all his son's wishes – all his honest wishes, that is. My view is that all the blame must fall on that greedy swine Corbolo. I won't have him in my house another moment. I'm going to sack him, as he so richly deserves.

[CORBOLO *returns to centre of stage.* ILARIO *catches sight of him.*]

ILARIO: Do you still dare to appear before me, you ugly brute?

CORBOLO: Don't be angry, sir – and above all, don't let your anger make you deaf to the voice of family feeling!

ILARIO: Why, you're weeping!

CORBOLO: You've more reason to weep than I have, sir. Your son . . .

ILARIO: Heaven save us!

CORBOLO: . . . is in danger.

ILARIO: Danger?

CORBOLO: Yes, danger of death, if something isn't done quickly.

ILARIO: What's that? What's that? Go on! Get on with it! Where is he?

CORBOLO: Pacifico caught him in adultery with his wife. Look, sir – the villain's standing there now, waiting for a chance to kill him with that spit. Those two young fellows there . . . and there . . . are relations of his, and he's waiting for his wife's three brothers to come and join them.

ILARIO: But where is the boy?

CORBOLO: Flavio? Those blackguards have got him besieged [*with a vague wave of the hand*] in there.

ILARIO: What do you mean, in there? Where is he?

CORBOLO: In Fazio's house.

ILARIO: Is Fazio in there too?

CORBOLO: If he was, I wouldn't be so worried. No, there's no one there but Fazio's daughter, a mere girl. You can imagine how much good she's going to be to him!

ILARIO: But if he was caught with Pacifico's wife in *there* [*pointing to*

PACIFICO's house], how is it that he's in *there*? [*Pointing to* FAZIO's *house*].

CORBOLO: I'll tell you the whole story, sir.

ILARIO: Yes, let's have it. Don't leave anything out – and none of your additions, mind, either!

CORBOLO: I'll tell you exactly what's happened – but first of all I'd like to explain something. You know that other story I told you, about Flavio being attacked and robbed of his clothes? It wasn't meant to do you any harm, but just to persuade you, with as little distress to yourself as possible, to give me the money he needs to get him out of the danger he's in. And because that didn't work, his life's in far more peril now than it was before.

ILARIO: Just tell me what's happened!

CORBOLO: Flavio thought Pacifico had gone out for the day, and Lena thought so too. So Flavio went to her room; and while they were in bed together that cuckoldy fellow, who must have been hiding somewhere, jumped out and threatened to kill him with that spit.

ILARIO: Oh! my heart!

CORBOLO: Flavio begged and pleaded, and offered him money too, until he agreed to spare his life.

ILARIO: That's better . . . that's better . . . if we can buy him off.

CORBOLO: But that's not the end of the story.

ILARIO: What else happened? Get on with it!

CORBOLO: Twenty-five florins was the sum they agreed on, to be paid before Flavio left the house. So he sent for me, and took off his gown and cap, and told me to go to Giulio and try to pawn them for the sum he needed, while he stayed there as a hostage. Then that young fellow Cremonino came along and put in his oar, as you know. The result is that Flavio's done for, God help him, unless you do something quickly.

ILARIO: But why should they do him any harm, if they've come to an agreement?

CORBOLO: I'll tell you, sir. Pacifico thought we were cheating him, and he became even more furious than he'd been before. He grabbed the spit again, and was going to kill him then and there, without giving him a chance to say anything.

ILARIO: That was where you made a bad mistake – you should have come and told me the whole story at once. But what happened in the end? Go on, damn it!

CORBOLO: I can't think how it was that Pacifico didn't kill him. You can believe me when I say God and the saints must have been looking after him.

ILARIO: But how could a cowardly rogue like that find the nerve to threaten my son's life?

CORBOLO: If your son hadn't grabbed up a stool and defended himself with that as he backed away towards the door and jumped out into the street, Pacifico would have killed him for sure.

ILARIO: But he did get away safely in the end, didn't he?

CORBOLO: I wouldn't say he was safe yet.

ILARIO: This business will be the death of me.

CORBOLO: That villain pressed him closely, and gave him no chance to get clear. In the end he had to take refuge in Fazio's house, and they've got him besieged in there now.

ILARIO: What audacity! What a beggarly, rascally, reckless villain!

CORBOLO: And he's planning to get together a crowd of other ruffians and force an entry.

ILARIO: Force an entry? I'm not so friendless nor so destitute that I can't put a stop to that, and show Pacifico up for the wretch he is!

CORBOLO: Don't take on too much, sir, when there's an easier way out. Causing a crowd to collect is against the law of our duke, and the penalty is at the discretion of the magistrate. Besides, it could easily lead to manslaughter. I quite believe you could stop Pacifico doing Flavio any physical harm – in fact the boot would more likely be on the other foot – but can you stop the mayor proceeding against Flavio if Pacifico lodges a complaint with him, as there's every reason to think he will? I'm sure you know all about the penalties laid down for adultery, and how much discretion the mayor has to increase them – not according to the degree of the offender's guilt, but the depth of his purse. Be careful, sir, that you don't end up in serious trouble, with your distress giving great pleasure to the hangers-on at court who're always on the look-out for cases like this, which give them a chance to go and ask the duke to make them a present of the fine-money. It's much better to part with twenty-five florins by agreement, without a fight, than to put yourself in danger of losing five hundred – perhaps even a thousand.

ILARIO: I'd better go and have a word with Pacifico, and see what's in his mind.

CORBOLO: No, no, sir – don't do that! He might be so carried away by his anger that he'd insult you in a way you could never overlook. Let me go – I think I know just what to say to him to make him quiet and respectful again. And then I can bring *him* over to *you*, which is much more suitable for your dignity.

ILARIO: You go, then.

CORBOLO: Wait here for me, sir.

ILARIO: But first of all listen to me, Corbolo. Make him an offer, but don't fix any exact sum of money. I want to attend to that myself. Make him a promise in general terms – you know what I mean.

CORBOLO: Yes, I know, sir. But it would be better not to quibble about the odd couple of florins.

ILARIO: Leave that side of it to me – I know more about it than you do.

[CORBOLO *goes over to* PACIFICO *and speaks softly to him.*]

ILARIO: I think it'll be a good idea if I go and talk to Fazio before I tackle Pacifico. I'd like to see whether Fazio intends to put up with this business of violence being offered to my son in his house. Besides, he'd be the right man to make peace in this case, for I know he has a lot of influence with Pacifico. I'll be able to find him at the barber's shop; he's always there, playing chess the whole day long.

[*Exit* ILARIO, *Right.* CORBOLO *leaves* PACIFICO, *crosses stage and beckons the two* GROOMS *over to him.*]

CORBOLO [*to* GROOMS]: I'm sorry, brothers, but you might as well go, and not waste any more of your time. My master, who sold the cheese to the Jews, tells me that they've changed their minds. They're getting a permit and they've paid the tax.

GROOMS: Ah well! It sounded too good to be true!

CORBOLO: You'll have to take the will for the deed . . . and it's true enough that I did my best for you.

GROOMS: We know that, and we'll always be grateful to you for it.

CORBOLO: God bless you, brothers!

GROOMS: Good-bye, Corbolo.

[*Exeunt* GROOMS, *Left.* PACIFICO *comes over to* CORBOLO.]

PACIFICO: Well, how did you get on?

CORBOLO: Very well indeed. You're going to receive twenty-five florins from Ilario, who'll beg you and implore you to accept them ... But that's if you do exactly what I tell you to do, and say exactly what I tell you to say, when you've got rid of that spit. Don't let's waste any time, now – go and put it away, and come straight back to me ... But wait a moment!

PACIFICO: What is it?

CORBOLO: Now that there's no doubt you'll get the money you've been promised, get your wife out of there, and leave those two lovers alone together for a bit before Menica comes back – or Fazio, come to that.

PACIFICO: There's plenty of time. If Menica does come back, I can easily find an excuse to get her out of the way again. And there's no need to worry about Fazio – he never gets back before sunset.

[CORBOLO, *with an impatient gesture, shepherds* PACIFICO *into* FAZIO's *house.* LENA's *voice is heard raised angrily inside the house a couple of times. Finally* LENA *and* PACIFICO *come out into the street.* LENA *crosses Right and goes into her own house.* PACIFICO *comes up to* CORBOLO *for further instructions.*]

CORBOLO: Go on, then – go and put that spit away! Then we can go and get the twenty-five florins from Ilario.

[PACIFICO *goes into his house. During the first part of the following speech* MENGHINO, FAZIO's *serving lad, enters Left and goes up to* FAZIO's *front door.*]

CORBOLO: All's well now. After so much toil, after so many dangers, the army of my lies is going to be victorious in the end – in spite of Fortune, which did its best to defend the contents of Ilario's purse from me. [*Catching sight of* MENGHINO] But where's that fellow going? Pacifico! Pacifico! Come out here quickly! Run, man, run! Only you can save us!

[*Enter* PACIFICO.]

PACIFICO: Here I am!

CORBOLO: Run, Pacifico, run! Go and make sure that fellow doesn't see Flavio!

PACIFICO: What fellow?

CORBOLO: What's the name of that lad who works here? – But what are you waiting for? If you go in, you'll see him! – But I remember now anyway. Menghino! That's it!

PACIFICO: Menghino? To hell with it!

CORBOLO: It's Menghino all right! [PACIFICO *goes into* FAZIO's *house, very slowly.*] What a paralytic idiot he is! But I'm still more of an idiot myself, to leave anything to him – he's as slow as a tortoise. – And now here comes Menica! Wherever I look, the enemy forces are getting thicker on the ground, and my heart fails at the thought of trying to resist their assault.

[CORBOLO *goes into* ILARIO's *house. Enter* MENICA, *Left, very out of breath.*]

MENICA: I swear to God that's the last time I ever do anything for Lena! She sent me off a good half mile the other side of Santa Maria degli Angeli; and I ran nearly all the way, so that I wouldn't be away too long, and now I'm so done up I can hardly move! I wouldn't have minded going all that way, if only I'd found the wretched woman I was looking for. I went from door to door like a beggar, asking for her everywhere, and no one had ever heard of anyone called Dorotea who gave lessons; and there doesn't seem to be a man called Pasquino in Mirasol or anywhere near it either. And worse still, my master ran into me on the way back, and wanted to know where I'd been – he's on his way here now with Ilario, *and* in a towering rage, I don't know why – and when I told him and explained that it was Lena who'd sent me there, he made a terrible scene, and threatened me with a good beating if I ever did anything for her again. And that's an order I don't mind obeying! Once I find somewhere to sit down, it'll take more than words to get me on my feet again.

[MENICA *goes into* FAZIO's *house. Enter* ILARIO, *Right.*]

ILARIO: I went to find Fazio, thinking he'd be just the man to make peace between Flavio and Pacifico. What I didn't know is that he's so much in love with that wretched woman that there's no getting any sense out of him. As soon as I told him that Pacifico had caught her with Flavio, he got into such a jealous rage that it's going to be more difficult to pacify him than her husband – But here he comes! [*Enter* FAZIO, *Right, trembling with fury so that he can hardly walk.*] – Come on, now, Fazio, move a little quicker;

we must get there before a worse scandal follows. Hurry up, sir, if you've any regard for me!

FAZIO: I can't and won't put up with it, Ilario! To think that after all the things I've done for that slut, and all the things I was going to do, she should have betrayed me like that! I'm going to have my revenge on her!

ILARIO: If she's wronged you, revenge yourself by all means. I'm not pleading her case, but just asking you not to let Pacifico attack my son in your house.

FAZIO: And so her new lover's a capricious boy, who's young enough to be her son. What can she expect from him, except that he'll boast about it and drag her name in the mire?

ILARIO: My boy didn't mean to offend you, Fazio. If he'd known how much she meant to you, I'm sure he would have shown her the same respect that he undoubtedly feels towards yourself.

FAZIO: So that's why she's been so bad-tempered and difficult with me this last couple of weeks!

ILARIO: Now just calm down for a minute and tell me this . . .

[The front door of FAZIO's house opens and MENGHINO's voice is heard inside.]

MENGHINO: I tell you I saw it myself, Pacifico! You can't hush it up now.

ILARIO [to FAZIO]: Ah, we've wasted too much time! Listen to all that shouting inside your house! Now you must help me, Fazio!

[MENGHINO comes out of FAZIO's front door, followed by PACIFICO.]

MENGHINO: I'm going to find my master and tell him what you've been up to!

PACIFICO: Listen to me, Menghino . . .

MENGHINO: I've heard enough already, and seen enough too!

PACIFICO: Don't try to stir up trouble like that . . .

FAZIO [to ILARIO]: Whatever can this mean?

PACIFICO: . . . or there'll be the devil to pay.

MENGHINO: I'm going to tell my master, if it's the last thing I do!

[ILARIO begins to move towards FAZIO's house. FAZIO checks him.]

FAZIO: No, no! Wait a moment – let's see what they're arguing about!

PACIFICO: Don't go, Menghino; stay here and listen to me!

MENGHINO: Let me go, Pacifico. Don't think you can stop me telling my master now!

[LENA *comes out of her house and addresses* MENGHINO.]

LENA: And what the blazes have you got to say that anyone wants to listen to? May you break your neck! What are you supposed to have seen, you ugly, half-witted donkey?

MENGHINO [*to* PACIFICO]: I saw Licinia and Ilario's son . . .

ILARIO [*aside*]: But he means Lena, not Licinia.

MENGHINO: . . . and they were in there, hugging and kissing each other . . .

LENA: That's a damned lie!

MENGHINO: But here's my master – I'm going to tell you the truth, sir! *I* won't be a traitor! Your daughter . . .

FAZIO: That's enough, you idiot! I heard you before. Do you want the whole neighbourhood to know about it too? – Ilario, you needn't think I'm going to let your son do me an injury like this without revenging myself on him as fully as I can. So much for that ridiculous story you told me about Lena and her husband!

ILARIO: That . . . that was what Corbolo told me . . .

FAZIO: But this isn't an insult to be passed over lightly – it's a very serious matter.

ILARIO: But listen, Fazio, I beg you . . .

FAZIO: Shame on you, Ilario! I'm amazed at you. Does this insult seem to you to be one I should ignore? You may be richer and better born than I am, but that doesn't mean I'm inferior to you in courage. Before Flavio leaves my house, I'm going to make an example of him which will show that a man in my position can't be trifled with!

ILARIO: By the paternal love which you feel as much as I do, I implore you to have mercy on me and on Flavio!

FAZIO: But it's that very paternal love that tells me I must be revenged!

ILARIO: By our ancient friendship, then!

FAZIO: You'd find this just as unforgivable as I do, if you were in my shoes. My honour, if you'll excuse me mentioning it, means more to me than your friendship. I'd rather lose all I have in the world than lose my honour, and without it I wouldn't want to live at all.

ILARIO: But isn't there one way in which we can save it?

FAZIO: Very well – let's settle this at one stroke. If your boy marries Licinia, and restores her honour, we can be friends again. But otherwise . . .

ILARIO: Stop there, Fazio! You've known me for fifty years now, and you know better than anyone what my way of life has been. You know I've always been a decent, law-abiding fellow, and that I've always been fond of you, always ready to show you respect and offer you my help – for I've given you some proof of it. Well, don't think I'm going to change now. Let me talk to Flavio and see exactly how things stand. And rest assured that I'll do whatever needs to be done to put things right and make good the insult which has been offered to you.

FAZIO: Let's go in then.

ILARIO: Lead on, and I'll follow you.

[FAZIO, ILARIO, MENGHINO *go into* FAZIO's *house*.]

PACIFICO: Well, Lena, now you can see where your wickedness and your whoring have led you!

LENA: And who made me a whore?

PACIFICO: You might as well ask a man on the way to the gallows who made him a thief. You became a whore of your own free will.

LENA: I became a whore because of your insatiable greed! If I hadn't hired myself out to a hundred different louts, just to keep you in food, you'd have died of hunger. And now, to reward me for the good I've done you, you reproach me with being a whore, you cowardly wretch!

PACIFICO: I reproach you with not being more modest and discreet about it.

LENA: Why, you great ponce! Do you talk to me about modesty? If I'd taken on all the men you've wanted me to – all the men you've constantly pestered me to accommodate – I'd have been a more public prostitute than the worst tart in the Gambaro! And when you thought that the front door wouldn't take the traffic, you wanted me to open up the back door for business as well!

PACIFICO: For the sake of peace, I suggested a course of action which I knew would give you great pleasure. I knew that if I'd tried to stop you you'd have been completely intolerable to live with.

LENA: Oh, go to hell!

PACIFICO: This life with you *is* hell! But it ought to be enough for you to be allowed to do what you like with yourself, while I look on and tolerate it, without disgracing us still further by setting up as a procuress – and a procuress of decent men's daughters, at that!

LENA: If I could stay young forever, it would be easy for me to go on maintaining both of us in the same old way. But the ants prepare for winter, and poor women like me must prepare for old age. They need to learn some profession well in advance, so that when the time comes they don't have to begin from scratch. And what art could I study that would be more profitable than this one, or easier for me to learn? Why should I wait until the last moment, when I shall be in real trouble, before I begin my training?

PACIFICO: I'd rather you'd done this to anyone else but Fazio, to whom we owe so much.

LENA: Why, you swine, I hope you break your neck! As if you didn't know about the whole thing from the beginning! Now that the plan's turned out badly, you're throwing the whole blame on me for something that's just as much your fault as mine. But if we'd got those twenty-five florins, you'd have wanted your fair share, *and* more.

PACIFICO: That's enough – here comes Menica.

[MENICA *comes out of* FAZIO's *house.*]

MENICA: Lena, how *could* you? Does Fazio really deserve a dirty trick like that from you?

LENA: What dirty trick? What am I supposed to have done to him?

MENICA: Not much, I suppose you'd say!

LENA: Nothing at all, compared with the misery he's caused me. There's no injury I could do him that he wouldn't deserve.

[PACIFICO *goes into his house.*]

MENICA: You've shown him what a spiteful nature you have, Lena, but you haven't done him any harm – far from it. You've been the cause that his daughter is getting a rich young fellow of good family for her husband – as fine a match as he could ever have chosen for her himself.

LENA: So is he going to marry her to Flavio?

MENICA: He's already done so. Ilario and he settled the whole thing in a couple of moments.

LENA: Although I hate that miserable old man worse than poison, I'm glad of any good that's come out of this affair for Licinia.

MENICA: If you stay in this filthy temper, Lena, you'll be the most ungrateful woman in the world. Fazio has every reason to feel just the opposite of what he does; but he loves you, Lena. He can't help it, and he can't hide the passion that's torturing him inside; he can't help regretting the horrible things he said to you this morning, which he reckons are what made you play that dirty trick on him. And he told me that when Ilario said Pacifico had caught you with Flavio, the shock and the grief of it nearly killed him; and when he found out that it wasn't you the young fellow had tousled, but Licinia, he began to feel better at once, and it was as if new life flowed into his veins. So there's no doubt he's ready to make it up with you, especially as the results of your stupidity have turned out to his advantage.

LENA: He can make it up if he likes; and he can take the whole thing as he pleases. If he wants to be the same to me as he used to be before, he'll find that I'll be the same to him.

MENICA: Good – and now I'll tell you the whole truth. Fazio has sent me to you with a message. He's your Fazio, as he always was, and begs you to be his Lena again. He invites you and Pacifico to a wedding feast this evening – and he doesn't see why Licinia and Flavio should be the only pair of happy lovers tonight.

LENA: I'll do whatever he wants. [MENICA *goes into* FAZIO'*s house.* LENA *turns to the audience.*] – And now, spectators, show us whether you liked our story, or found it a bore!

# THE STABLEMASTER

## (*Il Marescalco*)

*by*

## PIETRO ARETINO
## (*1492–1556*)

# PIETRO ARETINO

PIETRO ARETINO (1492–1556) was born in Arezzo (a dependency of Florence) in Tuscany. He was the son of a shoemaker and a famous beauty. After a rebellious youth, he made his first literary reputation as a lampoonist and erotic poet in the Rome of the Medici Popes, Leo X and Clement VII. Following a stay at the Court of Mantua from 1526–7, Aretino migrated to Venice where he found the ideal environment – an established printing and publishing industry, relative literary and journalistic freedom, a wealthy economy and the stimulus of many intellectual and artistic friends and enemies – for the full flowering of his astonishing literary talent, and not inconsiderable political influence.

Aretino's most important and admired production was the *Letters*, of which several hundred were collected and published and which provide a robust, shrewd and witty insight into the character of the Italian Renaissance, as remarkable and naturalistic as the *Life* of Benvenuto Cellini. He also wrote a handful of religious works; the scandalous *Sei Giornate* (dialogues about the seamier side of sexual life in the Italian cities); and several plays, of which the *Stablemaster* (*Il Marescalco*) exemplifies both his range of personal wit and fantasy and a type of the extravagant comedy of Renaissance theatre.

It was composed during his sojourn in Mantua and published in 1533. As well as its verbal ingenuity, it is notable for its serious psychological portrayal of character (especially Messer Jacopo) and for conveying deftly the many revealing social themes and relationships of a brilliant Italian court and town of the early sixteenth century.

A selection of Aretino's *Letters* is available in Penguin Classics (translated by George Bull) and there is a racy version of the *Dialogues* (*Sei Giornate*) by Raymond Rosenthal (George Allen & Unwin).

# CHARACTERS

in order of appearance

GIANNICCO, boy
STABLEMASTER, his master
MESSER JACOPO
AMBROGIO
NURSE of the Stablemaster
PEDANT
PAGE of the Knight
FOOTMAN of the Duke
COUNT
KNIGHT
JEW
JEWELLER
SON of Messer Jacopo
OLD WOMAN
CARLO, *dressed as a bride*
MATRON
LADY
MESSER PHEBUS
MAIDSERVANT of the Court
FOOTMAN of the Court

# ACT ONE

*A row of houses bordering on a square in Mantua. The* STABLEMASTER'S *modest house is on the corner of a street to the left and the house of the* COUNT *well to the right, also on the corner of a street so that a side-door is visible, as well as some of the interior courtyard. There are several houses and alley-ways in between. In the distance, there is a glimpse of the* DUKE'S *castle. It is early morning.*

[*The* STABLEMASTER *is standing outside his own front door, looking around the square, wearing an angry expression.*]

BOY [*offstage, singing*]:

My master's taking a wife,
My master's taking a wife in this town here,
In this town here;
He'll take her, he won't take her,
He'll have her, he won't have her when evening's near,
When evening's near.

STABLEMASTER: Where the devil is that brat? How can it be that he's never there when I want him?

[*Enter the boy,* GIANNICCO, *with great show of haste, holding his side.*]

BOY: I've got the stitch.

STABLEMASTER: I can't think why!

BOY: I didn't know you were there, master; congratulations!

STABLEMASTER: What do you mean, congratulations?

BOY: Don't you know?

STABLEMASTER: What d'you expect me to know?

BOY: Don't you know about the wife that the Duke's giving you?

STABLEMASTER: Ha, ha, the jokes they get up to at the palace!

BOY: You'll see whether it's a joke or not.

STABLEMASTER: Who told you this rubbish?

BOY: The nobles, the pages, the secretaries, the falconers, the door-keepers, and the flies on the wall.

STABLEMASTER: Silly palace gossip!

BOY: Serious promises, more like.

STABLEMASTER: Don't say that!

BOY: Oh, I'm glad about it.

STABLEMASTER: Why?

BOY: Because I am.

STABLEMASTER: Idiot!

BOY: Honestly, sir, everyone says that you're taking a wife and that you're telling people about it yourself.

STABLEMASTER: Will you stop saying that or won't you?

BOY: Whatever pleases your Lordship.

STABLEMASTER: Who's coming? Is that Messer Jacopo?

[MESSER JACOPO *crosses the square and joins them.*]

MESSER JACOPO: You always seem to be in conclave with your boy friend.

STABLEMASTER: Pox take him!

BOY: *A vobis!*[1]

STABLEMASTER: What do you say?

BOY: It'll be your fault if it does!

MESSER JACOPO: Very clever! Good enough for a stage comedy.

STABLEMASTER [*to* BOY]: Talk about something else than a wife, or I'll . . .

BOY: What do you want me to talk to you about? A husband? Anyway, if everyone says that the Duke is giving you a wife, why can't I say it too?

STABLEMASTER: Because, because.

MESSER JACOPO: You know, Giannicco's telling you something that I didn't dream would be news to you, and I was coming to congratulate you, because, apart from her beauty, virtue and birth, I hear that she is bringing you a dowry of four thousand crowns.

STABLEMASTER: Oh, it certainly would make a marvellous story, if I had to take a wife this very evening, and still didn't know a thing about it.

MESSER JACOPO: Good rulers, like ours, often do a favour to someone, before it's even crossed his mind that it's possible. The Duke

1. From you!

acts like this, so that anyone who serves him may be sure of being rewarded for his service, when he least expects it.

STABLEMASTER: The Duke plays better jokes than any other lord alive, God preserve him; but all the same he won't saddle *me* with this woman.

BOY: Do take her, do take her, sweet master.

STABLEMASTER: If it's to throw her down a well, I won't say no.

MESSER JACOPO: Down a well, did you say?

STABLEMASTER: Yes, that's what I said.

MESSER JACOPO: The greatest noble at our Court would think himself lucky if he could have her.

STABLEMASTER [*turning away*]: Good-bye.

MESSER JACOPO: Wait a moment.

STABLEMASTER: Leave me alone, please.

MESSER JACOPO: Wait, I pray you.

BOY: Listen to him, dear master.

STABLEMASTER: The pack-mule is lame in one foot, and I must see to him; nor will you make a fool of me! No, by God you won't.

MESSER JACOPO: Act like an idiot as usual, if you must.

STABLEMASTER: I serve the Duke too, remember.

MESSER JACOPO: Well, don't say I didn't warn you.

STABLEMASTER: Come, Giannicco.

BOY: I'm coming. He'll take her all right, messer.

[*Exeunt* STABLEMASTER *and* BOY, *as* AMBROGIO *approaches.*]

MESSER JACOPO: He's got no option. Oh dear, oh dear, how stupid he is! In my view, this business will be the ruin of him. But where are you going now, Ambrogio?

AMBROGIO: It's an extraordinary thing the way you're always talking to yourself; and always muttering, either that your servant's a thief, or that he's a drunk, or that he doesn't get up till nightfall, or that he licks his plate, or that he gambles, or that he chases after women, or that he never tells the truth, or that he can't be trusted with a message, or that it's hopeless to send him on an errand, and you even complain that he falls asleep on horseback: and now what are you grumbling about?

MESSER JACOIO: I was letting my mind wander on about the stablemaster. The Duke plans to give him a very beautiful, very rich wife, and he doesn't want her.

AMBROGIO: I can't believe it!

MESSER JACOPO: It's true; and he'd just about have crucified his boy a little while ago if I hadn't been there.

AMBROGIO: Why?

MESSER JACOPO: For telling him it was being said that he's taking a wife this evening.

AMBROGIO: Ha, ha, ha!

MESSER JACOPO: Anyone else would thank God for a chance like this, but he turns it down flat.

AMBROGIO: Our lords and masters always do good to those who don't deserve it, or those who don't recognize it.

MESSER JACOPO: Our lords and masters do other things that are more unpleasant.

AMBROGIO: We'll have to see what kind of front he'll put on when he actually marries her.

MESSER JACOPO: Can you imagine him dealing with the problem in any but a truly philosophical posture?

AMBROGIO: Ha, ha! Where will the wedding be held?

MESSER JACOPO: At the home of the Count.

AMBROGIO: Splendid, so let's meet again at the barber's shop, and then we can go to the wedding party together.

MESSER JACOPO: Agreed. Good-bye.

AMBROGIO: Good-bye.

[*Exeunt* AMBROGIO *and* JACOPO. *As they disappear, the* NURSE *enters the square from a side-street and the* BOY *from the house of the* STABLEMASTER.]

NURSE: Wherever are you going in such a bad temper? What has happened?

BOY [*mumbling*]: Damn it all, sod it all . . .

NURSE: I don't understand you; where's my foster-child?

BOY: The devil may know. Why not ask him?

NURSE: What a nice way to talk!

BOY: I don't want to stay with my master any more, and if I leave him, I'll . . . I'll . . .

NURSE: He treats you better than you deserve, you little dolt.

BOY: Well, I'll tell you this, and it's God's truth, he really wanted to have my guts for garters just now.

NURSE: Garters? And why, for God's sake?

BOY: For having told him that all Mantua is full of the news that the Duke is giving him a wife.

NURSE: What's this? What's this?

BOY: Gospel truth. And he swore, like a traitor, that he didn't want her; but he will have to take her, even if he bursts.

NURSE: O blessed saint Nafissa, lay your hands upon his head, *et in mulieribus ... nomen tuum ... vita dulcedo ... panem nostrum ... benedicta tu ...* if he takes her ... *ad te suspiramus ...* I'll behave like a little saint ... *et homo factus est ...* Tell me, Giannicco, my son, are you pulling my leg?

BOY: I'm not a sodding liar ...

NURSE: Don't swear, I believe you ... *sub Pontio Pilato, vivos et mortuos ...* my prayers, my fastings will bring it about; I'll make a vow before the Madonna of the Friars not to put any oil or salt in the cabbage on Fridays during March, and to fast during Ember weeks on bread and water ... *lacrimarum valle ... a malo.* Amen. For absolute sure, if he takes her, she'll be the support of my old age.[2]

BOY: Do you want to know anything else?

NURSE: Where're you going? Wait for me here, leave the whole thing to me.

BOY: I won't stay with him.

NURSE: Wait for me, I say.

BOY: I'll wait, but if he ... Enough, enough, I understand well enough, go.

[*The* BOY *goes into the house, leaving the* NURSE *alone.*]

NURSE: It's easy enough to make fun of dreams; but dreams aren't the nonsense some folk believe. In fact, I've no need to go to my spiritual father, instead I'll go to find my son; I'll certainly find him at the stable, because there's always some horse off its oats. But here he is. As my poor husband used to say, if a man has luck on his side, he doesn't need many brains.

[*The* STABLEMASTER *comes out of his house.*]

STABLEMASTER: Where are you going at this time of day?

NURSE: I was going to my confessor about something important.

2. The bastardized Latin is made up of phrases from several prayers, e.g. – 'Under Pontius Pilate, the living and the dead' ... 'the valley of tears' ... 'from evil'.

STABLEMASTER: What is it that's so important? Can you tell me?

NURSE: I can and I can't.

STABLEMASTER: Come on, tell me.

NURSE: I was going to get a dream explained, but because I've interpreted it on the way, I'm coming to you and not to him.

STABLEMASTER: Well then, describe your dream to me.

NURSE: Well, last night near daybreak I seemed to be in the garden at the foot of the fig-tree. I was sitting down while listening to a little bird that suddenly started singing and then a horrible man appeared who grew sick of the poor little bird's song, and began to throw stones at it. And the bird went on singing and he went on throwing, and while one was singing and the other flinging, I shouted at the man, and the man shouted at me. At the end the little bird was left up on the fig-tree. Do you understand it all?

STABLEMASTER: Easily, but what matters is the way you understand it now yourself.

NURSE: As I see it, the little bird that was singing is your boy. He was explaining to you sweetly about your wife. The horrible man is you, and you were threatening him as he explained things. I am, myself, the woman under the fig-tree, and I'll do and say all I can to get you to marry this girl. All the better for you if you do.

STABLEMASTER: It seems to me everyone in the world is interfering in my business. And now my own nurse is joining the conspiracy. But I must be patient and provided the Duke is pleased with me, I'll be happy enough; because it's a sign of affection when a master jokes with his servant.

NURSE: Come along, pull yourself together and leave your wicked ways.

STABLEMASTER: What wicked ways?

NURSE: You know what.

STABLEMASTER: Did I crucify Christ?

NURSE: No, but . . .

STABLEMASTER: What do you mean, no, but?

NURSE: I mean to say . . .

STABLEMASTER: What?

NURSE: That you've done something worse.

STABLEMASTER: In what way?

NURSE: You know just what I mean, you do. So now take my advice and marry her, my son, stop going around with young men and do something to restore your good name. Grow up and start a family of your own. There's only you at present. But if you marry, the Duke will give you a coat-of-arms; and you'll be properly known and respected by everyone imaginable.

STABLEMASTER: Oh God, oh God, how they torment me.

NURSE: You poor little fellow, do you know what happens when you take a wife?

STABLEMASTER: I don't know, and I don't want to know.

NURSE: You go to paradise when you take a wife.

STABLEMASTER: Yes, if hell is paradise.

NURSE: Now please listen to me and then you can make up your own mind what to do.

STABLEMASTER: Well go on; I'm listening.

NURSE: This is why getting married is like going to paradise. You arrive home, and your good wife comes to meet you all smiling at the top of the stairs. She gives you a good, heartfelt welcome, helps you off with your coat, and then embraces you joyfully. As you're all sweaty, she wipes you dry with some towels which are so soft and snowy that you are soon glowing comfortably all over. Then having put the wine to cool and laid the table, and fanned you for a while, she gets you to have a pee.

STABLEMASTER: Ha, ha!

NURSE: What are you laughing at, you great oaf? Once you've had a pee she sits you down to supper, and when you're nicely relaxed she whets your appetite with some tasty sauces and tit-bits that would make your mouth water even in the grave. And while you're eating, in the most agreeable way she keeps putting in front of you now one dish and now another, offering you all kinds of tasty morsel and saying: 'Eat this and now this, and if you love me try a little more for my sake.' And all her words are so honeyed and so sugared that they transport you not only to paradise but thousands and thousands of miles beyond.

STABLEMASTER: What about after supper, what does this wife do then?

NURSE: She calls her husband to bed, after he has swallowed his meal, and before he stretches out she washes his feet thoroughly in water boiled with bay leaves, sage and rosemary. As soon as she has trimmed his nails, and cleaned and dried him very nicely, she helps him to get into bed. Then she clears the table and tidies the room, and after saying her prayers, she gets in beside him, all affectionately. Next she embraces her beloved husband, kissing him again and again, and she says to him: 'My heart, my soul, dear hope, my own flesh and blood, let me be your own little girl, your jewel, your daughter.' And if a man's treated like this, isn't he truly in paradise?

STABLEMASTER: It doesn't seem so to me. But what's the point of all these caresses?

NURSE: The point of them all is to make sure that babies are started in a holy and proper way. Anyway, in the morning, your busy wife brings you your fresh eggs, and your white shirt, and while she helps you to dress, talking to you sweetly and kissing you, she fusses round you so lovingly that you have the same consolation from her as you would from the angels in paradise.

STABLEMASTER: Finished talking?

NURSE: Finished? I've hardly begun yet. Imagine, now, that it's winter time and you have come home wet through, covered in snow and frozen stiff. Your clever wife changes your clothes, thaws you out in no time with a good fire, and as soon as you're warm again, you find that dinner is ready. Her hot soup and the other nice things to eat revive you completely. If you happen to be worried about something, she acts very gently and says: 'What's the matter, what are you thinking about? Don't upset yourself. God will help us and look after us.' So all your sadness turns to joy. And then your babies start to arrive ... the little darlings, the little imps! O God, what comfort, what sweet tenderness a father feels when his little boy touches his face and his breast with those fond little hands, calling him daddy, my daddy, dear daddy! I've seen men longer in the tooth than you overcome by I don't know what kind of emotion at the sound of that 'daddy' ... but when shall I be able to see you acting like that?

STABLEMASTER: On St Bindo's feast-day; the feast that comes three days after the Day of Judgement.

NURSE: But haven't you seen what I've been trying to tell you?

STABLEMASTER: I've not only seen it. I've seen through it. You should talk to a poor wretch who is married and who in bed, or at table, in the morning or in the evening, outside and in, as if all the demons were in her body, is tormented by his wife's haughty behaviour, her obstinacy, and her uncharitableness. And I've heard it said that the pox with all its sores and boils and twinges, along with its sister, gout, is less of a punishment than having a wife . . .

NURSE [*interrupting*]: May God punish the one who told you that.

STABLEMASTER: And anyone who has a wife is a martyr . . .

NURSE: He deserves to be killed.

STABLEMASTER: And anyway a servant can easily do all those things you made such a song and dance about, and he can be told to bugger off whenever you like, and you can't get rid of a wife so easily.

NURSE: You certainly don't deserve a nice life. It'll serve you right to live in a filthy way with ill-washed sheets and linen all the time in your dirty stable-yards, with your uncouth friends. Now here comes your boy. He'll back me up in all I've said.

[*The* BOY *comes forward from the door of the house.*]

BOY: So help me, I wouldn't have believed it, just because I told you about your wife, you wanted to have me murdered.

STABLEMASTER: What are you yapping about now?

BOY: What's the harm in saying that you're taking a wife, when you'll still have me at your service?

STABLEMASTER: I don't like you saying it.

BOY: If you are to take a wife, can't I say so like everyone else?

NURSE: He's right, you know. He's talking sense.

STABLEMASTER: He's talking shit.

BOY: On account of saying one word about a wife . . .

STABLEMASTER: By God, I'll . . .

BOY: One shouldn't blaspheme on account of a wife.

STABLEMASTER: For Christ's sake, now I'm going to let you have it . . .

NURSE: Enough, you great madman.

BOY: I don't deserve to be beaten for talking about your wife.

STABLEMASTER: About a whore, you mean.

NURSE: That will do.

BOY: Why am I to blame if his lordship wishes to give you a wife?

STABLEMASTER: This is the end of me, I know.

BOY: The Duke is to blame for your wife, not Giannicco.

STABLEMASTER [*threatening* GIANNICCO]: Don't hold me back.

NURSE: Chastise him at the proper time and place.

BOY: It's because of his lordship that you're taking a wife, not because of me.

NURSE: That's the truth.

BOY: Yes, it's his Excellency who's giving you a wife, not me, your boy.

STABLEMASTER [*raising his hand*]: I'll give you something . . .

BOY: Good, I want you to give me something.

NURSE [*to both of them*]: You deserve everything you get. You mustn't let him be so cheeky. Get off home with you.

BOY: Cuckoo.

NURSE: Go home, you little fool.

STABLEMASTER: Go into the house, right now.

BOY: Yes, dear master, holy master, good master.

STABLEMASTER: You go in too, Nurse.

NURSE: If you want me to. Oh dear, oh dear!

[*Exeunt the* BOY *and* NURSE *leaving the* STABLEMASTER *alone.*]

STABLEMASTER: I'd have done better to stay in my old job, instead of being led astray by all the vanity of court life. I could enjoy a splendid life with what I used to earn, but instead I lead a lousy life and I'll end up losing everything. I was warned that in those cursed courts there's nothing but envy and treachery, and you get nowhere without influence. God help me, I'm done for. To be honest, his Excellency talked to me about it a month ago. I thought he was having a joke with me, but he was being serious. How can life be so cruel!

[*The* PEDANT *approaches from across the square.*]

PEDANT: *Bona dies. Quid agitis, magister mi?*[3]

STABLEMASTER: Forgive me, sir, for not seeing you, but I was miles away.

PEDANT: *Sis laetus.*[4]

STABLEMASTER: Please speak Italian. I've got other matters to think about than your astrology.

PEDANT: *Bene vivere et laetari:*[5] I bring you good news. It's very good, very good news.

3. Good day. How are you, master?
4. Be happy.
5. Live well and be merry.

STABLEMASTER: What good news can there be for me?

PEDANT: His Excellency, his most Illustrious Highness, loves you, and this evening he will secure you with the bond of matrimony and couple you to such a splendid young girl, that everyone *totum orbem*[6] will envy you.

STABLEMASTER: Are you talking seriously or just to try my patience?

PEDANT: *Per Deum verum.*[7] Our Lordship is giving you a wife. There's no doubt about that.

STABLEMASTER: I'll never agree to it.

PEDANT: Oh, my dear fellow, imagine you are reading the words of the holy Gospel.

STABLEMASTER: Is the Gospel against wives?

PEDANT [*with much humming and hawing*]: What do you mean, against wives? Quite the reverse, in fact. And just listen to what they teach. Let's consult the text of the Evangelist. *Id est*[8] the maker of heaven and earth, *coeli et terrae,*[9] says in the Gospel that the tree which does not bear fruit must be cut down and thrown in the fire. Hence our most magnanimous Lord Duke, in order that you, who are represented by the tree, should bear fruit, and that the human race should grow and multiply, has chosen a respectable consort for you to enjoy; and his Excellency has conferred *nobiscum*[10] about everything, and he has ordained that *ego agam oratiunculam,*[11] namely, that I compose the nuptial sermon, and speak to you in the common tongue.

STABLEMASTER: Oh, this really must be some diabolical conspiracy. No end of times I felt I would die of poverty, as most courtiers do. But I never thought my faults would be punished by the cruel penance of a wife. I'd as soon as thought of this as of flying.

PEDANT: Dear, unique, Stablemaster, recall and reflect judiciously on the Old Testament and, by the eye of faith, you will see what kind of people were expelled from the temples and interdicted *ignem et aquam.*[12] They were punished for being barren of offspring, and so guilty of frustrating the purposes of the world. The Prime Mover, the Giver of all things, marked and condemned them, and

| | |
|---|---|
| 6. the whole world. | 7. By the true God. |
| 8. Namely. | 9. heaven and earth. |
| 10. with us. | 11. I make a little oration. |
| 12. fire and water. | |

such was their evil fate that eventually they were mocked even by the ignorant populace, for art is mocked by art; as our Cato said. Now listen to the other side of the story. As the historian Dion, who has been translated by us grammarians from Greek into Latin and from Latin into our maternal language, narrates, recounts and explains, the great Octavius, known to all ages as Augustus, exalted to the stars and praised most fulsomely all those with an abundance of progeny. And *per antifrasim*,[13] he equally reproached and repudiated the sterile and useless. The aforesaid Dion also elucidates that it went hard with those who frequented the company of Augustus if they had no sweet offspring to show him.

[*The* BOY *joins them. He has been running and is out of breath.*]

BOY: Master, the horses are scrapping. They are murdering each other. Listen to the noise.

STABLEMASTER: See to things here. I'm just coming.

[*The* STABLEMASTER *leaves hurriedly.*]

BOY: What were you talking about to my master? Tell me, if it's decent.

PEDANT: About matrimonial copula.

BOY: What, sir? About scrofula?

PEDANT: I said copula. That means couplings.

BOY: Little cups?

PEDANT: Conjugal couplings.

BOY: Do you drink from them at breakfast, sir?

PEDANT: Either breakfast-time or bed-time, I was discussing with your master the subject of copulating with women. You see, the carnal copula is the first article of divine and human law, but concupiscence adulterates the law. So this evening his Lordship, I meant to say his most Excellent of Excellencies, the Duke, intends to arrange the incarnation of the marriage of your master.

BOY: I understand you. I've got your meaning. Yes, I see, you were at daggers drawn with him on account of the *in mulieribus*,[14] eh?

PEDANT: *Tu dixisti.*[15] You have said it.

BOY: Well then, will he take her or not?

PEDANT: With God's help I hope to convince him with such effica-

13. on the contrary.
14. amongst women.
15. You have said it.

cious arguments that we shall tame him. For, you know, *verba ligant homines, taurorum cornua . . .*[16]

BOY: You speak for yourself.

PEDANT: *. . . funes, idest vincula.*[17]

BOY: Oh good.

PEDANT: You don't penetrate such deep meaning?

BOY: Don't I?

PEDANT: Surely not.

BOY: Didn't you say that men bind grass, and chains bind fools?

PEDANT: Ha, ha!

BOY: Here's the master. Make sure we meet on the piazza, because I've got to talk to you.

PEDANT: Very well.

[*The* STABLEMASTER *comes back, mopping his brow.*]

BOY [*to the* STABLEMASTER]: You've spoilt our lovely, posh discussion.

STABLEMASTER: What a mad brute that Arab horse is.

PEDANT: Spirited steeds are always impatient with mules.

BOY: Listen, the nurse is calling you, listen. Here we are; we're coming.

STABLEMASTER: Good-bye, sir.

PEDANT: *Me vobis commendo.*[18]

BOY: Let's go at once, because I'm afraid that the cat may have eaten the partridge you stole this morning from the Duke's table.

16. Men are bound by words, the horns of bulls . . .
17. by ropes, namely ties.
18. I commend myself to you.

# ACT TWO

[*Scene as before. Later in the morning. The* BOY *and the* PAGE *are approaching each other as the* PEDANT *walks slowly on the other side of the square, oblivious to them.*]

BOY: While my master is arguing with his nurse about this wife of his, I will go to find the pedant with all his *hic, haec, hocs* and start an argument with him. Here's the knight's page.

PAGE: Who's there? That you, Giannicco?

BOY: Giannicco in person, my lad.

PAGE: I'd like to . . .

BOY: What would you like to do?

PAGE: Find some silly dodderer and tie these fire crackers on his back.

BOY: And I'd like to help you. Do you see that silly old fathead walking along over there?

PAGE: I see him, strutting along like a peacock.

BOY: That's him. He's the one who teaches little boys their prayers.

PAGE: So?

BOY: I'll attract the nitwit's attention, and meanwhile you come and tie your crackers on to him and set them alight.

PAGE: Ha, ha, ha, I couldn't have found anyone better than this soup-slurper, this bean-gobbler, this noodle-guzzler.

BOY: Follow me then, and keep close by.

PAGE: I'm coming.

[*As they walk up to the* PEDANT *the* PAGE *steps behind him without being seen.*]

BOY: Good morning, your most paternal Lordship.

PEDANT: Good day to you, and a good year as well.

BOY: I told the master's nurse that you'll do all you possibly can to make him take a wife, and she said that this will be good for your soul and what's more she'll give you four linen handkerchiefs and a pair of beautiful shirts. But will he take her or not?

PEDANT: I'm certain that he will take her for sure.

BOY: In that case, she'll be your slave.

PEDANT: Who will?

BOY: The nurse will. And I've told her that your Highness ...

PEDANT: Many thanks to you for saying Highness.

BOY: ... is a valiant fellow with a coat-of-arms of his own.

PEDANT: And with my *arma virum*[19] and my books I'm second to no one. But I must condole with you on the betrayal of your talents that was made when your education was neglected. As a scholar, you might have excellent merits.

BOY: I did have a good ferret, but it died three days ago. It was worth its weight in gold, and killed every pigeon in the place.

PEDANT [*starts talking, and suddenly jumps and shrieks as he is burnt by the fireworks*]: I said 'merits', not 'ferrets' ... Help, Jesus Mary ...

BOY [*to the* PAGE]: Push off and I'll find you later, you can be sure of that! Off you go!

PEDANT: Oh what an evil and ill-mannered way to treat a distinguished disciplinarian and philosopher of my sort!

BOY: Let me punish him. I'll beat him to a jelly.

PEDANT: A little pansy, a budding criminal like that dares to provoke a professor as erudite and noble as me?

BOY: Sir, it was only a practical joke. Practical jokes don't matter.

PEDANT: They don't matter? They matter so much when it comes to men such as me, that the Duke won't regard them as frivolous, oh no. Let me assure you of that most solemnly.

BOY: Don't upset yourself so much.

PEDANT: We can never control our immediate reactions because our anger stops us deliberating calmly. Now for God's sake go away, boy, I am going to lay a complaint before his Excellency, and then I swear to you, by the majesty of the toga, by the reputation of my rank, and by the dignity of my learning, that I'll give that page such a beating, I'll give him such a ...

BOY: No, no! For heaven's sake!

PEDANT: No?

BOY: Restrain yourself.

19. 'arms and the man' – the opening words of the *Aeneid*, which would be the Pedant's main stock-in-trade.

PEDANT: I have to go now if I want to finish reading the *Bucolics* to my disciples. *Dominus providebit.*[20]

BOY: You're going at the right time, but not in the right temper. Who's this trotting towards us? I think it's one of the footmen from court. I'll go back into the house.

[*Exit* BOY *as the* FOOTMAN *stops before the* STABLEMASTER'*s house.*]

FOOTMAN: This is his lodging. I'd better knock. [*Does so*].

STABLEMASTER [*appearing at the door*]: What do you want?

FOOTMAN: The Duke wants to see you.

STABLEMASTER: What does his Excellency want me for?

FOOTMAN: I'm not sure, but I think I know.

STABLEMASTER: Tell me what it is, I beg you, brother.

FOOTMAN: It's about your wife.

STABLEMASTER: That's the reward I get for all my service. It's cruel to hurt a man by making him take a wife against his will.

FOOTMAN: So the Duke is hurting you by making you rich?

STABLEMASTER: Please don't go on.

FOOTMAN: So you don't believe me when I tell you his Lordship will make you rich?

STABLEMASTER: The only one I believe is God but I know that these rulers have strange whims, and do extraordinary things. If I desired a wife and wanted to provide her with a dowry myself, and I sought his favour in a thousand ways and with a hundred thousand prayers, I would never get her. Yet because I don't want a wife, he wants to give me one against my will. Rulers are like women who run after those who flee from them and flee from anyone who pursues them, and they like nothing so much as to make all those who serve them fall into despair. Now let's be off.

[*Exeunt* STABLEMASTER *and the* FOOTMAN *as the* BOY *and the* NURSE *come out of the house.*]

NURSE: So the Duke insists on having his way.

BOY: Even a blind man could see that a mile off.

NURSE: What a worthy Duke he is! What a good Duke, a sweet, a holy and a lovable Duke! The most generous act he could possibly do is to make the Stablemaster take a wife, and set a good example

20. The Lord will provide.

to the rakes and rascals who are always dillying and dallying, who
ought to be burned in droves every day.

BOY: Be careful what you say, nurse!

NURSE: It's the likes of you who cause the trouble, you villainous
little pansies!

BOY: You'll be tossed in a blanket, if you go on like that.

NURSE: Who'd do that?

BOY: Everyone at court.

NURSE: Why?

BOY: Because courtiers are the enemies of women.

NURSE: Let them go and jump in the lake, the shameless crowd of
reprobates.

BOY: Here's Messer Polo, the local idiot, dressed up to the nines. He's
coming this way.

NURSE: Let's go back inside. If my son should come, everything
might be spoilt unless he finds us at home.

BOY: Let's go. I think I see him.

[*They go into the house as the* STABLEMASTER *and* AMBROGIO
*come round the corner and continue walking round the square.* SER
POLO *follows them, gesticulating at the* STABLEMASTER, *for a few
paces; then turns back and exits.*]

STABLEMASTER: Even the simpletons are laughing over my affairs,
and that idiot Ser Polo is mocking me. What a pass things have
come to!

AMBROGIO: I swear to God the Duke has done you a great favour.
He has treated you like a friend. Now take her and gain yourself
some advantage by pleasing him.

STABLEMASTER: You consider it an advantage to take a wife, eh?

AMBROGIO: A great advantage.

STABLEMASTER: Have you had a wife yourself?

AMBROGIO: I have, and I still have her.

STABLEMASTER: If she left you, you wouldn't go after her to get her
back again, would you?

AMBROGIO: Yes and no. But obey the Duke's orders and you won't
go wrong. Princes are the very devil, and we must pray God that
he doesn't get any fancies into his head, because if he does the only
people who'll be safe will be those who don't give a damn about
their honour. But let's not talk any more about rulers, because it i

more dangerous to take their name in vain than the Almighty's. To return to your wife . . .

STABLEMASTER: Don't say 'your' to me, if you want me to listen to you.

AMBROGIO: The woman who they say will be yours.

STABLEMASTER: That's better!

AMBROGIO: They tell marvellous stories about her virtues. And there's no doubt that if women had only an ounce of the loads of qualities attributed to them before they marry, those who take them would be really happy.

STABLEMASTER: Don't they stand up to the test?

AMBROGIO: Not at all, I'm afraid. To talk frankly, I was given to understand that mine was a wise Sibyl for wisdom and a cloistered angel, and when I had married her, the only thing she was good for was making sons for me without the slightest effort on my part, and I believe that those children I hold for my own, or to be exact that are held to be mine, are as much my offspring as Christ was St Joseph's.

STABLEMASTER: Why don't you kill her?

AMBROGIO: For what purpose should I kill her?

STABLEMASTER: To get rid of the shame.

AMBROGIO: That's a joke! Should I try to be wiser than those many great lords who not only do not chastise their wives for giving them horns, but treat their wives' lovers as their brothers and friends?

STABLEMASTER: She won't put it across me.

AMBROGIO: Well, to finish telling you about your . . .

STABLEMASTER: What did I say to you?

AMBROGIO: I don't recall.

STABLEMASTER: That you are not to say 'your'.

AMBROGIO: I'll do as you say. I say that the woman, or the wife, as you wish it, that the Duke wants to be yours, is praised to the skies by everybody.

STABLEMASTER: You swear to that?

AMBROGIO: I do.

STABLEMASTER: Shall I take her or not take her? Give me your honest advice.

AMBROGIO: Well, when . . .

STABLEMASTER: You're making a meal of it.

AMBROGIO: Do I have to give my opinion as to what I really think or just to please you?

STABLEMASTER: Say what you think.

AMBROGIO: Don't you take her. Don't you meddle with her, or else, by God, you'll regret it.

STABLEMASTER: Now I really do believe you and I certainly know that you are my friend, and I'm your servant for ever.

AMBROGIO: Let me tell you a little about what they're like!

STABLEMASTER: I'm listening.

AMBROGIO: You arrive home tired in the evening. You're thoughtful and full of those anxieties that plague all of us, and then your wife comes out to meet you: 'Do you think this is the time to come home?' she says. 'You've just left the tavern, or you've been with those whores. I know only too well. Is this the way you treat a good wife like me? Oh well, I knew it would be so.' You were looking forward to enjoying supper, but in the end you start to get angry; and if after putting up with it a while, you answer her back, she jumps down your throat: 'You don't deserve me,' she says. 'You aren't worthy of me.' And she makes more wild accusations, till you lose all desire to eat, and retreat to your bed. But after a thousand groans and moans, she gets in beside you and starts all over again. 'May the one who gave me to you be hanged,' she says. 'I could have married a Count, or a nobleman.' And beginning to go through all her family tree, till you'd think she was born a noble Gonzaga, such are the airs she puts on.

STABLEMASTER: So can the Duke really want me to take a wife? No, no, surely not.

AMBROGIO: Another time, you may happen to reproach her over one of the thousand things they do, all deserving of rebuke, and hardly have you opened your mouth, than she flies at you and screams: 'It didn't happen that way, you're missing the point, put your glasses on, you're beside yourself, cool down, I say. You're a half-wit, you're a shambles, pull yourself together. You're dreaming, you're raving, blockhead, dolt, wretch. A fine catch you are! A fine scarecrow! God must have made you only to forget you. D'you hear me? I'll say what I like to you. I'm not afraid!'

And unless the good husband closes his ears to this outcry, which gets all the louder the more she thinks he's listening, he would go deaf and mad all at once.

STABLEMASTER: Oh dear, oh dear, God help me!

AMBROGIO: It's agonizing to have to put up with their lies when they swear blind that geese are swans and that white is black. You can't make them change a word of it. White will still be black to them, even if they say it with their dying breath.

STABLEMASTER: They see whom they have to deal with, I think!

AMBROGIO: What torture it is when they start to gabble away, day in and day out and never let their tongues stay still. They talk the most dreadful, the silliest rigmarole that ever was heard, and woe betide anyone who interrupts their flow of words or doesn't listen to them. As to how envious they are, I can hardly tell you! As soon as they see a new fashion worn by another woman, they swell with rage and fume with anger. But they won't say a word to you about it – they expect you to know what they are thinking by instinct.

STABLEMASTER: To hell with them.

AMBROGIO: They're as wicked as Beelzebub. Everything they say is to spite you.

STABLEMASTER: May all women be wiped out!

AMBROGIO: As for their contrariness, I could hardly describe it. They are for ever grumbling and nagging.

STABLEMASTER: May they all be hanged.

AMBROGIO: As for their backbiting, you cannot imagine. They are always slandering other women. So-and-so has black teeth; someone else has too big a mouth; this one has a colourless complexion; that one is short; this one doesn't know how to speak properly; that one doesn't know how to walk; another flirts in church, and yet another is always ogling men from the balcony. And criticizing someone for one thing, and someone else for another, they act as if they themselves were completely virtuous, good mannered, and beautiful.

STABLEMASTER: I'm stupefied.

AMBROGIO: And wives are as disobedient as can be. A husband is like the mayor of Sinigaglia, the one who used to give orders but always had to carry them out himself.

STABLEMASTER: In view of all you've said, tell me this: once a man is married, is it better for him to live or die?

AMBROGIO: Well, there's a remedy for everything.

STABLEMASTER: What's the remedy, once you've taken a wife?

AMBROGIO: Send her packing, fair and square, the way people do . . . But to return to the argument, I say that if you happen to have a wife who's better-born than you, she will always be reproaching you about the social standing of her relations.

STABLEMASTER: I can already hear her calling me 'stablemaster' all the time.

AMBROGIO: If you get a wife who is richer than you, at every least thing that displeases her she'll say: 'If it weren't for me, you'd be in rags. I picked you up from the gutter. It serves me right! I had plenty of choice, God knows! And now I've been thrown on the scrapheap. Go on, take everything that's mine, devour me, eat me, drink me, consume all we've got . . .'

STABLEMASTER: I suppose this will happen every day on account of her dowry.

AMBROGIO: If you do dress her grandly everyone will murmur: 'Who does he think he is, who does she think she is?' If you send her out dressed modestly, they'll say: 'The wretch should be ashamed of himself, she gave him enough dowry to provide her with clothes. She is being stifled. She was a fool not to have become a nun instead.' If you admonish her for being too bold, you are called an ass; if you keep her on a loose rein, you are accused of neglecting your honour; if you allow her freedom, the whole neighbourhood murmurs against you; if you keep her locked up, everyone calls you jealous and brutal.

STABLEMASTER: How the devil is one to deal with them?

AMBROGIO: You'd better ask someone who knows!

STABLEMASTER: Oh God, what a business!

AMBROGIO: You don't know the half of what has to be put up with every day by those who are married. These are things that simply can't be told.

STABLEMASTER: Tell me something about the caresses they give their husbands.

AMBROGIO: Well, they may remove a hair from your back, or scratch a little scab for you with one finger, or take your shirt off for you, or set your hat on your head, or trim a nail for you and give you a clean handkerchief. This petty courtesy is the dust they throw in your eyes, so that it's impossible for you to perceive their treacheries. Ha, ha, ha!

STABLEMASTER: Why are you laughing?

AMBROGIO: I'm laughing, but I ought to be crying myself sick.

STABLEMASTER: Why?

AMBROGIO: Because I'm thinking of the way they look when they get up in the morning. All I can say is that even the barnyard fowls, which eat all kinds of muck, would find them disgusting. Even the doctors who specialize in unguents don't have as many little boxes of paste as they do and they never stop plastering, powdering and bedaubing themselves. I won't mention the handicraft they employ on their faces. First of all, they tighten the skin with astingents, and as a result, from being firm and smooth their faces become prematurely wrinkled and sagging, and their teeth as black as ebony.

STABLEMASTER: Ha, ha, ha!

AMBROGIO: But what about the way they varnish their faces with all that make-up? If only they were sensible enough to spread it evenly on their cheeks! When they slap it all in one place, they resemble those masks made in Modena.

STABLEMASTER: Oh the little fools! Tittle-tattlers! Bird-brains!

AMBROGIO: The architectural effort of adorning them is greater than a year's work on the arsenal at Venice. And now I want to make you laugh by telling you what happened to a certain lady who titivated herself foolishly.

STABLEMASTER: What happened to her?

AMBROGIO: It happened that with this madam, a kitten jumped on to her lap, and when she put her mouth down to kiss him, he put his paws, without cleaning them, on both her cheeks, and imprinted on them the marks of all his claws.

STABLEMASTER: Ha, ha, ha! Oh, if I had one of them (and I'd sooner God sent me through the gates of hell) what a sound beating I'd give her every time she painted her face in such fashion!

AMBROGIO: They can't be beaten just like that, you know.

STABLEMASTER: Why not?

AMBROGIO: Because they enchant you, they blind you, and they rob you of your senses.

STABLEMASTER: That's terrible.

AMBROGIO: Yes, and the devastation of Rome and Florence was nothing compared with the way they demolish, overwhelm and destroy their poor, trusting husbands. These men go about looking more filthy and foul even than our modern courtiers, so that they can afford to keep their wives richly adorned and attired, and they stay indoors for months and years on end, so that their wives can go to church or to parties and banquets looking like duchesses and empresses. And I know some men who have sold their possessions so that their wives may buy sables tipped with gold and strewn with jewels, and strings of pearls, regal necklaces, and pontifical rings. They sell all they've got and their wives buy all these temporal and spiritual treasures; and so at the end of the day, they end up with everything at the pawnbrokers.

STABLEMASTER: The beasts are better off than men.

AMBROGIO: What about those who let their decent horses draw the carriages of their wives and so have to ride on broken-down mules themselves, and if it weren't for the covering on the mules, which hides their sores, the people would run after them laughing and jeering.

STABLEMASTER: What cowards those husbands are!

AMBROGIO: I won't tell you about all the time lost by wives in discussing the way they should dress their hair, pluck their eyebrows, polish their teeth and arrange their dress. And they are for ever entertaining a coiffeuse, or a Jewish specialist on hats, fans, and perfumed gloves, or a herbalist, the effect of whose wares is not to preserve what little beauty they have, but in fact to make them old, shrivelled and rancid.

STABLEMASTER: Heaven help us!

AMBROGIO: But all their villainy – that's the only word for it – wouldn't matter, if only their benighted, bewildered and bamboozled husbands were able to make sure . . . I can't tell you.

STABLEMASTER: Tell me, sod it . . .

AMBROGIO: Of not growing horns.

STABLEMASTER: That too! Oh, it takes one's friends to tell the truth like this!

AMBROGIO: You've heard some of the hundreds and thousands of things I could say about wives. Now let me say something about the rulers of Venice. They deserve the highest praise for everything they do, of course. But when it comes to the sumptuary ordinances with which they restrain the unruly appetites of their women, they deserve even greater glory, because had they not imposed rules of moderation and restraint, all their riches couldn't suffice to adorn their wives for a single day, and remember the Venetians surpass all others in wealth as they do in prudence and power.

STABLEMASTER: And why is that?

AMBROGIO: Because of their extraordinary fads and fancies. For they are as beautiful as they are noble, and as noble as they are proud, and so when they dress fashionably they love to have innumerable frills and to use crimsons, slashed silks, embroideries, and jewels so lavishly that the treasure accumulated by Venetian enterprise would be consumed like snow under the sun.

STABLEMASTER: The comparison would be better if you said it would be consumed like the stablemaster is consumed when he remembers he has to take a wife. But understand that Venetian women have less need of ornaments than the angels, because they are incredibly beautiful.

AMBROGIO: That's true; and now do you want anything else from me?

STABLEMASTER: Anything else, eh? I don't know what else you could add. Your marvellous, blessed advice has made my mind up for me so strongly that I couldn't be forced to take her by all the dukes in the world, let alone the Duke of Mantua.

AMBROGIO: Good-bye then. Now wait there, because someone's coming for you, and I'm going.

[As AMBROGIO disappears round the corner, the STABLEMASTER is joined by the BOY and the NURSE.]

NURSE: There he is, all bedraggled. The Duke must have had him beaten.

BOY: No danger of that.

NURSE: Why not?

BOY: Because the Duke's too kind. But really he ought to have him hanged, God forgive me.

NURSE: Eh?

BOY: Yes, sir.

STABLEMASTER: Who's speaking to you?

BOY: I seemed to hear something.

STABLEMASTER: Don't you pull my leg.

NURSE: What's the reason you're so melancholy?

STABLEMASTER: I wish to hell I'd never been born.

NURSE: Oh, what on earth would you do if you had to swallow some medicine?

BOY: Yes, medicine is bitter, but a wife is sweet.

STABLEMASTER: Medicine drives the badness out of your body, while a wife drives all the goodness from body and soul.

BOY: Take it easy, what do you mean, goodness from the soul?

NURSE: What would you say if you were given a wife aged sixty, and you were only twenty-five, or rather if you were old, and had to take one of sixteen, as did . . . no, I won't say. What would you want to do then, eh?

STABLEMASTER: Then I'd share her with everyone!

BOY: Suits me!

STABLEMASTER: Boy, boy.

BOY: Master, master!

STABLEMASTER: You're a little fiend. Now, nurse, if you don't tell me some prescription to rid the Duke of this fantasy of giving me a wife, I'll throw myself out of a window, or I'll open the veins in my throat, or I'll give my body and soul to the devil himself.

NURSE: Don't do that, please don't, my son.

STABLEMASTER: I want to live my own life, to sleep with whoever pleases me, and to eat what I like, without being nagged by a wife all the time.

NURSE: If you go on being so stubborn you'll certainly come a nasty cropper. But I've thought of a way to stop the Duke talking about getting you a wife.

STABLEMASTER: Are you sure?

NURSE: I'm really sure.

STABLEMASTER: Dearest mother, how will you do it?

NURSE: By using spells.

STABLEMASTER: It isn't possible.

NURSE: Why not?

STABLEMASTER: Because I don't have any musicians among my friends.

NURSE: Your ears deceived you. I said spells.

STABLEMASTER: I was sure you said bells.

NURSE: Stuff.

STABLEMASTER: Well, then, are these enchantments worked by sorcery, or by necromancy?

NURSE: Necromancy, or sorceries, indeed! Come home and leave the arrangements to me. One day, when I'm gone, you'll realize what you've lost.

STABLEMASTER: What luck! ... if these enchantments save me from disaster, destruction and death, I vow to ...

NURSE: Well, hurry up then.

STABLEMASTER: I'm coming, I'm coming ... And as I was saying, I vow to make a pilgrimage all the way to the Holy Sepulchre, to Compostella, and to the world's end itself.

[*The* STABLEMASTER *follows the* NURSE *into his house. The* BOY *is left outside as the* COUNT *and the* KNIGHT *approach from the former's house.*]

COUNT: By my faith, sir, what a splendid joke for the Duke to give a wife to a man who has never seen a woman's shift.

KNIGHT: Yes indeed, and his Excellency won't let him see her before he actually marries her.

COUNT [*laughing*]: I have never seen anyone so unhappy about even the most dreadful misfortune as he is about taking a wife. I do believe that he would rather suffer ten strokes of the lash.

KNIGHT: Ten? A thousand, more likely. In the past, I've seen a score of people present a more cheerful face to the executioner, when he begs their pardon for what he has to do, than the stablemaster wears when anyone talks to him about this hoax.

COUNT [*laughing*]: Here is his boy. Let's ask him what his master is doing.

BOY [*singing*]:

> Open up, dear Marcolina,
> Tip-toe on your way,
> Open up, dear Marcolina ...

COUNT: Giannicco, how is your master?

BOY [*continues singing*]:

> Find me a husband, dearest mother, I can wait no more
> Find me a husband, dearest father, for I feel so ...

COUNT: What's your master up to, Giannicco?

BOY: Well, he's despairing, he's going to hang himself, he's tormenting himself cruelly, because he doesn't want the curse of a wife.
He's holding tight to his nurse, and she is teaching him some
bitchery that will rid him of such a nightmare.

KNIGHT [laughing]: You mean witchery!

BOY: Yes, my lord, something like that.

[The COUNT laughs more uproariously.]

BOY: Listen, my lord, and you listen too, sir. Here's the advice I've
given him . . .

COUNT: Go on, you splendid lad.

BOY: I've said that, if she's beautiful and rich, he should divide her in
half. In that way we will gain everything.

COUNT: In what way?

BOY: Let me tell you. To begin with, she'll be expensive to keep for
a few days, but then she'll attract some fine young cocks to our
home. So he'll be able to have the gay birds and I'll have the bird
he married. What do you say to that?

COUNT [laughing]: Solomon could not give him better advice!

KNIGHT [laughing]: What did your master say to that?

BOY: He wanted to boil me in oil. But I must go off and do an errand
for him in the castle. I see he is coming out of the house.

[He starts to sing.]

> The young widow when she sleeps alone,
> Has no cause to complain about me,
> She has no cause,
> She has no cause.

[The STABLEMASTER comes from the house towards the BOY who
runs off.]

KNIGHT: Let us pretend we are in a hurry and start to move on our
way. Welcome, stablemaster, I rejoice at all your good fortune.
Long may it continue!

COUNT: I'm delighted, stablemaster, over the favour the Duke has
shown you by giving you a rich and beautiful consort.

STABLEMASTER: I'd like my enemies to enjoy that kind of good
fortune and favour! But everyone has trouble in his life. Good-bye
to you.

KNIGHT: And that's not a joke.

[*Exeunt the* KNIGHT *and the* COUNT *as the* NURSE *appears at the door of the* STABLEMASTER's *house.*]

STABLEMASTER: Come outside, there's no one here.

NURSE: I'm coming.

STABLEMASTER: You are really sure that if I speak the words you tell me into his ear he won't talk to me about a wife any more, huh?

NURSE: No doubt about it. Now take this dust and do as I said. But tell me one thing: how will you make the crosses on the ground, without anyone noticing it?

STABLEMASTER [*bends down awkwardly as he is talking and scrawls on the ground*]: I'll let my hat fall off, and as I pick it up I'll make the crosses like this and this. Then I'll throw the dust behind him, while I am saying the words you've taught me.

NURSE: Now begin, and don't make any mistakes, and imagine that I'm the Duke.

STABLEMASTER:

> By Tobias I entreat thee,
> Let the Duke's ideas flee,
> Like the dust that blows so free,
> And of the wife he means for me,
> No more be heard on Epiphany.

NURSE: Too loud, and too much of a hurry.

STABLEMASTER:

> I entreat thee Epiphany
> By Tobias' wife who's not for me . . .

NURSE: Other way round. Despite everything, you're garbling it. I remember that it used to be murder to teach you to say your grace before meals, and you were eighteen years old before you knew the Hail Mary. Now start from the beginning.

STABLEMASTER:

> Wicked wife, I make my plea
> Banish such a fantasy . . .

God damn you, I wish to hell I'd never been born. I don't care if this is an enchantment or not. Curse all these spells and necromancy, for I won't take her, not till pigs fly. Go indoors, now – I want to say a few words to the schoolmaster.

[*The* PEDANT *approaches slowly*.]

NURSE: I see it all now! Oh dear, the devil has got hold of you and is making you do things all his way.

[*Exit the* NURSE. *The* PEDANT *approaches the* STABLEMASTER *in a towering rage*.]

PEDANT: These temerarious young adolescents, these effeminate Ganymedes are degrading our illustrious town. We guardians of the inheritance of Virgil are being intimidated by shameless jail-birds and brazen little pansies.

STABLEMASTER: What are you going on about?

PEDANT: It grieves and saddens me that the renowned city of Mantua, the *alma mater* that bore me, in the words of Virgil, is full of hermaphrodites. *Honorem meum nemini dabo*;[21] a cheeky boy, a bungling little thief, attached some paper crackers to my back, and then he set fire to them, and he has combusted my hair and dressed my vestment, *idest* my toga, with sulphur.

STABLEMASTER: Oh, what a stink! You look to me like the man who makes the gunpowder at Ferrara. Ha, ha, I'm laughing and I want to cry. Who was it?

PEDANT: That treacherous little miss, the knight's companion and secretary. I am going to his Excellency, and if he doesn't take up my case, posterity will hear about it because I'll record it all on paper.

STABLEMASTER: I'm certain the Duke will thrash him unmercifully when he hears about it.

PEDANT: When you think that it was we who brought from obscurity and darkness into light the ambiguous Priapic subtleties discovered by our daily and nocturnal studies! And we also dedicated to the knight our sententious macaronics, on account of whose witty style I was granted my laureate. It is a most difficult thing for an heroic orator to carry on living in this age of lead and iron. I wanted to discourse to you *ad unguem*[22] concerning your uxorial consort, but the fumosity of my choler impeded my eloquence; on another occasion I will report to you what our Prince, who is

21. I will sell my honour to no one.
22. fully.

most illustrious in arms, has confided to me. I am going to the castle and I will perambulate the cloister until vespers, and then I will exclaim *vocem magnam*:[23] the criminal will receive no mercy unless he genuflects before me to ask pardon, the young gallows-bird!

STABLEMASTER: Don't fight battles with a child, and let me solve my own problems, because I've got my paw caught in such a snare that it'll take all my determination to bite myself free. I am going indoors. Good-bye.

PEDANT: *Et ego quoque discedam. Vale.*[24]

23. in a loud voice.
24. And I am going as well. Good-bye.

# ACT THREE

*[It is early afternoon. The* BOY *is walking a little way from the* STABLEMASTER's *house towards the* JEW, *a fantastically attired pedlar carrying a tray of his wares and a drum.]*

JEW: Trinkets for sale. Lovely goods. Novelties galore. Who'll buy, who'll buy?

BOY: The fellow who's banging his drum to call people to buy his rubbish looks to me like that Jew with the bloodshot eyes and yellow face. Yes, it is him. I'd let him have it with a stone full on the chest if it weren't a crime to get at the Jews.

JEW: Lovely goods and trinkets for sale.

BOY: You're more than welcome, most reverend Abraham.

JEW: You do well to raise your hat to me, Giannicco.

BOY: It's the least I can do. But I want to make you rich as well.

JEW: I wish you could, dear boy.

BOY: D'you happen to have any little adornments for brides?

JEW: Well, I've only got fans, bonnets, make-up, perfumes, bracelets, necklaces, ear-rings, tooth-powder, pendants, belts and suchlike extravagances for husbands to buy.

BOY: If that's so, you must also have something extravagant for my master. He's got heartache, guts-ache and bellyache because he's taking a wife this evening.

JEW *[laughing]*: A wife, eh?

BOY: Yes, a wife, you treacherous dog . . . forgive me, your Lordship, it slipped out.

JEW: God will forgive you if you're telling me the truth.

BOY: It's gospel truth. I can't help it if you won't believe it. The Duke is making my master marry a beautiful bit of skirt tonight, at the Count's house, though he doesn't want to. And if you bring him your bazaar, he'll buy the lot. Please yourself whether you believe me and if not, you can go and play bellringers with yourself in a quiet corner.

JEW: There's nothing to lose by a short walk. I'll visit him, and if he doesn't want to buy anything I'll try someone else.

BOY: Don't say you heard it from me.

JEW: Why not?

BOY: It's a secret! Secret as a proclamation from the town crier!

JEW: As you say, pretty boy. Trinkets for sale, lovely things . . .

[*He moves off, crying his wares, towards the house of the* STABLE-MASTER *and starts to knock insistently and very loudly on the door.*]

BOY: I'll make my master wish he'd never been born; it's no more than he often does to me. Now the Jew's knocking at the door. I'll hide here to hear how politely he answers.

STABLEMASTER: Either I'm here, or I'm not here. If I'm here, I don't want to be. If I'm not here, why try to break the door down, you thieving old rascal?

JEW: Mind your manners!

BOY [*aside*]: That's the stuff. Report him!

STABLEMASTER: I stand by what I've said. Why don't you knock in a quiet sensible way?

JEW: I come to bring you a thousand pretty things, and you get on your high horse.

STABLEMASTER: And what should I do with your pretty things?

BOY [*aside*]: Stuff them up your behind.

JEW: Well, they are all for the wife who will be yours this evening. You won't believe what a beautiful little perfumed fan I've got her – just smell it!

STABLEMASTER: First that idiot and now the whole tribe of Jews are jeering at me. I've been taken for a fool, so I'll have to act the clown, or else I really will take leave of my senses.

BOY [*aside*]: Why not take leave of this world! That would *really* be a pity!

JEW: Don't worry, I'll let you have this bonnet for half-price. I wouldn't do that for anyone else.

STABLEMASTER: Please, leave me alone.

JEW: You have no judgement if you let this necklace out of your hand. It's all French workmanship, and look at the gold! The very finest, upon my word.

STABLEMASTER: I'll do something terrible!

BOY: Tie him up!

JEW: Now then, the bracelets will cost you ten crowns and four coppers; and I'll charge you nothing for the workmanship. [*Aside*] Whatever next? I'd do better business with a miser.

STABLEMASTER: You'll drive me out of my mind.

BOY: Ha, ha!

STABLEMASTER: I won't look at anything!

BOY: For God's sake, hit him! Then we'll see ...

JEW: This pendant is an antique, and it's worth a mint of money. But make your own price.

STABLEMASTER: Be quiet, Jew, I entreat you.

JEW: If you'll allow me to speak about it with a certain merchant, I'll give you six months to pay.

BOY: Oh, what a treat!

JEW: You don't accept? Well then, a year.

STABLEMASTER: You see what has happened through my terrible bad luck! One of those who crucified Christ makes a mockery of me and despite my position I'm not allowed to punish him. Yesterday too that ten-ton pig Mainoldo tripped me up in the middle of the court and made me fall head over heels, and I had to keep my temper.

BOY: What a shame!

JEW: They cost a hundred crowns, and the pendant alone is worth that. See what a beautiful colour this diamond has. It's the finest quality.

STABLEMASTER [*by now, scarcely containing himself*]: I don't want to give pleasure to my enemies, or I'd ... Enough, master Abraham. Go in peace!

JEW: I won't do anyone good by force. If you gave me two hundred for them, in cash, I wouldn't give them to you. I cheapened my goods by offering them to you, and all because of your boy.

STABLEMASTER: My boy, eh? It's the last straw.

[*Exit the* JEW.]

BOY: Someone's told me it's not true that the Duke is giving you a wife.

STABLEMASTER: Is that really you?

BOY: Yes, I think so.

STABLEMASTER: Do you know who I am?

BOY: Oh, you say the unkindest things.

STABLEMASTER: Unkind things, eh?

BOY: Yes, sir.

STABLEMASTER: Yes, sir, eh?

BOY: What are you getting at?

STABLEMASTER: Why have you been babbling about my affairs with the Jew?

BOY: The Jew? Me?

STABLEMASTER: The Jew, yes. You, yes.

BOY: God forbid; O the murderous Jews. May all those crooks and robbers be killed and burned like the one who was condemned when the emperor was here. The traitor is lying in his throat. It's a year since I last spoke with a Jew alone.

STABLEMASTER: Don't shout. I haven't got wax in my ears.

BOY: Now I remember, though, there was one of them I saw, who was dressed with frills all over his clothes and all festooned with bits of ribbon, and wore some gold ornament or other round his neck. The crawling trickster said to me: 'If that master of yours who has taken a wife wants to buy a golden carriage, all splendid and new, I'll sell it to him.' He swore it would be suitable for your horses, but I told him that yours aren't carriage-horses and so there was no point, and if I weren't frightened of going to prison, I'd have given him more than words.

STABLEMASTER [*somewhat mollified*]: You mustn't lift your hand in violence. But meanwhile what are they saying about my business?

BOY: Some say one thing, and some another.

STABLEMASTER: Indeed?

BOY: Indeed, yes. It's said by some that you're a fool, master, not to take her. But I've also heard from I don't know who that there's no wife at all.

STABLEMASTER: Oh, I wish to God that were so.

BOY: Master, this obstinacy will be your undoing. Please take a wife, please do. [*Under his breath*] If he's going mad before he's taken her, think what he'll do after he's lived with her a year or two. But here's one of the Duke's footmen.

[*The* FOOTMAN *comes running from the street leading towards the castle.*]

FOOTMAN: Would you have seen the jeweller?

STABLEMASTER: He was in the street a little while ago.

FOOTMAN: His Highness is asking for him.

STABLEMASTER: For what reason?

FOOTMAN: I don't know, by God. But I have to find him.

BOY [aside]: Perhaps he wants to win a gem or two at the gaming-table.

[Exit the FOOTMAN hurriedly.]

STABLEMASTER: I'm worried, I'm frightened, I'm terrified.

BOY: What of?

STABLEMASTER: Of the footman, because isn't it plain that he's going after the jeweller on account of me?

BOY: What do you mean, on your account?

STABLEMASTER: For the rings for my wife. For my ruination.

BOY: So he is, I expect. But if you do take her, what then? Saint Julian did worse than that when he killed his father and mother.

STABLEMASTER: He should have killed his wife. Cut your wife's throat and you go straight to heaven, flesh, bones and all.

BOY: All right then, if it'll get you to heaven, you'd better cut *your* wife's throat. It's quite the accepted thing in this world, anyway.

STABLEMASTER: How do you know whether it's the accepted thing or not?

BOY: Do we need Latin to learn things like that?

STABLEMASTER: Let's talk of something else. Go to the castle and spy out why the jeweller has been sent for by the Duke. Then come home, and I'll be waiting for you.

BOY: I'll do that, master: I'll go like a shot. But who are those two coming towards us chatting together? They look like the jeweller and the footman. I had better get a move on and arrive at the court before them.

[The BOY runs off towards the castle and the STABLEMASTER goes indoors as the FOOTMAN and a foppish JEWELLER approach from the other side.]

FOOTMAN: How should I know why the Duke is asking for you?

JEWELLER: If his Excellency wants to gamble with me today, I'm all set to win a fortune.

FOOTMAN: Take it easy, now.

JEWELLER: I'm sure I shall win. But what's the news you hear at Court?

FOOTMAN: That the Pope is going to Avignon, and not Nice; I meant to say Marseilles, and that the duke of Orleans has taken the Pope's niece as his wife, and everyone is absolutely amazed.

JEWELLER: That Pope is a fearsome Pope, and it's my opinion that he will turn the whole world topsy-turvy. But let them do as they please. Our Duke is the friend of everyone, and so there's never any upset in Mantua, God preserve him for a hundred years!

FOOTMAN: I had forgotten one thing. His Lordship is giving a wife to his stablemaster this evening. It's taking place in the Count's house.

JEWELLER: So he wants me on account of the rings, then. I must do the best I can for his Excellency! Look, let me show this little box of glorious and priceless jewels.

FOOTMAN: Be careful not to go out after nightfall.

JEWELLER: Why?

FOOTMAN: Because you'll have your jewel-box filched from you, and your life as well, and that matters still more.

JEWELLER: The jewel-box matters more.

FOOTMAN: What the devil, the jewel-box more!

JEWELLER: Yes, sir, it does. You know, I wouldn't sacrifice these jewels to save a thousand skins.

FOOTMAN: Yes, the skins of the grapes in your vineyards.

JEWELLER: I mean the skins of a thousand men.

FOOTMAN: You'd be right, if we're talking of some kinds of men!

JEWELLER: Even if they were men of my kind, I wouldn't worry, though it would be difficult to find ten like that, let alone a thousand.

[*The* FOOTMAN *bursts out laughing.*]

JEWELLER: Let us attend to these precious stones. Do you see this loose cameo?

FOOTMAN: I see it.

JEWELLER: I've been offered a hundred crowns for it.

FOOTMAN: A loose camel costs a lot, doesn't it? But what would it be worth mounted?

JEWELLER: I cannot say.

FOOTMAN: I heard about a camel that got loose and went to Pietole, and even that wasn't valued so highly!

JEWELLER: I'm talking about a cameo!

FOOTMAN: Yes, yes, I understand you now.

JEWELLER: Look here at this lapis lazuli. What a lovely ultramarine blue it is and only fifty crowns an ounce!

FOOTMAN: I'd hate my face to turn blue if I had leprosy, as if the sores of St Lazarus wouldn't be bad enough!

JEWELLER: No, no, lazuli, not lazari.

FOOTMAN: When you speak slowly I hear your words but when you say things in a hurry, my ears don't hear a thing.

JEWELLER: This is a carbuncle, a pair to the one at the treasury of San Marco. It is like fire. It is so pure and it shines so brightly that it dazzles the sight.

FOOTMAN: Away with a carbuncle. Take my advice, don't even think about having one.

JEWELLER: Why shouldn't I think of it?

FOOTMAN: Then you won't have to stay in bed. But now I had better tell my master that I didn't find you.

JEWELLER: Why so?

FOOTMAN: Do you expect me to go on talking to someone who has a carbuncle?

JEWELLER: I don't mean the kind you get on your neck. I'm talking about those stones which we jewellers value more than emeralds and diamonds. They are called carbuncles.

FOOTMAN: Oh·really?

JEWELLER: Yes, really.

FOOTMAN: Then it's all right.

JEWELLER: Now just admire this open-work necklace.

FOOTMAN: Let me try it round my neck.

JEWELLER: All right, but don't touch it with your hands, or it'll lose its shine.

FOOTMAN [*puts the necklace on*]: Now I really look like one of those popinjays who prance round their mistresses and must wear their necklaces to be as smart and foppish as they can. They like to wear them in full view and show off in front of everyone. To make a better show, they think their necklaces should be fine and fragile so they break if you lay a finger on them. But in fact necklaces should be like the one the King of France sent as a present to Pietro Aretino in Venice, and which weighs eight pounds.

JEWELLER: Who told you that?

FOOTMAN: Some good-for-nothing people who are bursting with envy over it.

JEWELLER: That king deserves to rule the whole world.

FOOTMAN: Do you have any chalcedonies?

JEWELLER: I have one waiting to be mounted. But look at this rosary of exquisite agates.

FOOTMAN: What are agates?

JEWELLER: They are stones just like these onyxes, these cornelians and these turquoises, which have great virtues when given as presents.

FOOTMAN: Make me a present of one, because I'd like to observe their virtues myself.

JEWELLER: I cannot do so.

FOOTMAN: Why not?

JEWELLER: The stone you want is promised. But have a good look at this mother of pearl. What do you think? Isn't it really majestic?

FOOTMAN: It seems to me the great-great-grandmother of pearls, not just the mother. It would split the ear of a cow, let alone a woman's.

[AMBROGIO *comes running from the direction of the castle.*]

AMBROGIO [*to* FOOTMAN]: You're a fast messenger, I must say! The Duke sent you off four hours ago and you're not back yet. [*To* JEWELLER] And you, Sir – his Excellency is calling for you very impatiently, so please be quick!

FOOTMAN: He was showing me enough stuff to sink a battleship.

JEWELLER: I have the Duke's service at heart, Sir!

AMBROGIO: Please, you must hurry up. You're both so slow, you must be related to the steed on which Our Lord rode into Jerusalem.

JEWELLER: Let's go then.

FOOTMAN: Yes, if you please.

[AMBROGIO *is left alone.*]

AMBROGIO: Anyone who doesn't become a courtier must be either a blockhead or Aristotle himself. Why should anyone want to go to the University of Bologna? Anyone who wants his sons to win their doctorates in three days should send them to court. It's a great centre of learning! You find so many kinds of men, so many different customs, such strange dispositions and such silly people all there together! And it's God's truth that scholars who are so sharp-witted and so knowing that they despise everyone else and trip everyone up soon become prize idiots when they mix with courtiers! At court, the cleverest man of all, the instant his lord and master wishes, will turn mental somersaults that are quite beyond the servile brain of a pasteboard courtier. A clever man can be made to believe things that even Simple Simon would laugh at. If anyone doubts this, show him the example of the stablemaster and the wife. Ha, ha! The poor fellow is worrying himself to death. But happy are those who are already idiots before they arrive at court, for at least they have no more problems to face.

[MESSER JACOPO *appears on the scene in time to hear the last few sentences of this soliloquy.*]

MESSER JACOPO: What's all this talk about wise men and fools?

AMBROGIO: I didn't see you there. I was talking to myself about the practical joke being played on our stablemaster. At the moment, he is looking for the confessor.

MESSER JACOPO: The confessor? Why's that?

AMBROGIO: Because he thinks that having to take a wife is the same as going to his own execution and he doesn't realize that it's all a great piece of nonsense.

MESSER JACOPO: It's not at all a nonsense. In fact, he's going to get a rich and beautiful young girl.

AMBROGIO: What do you think of our Lord Duke, then?

MESSER JACOPO: I think that God couldn't provide us with a better.

AMBROGIO: You're speaking like a wise man. But the Duke wouldn't be a Gonzaga if he weren't good, kind and generous. But where did you hear that his Excellency is giving the stablemaster a wife?

MESSER JACOPO: From a very good source.

AMBROGIO: What source?

MESSER JACOPO: A perfect source, I tell you.

AMBROGIO: Can you name the man?

MESSER JACOPO: Someone who knows what's what.

AMBROGIO: Who is this person, who knows it all?

MESSER JACOPO: My barber.

AMBROGIO [*laughing*]: You can certainly rely for information on the barber's shop. That's where all the messengers of the whole wide world dismount with their news. Now let's be on our way, so that we can be at the castle in time for the nuptial address.

MESSER JACOPO: Off we go then, and keep smiling – it's what we're paid for. But look, here's the town pedant. He's muttering his usual daft rigmarole to himself.

AMBROGIO: Let's walk away. If he tags on to us, he'll deafen us with his drivel.

[*The* PEDANT *approaches by himself and singing.*]

PEDANT:        *Scribere clericulis paro doctrinale novellis,*
                    *Rectis as es a, a, tibi dat declinatio prima.*[25]

The reception granted to me by his most Excellent Lordship has penetrated right to my intestines, my bowels, and my uterus. I was so moved, indeed, that I forgot to tell him the rash and insolentious scoundrelism shown me by that immoral little pig. But *ad rem nostram.*[26] His illustrious Magnanimity having chosen me for the preamble, the sermon and the speech at the nuptualities of our colleague, *nolo mirari,*[27] I want to go to consult the epistles of Cicero, and I hope to ingratiate myself with my audience, so that if I ask for the praetorship and the government of this golden city *omnio gratis et cito obtineam.*[28] But here comes that parricide of professors.

[*The* PAGE *runs up from the direction of the castle.*]

PAGE: Your Majesty, your Magnificence, your Lordship, have you seen my master, the knight?

PEDANT: Oh, you little wretch, you little catamite! Is it right and proper that you should make fun in public of the preceptor of the Mantuan *condiscipuli*?[29]

PAGE: What are you retching and catting about? Please tell me if you have seen the knight!

PEDANT: I swear to you by the Holy Gospel that I'll see you're given such a beating that it will be a lesson for all the other little nancy boys.

PAGE: Master, put this in Latin for me: there's a mouse peeing on my back.

25. The opening words of a medieval Latin grammar – regarded as comically old-fashioned by the scholars of Aretino's day.

26. To come to our business.

27. which is no wonder.

28. I may obtain all that I ask freely and immediately.

29. students.

PEDANT: You can go and pee yourself, you little beast.

PAGE: Good heavens, that's as easy as A.B.C., sir.

PEDANT [*spluttering with rage*]: It is most shameful that an impudent lad should provoke a noble scholar like me to anger! I'll . . .

PAGE: Is it true that it's all cock to have a K in the alphabet?

PEDANT [*lifting his hand*]: *Verum est*[30] that I'm giving you this . . .

PAGE: Using your fists, eh?

PEDANT: I cannot restrain myself from my urbane anger. Take that, and take this as well . . .

PAGE: By the body of Ch . . .

    [*He evades a rain of blows and bends down.*]

PEDANT: Put that stone down.

PAGE: I'll say what I . . .

PEDANT: I'll thrust your lies down your throat . . .

PAGE: You asked for it, you cowardly pedant.

PEDANT: Away with you, *maledictus homo*.[31]

PAGE: I've got you where I want you – and now, up yours!

    [PAGE *makes a rude gesture.*]

PEDANT: You raise your fingers to me? [*He totters away.*] Here is my little domicile and my modest refuge. My cerebellum is spinning! I'll go indoors *per requiescere aliquantulum*.[32]

              30. It is true.
              31. damned brat.
              32. to rest for a while.

# ACT FOUR

[*Late afternoon. The* STABLEMASTER *is alone at the door of his house.*]

STABLEMASTER: Giannicco ought to be back. O God, who would ever have thought that such a cruel fate would overwhelm me? How many wretched men have I consoled in my time, when their wives have caused the loss of their property and honour? How many things have I heard tell by one man or another, about one woman or another, and how many husbands have I seen disparaged with the words: 'I had his wife last night . . . the cuckold, the ninny, the silly fool.' And I've seen many who learn about the scandals their wives have inspired, and grow so ashamed that they suspect everyone they see talking of talking about them. So they never go out and about, not to church, nor to the piazza, nor to the court.

[*He pauses and starts as* GIANNICCO *appears suddenly.*]
I see my little blackguard, coming along laughing. Perhaps the Duke didn't send for him about the rings after all. [GIANNICCO *approaches him.*] Well then?

BOY: I wouldn't want to give you bad news. Your wife is still your wife.

STABLEMASTER: What do you mean 'still'?

BOY: All I know is that the jeweller went to the palace on your account.

STABLEMASTER: Are you certain it's not for someone else?

BOY: I've seen the rings.

STABLEMASTER: What does that prove? He's always displaying that jewellery of his.

BOY: Do you think I'm stupid? I saw the Duke take them.

STABLEMASTER: No, but sometimes one may mistake one thing for another.

BOY: Holy . . . you'll make me blaspheme.

STABLEMASTER: Perhaps when he saw you were there, he pretended to buy them.

BOY: He said he was buying them for you.

STABLEMASTER: Am I the only 'you' in the world?

BOY: He also said 'your master'.

STABLEMASTER: And the only master?

BOY: Interpret it your own way. I'm telling you that you should go to wash your beard and head, and tidy yourself up as quickly as possible, because tonight you have to go and take your wife and sleep with her. Is that clear?

STABLEMASTER: By all the saints! Oh hell and damnation! A wife? A wife for me? What have I done to deserve it?

BOY: But they are such charming rings. One has a red stone, like a boiled lobster, and the other is as green as parsley sauce.

STABLEMASTER: What's their colour matter to me? Oh my cursed fate, my squalid fate!

BOY: The name of the red one ends in 'uby'. It's cheruby or something like that. But I can't remember the name of the green one, something like cold or emerald. Anyway, I've told you about your wife, now it's up to you.

STABLEMASTER: Why should I care what the rings are called?

BOY: No reason at all, but it certainly concerns you to know that they cost a good four ducats.

STABLEMASTER: Four ducats, eh?

BOY: Four, or three and a half, more or less.

STABLEMASTER: It completely serves me right. I should have wasted my time grooming geese, rather than horses. I should have let the pimps, tipplers, prattlers and loud-mouth flatterers buzz about the courts without me. They're the ones who get the grace and favour, not a man like me. Now here they come looking for me.

[*They are joined by the* COUNT *and the* KNIGHT.]

COUNT [*addressing the* STABLEMASTER]: We are delighted to be of service to you, my gallant friend. The Duke has commanded us to take you at eight o'clock to the palace of the Count where preparations are being made for the wedding.

KNIGHT [*ingratiatingly*]: It's a wife and a wedding appropriate for a great lord, not someone of no position at all! So you will be under a permanent obligation to his Excellency . . .

STABLEMASTER: If a man is obliged to someone who ties a stone round his neck while he's drowning, I certainly do feel obliged to his Excellency. He must be a veritable Maecenas, as they say. But what have I done to deserve it? Heaven knows, I don't throw his kindness back in his face, like one courtier I could name, though I would sooner be thrown into the cesspool than take a wife.

BOY: What blasphemy! It would smell sweet enough to you if you were thrown in!

STABLEMASTER: Be quiet, or you'll get the worse of my temper.

BOY: I'll be silent as the grave!

COUNT: Stablemaster, I am fond of you, and one is always anxious to give the best advice to one's friends. Do you know what will happen to you, if the Duke were to hear you raving like this? He would throw you out for good, and that would be the end of it.

KNIGHT: He's not joking, my friend.

COUNT: Don't say I didn't warn you. As we all know, there is no one else in the whole world like our Duke of Mantua. He is the only prince who looks after and loves his servants and subjects, and raises them up in life. Why, the leading courtiers of the Pope and the Emperor are not dressed as well as you are dressed. You could have seen this with your own eyes when they were at Bologna. A loving word from his Highness is worth more than the actions of every other prince. It's only because he is magnanimous enough to treat us all as friends and companions that you dare to be so obstinate and disobedient.

KNIGHT: The Count is talking to you like a true friend. Remember that it won't be any use crying over spilt milk. Now that fortune beckons you, chase after her as hard as you can.

BOY: And if she bends over . . .

COUNT: Be quiet, you.

BOY: What do you mean, be quiet you? Can't I say what I like on my master's wedding day?

KNIGHT [*ignoring* GIANNICCO's *interruptions*]: The Count is perfectly right and all he wants is to help you. Believe him when he says that stablemasters are two a penny but the Duke of Mantua is unique.

COUNT: That's true, by God. If you're foolish, you'll be sorry when it is too late. Take her and have done with it. But men like you have to be forced to do what's best for them, because you are an ignorant lot. So I order you to take her, and be quick about it. I insist.

KNIGHT: It will be too late afterwards to say you're sorry.

COUNT: Do you know what is the worst thing in the world?

BOY [*interrupting*]: My master.

STABLEMASTER: Yes, I do know.

COUNT: What?

STABLEMASTER: To take a wife.

COUNT: Stuff and nonsense. I tell you that the worst thing one can do is to annoy one's rulers. It's far easier to lose a good prince than to find one. So don't make our prince lose his temper, because even though he likes to be very tolerant it's dangerous to provoke him too far. He will put up with quite a few affronts but eventually he will punish you for all of them, just when you think they are forgotten. Now I leave it to you to do what is right, because the next move is entirely up to you, isn't it?

KNIGHT: As the yokel said to the barber who was scalding him and asked if it hurt!

STABLEMASTER: You are driving me to blasphemy. What do you expect me to do with a wife? How can I live with her? Where can I take her? Who's to look after her new family? If I have to go on a journey, with whom can I leave her? Not with you, no, although you're very solicitous for your friends and relations. Tell the Duke he can hang, draw and quarter me but I won't take her. I'm a man, not a ram.

BOY: A ram doesn't *have* to have horns, does it, master?

STABLEMASTER: Now, be quiet there.

BOY: Whatever you say.

COUNT: Hush, boy. Now as for you, stablemaster, we'll report your idiocy to the Duke. If he orders us to knock all this obstinacy out of you, we'll do our duty.

KNIGHT: You always were a lunatic, and if it were up to me, I'd treat you like one.

COUNT: Let him go his way. He will have to eat the bread of repentance, the rogue.

STABLEMASTER: I'm an upright and respectable man in my station of life, as you are in yours, and it's very wrong of you to abuse me so.

KNIGHT: It's only wrong of us not to do more than that!

COUNT: Have things your own way, stablemaster. If the Duke commands it, and you still won't take her, then you'll lose your skin for it. Now let us return to court, sir.

KNIGHT: Let us return to court, Count.

STABLEMASTER: Oh what a fate! Shall I take her? I won't, by God! My evil fortune says I must, but I say I won't. But who is this who's coming slowly towards me? It's the professor.

[*The* PEDANT *approaches as the* COUNT *and the* KNIGHT *go off towards the castle.*]

STABLEMASTER: I didn't recognize you. Where are you going?

PEDANT: *Cogitabam, idest*[33] I was thinking of the innate goodness of our lord and master, our protector, and our monarch, whose benignity has imposed on my shoulders the burden of the oration for the ceremonies of your nuptials.

STABLEMASTER [*still distracted, and talking to himself*]: So, shall I take her or not?

[*Enter* MESSER JACOPO.]

MESSER JACOPO [*to* STABLEMASTER]: Even a blind man could see that you'll take her. Who wouldn't take her?

PEDANT [*to the* STABLEMASTER]: Let me tell you, dear colleague *per Deum,*[34] that she is one of the most renowned daughters of Mantua.

MESSER JACOPO: She needs must be good, since beauty without goodness is a house without a door, a ship without wind and a fountain without water.

PEDANT: Said in Seneca, in chapter XVII *de agilibus mundi.*[35]

BOY: What! Foul language from the schoolmaster?

MESSER JACOPO: Shut up, Giannicco. You are a fool, stablemaster. A fool, a fool! I'm saying it to you three times so that you hear me. Do you not know, you lunatic, that if your father had not taken a wife, you would not be here? And I have heard from the pulpit that it is better to have been born and go to hell, than never to have existed at all.

PEDANT: Augustine: *de Civitate Dei.*[36]

MESSER JACOPO: How can a man be as hopelessly obstinate as you

33. I was musing, that is.      34. by God.
35. A non-existent work.      36. *City of God.*

are? Don't you want to leave the city another person like yourself? After all, without you the horses would suffer a great inconvenience. I am thinking of all the wonderful cures that you work in cases of glanders, worms, cracks in the hoof, contractions, damage caused by bad shoeing, and many other things. So when your time comes and you are wasted by old age, or laid low by illness, if we don't have your children to take your place, we'll all feel the loss of them.

PEDANT: Oh, what a splendid discourse on progeny and fruitlessness!

MESSER JACOPO: Now come here, and listen to me as a friend should be listened to. For I want to describe to you just some of the contentment I have experienced because of my own wife's wisdom and capabilities and chaste love.

STABLEMASTER: Tell me about these miracles, but no lies mind.

PEDANT: Our messer Jacopo is neither mendacious nor loquacious. So listen to him and pay him attention.

MESSER JACOPO: Happy was the day when I took a wife in the year that the old Marquis, of munificent and glorious memory, became Captain-General of the Papal forces . . . I'm wrong, it was the year that his Excellency the present Duke was Gonfalonier, and I must then have been twenty or twenty-one or thereabouts, and I was on my uppers, as nearly all courtiers are, and then my good wife came along. I cannot help crying when I remember it . . .

BOY: Don't cry, sir.

PEDANT: It is only human nature.

STABLEMASTER: What a to-do about nothing!

MESSER JACOPO: My good wife came along, and she welcomed me to her honourable abode, which was well supplied with soft beds and comfortable furnishings, and so helped to restore me from death to life. And so as the days passed and I began to savour all these comforts and conveniences, I grew into a different person, and as she prudently sensed my natural wants and inclinations, she said, decreed and effected everything just as I wanted it, even if I didn't know how to ask. Then some illness or other struck me down; and dear God what care, dear God what solicitude, dear God what love she poured out in answer to my needs. She didn't eat, she didn't sleep, she never rested a moment, rather she started to her feet in response to my slightest sigh and slightest stir. 'What grieves you? What is your pleasure?' she would ask. And: 'What is worrying you?' And when she gave me my gruel, and my bread and soup, she murmured such sweet entreaties that she made food which had seemed bitter to me turn to honey. And whoever saw her, all anxious and worried, asking the doctor about my health, would have been able to understand the nature of a wife. And as for the redoubled love and tenderness I knew after I was better, how could I ever describe it to you?

PEDANT: Aristotle has a similar dialogue in the *Ethics*.

STABLEMASTER: If there is still more to tell us, please hurry up about it.

MESSER JACOPO: Gently please! Well then, let me say that you could not find any nourishing food or cordial that my most sweet wife did not set before me. I got better, thanks to God's mercy, and my first male child was born to me, and this made me so happy that I forgot about the court, and about the work and rewards, and I changed from being a busy courtier to a lover of peace and quiet, and I never left my home, or if I did, every instant till my return seemed to me like a whole day. And as my boy grew up, when I saw him playing at meal-times, in the parlour or in his bed, I knew a joy beyond belief.

PEDANT: As Virgil says: *mihi parvulus aula luderet Aeneas.*[37] Dido, the queen of Carthage, would never have plunged the truculent steel into her milky and ivory bosom, if she had had from Aeneas a little boy who could play with her in her house.

BOY [*in mock admiration*]: You know the Bible, the New Testament and everything by heart, professor.

PEDANT: These are not passages for adolescent boys. Do not interrogate me further, because I will not reply to you.

STABLEMASTER [*despairing*]: Children and crackpots spoil any home.

BOY: And what about chickens?

MESSER JACOPO [*confused by these interruptions*]: I no longer remember what I was saying . . .

BOY: The professor here has made you wander from the subject. Let him talk, professor.

STABLEMASTER [*laughing hysterically*]: What marvellous jokes for a comedy!

37. A little Aeneas would have played in my halls. A correct quotation from the Pedant this time.

MESSER JACOPO: I'll finish my talk with you another time. Let me just say for now that I advise you to take this step, because a man with no wife is like a fly with no head.

PEDANT: Plutarch in the Dream of Scipio[38] said the very same.

MESSER JACOPO: Let me tell you about when, because of the business you know about, I was in danger of being banished, but because of the clever efforts of my dear wife not only was I not banished but within a week I was pardoned. Nor should you think ill of it that she took our baby son in her arms and went before the Duke so humbly that she made everyone weep at the loving tenderness of her words.

STABLEMASTER: Indeed I like to think that you haven't told us half of it. But do you really think that one swallow makes a summer? If there were a hundred men here with their wives, all anxious to tell the truth, what do you think they would say about them?

MESSER JACOPO: I do not deny that there are bad wives, because even among the Apostles there was a Judas.

PEDANT: *Omnis regula patitur exceptionem*,[39] to say it in Latin.

MESSER JACOPO: But the wife who's promised to you is an angel, truly an angel, and they say there's no other woman to equal her.

BOY: If she's an angel, do take her, master.

STABLEMASTER [*to* BOY]: If you say any more, I'll smash your bones with my fists, I'll skin you with my nails, and I'll tear your eyes out with my fingers.

PEDANT: *Irascimini, et nolite peccare*,[40] as it's written in the Apocalypse.

STABLEMASTER: I don't want to quarrel with you, Messer Jacopo, so I tell you not to say any more to me, if you want to stay my friend. I'm talking to you frankly.

MESSER JACOPO [*starting to grow angry*]: What does your friendship matter to me? I've been advising you like a brother. I repeat: carry on in this way and one day you'll be left flat, to scratch your arse and regret your foolishness. And if his Lordship stops looking after you as he does now you'll have to go around dressed in rags, and

38. The Dream of Scipio is by Cicero, not Plutarch.
39. There is an exception to every rule.
40. Be ye angry, and sin not. This verse comes from Ephesians, IV, 26, not from the Apocalypse.

you'll die if you can't put on your leather apron again, and kiss the horses' feet every day.

STABLEMASTER: I'm a respected citizen.

MESSER JACOPO: I don't mind what you are so long as I don't have to be your friend. Now, master, let's go along to the Palace. Giulio Romano may be showing some beautiful painting there.

PEDANT: *Eamus*.[41] What a beautiful edifice is the palace created from the design of Giulio's little model. He has emulated the ancient perspective of Vitruvius.

MESSER JACOPO: Let's go.

[*Exeunt* MESSER JACOPO *and the* PEDANT.]

STABLEMASTER: I feel the urge to go behind that old dodderer and knife him, and that would teach him to argue with me that I should take a woman whom he'd be only too anxious to refuse. It's always the case that someone who has accidentally broken his neck wants everyone else to break theirs. But I know something about it too.

BOY: You teach the old man a lesson. He's a wicked old man, a real villain. But here's the jeweller. He wants you.

[*The* JEWELLER *arrives from the castle as the* NURSE *appears from inside the house.*]

JEWELLER: Come over here and touch it. It'll bring you luck. Knowing that they were being bought for you, I've got you two gems that would grace the Turkish helmet that the jeweller, Luigi Cavorlino, made in Venice. And what a charming gentleman and perfect companion he is!

STABLEMASTER: Go away. Go and see to your business.

[*Incensed by this dismissal, the* JEWELLER *tries to impress the* STABLEMASTER *by launching into a rigmarole of high-flown nonsense.*]

JEWELLER: My business is that of my friends. But you must be in a strange mood because the moon is on the wane. Let me go to see the medals and the statues and the vases that the abbot found in an ancient latrine. I understand that among them there's the head of St Joseph from the hand of Polyclitus, and a foot of the Nunc Dimittis from the hand of Phidias.

And when I've seen everything, I'll prepare to go to Venice to barter ten thousand plasmas for garnets and pearls, with which

41. Let us go.

I'll embroider my gold robe, row upon row. And whoever says that it was made from such rubbish as the trappings of the horse of the great Condottiere, Bartolommeo Colleoni, is lying in his throat. I'm a Catholic knight, and an apostolic jeweller. Do you understand me, Stablemaster?

STABLEMASTER: I understand you. Now go away. What an ass the man is! And what does my nurse want, trotting up to me like this?

BOY [knowingly]: I know what she wants.

STABLEMASTER: You little beast.

BOY: I know for sure.

STABLEMASTER: What does she want?

BOY: She wants you to take her to the wedding.

STABLEMASTER [slapping GIANNICCO hard]: Take this for the wedding, this for wives, and this for husbands.

BOY: Do you want to murder someone for doing you a favour?

STABLEMASTER [redoubling his blows]: Take this for your favours, this for your services, and this for all your desserts.

NURSE: Oh, don't let people see you doing that in public! Enough is enough.

    Stand back, Stablemaster, and you get up, Giannicco, and I want no more from either of you.

STABLEMASTER: You traitor!

BOY: I'll tell on you, wait and see. You dare to beat me, eh?

NURSE [to STABLEMASTER]: Stop, I tell you. Are you not ashamed to run after him like that?

STABLEMASTER: You little swine!

BOY: I'll tell everybody.

STABLEMASTER [to the NURSE]: And you're a bitch!

NURSE: Now then, keep your temper.

BOY: That's enough! That's enough!

STABLEMASTER: Leave me alone, you old witch, or by the body of . . . or I'll run out of patience.

NURSE: It's wrong to treat you kindly. How much more must I take from a lunatic who wants to devour us all? To hell with you! If I want to, I shall go straight home, and that'll be the last you see of me.

STABLEMASTER [shouting after the NURSE as she leaves]: You hideous

167

old hag. Go to hell. Now I'm rid of all the lot of them, the Count, the knight, the boy, the nurse and that shit-bag Jacopo. Now I'll see who will force me to take a wife. If the Duke ordered me to risk my life for him, I would be as happy to do that as I am miserable to have him commanding me and wheedling me to take a wife. By heavens, I won't take her! My God, he won't give the stablemaster a wife. No, no, no! He'll have to think of some other plan. If he wants me dead, let him dispatch me at once, and not keep me in suspense like this.

[*All leave except the* STABLEMASTER *who is joined by the* FOOT-MAN.]

FOOTMAN: I'm glad to see you.

STABLEMASTER: Same to you.

FOOTMAN: Oh, that's a cold answer. Aren't I your friend?

STABLEMASTER: Please don't aggravate me.

FOOTMAN: How come, aggravate you? You ought to be dancing in the street, and instead you're almost crying!

STABLEMASTER: Why dancing?

FOOTMAN: Because of your wife, her dowry, and his Excellency's favour.

STABLEMASTER: Stop tormenting me, I beg you.

FOOTMAN: You'll give me a nice present for my good news, won't you?

STABLEMASTER: If you weren't the Duke's footman, I'd either shut you up or do something worse. And if you stir me up I'll forget all my respect, and perhaps, perhaps . . .

FOOTMAN: What's all this huffing and puffing about? I've no great respect for you, and if it weren't beneath me to deal with a work-man, who just about knows how to use a hammer and nails, let alone a sword, I'd cut your coat to ribbons. You are going to take her and keep her, whatever you say. Yes, a wife, a wife. Am I speaking plainly enough?

STABLEMASTER: Try as he may, a man can't just get on with his own business. Thanks to these trouble-makers, he's never safe from attack.

FOOTMAN: What do you say?

STABLEMASTER: I'm taking my leave of you. Good-bye now.

FOOTMAN: Marriage will be a fine thing for her, I can see! I don't

know who should despair more – your wife of you or you of her.
Just accept her, and don't make such a song and dance about it.
[*The two talk almost in unison.*]

STABLEMASTER: O God, O Christ, O Jesus! Why am I tormented so much? I beg you, brother, either change the subject or go away.

FOOTMAN: Let's talk about your future happiness with your wife.

STABLEMASTER: I can't go on living . . .

FOOTMAN: She's very beautiful . . .

STABLEMASTER: It's the end of the world . . .

FOOTMAN: Four thousand crowns and more . . .

STABLEMASTER: I'll have to go into exile.

FOOTMAN: Partly in possessions, and partly in money . . .

STABLEMASTER: It doesn't stop . . .

FOOTMAN: She's a lady . . .

STABLEMASTER: Patience . . .

FOOTMAN: So very young . . .

STABLEMASTER: I bid you good-bye. I'm going into my house, so you'll have to leave me alone.

FOOTMAN [*laughing, as he calls after the* STABLEMASTER *who walks away*]: Don't forget the little present!

I have obeyed the Duke and teased the stablemaster. How he's suffering! Now I'll go back to the court.

# ACT FIVE

[MESSER JACOPO *leads in his* SON, *to whom he is talking as they walk towards the* STABLEMASTER.]

MESSER JACOPO: I've enjoyed a long friendship with the stable-master and I couldn't stay angry with him, even if I wished. After all, he's a good fellow and he deserves to be loved. I'll wait until he comes out of his house, and my eldest son will be the means by which I'm reconciled with him and prevail upon him to take a wife for love. Then he won't be forced to take her, which would do him no good at all. But I see him coming.

STABLEMASTER: I'd be wise to leave this town and escape from all my torments. But here's the scourge of my life!

MESSER JACOPO: Sir, a few words between friends don't matter at all! So let's stop being angry and instead talk sensibly to each other.

STABLEMASTER: I'm certainly not angry now and I am as much your friend as ever, provided that you don't go on about something I can't stand being mentioned . . .

MESSER JACOPO: Here is one of the first fruits gathered from my own marriage tree. Just look at him. He's my very life, the staff and comfort of my old age, my very eyes and ears! This is my son and my friend and my brother. He looks after me, serves me, guides me, and when I'm at the end of my days, please God, he will be like a father to me rather than a son, and just as I sustain our little family now, so will he when the time comes.

STABLEMASTER: May God preserve him for you! Myself, I'm not so fortunate as to hope for a son like that.

MESSER JACOPO: Let me go on. The boy sings nicely, he plays music, he rides, he fences, he writes a good hand, knows his letters, dances well, has the table manners of a gentleman and could attend the person of the sultan himself. If you had a boy like that wouldn't you value him as much as an artist might value the generosity of the Duke of Mantua?

STABLEMASTER: Be quiet for a moment. Here come the count and the knight. What's going to happen?

MESSER JACOPO: Off with you, my son. It's time to break in the young horses.

SON: Father, the tailor is a treacherous fellow.

MESSER JACOPO: Why is that?

SON: Because I was hoping to wear my new clothes tomorrow morning, and the cloth hasn't even been cut yet.

STABLEMASTER [to himself]: I'm frightened, really frightened.
[The SON leaves and MESSER JACOPO and the STABLEMASTER are joined by the KNIGHT and the COUNT.]

COUNT [to the STABLEMASTER]: Do you wish we were dead?

KNIGHT: Here we are, more your friends than ever.

MESSER JACOPO: He's as docile as a lamb.

COUNT: Forgive us for what we said to you a little while ago.

KNIGHT: We went too far, but only because we love you.

MESSER JACOPO: And I went too far as well.

STABLEMASTER: Your lordships are my masters, and servants aren't allowed to feud with their masters. So long as you don't speak to me about a wife, I'm ready to put up with anything.

COUNT: Brother, we thank you, and we approach you on behalf of the Lord Duke. Through us, he begs you – he doesn't command you – to say yes and to marry the girl this evening.

STABLEMASTER: I'm at death's door . . .

KNIGHT: That's silly nonsense.

STABLEMASTER: What a punishment.

COUNT: Now listen to us. In a moment you will bless us for what we have to say and do.

STABLEMASTER: Go on, I'm listening.

COUNT: His Excellency has given you the ring and now besides the other favours he does you he wants to make you a knight. That's an honour even for a king.

MESSER JACOPO: And what more would you wish for? Do you want jam on it?

KNIGHT: Certainly to dub someone a knight is to give him the noblest title possible, even if he's a prince.

STABLEMASTER: This is even worse than talking about a wife.

COUNT: Lunatic!

KNIGHT: Surly wretch!

MESSER JACOPO: Silly ass!

STABLEMASTER: Me a knight of the golden spurs? I agree with the jeweller. He's a blessed idiot, but all the same he's kept enough of his wits not to want to be called a knight, because the only benefit it brings is to put you at the prince's right hand, and that is sometimes a great inconvenience.

COUNT: What an idiot!

STABLEMASTER: I know that when a ruler wants to toss someone a bone he makes him a knight. The title is very suitable for someone who is rich enough and only wants a bit of reputation!

KNIGHT: It is suitable for everyone. It was devised not only to dignify the nobility, but to ennoble others as well.

STABLEMASTER: My lords, a knight without a private income is a bare wall that everyone pees against.

MESSER JACOPO: He's raving mad.

KNIGHT: If he made a will it certainly wouldn't count.

COUNT: Let's change the subject and talk about his spouse. She is learned, you know . . .

KNIGHT: That's true. And she composed the words for that madrigal that everyone is singing. The one with the tune by Marchetto.

MESSER JACOPO: I sing it all the time.

STABLEMASTER: So she is educated then?

COUNT: Very much so.

STABLEMASTER: And a poetess?

COUNT: As you heard.

STABLEMASTER: I heard it all right. I feel it, too. She composes, does she? When women begin to write songs, husbands start to feel a weight on their foreheads. I learned the other day from two young ladies who were reading the *Furioso*, where Ruggiero had his meeting with the enchantress Alcina . . .

COUNT: The point is that this one only reads the lives of Fathers of the Church, and one day we'll be lighting candles to her statue, as we do to Sant' Elena.

STABLEMASTER: Let me finish.

KNIGHT: Make up your mind for once and all. It will be the best thing for you.

STABLEMASTER: You go on, because I'm not saying a word, am I?

COUNT: Now let's talk seriously.

STABLEMASTER: Please, listen to a word or two from me, and then you can say as much as you like.

COUNT: Say what you have to.

STABLEMASTER: The young ladies were not only reading Ariosto, but, I don't want to say it, they had another book . . .

KNIGHT: What book?

STABLEMASTER: The book, where you find they depict the kind of birds you find in velvet nests . . .

KNIGHT: And then?

STABLEMASTER: Just looking at them made them all hot and bothered.

[*The* KNIGHT *bursts into a peal of laughter.*]

COUNT: You make too much of a song and dance about things. I ask you if you are so blind you don't see how lucky you are to fall in with a woman who's worth so much?

STABLEMASTER: You mean am I so blind I don't see how unlucky I would be to fall in with a woman who's worth very little.

COUNT: Everyone knows how good and able she is.

KNIGHT: If she were otherwise, the Duke wouldn't be giving her to you.

STABLEMASTER: Oh, these rulers of ours! They are all wicked brutes! I can't stand any more.

COUNT: How many wives do I know whose husbands would be beggars without them.

STABLEMASTER: How many husbands do I know who would be basking in the sun but for their wives.

MESSER JACOPO: There's nothing worse than . . . I won't say it.

STABLEMASTER: Do say it.

MESSER JACOPO: Than refusing to pour the wine of life into its cup.

STABLEMASTER: You perceive the mote in my eye, but you don't feel the beam in your own.

COUNT: We are wandering from the point. Have you had a talk with Messer Jacopo about the happiness given by a wife?

STABLEMASTER: Yes, I have.

COUNT: What conclusion did you come to?

STABLEMASTER: That he wants to see me dead!

MESSER JACOPO: Dead?

STABLEMASTER: Yes, dead, because he's advising me to do what Ambrogio, who's a good and honest man, advised me against. Ambrogio told me exactly the opposite of what you said to me.

KNIGHT: Ambrogio, eh?

MESSER JACOPO: Do you believe Ambrogio?

COUNT: Do you put faith in Ambrogio?

STABLEMASTER: I believe Ambrogio, and I put as much faith in him as in the word of God, and now something else comes to mind.

COUNT: What else?

STABLEMASTER: Something that I saw done by a girl at court.

COUNT: What did she do?

STABLEMASTER: Put all the palace in an uproar, just over a broken fingernail. But when she had her ears pierced to wear some rubbishy earrings or other, she laughed more happily than I would laugh if . . . if the Duke were to think about something other than getting me married.

COUNT: What do you mean by this?

STABLEMASTER: That wives are the sort of goods on which you can lose all your money.

COUNT: Yours isn't the sort of woman who pierces her ears. She is not one of them.

STABLEMASTER: If she pees like the others, she must be one of them.

KNIGHT: What a man!

STABLEMASTER: What a man, eh? Believe me, whether she dresses like a queen or not, I don't suppose she'll be different from any other woman when it comes to all the usual vanities. God damn them all, I say.

COUNT: Let us get everything settled here and now. What must be, must be, understand that. You are destined to take a wife this evening.

[*The* PEDANT *arrives suddenly and addresses himself to the group.*]

PEDANT: *Sapiens dominatur astris.*[42]

STABLEMASTER: There's the man who'll do his best for me; what do you say, schoolmaster?

PEDANT: I say that the sages are ruled by the astral bodies, the stars; and therefore it is necessary for you to take her. Read Ptolemy, Albumazar and the other astronomers concerning how we are

42. The learned man is ruled by the stars.

guided by fate and what has been ordained by fate, and written in the stars.

COUNT [*to the* STABLEMASTER]: What do you say to that?

STABLEMASTER: I say you stuff Albumazar and Ptolemy and all the astrologers who are or ever will be up my arse.

KNIGHT: Ha, ha, ha!

MESSER JACOPO: Schoolmaster, listen, use your philosophy to persuade him to take her. You can take your time.

PEDANT: Willingly, *liberter, quis habet aures audiendi audiat*:[43] listen to me, my colleague, *quia amici fidelis nulla est comparatio*.[44] Everything is the will of God, and especially marriages. He always has a hand in them. *Et iterum*,[45] again, I tell you that this wedding of yours was made in heaven this morning and will be made below this evening. This is because, as I said, God has a hand in it.

STABLEMASTER: It would be much better for me and more honour to mister God Almighty if he had put his hand to writing me a cheque for a thousand ducats.

COUNT: But hasn't he done just that, since he has seen to it that you are to get four thousand as a dowry?

PEDANT: Let me finish, please. Stablemaster, I tell you that there could be born a son *seminis eius*.[46] And from the maternal womb he would inherit that beautiful grace possessed by Alfonso d'Avalos, whose martial and Apollinarian presence makes us appear like tailed apes. And this *acerrimus virtutum ac vitiorum demonstrator*[47] spoke well, when he said that, while his natural liberality stripped him naked, he thereby shone out more splendidly than the Roman Fabricius did in his pauperdom, although *veritas odium parit*.[48]

KNIGHT: Take notice of that . . .

COUNT: Be warned . . .

MESSER JACOPO: Mark it well . . .

STABLEMASTER: I do notice, I've been warned, I mark it well.

PEDANT: And who knows if he will not learn that bold eloquence

---

43. Willingly, who has ears to hear, let him hear.
44. because there is nothing like a faithful friend.
45. And again.
46. of you.
47. acute judge of virtues and vices.
48. truth begets hatred.

with which the invincible Duke of Urbino addressed *Carolus quintus Imperator*[49] as he told him of the Italian battles fought by Italic, Gallic, Spanish and Germanic soldiers, to the astonishment of his Majesty, as Fabius Maximus once astonished the Senate and people of Rome, telling with what skill he had kept at bay Hannibal the Carthaginian.

KNIGHT: Now he has started giving us a lesson.

PEDANT: You're right.

COUNT: What a fine thing is the discourse of learned men.

STABLEMASTER: It's all stuff and nonsense.

PEDANT: This son might even approach the qualities of the Medicean Alessandro, that second Alexander the Great, or those of the dread signor Giovanni de' Medici, terror *hominumque deumque*,[50] and of Paolo Luzzasco, his teacher and disciple. And in goodness and munificence he might be like Massimiliano Stampa. Now *pictoribus atque poetis*:[51] and as a poet in Hebrew, Greek, Latin, and Italian he might be like Fortunio of Viterbo.

KNIGHT: You know many famous names.

PEDANT: *Ego habeo in catalogo*[52] all the names *virorum et mulierum*[53] *illustrium*, and I have learned them by heart. Thus as regards poets, he could be Bembo, *pater Pieridum*,[54] or Malza the Modenese, who made the streams stand still with his flute, or the erudite Giuidiccione of Lucca, or indeed the mellifluous Alamanno of Florence, or the elegant Cappello of Adria, as well as the youthful Veniero; or finally the sprightly Tasso.

STABLEMASTER: What's the use to me of all these names?

PEDANT: For embroidery, because they are like so many pearls, unions, sapphires, hyacinths, and rubies. More still? Well, he may be like the miraculous Camillo, who diffuses knowledge as the skies shed light, or the famous Bevazzano of Venice, or even the marvellous Aretino himself, or a Giovanni Pollio of Arezzo. Stop and think: he could be the witty Firenzuola, or Fausto, who has so much learning that it would sink a battleship. Or the good Antonio Mezzabarba, whose legal studies have kept him too long

49. Emperor Charles the Fifth.
50. of men and gods.
51. as for painters and poets.
52. I have in my list.
53. of illustrious men and women.
54. father of the Muses.

from the muses, or else Ludovico Dolce, who adorns the world so greatly today.

COUNT: You sound like a parish priest reciting the litany to the yokels.

[*The* KNIGHT *and* MESSER JACOPO *laugh dutifully.*]

PEDANT: What do you think of the comedy put on for all those princes at Bologna by Ricchi? The one he wrote in his early adolescence in imitation of the good old Greeks and Romans?

STABLEMASTER: To hell with all this!

PEDANT: Did you not see the Roman academy represented in San Petronio? Didn't you admire Giovio as another Paduan Livy, another Crispus Sallustius? I myself saw a rich mine of learning in Claudio Tolomei. And there I came to know Cesano, so free and resolute; and everybody knows our Gian Giacomo Calandro, our Statius, and the honourable Fascitello, the chief luminary of the great San Bendetto of Norcia.

KNIGHT: We'll be here until nightfall.

COUNT: The stablemaster's bursting.

MESSER JACOPO: Ha, ha, ha!

PEDANT: Shush, *silentium; si pictoribus* . . .[55]

STABLEMASTER: Oh dear, what a way to die!

COUNT: Ha, ha, ha!

PEDANT: *Si pictoribus*,[56] well, in that case he will be a Titian *emulus naturae immo magister*,[57] he will certainly be a fra Sebastiano, the inspired painter of Venice. Or perhaps he'll be a Giulio Romano of the Pope's court, and the pupil of Raphael of Urbino. And in sculpture, which I should have mentioned first (though its preeminence is not yet fully decided), he may be half a Michelangelo, or a Jacopo Sansovino, *speculum Florentiae*.[58]

STABLEMASTER: Gentlemen, by your leave, I shall sit down . . . now go on with the comedy if you like.

COUNT: Ha, ha!

KNIGHT: Ha, ha, ha!

MESSER JACOPO: Ha, ha, ha, ha!

55. silence; as for painters.
56. As for painters.
57. a rival of nature or rather its master.
58. mirror of Florence.

PEDANT: Yes, do be seated, dear colleague; be seated, brother. Now then, no doubt in Vitruvian architecture he will be the elder Baldassare of Siena, or a Serlio of the university city of Bologna, or a Luigi Anichini of Ferrara, inventor of engraving on Oriental crystal. In harmony, he'll be a Hadrian, a veritable force of nature. He'll be like the priest Lauro, or a Roberto, *et in cimbalis bene sonantibus*[59] a Giulio of Mutina, and a Marcantonio. Don't you realize that he may indeed play like the Milanese Francesco or the Mantuan Alberto? And in medicine he may be an Aesculapius of a doctor like Polo of Vicenza, and be made a Roman citizen by the Senate in the Capitol.

STABLEMASTER: Ring down the curtain, for the first act is finished.

KNIGHT: Ha, ha, ha, ha!

COUNT: Ha, ha ha!

MESSER JACOPO: Ha, ha!

PEDANT: And certainly, most certainly he will have the integrity, fidelity and ability possessed by messer Carlo of Bologna, on whose prudence the soul of the most Excellent Duke Massiano so happily relies. *In tandem*[60] he might equal the most upright Aurelio, or the splendid knight Vincenzo of Fermo, and share in the good breeding, possessed not only by Ottaviano dei Ceresara, but by all the gentlemen at the court of his Excellency; and if it is a female that God ...

STABLEMASTER: Save me!

PEDANT: ... wills, she will have the qualities of the famous Marchioness of Pescara.

KNIGHT: You really ought to be put in a straitjacket.

PEDANT: Why?

KNIGHT: Because God Himself could scarcely create a woman with a single one of her thousand glorious attributes. Unless there came back to earth madonna Bianca, the wife of Count Manfredi of Collalto, whose presence is now as welcome in heaven as once it was on earth.

COUNT: The bride is another such, and the stablemaster could not be the husband of a better wife nor she the wife of a better husband.

MESSER JACOPO: You speak the truth.

STABLEMASTER: Now you see, dear *hic, hoc, haec*, all your rigmarole gets us nowhere.

59. and upon the well-sounding cymbals.　　60. Finally.

PEDANT: *Certum est*[61] that she was suckled by the ten muses.

KNIGHT: Professor, there are only nine muses, unless you want to add your house-keeper.

PEDANT: What do you mean nine? Count them for yourself: Clio one, Euterpe two, Urania three, Calliope four, Erato five, Thalia six, Venus seven, Pallas eight and Minerva nine. *Verum est.*[62]

STABLEMASTER: That's the end of the second act.

KNIGHT: Ha, ha, ha!

COUNT: Ha, ha, ha, ha!

MESSER JACOPO: Ha, ha, ha, ha, ha!

STABLEMASTER: I don't think the joke is at all funny.

PEDANT: Though my oration is *ex abrupto*,[63] I won't forget to tell you that the girl you create will surely possess the prudence, the presence and the magnificence with which the Venetian ladies so stupefy stupendous Venice.

STABLEMASTER: If I thought I would have a girl who looked even like one of their old shoes, I would kneel down and give her the ring.

KNIGHT: Praise be to Mahomet, now you've found something feminine that is to your taste.

PEDANT: Now may Christ protect you from evil, honourable stable-master.

STABLEMASTER: Listen, all of you! The only answer I can give our pedagogue is that if these children he wants to see born of me were to be males, they might well turn out to be gamblers, pimps, thieves, traitors and cowards; and if they are females, then at best, whores. Now good-bye.

COUNT: Wait a moment. You're a man and she's a woman of such a kind that you can expect nothing but good behaviour and virtue from your sons and daughters.

PEDANT: You have spoken wisely, because *arbor bona bonos fructus facit.*[64]

STABLEMASTER: Some good fathers and good mothers have wicked children, and it's a wise man knows his own children.

---

61. For certain.
62. You're right!
63. Unprepared.
64. a good tree produces good fruit.

COUNT: Let's go into your house, and after we've had a good discussion, you'll admit yourself that it's best to please and obey the Duke.

PEDANT: *Bene, bene!*[65]

KNIGHT: Let us go.

STABLEMASTER: Whatever pleases your lordships.

KNIGHT: After you, my lord count.

COUNT: After you, my lord knight.

KNIGHT: No, you first, my lord

COUNT: No, you first, sir.

KNIGHT: But my lord . . .

COUNT: But sir . . .

PEDANT [*pushing his way forward*]: *Cedant arma togae.*[66]

MESSER JACOPO: I defer to you, schoolmaster. These Lombardian, Spanish and Neapolitan courtesies no longer mean anything.

> [*Exeunt omnes. Round the corner by the house of the* COUNT *appears a little group including* CARLO, *the Duke's page, dressed as a bride, the* MATRON *and a* LADY. *They walk past an* OLD WOMAN *who has been standing there quietly.*]

OLD WOMAN: The greatest show on earth! The Duke has informed the whole court that this evening he is giving a wife to his stablemaster. Seeing that everyone believes it's true, he has had Carlo da Fano dressed up as the bride that the Duke is supposed to have chosen for him. Ha, ha, ha, here they come!

CARLO: I've worked a miracle. From being a male I've become a female. Ha, ha! And now the stablemaster has to give me the ring! Ha, ha, ha!

MATRON: Heavens above, but everyone would believe that you really were a girl, going by your airs and graces and the way you walk and talk. Ha, ha!

LADY: By the holy cross, you're right! For one thing, he didn't need any make-up on his cheeks.

MATRON: You know what to do with your eyes?

CARLO: Lowered like this!

MATRON: Good.

CARLO: With my head held meekly and slightly inclined in this way, right?

65. Good, good!   66. Let arms give way to the toga

MATRON: Right. Look thoughtful, modest and respectful, and when the bridegroom approaches, stare down at the ground and on no account look into anybody's face. And when the question is put, don't say 'yes' until you're asked for the third time. Understand?

CARLO: Yes, my lady.

MATRON: Rehearse it a bit.

CARLO: With my eyes lowered like this, my mouth this way and curtsying so, when I'm asked the third time I shall reply: y-y-yes!

LADY: May I die if I have ever seen a bride play her part so well! Ha, ha, ha!

MATRON: Don't spoil it by laughing.

CARLO: I won't!

LADY: Remember to stick your tongue in his mouth, for that's what the Duke wants you to do.

CARLO: I shan't forget.

LADY: Now here is the Count's house; proceed inside, matron.

MATRON: After you, dear lady.

LADY: After you, dear matron.

MATRON: No you.

LADY: It should be you first.

OLD WOMAN: It should be me, since I'm the oldest.

CARLO: It should be me, since I'm the bride.

MATRON: So he is; well, go along with you, bride. The rest of us will follow all together.

> [*They all enter the house of the* COUNT. *The* STABLEMASTER *comes to the door of his house and round the corner arrive* MESSER JACOPO, *the* COUNT, *the* KNIGHT *and* PEDANT.]

COUNT: We have been ordered, if you won't come out for love, to bring you with us by force.

KNIGHT: You will forgive us. One must obey the Duke. Nothing else matters at all.

MESSER JACOPO: If you come to any harm, don't say afterwards that it wasn't your fault.

STABLEMASTER: All right then, you obey the Duke and murder me. Put me out of my misery now.

COUNT: Take these rings. There's an emerald and a ruby. The Duke is giving them to you.

STABLEMASTER: May the malediction of these rings fall on . . .

KNIGHT: Let's get on with this gradually, until everything's in order.

STABLEMASTER: You are going to a celebration, and I'm going to my execution.

MESSER JACOPO: Still the same nonsense?

KNIGHT: Here's the Count's house. Let's enter. And later in front of the door, on this beautiful piazza, I want you to marry her, so that in a thousand years' time it may be said: here the Lord Duke's stablemaster of beloved memory married my lady so-and-so . . .

STABLEMASTER: No, what will be said is: here the Lord Duke's stablemaster was sent to his death, thanks to his loyal service . . .

COUNT: Enough of all that. You go first, bridegroom.

STABLEMASTER: That's an honour I don't care for.

PEDANT: One must observe the right decorum for particular occasions. As I shall observe it *etiam* in the oration which his Excellency has imposed upon me to make for your marriage: *igitur*, therefore you go in first, *tamen* and notwithstanding, go first, bridegroom.[67]

STABLEMASTER: Mock me, ridicule me, scorn me. I put up with it all, because I have to.

COUNT: Everyone come along.

[*They all enter the house of the* COUNT. *Round the corner appear* AMBROGIO *and* MESSER PHEBUS.]

AMBROGIO: I would rather do without mass, sermons and vespers for a whole year than miss this entertainment.

MESSER PHEBUS: I quite agree – but do you know what I'm afraid of?

AMBROGIO: No.

MESSER PHEBUS: That his obstinacy will make the Duke lose his temper, and as a result he'll send him to the gallows.

AMBROGIO: Isn't he sending him to the gallows by giving him a wife?

MESSER PHEBUS: I think that he's sending him to paradise, because she's rich and beautiful. I wish to God I could take his place.

AMBROGIO: You ought to learn a bit more about life!

MESSER PHEBUS: What do you mean by that?

AMBROGIO: Simply that if you knew what it was like to have a wife, you would try to get out of it, just like the stablemaster.

67. also . . . therefore . . . nonetheless.

MESSER PHEBUS: What's it like then?

AMBROGIO: Have you ever had the amorous complaint?

MESSER PHEBUS: What is that?

AMBROGIO: The pox.

MESSER PHEBUS: Why do you call it the amorous complaint?

AMBROGIO: Because it is caught from between the thighs of *omnia vincit Amor*.[68]

MESSER PHEBUS: And what's it matter if one catches what almost everyone has got? If I had it, would you accuse me of stealing it?

AMBROGIO: That's not why I said what I did.

MESSER PHEBUS: Why did you say it?

AMBROGIO: To make you realize what a wife is like, by means of an example.

MESSER PHEBUS: Go on, tell me.

AMBROGIO: A wife in a home is like the pox in your body. Just as with the pox you feel pain now in one of your knees, now in an arm and now a hand, so in the house where a wife is living, something is always lacking to your peace and quiet, and a man who has a wife is like one who has caught what I said, because either she's raging here or got her heels dug in there, and she is always in a temper or a tantrum; she's always either over-dressed or sluttish, and there never was nor ever will be a husband married to a wife without an 'if' or a 'but'. Just as there never was a man, nor will be, who has the clap without being left with a nasty little twinge here and a nasty little twinge there. But look, here are the stable-master's boy and the nurse.

[*The* BOY *and the* NURSE *approach from the house of the* STABLE-MASTER.]

AMBROGIO: What shall we do, my pretty lad? Are you going to make it up with your master and come to the wedding?

BOY: We have made it up, and the wedding can go ahead, because I could never live with anyone else, and although he was unjust to me, I don't want to leave him.

AMBROGIO: Wisely said.

NURSE: And I say the same, and I don't care a jot for all the rude things he's said to me, since after all I brought him up, and his marriage will mean that we're at peace again.

68. love conquers all.

MESSER PHEBUS: That's clear.

NURSE: Once his bad temper's over, he's the best man in the world.

AMBROGIO: Please let's go straight away so that the holy ring isn't given away before we're there.

MESSER PHEBUS: Let's go down this alley and we'll find the way into the Count's house through the back door.

*As they disappear down an alley near the house of the* COUNT *the* FOOTMAN *crosses the square to the front of the house.*]

FOOTMAN: Will all this fuss about the stablemaster's wedding last for ever? All day long I have trotted here and there for him, and now that I was getting ready for a quick game of cards, the Duke has commanded me to go flying to the Count to tell him that he must arrange for the wedding ceremony to take place immediately. This is his door. I'll knock loudly.

[*He bangs at the door three times and a girl's voice answers from the upstairs window.*]

SERVING GIRL: Who's down there?

FOOTMAN: Come to the window.

SERVING GIRL: Who's knocking?

FOOTMAN: One of the Duke's footmen.

SERVING GIRL: What do you want?

FOOTMAN: Is that you, my heart?

[*She looks out of the window and smiles.*]

SERVING GIRL: Yes, dearest treasure.

FOOTMAN: Tell the Count that he must get the ring on to the bride's finger at once, this minute. It's on the Duke's orders.

SERVING GIRL: I'll tell him . . . [*She sighs deeply.*]

FOOTMAN: What was that sigh for?

SERVING GIRL: It only means I wish the ring were yours to give to your little blossom.

FOOTMAN: I shall keep my word. But remember your promise too.

SERVING GIRL: Three o'clock by the stable door, right?

FOOTMAN: Yes, madam.

SERVING GIRL: Three o'clock, you understand?

FOOTMAN: I understand, my love, my queen.

SERVING GIRL: Cross your heart and hope to die . . .

FOOTMAN: Yes, my dearest.

SERVING GIRL: Don't get the time wrong.

FOOTMAN: Get it wrong? How could I, dear heart?

SERVING GIRL: Make sure you don't fall asleep.

FOOTMAN: Of course not, my sugar plum, my lovely peach.

SERVING GIRL: Don't forget, three o'clock.

FOOTMAN: I won't forget, my milk-white dove, my priceless jewel.
Let me blow you a kiss. [*To himself.*] That's a joke on the little slut,
because I won't be there to meet her at three o'clock and not at four
o'clock either. But what's all this crowd? I'll go this way.

> [*As he leaves, on to the piazza from inside the house of the* COUNT
> *come the* COUNT, KNIGHT, MESSER JACOPO, PEDANT, MESSER
> PHEBUS, AMBROGIO, STABLEMASTER, BOY, NURSE, MATRON,
> BRIDE, LADY *and the* OLD WOMAN.]

COUNT [*to the* STABLEMASTER]: There's nothing to do but put a
cheerful face on it.

KNIGHT: That's what I keep telling him.

STABLEMASTER: To suffer death a single time without a wife would
be a mercy to me; but to make me suffer a thousand living deaths
with a wife is crueller than anything Nero ever thought of.

COUNT: There's the bride with her beautiful companions! Damn it!
She *is* lovely!

KNIGHT: Good heavens, the luck some people have!

STABLEMASTER: Oh dear, I'm dying, I'm bursting . . . I commend
. . . my spirit!

COUNT: Smelling salts, smelling salts! Loosen his belt! Stablemaster!
Stablemaster!

KNIGHT: This is the strangest thing in the world! Other men come to
life when they see a beautiful woman, but this man dies!

COUNT: He's not drawing breath at all.

BOY: Master, have recourse to Our Lady of St Peter's . . .

NURSE: If he recovers from this sudden affliction, I vow to say the
prayer of Saint Alexis every morning coming downstairs.

PEDANT: *Altaria fumant,*[69] because *sine Ceres and Bacchus friget Venus;*[70]
don't lose heart, dear friend.

COUNT: Bathe his wrists.

STABLEMASTER: Ah, my heart!

KNIGHT: Come, there's nothing wrong with you.

69. the altars are smoking (are ready for the sacrifice).
70. without food (Ceres) and wine (Bacchus) love (Venus) grows cold.

PEDANT: Vapours coming from the brain!

NURSE: How quickly his colour has come back!

BOY: Oh, he does have a strong constitution.

STABLEMASTER: Are you here, nurse? And you, dear Giannicco?

NURSE: I don't really mind it when you're naughty . . .

BOY: You wouldn't find another boy like Giannicco easy to come by . . .

STABLEMASTER: I didn't see you, Messer Jacopo.

MESSER JACOPO: I can't let you down. That's why I'm here.

COUNT: That's enough now. Let's get on with our business.

KNIGHT: With this magnanimous enterprise.

COUNT: Schoolmaster, you will deliver the sermon. Here now! Bring the bride here, so that the Duke's wishes for them both may be carried out. And you, stablemaster, you'll be happy to obey him, won't you?

STABLEMASTER: No, my lord.

COUNT [*brandishing a dagger*]: Either you say yes, or I'll cut your throat with this.

KNIGHT: He really wants to have his funeral at the same time as his wedding!

STABLEMASTER: Don't upset me. I'll tell you why I can't take her.

COUNT: Why?

STABLEMASTER: I have got a hernia that's opened up.

KNIGHT: Close yourself, then, if you've opened up, ha, ha!

STABLEMASTER: If you don't believe me ask my . . . ask my nurse – I won't say 'Ask my boy.'

NURSE: I won't have this lie on my conscience. It's not the truth.

BOY: That's the way, nurse, stick to the truth.

COUNT: Enough of these childish delays. We've got to get this finished today.

STABLEMASTER: Bring her here, bring her over here! Oh, my sins! My miserable sins!

KNIGHT: Come, ladies, bring the bride over to us.

MATRON: Here she is, my lord.

COUNT: It's your job, schoolmaster, to intone the wedding service.

STABLEMASTER: I'm sweating, and yet I'm shivering.

PEDANT: The frugal nature of our temperate banquet does not inspire me to attempt a lofty flight; but let us commence in Latin

nevertheless, because Cicero in the *Paradoxes* forbids one to speak
in the common tongue concerning sacrosanct matrimony.

COUNT: Speak to us as commonly as you can, because your Latin
rigmarole is too constipated for us to understand.

AMBROGIO: His lordship the Count speaks the truth.

PEDANT: Do you wish that I should be failing in oratorical gravity?
It is necessary first to take a few paces, looking now upwards and
now downwards, in the manner of Demosthenes. *Silentium*.[71]

*In principio creavit Deus caelum et terram.*[72] *Praeterea*[73] besides this
he made fishes for the water, *et inter aves turdos, et inter quadrupedes
gloria prima lepus.*[74] I say that the Lord God once he created the
heaven and the earth, made the fish for the seas, the birds for the
air, and for the woods, the bucks and stags. *Ulterius ad similitudinem
suam*[75] he mixed from clay the female and the male, *postea*[76] he
contracted them, *idest*[77] he joined them together, so that they
should increase and multiply without adultery *usquequo*,[78] until they
filled the thrones that the proud and profane followers of Lucifer
had vacated, and he made *principaliter*[79] the man to trample down
the lion and the dragon and he made him a rational animal with
sight and touch and the other senses *solum*[80] so that he might be
different from the beasts in his appetites, and *ideo*[81] he joined him
to the woman, in Genesis, where it treats of Adam and Eve. For
which reason, the most excellent Highness of our most illustrious
Duke at this moment joins his most celebrated stablemaster with
this most beauteous lady, *cui*, to whom I turn and say: 'Does it
please you, most beauteous lady, to take for your legitimate spouse
the unique stablemaster of his most excellent Excellency?'

STABLEMASTER: O God, please strike her dumb . . .

71. Silence.
72. In the beginning, God made heaven and earth.
73. And then.
74. and then the thrush and the hare, the outstanding glory among birds and
quadrupeds.
75. Furthermore to his likeness.
76. then.
77. that is.
78. until.
79. lord of all.
80. only.
81. therefore.

PEDANT: Does it please you, most exemplary and moral lady, to take for your perpetual husband the personal stablemaster of the most Illustrious and most Excellent Lord Duke Federico, first duke of Mantua?

STABLEMASTER: Oh God, if you did, it would be a marvellous miracle!

PEDANT: Does it please you, most delicious lady, to take for your singular consort the stablemaster *de Nobilibus*?

BRIDE: Y-y-yes!

STABLEMASTER: Now pluck out my other eye!

PEDANT: *Spectabili viro domino Marescalco placet vobis,*[82] does it please you to take for your spouse, wife, helpmeet and consort . . .

STABLEMASTER: Haven't I said to you that I can't, because I have a hernia that's opened up?

BOY: Nonsense, he's closed up as tight as can be!

COUNT: If you don't say 'yes' you'll force me to kill you.

BOY: Say 'yes', master.

[COUNT *threatens him with dagger.*]

NURSE: Spare him, my lord Count!

STABLEMASTER [*whispering*]: Yes, my lord, she pleases me, I want her. Mercy!

COUNT: Speak up.

STABLEMASTER [*louder*]: She pleases me, I want her, mercy, yes, my lord!

KNIGHT: *Te Deum Laudamus.*[83]

COUNT: Kiss each other as you put on the ring.

BRIDE [*backing away*]: Oh! Oh!!

MATRON: I never saw any woman more modest.

KNIGHT: We'll see how she looks tomorrow!

COUNT: Kiss her, close.

BOY: Here it comes!

[*The* 'BRIDE' *comes forward and kisses the* STABLEMASTER *warmly.*]

STABLEMASTER: A French kiss, eh? So I've been deceived. She may be a martyr one day, but neither God nor his Mother could make her a virgin. I'll be joining the cuckolds' club. There's no doubt about that. I'll just have to be patient.

82. Renowned lord stablemaster, does it please you.
83. We praise thee, O God.

LADY: Ungrateful brute!

STABLEMASTER: Put not your trust in princes ... there's a true saying.

BRIDE: He must be a beastly man.

STABLEMASTER: But I want to see what goods I've paid for despite myself.

PEDANT: 'In spite of' is better.

STABLEMASTER [*inspecting his* 'BRIDE' *at close quarters*]: Stay still, don't move, come here, more, more. Oh, very good!

BRIDE: Ha, ha, ha.

STABLEMASTER: O what a dolt, what an ox, what a blockhead, what a simpleton I am! It's Carlo the page, ha, ha, ha!

COUNT: What the devil, Carlo!

KNIGHT: Let's see him! It is Carlo, by God, ha, ha, ha!

COUNT: So we've been had?

KNIGHT: We've been had, ha, ha, ha!

AMBROGIO: Indeed yes, we are really a lot of boobies, the prize fools of Mantua, ha, ha, ha!

MESSER PHEBUS: It's really quite a saga, ha, ha, ha!

PEDANT: Is it a young man? *In fine nemo sine crimine vivit.*[84]

NURSE: Isn't the wicked rascal chuckling to himself?

STABLEMASTER: It doesn't matter. It's better for me to watch you all laughing over this lie than for you to see me weeping over the truth.

NURSE: The frog could never be enticed from the marsh.

PEDANT: Aesop in the fables.

MESSER JACOBO [*laughing*]: You're not so reluctant now, are you, Stablemaster?

[*The Count's* FOOTMAN *appears at the door of the house.*]

FOOTMAN: All of you come into the house, because dinner is ready and you can finish laughing at the joke afterwards.

COUNT: First the bride, then the ladies, and then you, madam.

[*Addressing* OLD WOMAN.]

KNIGHT: Go in after them.

STABLEMASTER: I'm going first because I'm the *quondam*[85] bridegroom; come, dear friends.

84. The conclusion is that no one lives without sinning.
85. 'Sometime' or 'former'.

PEDANT: Everybody wants to be called quondam, as if any common fellow deserved the name quondam! It has so many meanings this quondam, so many.[86]

COUNT: What are you babbling about, schoolmaster? Give a hero's farewell to the crowd and come along for some scoff. Let's go, dear knight.

PEDANT: Neither I nor any of mine was ever a comic and I don't think any of this is a laughing matter, so I don't know what you mean by 'scoff'.

BOY: Ha, ha, ha!

PEDANT: What are you laughing at, you little ass?

BOY: I'm laughing as you're not used to army ways, because in soldier's jargon to scoff means to eat for free.

PEDANT: Certain?

BOY: Absolutely certain.

PEDANT: Homer, the father of our Greek studies, died because of a similar enigma. I thank you for having explained to me such a strange cipher that even Averroes wouldn't have understood it.

BOY: Aren't I learned?

PEDANT: You have a speculative mind. Go inside, and I'll follow at once.

BOY: Be quick about it; or you'll be eating with gloves on.

PEDANT: How can I eat with gloves on when I haven't got any?

BOY: I'll have to be paid for it if you want me to explain that one as well.

PEDANT: We'll talk about it again later.

BOY: Look over there [pointing to audience], and say nasty things about wives, and everyone will be obliged to you.

PEDANT: Yes?

BOY: Yes, sir.

[The PEDANT is left alone.]

PEDANT: The serving boy has advised me to ingratiate the audience, and I agree, because to use an appropriate form to take one's leave from the rest of the company, matrimony must be criticized so as

---

86. The PEDANT apparently objects to the uneducated STABLEMASTER using a Latin word. 'Quondam' is a slightly pompous word for the ex-holder of an official position – also it often means 'the late' of someone who has died – also it can relate to an unspecified time in the future as well as the past.

to balance my praise of it in my nuptial sermon. So I am cogitating how I can set about it. I think, I've thought, now I'll explain.

Spectators, we intend, with God's help, as no studies of this problem exist, to compose a comedy on the stablemaster's case in four parts. In the first part, we will deal with the happiness of those whose wife has died. In the second, we will talk about the unhappiness of those whose wife won't die. In the third, we will describe the misfortunes that befall those who must take a wife. Fourthly, and lastly, we will conclude with the beatitude of those who have no wife, don't want one, and never had one. *Isto interim,*[87] what did I mean to say? Please remind me: I meant to say . . . ha, ha, I've got it; *isto interim. Valete et plaudite.*[88]

87. Meanwhile.
88. Meanwhile. Good-bye and applaud.

# THE DECEIVED

## (Gl'Ingannati)

*by*

GL'INTRONATI DI SIENA
*A sixteenth-century Literary Society*

# GL'INTRONATI DI SIENA

The INTRONATI of Siena, a sixteenth-century literary and dramatic society, claim collective responsibility for *The Deceived* (*Gl'Ingannati*) on the title-page of the first edition, which appeared in 1538. Whether the play is really the product of a collaboration, and if so of how many hands, cannot now be determined. *The Deceived* enjoyed great contemporary success. By the end of the sixteenth century it had run through twenty Italian editions, and been translated into French, Spanish and Latin. Shakespeare's *Twelfth Night* is visibly indebted to *The Deceived* for the greater part of its plot and for its most memorable character. There are several routes by which the story could have reached Shakespeare, but the following seems the most probable. Bandello had turned it into a long short story in his *Novelliere* (1554); Belleforest had translated Bandello's version into French in his *Histoires Tragiques* (1570); and Barnabe Riche had translated Belleforest's version into English in his *Apolonius & Silla* (1581). Whether Shakespeare learned of the story at fourth hand through Riche or by some other, more direct means, there can be no doubt that Viola is lineally descended from Lelia, and bears a strong family likeness to her.

Long extracts from *The Deceived* have been translated on two occasions to illustrate the connection with *Twelfth Night* – once in *Gl'Ingannati and Aelia Laelia Crispis* by T. L. Peacock, 1862, and once in Volume II of *Narrative and Dramatic Sources of Shakespeare* by Geoffrey Bullough, 1958. But the present translation is the first complete one into English. The Italian text on which it is based is that edited by I. Sanesi and published by G. Laterza in 1912.

# CHARACTERS

in order of appearance

GHERARDO, Isabella's father, an old merchant
VIRGINIO, father of Lelia and Fabrizio, an old merchant
CLEMENZIA, Lelia's old nurse
LELIA, Virginio's daughter, in love with Flamminio
SPELA, Gherardo's manservant
SCATIZZA, Virginio's manservant
FLAMMINIO, a young nobleman, in love with Isabella
PASQUELLA, Gherardo's maidservant
ISABELLA, Gherardo's daughter
GIGLIO, a Spanish soldier
CRIVELLO, Flamminio's manservant
MESSER PIERO, Fabrizio's tutor
FABRIZIO, Lelia's brother
STRAGUALCIA, Fabrizio's manservant
L'AGIATO, an innkeeper
FRULLA, another innkeeper
CITTINA, Clemenzia's little daughter

# ACT ONE

*A street in Modena. The frontages of five buildings can be seen – the large houses of* VIRGINIO BELLENZINI *and* GHERARDO FOIANI, *two rich elderly merchants, a small house belonging to* CLEMENZIA, *the old nurse of the Bellenzini family, and two inns. The sequence from left to right is as follows:*

| Clemenzia's<br>house | Virginio's<br>house | Mirror<br>Inn | Fool<br>Inn | Gherardo's<br>house |

[GHERARDO *and* VIRGINIO *enter Left, talking earnestly. During the following conversation, they walk slowly over to* VIRGINIO'*s house and continue talking outside the front door.*]

GHERARDO: Well then, Virginio, since you want to oblige me in this matter, as you say, please fix the earliest possible date for this wedding we've been talking about for so long, and get me out of the tangled web in which I've somehow become involved without meaning it to happen at all. If there's some obstacle in your way, like not having enough money for the wedding clothes – and I know you lost everything in that wretched sack of Rome – or some difficulty of the same sort over wedding decorations for the house, or the celebrations in general, don't hesitate to tell me. I wouldn't mind spending a few *scudi* extra to speed things up by a month, say, and get what I want a little quicker, for neither of us is exactly in the springtime of his days – it's summer with us, if not . . . and so the longer we wait the more time we lose. And don't be surprised, Virginio, that I come worrying you like this, for I swear to you that since I got this idea into my head, I can't sleep for more than half of every night; and to prove that's true, see how early I got up this morning, and what's more before I came to see you I went to the cathedral and heard the first mass there, because I didn't want to wake you up any earlier. And if you've changed your mind, or come to the conclusion that your daughter's age wouldn't suit mine, being well into the forties or perhaps a little bit more than that, don't be afraid to say so. I'll know what to do, I'll look elsewhere, and that'll save both of us a lot of trouble, because as you know I've other friends who'd be glad to see me become a member of their family.

VIRGINIO: The things you've mentioned, Gherardo, wouldn't stop me marrying my daughter to you today, if I were in a position to do so. When Rome was sacked, I did lose nearly everything, including my son Fabrizio, unfortunately; but I've still got enough of my fortune left, thank God, to be able to pay for the clothes and the other expenses of my daughter's wedding, without troubling anyone for assistance. And don't think I'll go back on my promise to you, as long as the girl's happy about the match, for as you know it's not good for a merchant to break his word.

GHERARDO: That's a principle that gets more lip-service than anything else among the merchants of the present time; but I'm sure you're not like that. But seeing myself put off from today to tomorrow, and then from tomorrow to the day after, it does make me wonder if there's something or other wrong; and I know you're man enough to be able to get your daughter to do anything you please, if you really want to.

VIRGINIO: Let me explain. You know I had to go to Bologna to clear up some business I had with Messer Buonaparte Ghisilieri and the Cavaliere da Casio. And as I'm a widower and was living in the country at the time, I didn't want to leave my daughter in charge of the servants, so I sent her to the convent of San Crescenzio, where her aunt Camilla is a nun. And she's still there, for as you know I only got back last night. And now I've sent my servant to tell her to come home.

GHERARDO: Are you sure she's still in the convent and not somewhere else?

VIRGINIO: What d'you mean, am I sure? Where do you expect her to be? What sort of question is that?

GHERARDO: I'll tell you. I've been out there several times in connection with my own affairs, and I've asked to see her, but the sisters wouldn't let me, and some of them said she wasn't there.

VIRGINIO: That's because the good sisters want to make a nun of her, so that the convent will inherit the little I've got left, when I come to die. But that cock won't fight, for I'm not so old that I can't have a couple more children, if I get married again.

GHERARDO: Old, indeed! I can assure you that I feel every inch the man I was when I was twenty-five, especially in the morning, before I've had a piss. It's a case of

> 'To have a hoar head and a greene tail'

as the old poet says.

And I'd be sorry if any of these beardless boys we see swaggering round Modena with tall plumes in their caps after the Guelph style, and their sword at their side, and their dagger behind, and silk tassels on their scabbards – why, I'd be sorry to see them beat me at anything, unless perhaps it was running races.

VIRGINIO: There's nothing wrong with your spirit or your courage, but I don't know about your strength.

GHERARDO: You'd better ask Lelia about that, after our first night together.

VIRGINIO: Now, for God's sake, use a bit of sense. She's only a child, and it's no good going at it like a bull at a gate the very first time.

GHERARDO: How old is she, exactly?

VIRGINIO: She was just thirteen at the time of the sack of Rome, when she and I were prisoners of those bastards.

GHERARDO: Then she's just right for me. I wouldn't want her to be any older or any younger. I've got the finest clothes and the finest jewels and the finest necklaces and the finest other ornaments for a girl of any man in Modena.

VIRGINIO: I'm glad to hear it. I'm happy to hear of any good fortune that comes her way – and yours.

GHERARDO: Hurry it up as much as you can.

VIRGINIO: As far as the dowry is concerned, what's been agreed has been agreed.

GHERARDO: You know I wouldn't change my mind about that – But I must be going.

VIRGINIO: God be with you. [GHERARDO *goes into his house.*] – Why, here's her nurse – that saves me the trouble of sending for her to tell her to go and fetch Lelia.

[CLEMENZIA *comes out of her house. She does not see* VIRGINIO *at first.*]

CLEMENZIA [*soliloquizing*]: I can't think what can be meant by the way my hens have been cackling this morning, as if they wanted to wake up the whole household, or lay so many eggs that they'd make me a rich woman. Something strange must be going to happen today, for they never create that sort of din unless either I'm going to hear something bad or something bad's going to happen to me.

VIRGINIO: She must be conversing with the angels, or with the holy father superior at San Francesco's.

CLEMENZIA: And another thing's happened to me that I can't see the meaning of; though my confessor tells me that I'm wrong to think of such things or believe in omens the way I do.

VIRGINIO: Why are you standing there mumbling like that? Epiphany's come and gone![1]

CLEMENZIA: Oh! Good morning, Virginio. As I hope to be saved, I was coming to pass the time of day with you. But you must have got up very early today. Welcome to you, anyway.

VIRGINIO: But what were you muttering just now? Were you planning to wheedle me into giving you a measure of grain or a bottle of oil or a piece of fat bacon, the same as usual?

CLEMENZIA [*sarcastically*]: Yes, of course! And what an open-handed hero your honour must be to need all this wheedling! Perhaps your honour is saving up for his children's sake?

VIRGINIO: What *were* you saying, then?

CLEMENZIA: I was saying that I didn't know what it could mean that a dear little kitten of mine, which had been lost for a fortnight, suddenly turned up again this morning; and then while she was playing with a mouse that she caught in that dark little room of mine, she spilt a bottle of good wine that the preacher at San Francesco's gave me for doing his laundry.

VIRGINIO: It's a sign of a wedding. And you'd like me to give you another one, wouldn't you?

CLEMENZIA: You're right there.

1. The feast of Epiphany was celebrated by the giving of presents – and Virginio suspects that Clemenzia is about to ask him for something. The word 'epiphany' was also used to denote an old hag.

VIRGINIO: See what a good thought-reader I am! But how's your young mistress, Lelia?

CLEMENZIA: Poor girl! Better for her if she'd never been born!

VIRGINIO: Why?

CLEMENZIA: 'Why?' indeed! Isn't Gherardo Foiani going round telling everyone that she's to marry him and that it's all arranged?

VIRGINIO: What he says is true. And why not? Don't you think she'll be well placed, in an honourable house, with a rich husband who lacks for nothing, and no one else in the family? There'll be none of the usual cat-and-dog business between mother-in-law and daughter-in-law and sisters-in-law. And he'll treat her like a daughter.

CLEMENZIA: That's just it – young women want to be treated like wives and not like daughters. They'd rather have someone who'll torment them and bite them and tear their clothes first in one place and then in another than someone who'll treat them like a daughter.

VIRGINIO: Do you think that all women are the same as yourself? – You and I should know each other well enough by now, eh? – But that's all nonsense, and anyway Gherardo has every intention of treating her like a wife.

CLEMENZIA: Why, isn't he well over fifty?

VIRGINIO: What does that matter? I'm not far off the same age myself, and you should know whether I can still keep my lance steady in the rest or not!

CLEMENZIA: Oh! There aren't many in your class. But if I thought you really meant to give her to him, I'd drown her.

VIRGINIO: Clemenzia, I've lost the little I used to have, and now I've got to make the best of things. If Fabrizio turns up one of these days, and I've given everything to her, he'll die of hunger, and I shouldn't want that to happen. Now I'm marrying her to Gherardo on condition that, if Fabrizio doesn't come home within four years, he'll have one thousand florins for her dowry, but if the boy does reappear, Gherardo will only get two hundred and find the rest of her dowry himself.

CLEMENZIA: The poor girl! It's a pity I can't have a word with her.

VIRGINIO: What the devil do you mean by that? How long is it since you last saw her?

CLEMENZIA: More than a fortnight. I was planning to go there today.

VIRGINIO: I believe the sisters want to make a nun out of her, and I'm afraid they may have been stuffing her head with nonsense, as they generally do. Go and see her now, Clemenzia, and tell her from me that she's to come home at once.

CLEMENZIA: Do you know, I'd like you to lend me a few pence to buy a cord of firewood, for I haven't a single stick left in the house.

VIRGINIO: To hell with it! Be off with you, and I'll buy the wood for you myself! Go!

CLEMENZIA: But I must go to mass first.

[VIRGINIO *glares at* CLEMENZIA *and goes into his house.*]

[LELIA *enters Right, dressed as a boy. She walks over towards* CLEMENZIA's *house.*]

LELIA: I can't think where I found the nerve to come out alone like this at this time of day, knowing what I do about the bad habits of the wicked young men of Modena! It would serve me right if one of those reckless young idiots grabbed hold of me and dragged me into a house somewhere to find out whether I'm really a boy or a girl! That would teach me to go out on my own in the early hours like this! But the cause of all this turmoil is my love for that ungrateful brute Flamminio. Talk about bad luck! I'm in love with a man who hates me and never has a good word for me; I serve a man who doesn't even know who I am! And to make things worse, I'm helping him to court another girl, without a hope – and this is what no one will ever believe – without a hope of any satisfaction beyond what I can get out of feasting my eyes on him! Well, it's worked all right so far; but what can I do now? What plan am I to follow? My father's come home and Flamminio's come to live in town – and I can't go on like this in Modena without being recognized. And if I am, I shall be ruined for ever, and become a byword in the whole city. And that's why I've come out so early, to consult my nurse. I was looking out of the window, and saw her coming this way, and I want to ask her to help me choose the best course of action. But first of all let's see if she knows me in these clothes.

CLEMENZIA [*looking offstage, Right*]: Why, Flamminio must be back in town, for there's the door of his house open. Oh! if Lelia knew that, how she'd long to be back in her father's house – But who's this young sprig who keeps crossing my path this morning? Why do you keep on getting under my feet? And why don't you go away? What are you hanging around for? What do you want with me? If you knew what I think of the likes of you!

LELIA: I wish you good day, Madame Spindle-Fiddler!

CLEMENZIA: Be off with you! I'm sure you've just given somebody a good night – so take your good days to the same address!

LELIA: Since you think I've given someone else a good night, I'll give you a good day, if you'd like me to.

CLEMENZIA: Don't pester me like that! I've had such a morning ... if you pester me today, I'll ... I'll ... I won't tell you what I'll do.

LELIA: Is the father superior at San Francesco's waiting for you? Or are you on your way to see Fra Cipollone?

CLEMENZIA: May you break your neck! and the sooner the better! What concern of yours is it what I do or where I go and where I stay? What father superior d'you mean? or what Fra Cipollone?

LELIA: Oh! don't lose your temper, Madame All-Blow-and-No-Go!

CLEMENZIA [aside]: (I know this brat all right, and I'm sure I've seen him hundreds of times, but I can't tell where.) Tell me, my lad, how is it that you know me so well, and claim to know so much about my affairs? Put your hood down so that I can see your face.

LELIA: Come now! Are you pretending not to recognize me?

CLEMENZIA: If you keep your face covered up like that, how do you expect me or anyone else to recognize you?

LELIA: Come a little farther over here.

CLEMENZIA: Where?

LELIA: This way ... Do you know me now?

CLEMENZIA: Are you Lelia? Oh, poor Clemenzia, then! Poor, unhappy Clemenzia! Yes, it is Lelia! What does this mean, my child?

LELIA: Keep your voice down! Are you mad, or something? I'll go straight off and leave you here, if you shout like that!

CLEMENZIA: And no shame at all! Oh, Lelia, have you become a woman of the world, as some people call it nowadays?

LELIA: Yes – I'm a woman of the world, all right, if it's this world you're talking about. How many women of the other world have you seen? I've never been there in my life, that I can remember.

CLEMENZIA: Well, then, have you lost your virgin name?

LELIA: Not so far as I know – not in Modena at least. Not the *name* of virgin – but if you want to know about anything else, you'd better ask the Spaniards who held me prisoner at Rome.

CLEMENZIA: Is this the respect you show to your father, to your family, to yourself and to me, who brought you up? I'd like to strangle you with my own hands! Now come straight indoors with me, for I can't bear it that you should be seen in those clothes.

LELIA: Oh! don't be so impatient!

CLEMENZIA: But aren't you ashamed to be seen dressed like that?

LELIA: Am I the only one? I've seen dozens of them at Rome. And here at Modena, too, how many women do you suppose go out every night about their own affairs dressed like this?

CLEMENZIA: But those are wicked women!

LELIA: And among all those wicked women isn't there room for one good one?

CLEMENZIA: Tell me why you're going about like that, and why you left the convent. And if your father knew about it, wouldn't he kill you, you wretched girl?

LELIA: That'd be one way out of my troubles. Do you think I love life so much?

CLEMENZIA: But why are you doing this? Why?

LELIA: If you'll listen, I'll tell you; and you'll hear the whole story of my misfortunes, and the reason why I left the convent and put on these clothes, and the help I'm hoping to get from you. But come over here. It'd be a pity if some passer-by recognized me from the fact that I'm talking to you.

CLEMENZIA: You're making me quite ill with worry. Tell me quickly, or I'll die of desperation. Oh dear! Oh dear! Oh dear!

LELIA: Well, as you know, my father lost everything in that miserable business of the sack of Rome; and together with his property he lost my brother Fabrizio. Before that, he'd placed me in the household of a certain noble lady, but now he didn't want to be left on his own, so he took me away again, and as we'd no alternative we came back to Modena, to the old family home, where we could get away from all that ill fortune and live on the little we had left. And you know that my father was regarded as a friend of Count Guido Rangone, and some people looked askance at him for that reason.

CLEMENZIA: Why are you telling me these things which I know better than you do? I know very well that it was because of what you've just said that you went to live on your farm at Fontanile; and I went there too to keep you company.

LELIA: That's right. And you know that for all that time I had a hard and difficult life, shut off from thoughts of love, and almost shut off from humanity; for I thought everyone would be pointing at me because I'd been in the hands of the soldiers, and however honourably I lived, I didn't see how I could escape calumny. You know that, because you often used to scold me for it, and encourage me to lead a gayer life.

CLEMENZIA: If I know it, why say it? Get on with your story!

LELIA: If I hadn't repeated this to you, you couldn't have followed the rest of it. About that time Flamminio Carandini became a close friend of my father's, because he belonged to the same party. He used to come and see us every day, without fail; and sometimes he used to look at me very secretly, and sigh, and lower his eyes. And you were the first to draw my attention to this. Then his manners, his words and his ways began to please me much more than before; but I still had no thoughts of love. But as he went on coming to see us, with many kind actions and signs of his love, seeking my company, gazing at me and sighing deeply, I realized that he'd taken more than an ordinary fancy to me. And though I'd never been in love before, he seemed to me worthy to have my heart, and I soon reached the stage where my one idea of bliss was just to see his face.

CLEMENZIA: I knew that too.

LELIA: And you know that when the Spaniards finally left Rome my father went back there, partly to see if any of our property could be recovered, but mainly to try and get news of my brother. And as he didn't want to leave me alone, he sent me to Mirandola to stay with my aunt Giovanna until he came back. You know how sad I was to leave my Flamminio, for you dried my tears often enough. I stayed at Mirandola for one year. Then, as my father had come home, I returned to Modena, more than ever enamoured of the man who'd been my first love and made me so fond of him, and expecting him to be still as much in love with me as he'd seemed to be earlier on!

CLEMENZIA: You silly girl! How many men d'you know here in Modena who'd stay in love with the same woman for a whole year, instead of making fools of poor girls and giving them the go-by at the rate of one a month?

LELIA: Well, when I found him, he remembered me just as well as if he'd never seen me in all his life; and what's worse, he'd set his heart and soul on winning the love of Gherardo Foiani's daughter Isabella, who's a beautiful girl, and her father's only heir, unless the old fool's planning to get married again and start another family.

CLEMENZIA: He's planning to marry *you*, in fact, and he says that your father's promised that he can have you. But what you've told me doesn't seem to have much to do with your disguising yourself as a boy and running away from the convent.

LELIA: Just let me finish, and you'll see that it has a great deal to do with it. But first of all I'll say this: Gherardo Foiani will never have *me* for a wife! Well, when my father came back from Rome, he had to ride over to Bologna in connection with a scheme of the Count's; and as I didn't want to go back to Mirandola, he put me in the nunnery of San Crescenzio with Sister Amabile, who is a relation of ours, to stay there until he came back, which he expected to do pretty soon.

CLEMENZIA: I knew all that.

LELIA: While I was there, I noticed that the reverend mothers of the convent never talked about anything but love, and this encouraged me to tell Sister Amabile my own story. She had pity on me, and arranged for Flamminio to come and speak to her and to various other nuns, so that I could hide behind the curtains and feast my eyes with the sight of his face and my ears with the music of his voice; for that was all I wanted. And one day when he came I heard him say how much he missed a young page of his who had just died. He said what a fine young fellow he'd been, and what a devoted servant, and added that if he could find another like him he'd be the happiest man in the world and would give him whatever he asked.

CLEMENZIA: Oh dear! I don't like the sound of that boy at all. I'm sure he means trouble for me.

LELIA: It crossed my mind at once that *I* might be the lucky young fellow who'd take his place. As soon as Flamminio had gone, I told Sister Amabile about the idea I'd had. And as Flamminio wasn't living in Modena itself at that time, I thought I'd see if I could get him to take me on in place of the other boy.

CLEMENZIA: Didn't I say that boy meant trouble? Oh, I'm done for now!

LELIA: Sister Amabile encouraged me, and told me what to do. She lent me some boy's clothes that she'd just had made for herself, so that she could go out about her own business in disguise sometimes as they all do. And so early one morning, dressed like this, I ventured out of the convent – it's well outside the town, which was very convenient and gave me all the more courage. And I went to the building where Flamminio was living, which as you know isn't all that far from the nunnery, and waited outside until he came out. And here at least I can't complain of my luck, for he caught sight of me at once, and asked me very civilly where I came from and whether I wanted anything.

CLEMENZIA: And didn't you fall down dead for the shame of it?

LELIA: Certainly not. Love found me the words to say and I spoke out boldly and told him that I came from Rome, that I'd lost everything, and that I was seeking my fortune. He looked me up and down until I was afraid that he'd recognize me; but then he said that if I'd like to stay with him he'd be glad to keep me and would treat me handsomely. And though I did feel a little shame, I agreed.

CLEMENZIA: You make me wish I'd never been born. What good did you think all this lunacy was going to do you?

LELIA: What good, did you say? D'you think it means nothing to a woman who's in love with a man to see him all the time, speak to him, touch him, hear his secrets, see all his friends, talk to him, and be sure of one thing at least – that if you're not enjoying the benefits of his love, no one else is enjoying them either?

CLEMENZIA: These are silly little girl's tricks, and can't do anything but add fuel to the flames – unless you're really sure that they'll stand you in good stead with your lover. And what sort of service do you give him?

LELIA: I serve him at table and in his room. And I know that I've made him so fond of me, in the couple of weeks I've been with him, that if he liked me equally well in skirts I'd have nothing to complain about.

CLEMENZIA: Tell me: where do you sleep?

LELIA: In a little room next to his, on my own.

CLEMENZIA: And suppose one night he's taken by a wicked, un-natural temptation and calls you to his bed?

LELIA: I won't cross my bridges before I come to them. If that did happen, it'd be time enough to think about it and decide what to do.

CLEMENZIA: What will people say if all this comes out, you naughty child?

LELIA: How are they to know, unless you tell them? Now this is what I'd like you to do, since I know my father came home last night, and I'm afraid he'll send for me – I'd like you to manage things so that he doesn't get in touch with the nunnery for four or five days; or you could tell him that I've gone to Roverino with Sister Amabile, and I'll be back in a few days' time.

CLEMENZIA: What's the point of that?

LELIA: I'll tell you. Flamminio, as I was saying just now, is in love with Isabella Foiani, and he's always sending me to her with letters and messages. She thinks I'm a boy, of course, and she's fallen so madly in love with me that she shows me all the kindness you can imagine. I've told her that I won't love her unless she makes Flamminio fall out of love with her – and I think I've pulled it off. I hope that in three or four days it'll all be over and he'll give her up.

CLEMENZIA: Now listen, Lelia – your father's already told me to fetch you. You come along to my house, and I'll send for your clothes, for I can't stand people seeing you like that, and if you won't I'll tell your father.

LELIA: You'll force me to go somewhere where neither you nor he will ever see me again. *Please* do what I say! [*Catching sight of* GHERARDO *coming out of his house, followed by his servant* SPELA.] But I can't finish my story now; Flamminio's calling me – Yes, sir! – Go home and wait for me, Clemenzia, and I'll be with you in an hour's time. And listen! Any time you want to see me, be sure to ask for Fabio Alberini, for that's the name I'm using. Mind you get it right! – Coming, sir! – Good-bye, Clemenzia!

[LELIA *puts her hood up again, runs across stage past* GHERARDO, SPELA, *and exit Right.*]

CLEMENZIA: The fact is that she saw Gherardo coming along the street; and that's why she ran away. Now what am I to do? It wouldn't be right to tell her father about this, but I can't let her stay as she is either. I'll have to wait till I see her again.

[GHERARDO, SPELA *cross towards* CLEMENZIA's *house*.]

GHERARDO: If Virginio's as good as his word, I'm going to treat myself to the merriest time any man ever had in this city of Modena! What do you think, Spela? Haven't I got the right idea?

SPELA: It'd be an even better idea, sir, since you ask me, if you did something for your nieces and nephews, who are nearly starving, or for me, since I've served you for many years and haven't been able to put aside so much as the price of a pair of shoes. I'm afraid this new wife of yours will turn you out of doors, or make you a . . . I forget what I was going to say.

GHERARDO: You just see if she doesn't find herself well provided for! She won't be complaining of short measure from me!

SPELA: I quite believe it, sir; for what she might get from someone else in fine heavy coin she'll get from you in pence and halfpence.

GHERARDO: But here's her nurse. Be quiet now, and I'll wheedle some news of Lelia out of her.

CLEMENZIA [*aside*]: There's a fine handsome Adonis for you, to be wanting to marry a sweet young girl in her teens! Who could believe that the right place for her was in the hands of that croaking old fool? As I wish to be saved, I'd strangle her rather than let her be given to that musty, mouldy, dribbling, rancid, snotty old idiot. But I'll have a bit of fun with him. [*To* GHERARDO] Good morning and good day to you, Gherardo! And God bless your fresh young face!

GHERARDO: And God send you a hundred thousand ducats, Clemenzia, and then a second hundred thousand to keep them company!

SPELA: It would be better if they came *my* way.

GHERARDO: Oh Spela, how happy I'd be if I could be Clemenzia!

SPELA: So that you could have tried your luck with many different husbands, instead of with a single wife, d'you mean? Or have you something else in mind?

CLEMENZIA: And how many husbands am I supposed to have had, Spela, may the crows peck out your eyes! Are you jealous because you weren't one of them?

SPELA: That's right! It's easy to see what a jewel I've missed!

GHERARDO: Be quiet, you fool! That wasn't what I meant at all.

SPELA: What did you mean, then?

GHERARDO: If I'd been Clemenzia, think how many times I'd have hugged, kissed and dandled my sweet Lelia, who's all made up of sugar and gold and milk and roses and . . . and . . . I don't know what else.

SPELA: Oh! Oh! Master, we must go straight home! Come on now! Quickly!

GHERARDO: Why?

SPELA: You've got a fever and it's not good for you to be out in the open air like this.

GHERARDO: Fever, indeed! May Heaven send you something worse! What fever! I feel perfectly well.

SPELA: And I say that you've got a fever. I know the signs very well. It's a nasty attack, too.

GHERARDO: But I feel all right.

SPELA: Does your head ache?

GHERARDO: No.

SPELA: Let me feel your pulse . . . Have you a pain in your stomach, or can you feel any fumes rising up into your brain?

GHERARDO: You're talking like an idiot. Are you trying to make a fool of me? I tell you I've no pains at all, except a little heartache for my honey-sweet Lelia.

SPELA: I can tell you've got a fever and are very ill with it.

GHERARDO: What makes you think that?

SPELA: What makes me think that? Can't you tell yourself that you're crazy, raving, at your last gasp, and that you don't even know what you're saying?

GHERARDO: Such is the will of the love god – eh, Clemenzia? 'Omnia vincit Amor!'[2]

SPELA: My word! There's a fine Neapolitan saying for you! Facetis manum,[3] you fellows! There's no more to be said!

GHERARDO: That heartless little traitress, your foster-daughter . . .

SPELA: It's not fever after all, but softening of the brain. Heaven help us! Poor Spela! What am I to do?

2. 'Love conquers all things.'
3. A piece of incomprehensible dog-Latin.

GHERARDO: Oh Clemenzia, I'd like to hug you and kiss you a hundred times!

SPELA: It's a case for a strait-jacket – didn't I say so?

CLEMENZIA: Now don't get any ideas like that into your head, for I don't like being kissed by old men.

GHERARDO: Do you think I look as old as that?

SPELA: Whatever do you mean? My master's still got a fine set of eyes and a good pair of teeth.

CLEMENZIA: Well, you can't be as old as people think you are, and that's a fact.

GHERARDO: Tell Lelia that! And if you make her like me, I'll give you a new veil.

SPELA: My master's a generous fellow! What'll you give me, sir?

CLEMENZIA: If the Duke of Ferrara liked you as well as Lelia does, you'd be on velvet! But you seem bent on making a fool of her. If you were really fond of her, you wouldn't keep her in suspense like this, and you wouldn't try to stop her happiness.

GHERARDO: Stop her happiness? I'm trying to give her happiness, not to stop it for her.

CLEMENZIA: Then why have you been shilly-shallying for a whole year about whether you want to marry her or not?

GHERARDO: What! Does Lelia think that the delay is my fault? If I don't remind her father about it every day . . . if it isn't my dearest wish . . . if I'm not longing for it to happen today rather than tomorrow . . . why, I hope you'll soon see me on my way to the graveyard!

CLEMENZIA: As to that, God's will be done! I'll tell her everything you've said. But do you know something? She'd rather you dressed a bit differently from that – she thinks you look like an old sheep.

GHERARDO: 'Sheep'? Why, what harm have I done her?

CLEMENZIA: It isn't that – it's because you always go around wrapped up in all those furs.

SPELA: So perhaps he'd better have his skin flayed off to please her better? Or at the very least he could walk round Modena stark naked! Did you ever hear such rubbish?

GHERARDO: No man in Modena has got such fine clothes as I have, at home. Thank you for mentioning it. I'll make sure that before long she does see me dressed very differently. But where can I see her? When is she coming back from the nunnery?

CLEMENZIA: You can see her at the Bazzovara gate. I'm going to fetch her now.

GHERARDO: Can't I come with you? We could have a chat as we go.

CLEMENZIA: No, no! What would people say?

GHERARDO: Oh love, oh love, how cruelly you shake me!

SPELA [aside]: Old fool, old fool, how very sick you make me!

GHERARDO: Happy, happy nurse!

SPELA [aside]: Mad – and getting worse!

GHERARDO: Lucky Clemenzia!

SPELA [aside]: Senile dementia!

GHERARDO: Oh blessed, bounteous breast!

SPELA [aside]: Oh doddering old pest!

GHERARDO: May your good fortune never pass away!

SPELA [aside]: And may a bull-dog tear your arse away!

GHERARDO: Well, Clemenzia, it's time you were off! Good-bye! [Exit CLEMENZIA.] Come with me, Spela; I want to go and make some important changes. I've decided to alter my style of dress so as to please my wife.

SPELA: I don't like the sound of that.

GHERARDO: Why not?

SPELA: Because you're giving in to her already. It's clear enough who's going to wear the breeches.

GHERARDO: Go to the apothecary's and get me a box of civet, for I'm going to devote my whole life to love.

SPELA: What about the money?

GHERARDO: Here's a *bolognino*. [*Gives small coin, at which* SPELA *looks incredulously*.] And be quick about it. I'm going back home.

[GHERARDO *crosses to his own house and goes indoors*.]

SPELA: If ever anyone wanted to find room for all the follies of the world in a single sack, he could just stuff my master into it and be sure he'd got them all. And it's worse now that this madness of love has got into him. Combing himself all the time – pulling out odd hairs with tweezers – prowling around trying to get a sight of his lady. If there's any sort of festival late at night, he's there, armed with a funny curved dagger; he sings all day in his dirty, cracked old voice, to the music of a lute that's more out of tune than he is himself. And he's even taken to writing sonnets and odes, and groundelays and madrigials, and long letters in rhyme which *he* calls 'pizzles'⁴ (and serve him right if his own fell off!). And a hundred other comic acts which would make a donkey laugh, let alone a dog. And now he wants to scent himself with civet! In God's name, wouldn't it make anyone get his ballocks knotted? – But here's Scatizza, back from calling on the nuns.

[*Enter* SCATIZZA, VIRGINIO's *servant.*]

SCATIZZA [*soliloquizing*]: Well, one thing I must say: fathers who make nuns of their daughters must be fine old gentlemen of the time of Bartolommeo Colleoni.⁵ Do you know, they genuinely believe that the girls spend their lives kneeling before the crucifix and calling on God to bless the man who put them inside? The girls say their prayers all right, to God and to the Devil as well, but what they pray for is that the man who put them there may break his neck.

SPELA: I'd like to hear the rest of this story.

SCATIZZA: I went into the visitors' parlour, and knocked at the little hatchway they have there so that they can pass messages through without anyone seeing them. The next second the whole room was full of nuns – all young ones, and all as pretty as angels. So I began to ask for news of Lelia – and what happened? Laughing from one side, giggling from the other; and all of them making fun of me and my message, as if I'd been a stuffed dummy.

SPELA [*falsetto*]: 'Good morning, Scatizza! And where have you come from? Oh! I believe you've got some sugar plums in there! Give me a couple!'

SCATIZZA: May the devil fly away with you and with your lunatic of a master!

SPELA: But let's talk about you! Where have you come from?

SCATIZZA: From a visit to the nuns of San Crescenzio.

SPELA: That's fine. What's the news of Lelia? Has she come tripping back to her father's house?

SCATIZZA: May the gallows come tripping back to her father's

4. i.e. 'epistles'.

5. A famous general of mercenaries, 1400–75. The point here is that his name is very near in sound to the Italian word 'coglione', which means a testicle, or, in popular slang, an idiot.

house and take you for a ride! I know that with God all things are possible – but is it really possible that your halfwit of a master thinks he's going to have Lelia for a wife?

SPELA: Why? Doesn't she want him?

SCATIZZA: I'm sure she doesn't. Do you think that a dish like her should be set before an animal like him?

SPELA: She may be right, at that. But what did she say?

SCATIZZA: Nothing – nothing at all. What the devil d'you expect her to say, when I couldn't even see her? As soon as I got to the convent and asked for her, those villainous nuns were all round me, and I could see they wanted to play some silly trick.

SPELA: Trick, indeed! They wanted to trump your ace. You don't know what they're like.

SCATIZZA: I know them better than you do, may they rot in hell! Listen to this! One said I looked ill, and was it for love of her? Another asked me if I'd marry her. Another said they'd put Lelia to soak up in the dormitory, and she wouldn't be dry yet awhile; another said they were wringing her out in the cloisters.

Another said: 'It's a pity your father never had a son!' *I* nearly said: 'It's a pity my father isn't here to show you his pr- pr- practical gifts!' But it was clear enough that they were pulling my leg, and didn't intend to let me talk to Lelia.

SPELA: You *were* a coward! You ought to have gone in and insisted on looking for her yourself.

SCATIZZA: Devil take it! Go in there alone? Get away from me, before you ruin me for ever! Why, there isn't a stallion in the Maremma who could cope with their carryings-on, if he went in there alone! To hell with all nuns! But I can't stay here; I've got to go and report to my master.

SPELA: And I've got to go and buy some civet for *my* old fool.

[SCATIZZA *goes into* VIRGINIO's *house. Exit* SPELA, *Right*.]

# ACT TWO

*Scene as before.*

[*Enter Right* FLAMMINIO, LELIA.]

FLAMMINIO: It's a strange thing, Fabio, that up to now you haven't been able to get a better answer from my cruel, ungrateful Isabella. And yet she always receives you so gladly and welcomes you so warmly that I can't think she really hates me. And I've never done anything to upset her, so far as I know. Can't you work out from the things she says what it is that she's got against me? Tell me again, Fabio: what did she say yesterday when you took my letter to her?

LELIA: I've told you all that twenty times already.

FLAMMINIO: Ah! Tell me again. What difference does it make to you?

LELIA: Why, it does make a difference to me, because I can see it causes you displeasure, and that gives as much pain to me as it does to you. I'm your servant, and I should never do anything but what may please you. If I go on repeating her answers to you it may make you hate me.

FLAMMINIO: Don't think that, my dear Fabio, for I love you like a brother. I know that you're fond of me, and you can rest assured that I'll always look after you. Time will show that what I've said is true. Say your prayers and have faith in God . . . but what *did* she say?

LELIA: She said what I told you before – that the greatest kindness you could do her would be to leave her alone, and not think about her any more, because her heart belongs to someone else; that she doesn't ever want to see you again, and that it's a waste of time and effort for you to court her, because at the end of it all you'll find you are no further ahead than you were at the beginning.

FLAMMINIO: But what do you think, Fabio? Does she really mean all

215

these things, or is it just that she's angry with me about something? She used to show me some signs of favour, from time to time – though that was some time ago. And I can't believe she really hates me when she's always prepared to receive my letters and my messages. I'm ready to go on courting her till I die. We'll see what'll come of it. What do you say, Fabio? Do you think I'm right?

LELIA: No, sir.

FLAMMINIO: Why not?

LELIA: Because, if I were you, I'd want to serve a lady who would welcome my attentions. A man like you, noble, talented, pleasant-spoken, and handsome (as you undoubtedly are) – how can you ever be short of ladies' company? Take my advice, sir. Leave her, and take up with a mistress who'll love you. You'll find there are plenty of them, and some of them may be as beautiful as Isabella. Tell me – don't you know of anyone in this town who'd be glad of your love?

FLAMMINIO: Yes, of course. Among others there's one called Lelia. She's very like you in face, by the way; it's struck me many a time. She's considered to be the prettiest, cleverest, sweetest-mannered girl in Modena. I must point her out to you some time. She'd be very happy if I showed her a little friendship. She's rich, too, and has been at court. I loved her for nearly a year, and she was very kind to me; but then she went off to Mirandola. And now my fate has made me fall in love with Isabella, who is as cruel to me as the other one was kind.

LELIA: Well, sir, all that's happened serves you right, because if you've got someone who loves you and you won't look at her, it's only fair that someone else should refuse to look at *you*.

FLAMMINIO: What do you mean?

LELIA: If that poor girl was your first love, and still loves you more than ever, why have you deserted her to go and court someone else? That's a sin, and I don't know whether God can ever pardon it. Oh, Signor Flamminio! You're certainly doing something very wrong.

FLAMMINIO: You're still a child, Fabio, and you can't be expected to understand the full force of love. But I'll tell you this: I can't help loving Isabella – I can't help adoring her. I can't and won't think of anyone else. So go back and talk to her again, and see if you can wheedle out of her what it is that she's got against me that makes her hate me so much.

LELIA: You're wasting your time.

FLAMMINIO: I like wasting it!

LELIA: You'll get nothing out of it.

FLAMMINIO: Never mind!

LELIA: Stop thinking about her!

FLAMMINIO: I can't. Go and see her, I beg you.

LELIA: I'll go, sir, but . . .

FLAMMINIO: And come straight back with the answer. I'm going to the cathedral.

LELIA: I'll do what I can.

FLAMMINIO: Fabio, if you manage this for me, you won't regret it!
    [Exit FLAMMINIO, Right. PASQUELLA comes out of GHERARDO's house.]

LELIA [aside]: It's as well he's gone, for here's Pasquella coming to look for me.

PASQUELLA [aside]: I don't believe any job in the world can be more difficult or more unpleasant for someone like me than serving a young lady who's in love – especially one who's got no mother, sisters or anyone else to keep her in check – and that's my mistress. These last few days she's got such a passion, such an itch of love on her that she can't stay still either by day or by night. All the time she's scratching herself where it itches, she's stroking her thighs, she's running to the loggia, she's dashing to the window, and upstairs and downstairs – it's as if she had quicksilver under her feet. Heaven help us! I've been young and in love myself, and managed to do a little something about it, too; but I used to get some rest from time to time, even then. At least she might have taken a fancy to a proper man – someone who'd reached maturity, as they say, and would have known what to do with himself and been able to get all this nonsense out of her system. But she's got involved with a young sprig who looks as if he'd hardly know how to do up his own clothes without help, if they came undone. And all day long she sends me out to look for this fine lover of hers – as if I hadn't plenty of work to do in the house. Can Flamminio really believe that all these messages to and fro are for *his* benefit? But I believe that's the boy coming in this direction now. That's

lucky! Fabio! God send you a good day! I was just coming to look
for you, my pet.

LELIA: And God send you a thousand *scudi*, dear Pasquella. What is
your lovely mistress doing, and what did she want with me?

PASQUELLA: What do you think she's doing? Weeping, going into
a decline, fading away – and all because you haven't been to see her
yet this morning.

LELIA: Why, does she want me to visit her before daybreak?

PASQUELLA: She'd like you to stay with her for the whole night, if
you ask me.

LELIA: Oh! I've other things to do. I've my own master to serve.

PASQUELLA: Oh! If she sent for your master, I'm sure he wouldn't
need asking twice! Do you sleep with him, by the way?

LELIA: Would to God that I were so far advanced in his favour! Then
I shouldn't be in my present unhappy state.

PASQUELLA: Oh! Wouldn't you rather sleep with Isabella?

LELIA: Not I!

PASQUELLA: You're not telling the truth!

LELIA: I wish I weren't.

PASQUELLA: Well, no more of that, then. My mistress asks you to
come and see her as soon as you can. Her father's not at home, and
she has something important to speak to you about.

LELIA: Tell her she's wasting her time unless she gets rid of Flamminio
and his love for her first. She knows it means my ruin otherwise.

PASQUELLA: Come along and tell her yourself.

LELIA: But I tell you I've got other things to do. Can't you hear me?

PASQUELLA: What else have you got to do? Come along with me
quickly, and you can be back here in a moment.

LELIA: Oh! You're really pestering me now! Be off with you!

PASQUELLA: So you won't come?

LELIA: No, I won't. Can't you understand?

PASQUELLA: Really and truly, Fabio, you're far too conceited. I'm
going to tell you something – you're very young and you don't
know when you're well off. You won't always have those looks.
Your beard will grow; the colour will leave those cheeks, the red
will leave those lips, and you won't have everyone running after
you like this. Then you'll recognize how silly you've been, and
you'll be bitterly sorry when it's too late. Tell me this: how many

men do you think there are in this city who'd be overjoyed if Isabella looked at them? You turn up your nose at your own good fortune, even when it arrives with bells on.

LELIA: Why doesn't she look at some of those other people then and leave me alone, since I'm not interested?

PASQUELLA: Good heavens! It's certainly true that young men don't have much sense!

LELIA: Come on now, Pasquella. Don't preach any more – it's no good!

PASQUELLA: Conceited little monkey! And soon you'll have nothing to be conceited about! – But sweet Fabio, darling Fabio, won't you do me this favour and come with me now, quickly? Otherwise she'll only send me out to look for you again, and she won't believe I've really given you the message.

LELIA: All right, then! Go on home, Pasquella, and I will follow you. I was only joking.

PASQUELLA. When will you come, my sweet?

LELIA: Soon.

PASQUELLA: How soon?

LELIA: Before long. Be off with you, now.

PASQUELLA: I'll wait for you at the front door, mind!

LELIA: Yes, yes!

PASQUELLA: Listen! I shall be very angry if you don't come.

[*Exit* LELIA, *Left. Enter* GIGLIO, *a Spanish soldier, Right, and walks towards* GHERARDO'*s house.*]

GIGLIO: By my life – the well-fortuned old woman who have the most pretty girl of this town for her mistress! Oh if I could speak that girl two words without witnesses! I vow by the virginity of all the cardinals in Rome that I shall make her to shriek like the she-cat in the mating season. But let me see if with some flattery I can get myself on terms with this old jade, that I can achieve something with her mistress. – Good morning, sweet pretty madame Pasquella. And where have you come from thus early?

PASQUELLA: Why, good morning, Giglio. I've just come from mass. And where are you going?

GIGLIO: I search my fortune – I look for some woman who will do me kindness.

PASQUELLA: What an idea! I never heard of any of you Spaniards being short of women! Every one of you has at least a dozen running after him.

GIGLIO: In truth I have two; but I cannot go to them without peril.

PASQUELLA: Ah yes! They must be noble ladies, who come from some extinguished family.

GIGLIO: Yes, my faith; but I want to find a mother who wash my shirts and iron my doublet and hose and who treat me like a son, and I help her every way.

PASQUELLA: Go on looking, and you're sure to find one. A man who has all these ladies at command can hardly lack for serving-women when he wants them.

GIGLIO: She is found already, if you please.

PASQUELLA: Who is she?

GIGLIO: Yourself and no other.

PASQUELLA: Why, I'm much too old for you!

GIGLIO: Old? I vow to the Virgin of Montserrat that to me you seem a girl of fifteen or twenty summer. You not say 'old' again, or I get angry! If you want to do me some pleasure, you soon see whether I treat you like young or like old!

PASQUELLA: No, no! None of your farmyard ways here! I don't want to get mixed up with Spaniards. Horseflies, I call you – if it isn't bite, bite, it's buzz, buzz. It's like dealing with hot coals – we may get burnt and we certainly get dirty. We've had enough to do with you to teach us a lesson; and we know you well enough now, thank God, to be sure that there's nothing to be gained from you.

GIGLIO: Gain, is it? I swear to God that you shall gain more with me than with the first gentleman of this town! Although I appear before you thus down on my luck, I am of the best well-born hidalgos of all Spain.

PASQUELLA: It's a marvel he didn't say knight or lord, for that's what all the Spaniards who come over here make themselves out to be. And just look at them!

GIGLIO: Pasquella, accept of my friendship, and you will not regret!

PASQUELLA: And I suppose you'll make a countess of me, will you?

GIGLIO: All I ask is this; you be my mother. And I shall gladly be your son, and sometimes your husband too, if it like you.

PASQUELLA [giggling]: Oh, leave me alone!

GIGLIO [*aside*]: She laugh now; it is going to be all right.

PASQUELLA: What was that?

GIGLIO: I give you a rosary, to say your prayers all night.

PASQUELLA: Where is it?

GIGLIO: See here.

PASQUELLA: Oh! It's one of those paternoster rosaries! Why don't you give it to me?

GIGLIO: If you be my mother, then I give.

PASQUELLA: I'll be anything you like, if you give it to me.

GIGLIO: When can we talk together one hour?

PASQUELLA: Whenever you like.

GIGLIO: Where?

PASQUELLA: Oh! I don't know where!

GIGLIO: Is some room in your house where I could come this evening?

PASQUELLA: Yes, there is. But suppose my master found out?

GIGLIO: Nonsense! He not know anything!

PASQUELLA: All right! I'll see what can be arranged this evening; you walk past the door and I'll tell you whether you can come in or not. Now give me the rosary. What a beauty it is!

GIGLIO: Right! I be ready at sunset.

PASQUELLA: Yes, yes! But give me the paternosters!

GIGLIO: I bring them when I shall come there; for first of all I want to have them a little perfumed.

PASQUELLA: I'm not worried about that sort of thing. Give them to me as they are; I don't want any more perfume on them than they've got.

GIGLIO: But see here! This bit is damage. I get gold put on there, and give you this evening. What else you want, except that it be yours?

PASQUELLA: It'll be mine when I get it. My word, this is putting a lot of trust in a Spaniard's promises! These fellows are hard nuts to crack, and when you do crack them there's nothing inside.

GIGLIO: What you say, mother?

PASQUELLA: I must go home – my mistress is waiting for me.

GIGLIO: Stay a little while! You have a great haste. What must you do for your mistress?

PASQUELLA: Why, what do you think? These blessed girls today are in love before we get them dry behind the ears, and they want to handle all sorts of implements before they've even learned to thread a needle.

GIGLIO: What she want to do? What mean these words?

PASQUELLA: Words, indeed! It's not words she wants, but action.

GIGLIO: But tell me, if you please. With whom is she in love? But it cannot be true, she is still too young.

PASQUELLA: I wish it weren't true, or at least that she'd made a more equal choice.

GIGLIO: Tell me, by your life – who is it?

PASQUELLA: I shouldn't tell you ... well, be sure you keep it to yourself. You know that boy who serves Flamminio de' Carrandini?

GIGLIO: What! that lad who go all dressed in white?

PASQUELLA: Yes, that's him.

GIGLIO: God help us all! What she plan to do with him? He not look like doctor for her trouble – more like patient.

PASQUELLA: Well, you heard what I said.

GIGLIO: And is the boy loving the young lady?

PASQUELLA: Ye-es. A bit.

GIGLIO: Her father not know what go on?

PASQUELLA: I don't think so. In fact he's found the boy in his house a couple of times, and he's made a great fuss of him – taken him by the hand, chucked him under the chin, as if he were his own son. And he says the boy reminds him of Virginio Bellenzini's daughter.

GIGLIO: The old pig, the dirty bastard! Yes, I know what he want.

PASQUELLA: Why, you've made me late. I must go.

GIGLIO: Be sure that I will come tonight; and don't forget your promise.

PASQUELLA: And don't you forget the paternosters!

[*Exit* GIGLIO, *Right. Enter* LELIA, *Left, and runs quickly across to* PASQUELLA, *who takes her into* GHERARDO's *house. Enter* FLAMMINIO's *servant* CRIVELLO, *Right, and* FLAMMINIO *following him.*]

FLAMMINIO: Crivello, you still haven't been to look for Fabio; and he still hasn't come back. I don't know what to make of his taking such a long time.

CRIVELLO: I was going, sir, and you called me back. It's not my fault.

FLAMMINIO: Go now, then; and if he's still in Isabella's house, wait till he comes out and tell him to come back here at once.

CRIVELLO: But sir, how am I to know whether he's there or not? Do you want me to knock at her door and ask for him?

FLAMMINIO: What an idiot! Do you really think that would be the right thing to do? I'll tell you this – I haven't a single servant in my household who's worth twopence except for Fabio. God grant that I may be able to look after him as he deserves. – But what are you muttering about? What did you say, you idle rogue? Isn't it true?

CRIVELLO: What do you expect me to say, sir? I agree with everything. Fabio's a fine lad, Fabio's good-looking, Fabio serves you well. Fabio in your house, Fabio in your lady's house. Fabio is everything, Fabio does everything. But . . .

FLAMMINIO: But what?

CRIVELLO: Maybe he does too much. I don't know about some of the things . . .

FLAMMINIO: What things? What d'you mean?

CRIVELLO: You shouldn't trust him with all your things the way you do. He's a foreigner, after all, and might let you down.

[SCATIZZA *comes out of* VIRGINIO's *house.*]

FLAMMINIO: I wish I could trust you other servants in the same way. – But there's Scatizza – you can ask him whether he's seen Fabio. I'll be at the Porrini.

[*Exit* FLAMMINIO, *Right.*]

CRIVELLO: Hallo, Scatizza. Have you seen Fabio?

SCATIZZA: Who? Your little sight for sore eyes? The young bastard! You've a fine job on your hands, looking for him!

CRIVELLO: Where were you going?

SCATIZZA: To find my old master.

CRIVELLO: He went by here just now.

SCATIZZA: Where was he going?

CRIVELLO: That way. Come on, and we'll find him. Come on, now! I've got a fine story to tell you, something that really happened to me with my Caterina, the funniest thing you ever heard!

[*Enter* SPELA. CRIVELLO *draws* SCATIZZA *aside and whispers to him during the following speech from* SPELA.]

SPELA [*soliloquizing*]: Can there be anything in the world worse than

223

to serve a master who's off his head? Gherardo sent me off to buy him some civet. When I asked the apothecary for it, and told him that all the money I'd got was one *bolognino*, he said I must have got my instructions wrong: that Gherardo probably wanted a box of ointment for the mange, which he certainly needed, and that he knew that Gherardo didn't use civet. So to make him believe me, I started to tell him about the new love that's come into my master's life. Then he and some young fellows who were in his shop laughed at me till they nearly died. And then he told me to take him a box of asafoetida.[6] So I came away, followed by their mocking laughter. Well, if the master wants any civet, he'll have to give me some more money.

[*Exit* SPELA. CRIVELLO, SCATIZZA *come forward again, laughing.*]

CRIVELLO: Well, now you've heard the whole story. And if you'd like to come with me next time, I'll find you a girl too.

SCATIZZA: Yes, see if you can. I promise you that if you can find me a girl I like I'll see to it that we have the best time in the world. I've got the keys of my master's barn, his cellar, his larder and his woodshed. If you'll help me to find some fodder for my donkey, I'll see to it that we live like lords. In any case, there's no other way of getting anything out of masters like ours.

CRIVELLO: I'll do what I said: I'll tell Bita to find you a wench, and the four of us will have a wonderful time during the carnival.

SCATIZZA: But we're right at the end of the carnival already!

CRIVELLO: Well then, we'll have a wonderful time during Lent, while our masters go to church and sit there ogling the girls – But look, Gherardo's front door is opening!

[LELIA *comes out of* GHERARDO's *house, and turns to speak to* ISABELLA, *who appears in the doorway.*]

CRIVELLO [*moving to one side*]: Come over here!

SCATIZZA: Why?

CRIVELLO: Oh, out of respect, of course!

LELIA: Remember what you promised me, Isabella!

ISABELLA: And don't you forget to come and see me! But come a little closer – I want to tell you something.

CRIVELLO: If I were in that little pansy's shoes, my master would have something to forgive me.

6. An evil-smelling medicine.

SCATIZZA: You'd help yourself to your master's dish, would you?

CRIVELLO: What do you think?

LELIA: What else can I do for you?

ISABELLA: Listen!

LELIA: I'm listening!

ISABELLA: Is there anyone outside there?

LELIA: Not a soul.

CRIVELLO: What the hell does she want?

SCATIZZA: They're much too familiar.

CRIVELLO: Keep still and watch them.

ISABELLA: Just one more word!

CRIVELLO: They're getting very close to each other.

SCATIZZA: They certainly are!

ISABELLA: Listen . . . I'd like . . .

LELIA: What would you like?

ISABELLA: I'd like . . . Come closer!

SCATIZZA [*falsetto*]: Closer, you cruel little thing!

ISABELLA: Make sure that there's no one there.

LELIA: I have looked. There's no one there at all.

ISABELLA: Oh! I'd like you to come back after dinner when my father will be out.

LELIA: I will – but if my master comes by when you're sitting at your window mind you look angrily at him and close the shutters.

ISABELLA: If I don't do what you ask, you needn't be fond of me any more.

SCATIZZA: What the devil is she doing with her hand?

CRIVELLO: My poor master! I know what's coming next.

LELIA: Good-bye.

ISABELLA: But listen – must you go now?

SCATIZZA: Kiss her, you fool!

CRIVELLO: She's still afraid of being seen.

LELIA: You'd better get back indoors.

ISABELLA: I want you to do something for me.

LELIA: What?

ISABELLA: Come just inside the door for a moment.

[LELIA *steps into the doorway.* ISABELLA *kisses her.*]

SCATIZZA: That's that, then.

[LELIA *tries to break away.*]

ISABELLA: Oh! You're cruel!

LELIA: Someone'll see us.

[ISABELLA *kisses her again.*]

CRIVELLO: Oh God! I wish I had half your luck, dammit!

SCATIZZA: Didn't I say that he'd kiss her in the end?

CRIVELLO: I'll tell you one thing – I wouldn't have missed the sight of that kiss for a hundred *scudi.*

SCATIZZA: I know. I wish I'd been on the receiving end of it myself!

CRIVELLO: My word! What will my master say when he hears about this?

SCATIZZA: To hell with it! You can't tell him that!

ISABELLA: Forgive me! You're so lovely and I love you so much that I'm doing something that may make you think that I'm not a good girl. But God knows I can't help it.

LELIA: Don't ask my forgiveness, my lady. I know only too well how I stand myself and what love has led me to do.

ISABELLA: What has love led you to do?

LELIA: Why, to deceive my master, which is very wrong of me.

ISABELLA: Oh, damn your master!

CRIVELLO: This is what comes of trusting these blasted women! It serves him right! I can see now why the smug young brat encouraged his master to give up this love affair.

SCATIZZA: Well, everybody looks after number one. And when you come down to it, all women are the same.

LELIA: It's getting late – I've got to go and find my master. Good-bye.

ISABELLA: One more word! [*Draws* LELIA *inside and kisses her again.*]

CRIVELLO: Ah! That makes two! – May your weapon lose its edge and let you down in your hour of need.

SCATIZZA: My God! I've got such a swollen leg that I'm afraid it's going to discharge any moment.

LELIA: You'd better shut the door now. Good-bye!

ISABELLA: I give myself into your hands.

LELIA: And I'm all yours. [ISABELLA *withdraws and shuts the door.*] It's true that I'm having a great joke with this girl who believes I'm a man; but on the other hand I want to get out of this tangle and I don't know how to begin. Now that she's reached the kissing stage, I can see that she'll take the first opportunity to go further along the same road. That means I'll lose everything, and all my tricks will be discovered. I'll go and ask Clemenzia what she thinks. But here comes Flamminio.

CRIVELLO: Scatizza, my master told me to wait for him at the Porrini. I'll go and give him this glad news! If he doesn't believe me, I hope you'll back me up.

SCATIZZA: You can rely on me. But if I were you I'd keep quiet for now, and then I'd always have this hanging over Fabio's head to make him do what I wanted.

CRIVELLO: Yes, but I hate him. He's ruined me.

SCATIZZA: Well, do as you think best.

[SCATIZZA *goes into* VIRGINIO's *house.* CRIVELLO *is leaving stage Right when* FLAMMINIO *enters, brushing past him without giving him a chance to speak.* CRIVELLO *remains in wings while* FLAMMINIO *walks over to* LELIA. *As he comes up to* GHERARDO's *house,* ISABELLA, *at window, pointedly averts her gaze and closes shutters.*]

FLAMMINIO: How can I be so far out of my mind and respect myself so little that I must love a woman who despises my love and serve a woman who tortures me, scorns me, and won't even honour me with a glance? Am I so vile and so ignoble that I can't get this shame and this torment off my back? But here's Fabio. Well, what have you done?

LELIA: Nothing, sir.

FLAMMINIO: Why have you been such a time about it, then? You aren't going to turn into a useless young rogue, are you?

LELIA: I took a long time because I tried hard to speak to Isabella.

FLAMMINIO: And why didn't you speak to her?

LELIA: She wouldn't listen to me. And if you'd take my advice, sir, you'd look elsewhere and arrange things differently. From what I've been able to see so far, you're wasting your time here, for she's absolutely determined not to do anything to please you.

FLAMMINIO: That's God's own truth. Just a moment ago, when I passed her window, she jumped up as soon as she saw me coming and swept away from the window with as much haste and as much revulsion as if she'd seen some horrible and terrifying sight.

LELIA: Let her go, I say, sir. I can't believe that in all this city there isn't some other girl who deserves your love just as much as she does. Have you never had a fancy for any other woman but Isabella?

227

FLAMMINIO: I wish I never had! I'm afraid that's the source of all my trouble, because I did love Lelia very dearly – Virginio Bellenzini's daughter, you know; I told you about her before. And I'm afraid that Isabella may think I still love her, and won't see me for that reason. But I'll show her that I don't love Lelia any more – that I hate her in fact, and can't even bear to hear her name mentioned. And I'll swear never to go anywhere where I might meet her again. And I want you to tell Isabella all this, Fabio.

LELIA: Oh God!

FLAMMINIO: What's wrong? You look faint. Have you got a pain?

LELIA: Oh God! Oh God!

FLAMMINIO: Where does it hurt?

LELIA: My heart!

FLAMMINIO: How long has it been going on? Here, lean on me. Have you got a pain in the stomach?

LELIA: No, sir, no.

FLAMMINIO: Do you feel sick?

LELIA: No, no – it's my heart that aches, I tell you.

FLAMMINIO: And my heart aches too – more than yours, perhaps. But you've gone quite pale. Go home and put a hot cloth on your chest, and get someone to rub your back, and it'll soon pass. I'll be there before long, and I'll get the doctor if you need him; he'll take your pulse and see what's wrong with you. Give me your arm! You've gone all cold! Come on now! go home slowly. [Aside] – What a strange life this is! I wouldn't lose this lad for anything in the world. I don't think there's ever been a cleverer, better-mannered servant anywhere than this one. And what's more, he seems so attached to me that if he were a woman I'd think he was ill for love of me. [To LELIA] Go on home now, Fabio, and mind you warm your feet. I'll be back soon. Tell them to lay the table.

[Exit FLAMMINIO, Right. CRIVELLO joins him as he goes off stage.]

LELIA: Well, now you've heard it all with your own ears, from Flamminio's ungrateful lips – you've heard just how much he loves you! Poor, unfortunate Lelia! Why waste any more time in the service of this cruel man? You achieved nothing with your patience, your prayers, or the kindness you showed him earlier on; and now you've achieved nothing by deceit. Poor, poor Lelia!

Rejected, driven away, shunned and hated! Why should I serve a man who rejects me, why seek a man who drives me away, why follow a man who shuns me, why love a man who hates me? Oh Flamminio! nothing pleases you except Isabella! You don't want anything but Isabella! Very well then – win her, keep her if you will. I'll leave you or die in the attempt – I won't serve him any more, or wear these clothes, or even see him again, since he hates me so much. I'll go and find Clemenzia, who's waiting for me in her house, I know, and with her help I'll decide what to do with my life.

[LELIA *runs across to* CLEMENZIA's *house and goes in. Re-enter* FLAMMINIO, CRIVELLO, *Right.*]

CRIVELLO: If it's not as I say, sir, don't just cut out my tongue – hang me up by the neck! I've told you the truth, sir.

FLAMMINIO: How long ago was this?

CRIVELLO: When you sent me to look for him.

FLAMMINIO: What happened? Tell me again, for he says he wasn't able to speak to her.

CRIVELLO: You wouldn't expect him to tell you the truth! Well, while I was waiting to see if he was prowling round her house anywhere, I suddenly spotted him coming out of the door. He was just going to move away, when Isabella called him back again. They looked round carefully in case anyone outside was watching – they couldn't see a soul – and then they kissed.

FLAMMINIO: How was it that they didn't see you?

CRIVELLO: I'd moved into that portico opposite, so that I was out of sight.

FLAMMINIO: And how did you see them?

CRIVELLO: With my eyes, sir. Do you think I could have seen them with my elbow?

FLAMMINIO: And he kissed her, did he?

CRIVELLO: I don't know whether she kissed him or he kissed her; but I know they kissed each other.

FLAMMINIO: Did they really put their faces so close together that they could kiss each other?

CRIVELLO: Not their faces, sir – their lips.

FLAMMINIO: Oh God! Can two people put their lips together without putting their faces together?

CRIVELLO: If people had their mouth in their ear or the back of their neck, maybe they could; but as things are, I doubt it.

FLAMMINIO: Be sure that you did see everything clearly, and don't come back later and say 'it seemed as if . . .' or 'I thought I saw . . .', because this is a terrible thing that you're saying.

CRIVELLO: Not so terrible as a raging lion.

FLAMMINIO: How did you see them?

CRIVELLO: Wakefully, with open eyes, seeingly, and having nothing else to do but look.

FLAMMINIO: If this is true, you've killed me.

CRIVELLO: It is true. She called him to her, he went right up to her, she put her arms round him, she kissed him. [*Aside*] Now die if you must!

FLAMMINIO: No wonder the traitor denied that he'd been to her house! Now I can see why the bastard encouraged me to have nothing more to do with her – he wanted her for himself. If I don't revenge myself – if I don't make him an example for all time to all my servants that it doesn't pay them to betray their masters, I'll give up all claim to be a man . . . But after all, if I've no other confirmation, I'm not going to take your word for it. I know that you're a villain and that you must hate him. You're doing this to get rid of him, to get him out of my house. But I swear by the God I worship that I'll make you tell the truth or I'll kill you. Now tell me! Did you see him?

CRIVELLO: Yes, sir.

FLAMMINIO: Did he kiss her?

CRIVELLO: They kissed each other.

FLAMMINIO: How many times?

CRIVELLO: Twice.

FLAMMINIO: Where?

CRIVELLO: Inside there, in the hall.

FLAMMINIO: You're lying! Just now you said it was in the doorway!

CRIVELLO: I meant near the door.

FLAMMINIO [*beating him*]: Speak the truth!

CRIVELLO: Ow! Ow! I'm sorry I told you now.

FLAMMINIO: But was what you told me true?

CRIVELLO: Yes, it was, sir. But I was forgetting – I've got a second witness!

FLAMMINIO: Who is it?

CRIVELLO: Messer Virginio's servant Scatizza.

FLAMMINIO: Did he see it too?

CRIVELLO: He saw the same as I did.

FLAMMINIO: And if he denies it?

CRIVELLO: You can cut my throat.

FLAMMINIO: I will.

CRIVELLO: And if he confirms it?

FLAMMINIO: That'll be two throats to cut instead of one.

CRIVELLO [*terrified*]: Oh God! What for!

FLAMMINIO: I don't mean your throat, dammit – Isabella's and Fabio's.

CRIVELLO: And you can burn the whole house, with Pasquella and everyone else that's in it.

FLAMMINIO: Let's go and find Scatizza. If I don't make Fabio pay in full for this – if I don't make Modena talk of me ... I'll be so revenged! The treacherous bastard! You can't trust anyone!

[*Exeunt* FLAMMINIO, CRIVELLO.]

# ACT THREE

[*Enter Right* VIRGINIO's *son* FABRIZIO, *with his tutor* MESSER PIERO *and his servant* STRAGUALCIA. *They walk slowly across the stage towards the inns, Centre, looking curiously about them as they go.* FABRIZIO *is very like his sister* LELIA *in appearance.*]

MESSER PIERO: This town seems to have changed completely since I last saw it – though the truth is that I was only here for a short time in transit. I was with the delegation from Ancona, and we stopped at the 'Guicciardino'. We spent six days there in fact. Do you recognize anything, Fabrizio?

FABRIZIO: No – it's as if I had never been here at all.

MESSER PIERO: I can quite believe it, seeing how small you were when you left Modena. But I remember this street now, and know where we are. [*Pointing over heads of audience.*] That's the Rangoni Palace; that's the main canal; and over there is the cathedral. Fabrizio, have you ever heard people say: 'Who do you think you are – the mayor of Modena?' – or 'He's carrying on as if he were the mayor of Modena!'?[7]

FABRIZIO: Yes, hundreds of times. I'd like to see this famous mayor.

MESSER PIERO: Then look over there towards the cathedral . . . What do you see?

FABRIZIO: A statue of a small man on an enormous horse . . . an enormous mare, rather – the sculptor's made that *quite* obvious . . . Oh! I see! You mean that *she*'s the mare of Modena!

MESSER PIERO: That's it!

FABRIZIO: Is that a local joke?

MESSER PIERO: Precisely.

FABRIZIO: I've also heard people say that something's 'no better

_____
7. There was a historical mayor of Modena whose arrogance had become proverbial.

232

than bear-leading in Modena'.[8] What does that mean? and can you show me the bear?

MESSER PIERO: These are ancient sayings *de quibus nescitur origo*.[9]

FABRIZIO [*looking round again*]: You know, Messer Piero, there's something I very much like about Modena.

STRAGUALCIA: And there's something I like even better – [*Sniffs*] – that wonderful smell of roast meat cooking close at hand. It makes me feel quite faint.

MESSER PIERO: Aha! Do you not remember the words of Cantalicius? – '*Dulcis amor patriae.*'[10] And what says our Cato? – '*Pugna pro patria.*'[11] These are true words. In sum, there's nothing so sweet as a man's own native land.

STRAGUALCIA: I wonder if the local wine isn't sweeter still! I wish I had a glass of it now – this luggage is breaking my back.

MESSER PIERO: The roads seem to have been completely relaid. When I was last here they were all dirty and muddy.

STRAGUALCIA: Are we going to count the cobblestones? It'll take rather a long time. I'd rather we found somewhere to have dinner, myself.

MESSER PIERO: *Iandudum animus est in patinis.*[12]

FABRIZIO: What arms are those with a device like a brace and bit?

MESSER PIERO: That's the emblem of the City of Modena, and it's called the Brace. And just as the popular war cry in Florence is 'a Lion! a Lion!', and in Siena it's 'a Wolf! a Wolf!', so here you'll hear the crowd shout 'a Brace! a Brace!'

STRAGUALCIA: A brace of fat capons is what I ought to be shouting for!

FABRIZIO: There's one I do know. That's the Duke's coat of arms.

STRAGUALCIA: Messer Piero, do you think you could carry this bag for a bit? My lips are so dry that I can't speak.

MESSER PIERO: Come on, now! You can quench your thirst later.

8. 'Bear-leading in Modena' was an expression for a disastrous and discreditable enterprise.

9. 'The origin of which is unknown'. The first of a series of Latin tags from the pedantic tutor. They contain a fair number of grammatical and other mistakes – perhaps the work of a careless copyist.

10. 'Sweet is the love of one's country.'

11. 'Fight for your country.'

12. 'His heart is ever in the kitchen.'

STRAGUALCIA: 'And when I die, don't bury me at all,
    Just . . .'

FABRIZIO: Well, at first sight I like Modena very much. How about you, Stragualcia?

STRAGUALCIA: To me it's a heavenly paradise, with nothing to eat and nothing to drink. Come on, now, sir! Don't let's waste any more time on seeing the sights; we can do that later.

MESSER PIERO: Another thing you can see in Modena is the finest bell-tower in the whole world.

STRAGUALCIA: Didn't the Modenese want to make a sheath to go over the top of it? Is it the one that's supposed to have a shadow that'll send you mad?

MESSER PIERO: Yes, that's the one.

STRAGUALCIA: Then I shall spend the whole day safely in the kitchen. If anyone wants to go to the bell-tower, good luck to him! But now let's find somewhere to stay.

MESSER PIERO: You seem to be in a great hurry!

STRAGUALCIA: Dammit! I'm dying of hunger. I've had nothing to eat today except half a chicken which was left over in the boat.

FABRIZIO: Let's look for someone who can show us the way to my father's house.

MESSER PIERO: No. I think we should start by going to an inn and making ourselves comfortable. After that it will be more convenient to look for your father.

FABRIZIO: Very well. These must be the inns.

[L'AGIATO, *host of the 'Mirror' inn, and* FRULLA, *host of the 'Fool',
appear in their respective doorways.*]

L'AGIATO: Ah, gentlemen! This is the inn for you, if you're looking for somewhere to stay. Come to the 'Mirror'!

FRULLA: Ah! Welcome to you all! You've stayed with me some other time, I think. Don't you remember old Frulla? Come in here, where all the gentlemen of your sort come to stay.

L'AGIATO: Come with me. You'll have good rooms, a good fire, excellent beds, and you shall lack for nothing that you can have.

STRAGUALCIA: I could have told you that!

L'AGIATO: 'Lack for nothing that you can want,' I should have said.

FRULLA: I'll give you the best wine in Lombardy, partridges as plump as that [*expressive gesture*], sausages as long as this, pigeons, chickens and whatever else you ask for; and you'll have a good time!

STRAGUALCIA: That's what I want!

MESSER PIERO [to L'AGIATO]: What do you say to that?

L'AGIATO: I'll give you calves' sweetbreads, mortadella, wine from the hills; above all, you shall have everything delicate about you.

FRULLA: I'll give you less delicacy and more stuff to get your teeth into. If you come to me, I'll treat you like gentlemen and you can pay me what you like. At the 'Mirror', now, you'll find even the candles on your bill. It's up to you, gentlemen!

STRAGUALCIA [to FABRIZIO]: Let's do as he says, master; it'll suit us better.

L'AGIATO: Take my advice, gentlemen, if you want to be comfortable. Do you want people to say that you lodged with the 'Fool'?

FRULLA: My 'Fool' is twenty times better than your 'Mirror'!

MESSER PIERO: *Speculum prudentia significat iusta illud nostri Catonis 'Nosce teipsum'.*[13] Do you understand, Fabrizio?

FABRIZIO: Yes, I understand.

FRULLA: See who has more guests, L'Agiato or myself.

L'AGIATO: See who has more worthy gentlemen among his guests.

FRULLA: See where they are better treated.

L'AGIATO: See who offers the more delicate service.

STRAGUALCIA: What's the point of all this talk about delicacy? Just this once, I'd like to fill my belly properly and worry less about being delicate. All this delicacy is something for the Florentines.

L'AGIATO: All the Florentines lodge with me.

FRULLA: They used to at one time, but for the past three years they've all come to the 'Fool'.

L'AGIATO: Listen, my lad – put that bag down; I can see it's wearing you out.

STRAGUALCIA: Don't worry about that. I don't want to lighten my shoulders before I'm sure of loading up my belly.

FRULLA: Would a couple of capons help? Here! These are for you!

STRAGUALCIA: Good, good! As a starter, of course.

L'AGIATO: Look at this ham! Did you ever see such a colour?

MESSER PIERO: It's not bad, I must say.

13. 'A mirror should be regarded as signifying wisdom, according to our Cato's saying: "Know thyself!".'

FRULLA: Who knows about wines?

STRAGUALCIA: I do, I do, better than a Frenchman.

FRULLA: Try this one; if you don't like it, there are ten others I can let you have.

STRAGUALCIA: Frulla, you seem to me to have more experience than this other fellow, who shows us the ham he uses to give people a thirst before he's made sure we like his wine. [*drinking*] – Oh, master, master, it *is* good! – Take the bag, Frulla.

MESSER PIERO: Just a moment. What have you to say now, L'Agiato?

L'AGIATO: I say that gentlemen don't care so much about stuffing their bellies. They like small helpings of good, delicate food.

STRAGUALCIA: He must be running a hospital, or a special inn for sick people.

MESSER PIERO [*to* L'AGIATO]: You're right, in a way. What can you give us?

L'AGIATO: Ask for anything you like.

FRULLA: I must say that I'm surprised at you gentlemen. When there's plenty of food on the table, a man can eat as much or as little as he likes; which is not the case when there's only a little. And then your appetite may grow while you're eating, and in the end you have to fill up with bread.

STRAGUALCIA: There's more wisdom in you than in a whole shelf-ful of law-books. I never met a man who understood my needs like you do. I can see we're going to be friends.

FRULLA: Go into the kitchen and have a look round, my lad.

MESSER PIERO: *Omnis repletio mala, panis autem pessima.*[14]

STRAGUALCIA: Useless, idle pedant! I'll knock your teeth in one day, I swear it!

[STRAGUALCIA *goes into the* 'Fool'.]

L'AGIATO: Come inside, gentlemen! It isn't wise to stand about in the cold.

FABRIZIO: We're not such chilly mortals as all that!

FRULLA: You should know, gentlemen, that the 'Mirror' used to be the best inn in all Lombardy. But since I opened the 'Fool', the 'Mirror' doesn't get ten guests in a year. My inn's the most famous one anywhere, now. Crowds of Frenchmen come here, and all the Germans who pass through Modena.

14. 'All overeating is bad, but overeating with bread is the worst.'

L'AGIATO: That's not true – the Germans go to the 'Boar'.[15]

FRULLA: Everyone from Milan, Parma and Piacenza comes to my inn.

L'AGIATO: The Venetians, the Genoese and the Florentines come to mine.

MESSER PIERO: Where do the Neapolitans go?

FRULLA: They come to me.

L'AGIATO: No, no, gentlemen – most of them go to the 'Cupid'.

FRULLA: And how many of them lodge with me?

FABRIZIO [*interrupting*]: Where does the Duke of Malfi stay?

L'AGIATO: Sometimes with me, sometimes with him; sometimes at the 'Sword', sometimes at the 'Cupid', according to his fancy.

MESSER PIERO: What about people from Rome? We come from there ourselves.

L'AGIATO: They come to me.

FRULLA: It's not true – you won't find one Roman there in a whole year. There are one or two old cardinals who go to the 'Mirror' from force of habit; but all the new ones come straight to the 'Fool'.

[*Re-enter* STRAGUALCIA.]

STRAGUALCIA: Wild horses wouldn't drag me away from this place. The others can go where they like. Master, there are so many cooking-pots around the fire, such tasty dishes, such delicacies, such mouth-watering morsels, so many spits laden with partridges, thrushes and pigeons, such fine kids and capons, fresh out of the cooking-pot, such abundance of roast meat, such savouries, such heavenly tit-bits, such pastries and pies, that if the inn-keeper were waiting for Carnival to begin, or for the whole court of Rome to arrive here, he'd be well supplied.

FRULLA: Have you had a drink?

STRAGUALCIA: I have! The wines here are wonderful!

MESSER PIERO: *Variorum ciborum commistio pessima generat digestionem.*[16]

STRAGUALCIA: *Bus asinorum, buorum, eunuchorum, tato, potato idiotibus!*[17] You would start complicating things. A plague on you

15. Perhaps a reference to the tradition of German greediness.
16. 'A mixture of various foods is the worst thing for the digestion.'
17. The servant produces a string of meaningless words meant to sound like Latin, with an insulting ring about them.

and on all other pedants in the world! What a villainous face you have! [*To* FABRIZIO] Master, let's go in here.

FABRIZIO: Where do the Spaniards go?

FRULLA: I don't have anything to do with them. They go to the 'Highwayman'.[18] But what's the point of all this talk? All travellers come to my inn, except for the Sienese, who are so closely linked with the people here that as soon as one arrives he finds himself surrounded by friends who take him to their own house. But apart from that, you'll find that lords and nobles, rich and poor, soldiers and good companions, all come to me at the 'Fool'.

L'AGIATO: I'll tell you this: lawyers, judges and virtuous friars all come to my inn.

FRULLA: And I'll tell you this: there aren't many days in the year when one of the guests at the 'Mirror' doesn't move out and come to me.

FABRIZIO: What shall we do, Messer Piero?

MESSER PIERO: *Etiam atque etiam cogitandum.*[19]

STRAGUALCIA: Here's good news for you, stomach – make the most of it! This is one time I'm going to be able to fill you up.

MESSER PIERO: You know, Fabrizio, we haven't much money with us.

STRAGUALCIA: Messer Piero, the owner of this inn [*pointing to the* 'Fool'] has got a little son who looks as beautiful as an angel.

MESSER PIERO [*briskly*]: Well! let's make a move. This is the place for us. Anyway, Fabrizio, your father will pay the bill, once we've found him.

STRAGUALCIA [*aside*]: I picked the right bait to catch that wily old bird this time, didn't I? Well, I've had three drinks and only mentioned one of them. I won't leave the kitchen till I've tasted everything I can see; and then I'll have a snooze by that beautiful fire. And to hell with everyone who puts things by for a rainy day!

[FABRIZIO, MESSER PIERO *and* STRAGUALCIA *go into the* 'Fool'.]

L'AGIATO [*threateningly*]: You've done this once too often, Frulla. One of these days it'll come to a fight; and I don't mind if it does.

FRULLA: Whenever you like – now if it suits you!

[*They glare at each other and go indoors.* CLEMENZIA *runs out of*

18. Perhaps a reference to the looting habits of Spanish soldiers.
19. 'This needs repeated consideration.'

VIRGINIO's *house, pursued by her master, who is in a towering rage. She runs across the stage and he catches up with her outside* GHERARDO's *house.*]

VIRGINIO: Is this how you've taught my daughter to behave? Is this the respect she shows for my honour? Oh God! Can it be for this that I've weathered so many storms? [GHERARDO *looks indignantly out of upper window, and retires behind curtains.*] To see my fortune without an heir, my family dispersed, my daughter a whore? To become a fable in the mouths of the crowd? Not to be able to show my face in public – to have boys pointing at me, old men mocking at me, the Intronati[20] making a comedy about me? To be the hero of one story after another and have all the women in town talking about me? And don't they know how to tell a story! Don't they enjoy scandal! I expect it's common knowledge already – it stands to reason, because it's enough for one of these women to find something out and then the whole town knows about it within three hours. Unhappy father that I am! Unfortunate, wretched old man, who's lived too long. What am I to do? What thoughts dare I think?

CLEMENZIA: You'd do well to make as little noise about it as you can, and try to get her back home again without the whole city coming to know of it. But I wish that Sister Novellante Ciancini had as little breath to tell her story as I have faith to believe it! Lelia going around dressed as a man indeed! Mind the good sisters aren't telling you that tale in the hope that you'll make a nun out of her and leave all your money to them.

VIRGINIO: But how can it be a lie? She even told me that Lelia's got a job as a serving boy with a nobleman of this city, and that he doesn't know that she's a woman.

CLEMENZIA: All things are possible; but I can't believe it!

VIRGINIO: And *I* certainly don't believe that he hasn't noticed she's a woman.

CLEMENZIA: I'm not talking about that.

VIRGINIO: *I'm* talking about it, though, because it affects me . . . but it's all my own fault, really, for entrusting her to you to bring up, though I knew what you were like.

20. The Intronati were a literary society, and the present play is in fact one of theirs. (*Translator's note.*)

CLEMENZIA: Don't let's have any more of that, Virginio. If I've been a bad woman, you made me one. You know very well that until you came along I'd never been unfaithful to my husband. But you've no idea how a girl needs to be treated. Aren't you ashamed of yourself for trying to marry her off to a croaking old man who's old enough to be her grandfather?

VIRGINIO: And what's wrong with old men, you wretched creature? They're a hundred times better than the young ones!

CLEMENZIA: You must be going out of your mind! And what's more, people are beginning to notice, and that's why they tell you these silly stories.

VIRGINIO: If I can find her, I'll drag her home by the hair.

CLEMENZIA: Then you'll be planting the horns on your own forehead when you could have kept them under your cloak.

VIRGINIO: I don't care. It's bound to come out anyway. And I'll wrench those horns off again soon enough.

CLEMENZIA: You must make your own arrangements – but mind you don't get a headache.

VIRGINIO: I've got a description of the clothes she's wearing. I'll go on looking for her until I find her. That'll be enough for a start.

CLEMENZIA: Do what you like then. But I must go – there's no point in my talking to deaf ears.

[*Exeunt* VIRGINIO, CLEMENZIA. FABRIZIO *and* FRULLA *come out of the 'Fool'.*]

FABRIZIO: While my two servants have a rest, I'm going to have a look at the town. When they wake up, tell them to come along towards the main square.

FRULLA: You know, sir, if I hadn't just seen you put those clothes on, I'd have been ready to swear that you were a young man who's in the service of a nobleman of this city. He wears white, just like yourself, sir, and he looks so much like you that you could be taken for him.

FABRIZIO: Perhaps I've got a brother I don't know about?

FRULLA: Maybe.

FABRIZIO: Please tell my tutor to look for the person we've come to see.

FRULLA: Leave it to me, sir.

[FRULLA *goes into the 'Fool'. Enter* PASQUELLA.]

PASQUELLA: Why, there he is! I was afraid I'd have to search the whole city before I found him – Fabio, I'm glad to have found you here. I was coming to look for you, and now you've saved me the trouble. Listen, darling, my mistress wants you to come to her at once, for a matter that concerns you both. I don't know what it can be!

FABRIZIO: But who is your mistress?

PASQUELLA: You should know by now! You two seem to be closely enough attached to each other!

FABRIZIO [*laughing*]: I'm not so attached as all that – but if she'd like me to attach myself to her, I will, and the sooner the better.

PASQUELLA: You're a cowardly couple. I only wish I were young enough to get a bit of the same for myself. If I were in the same situation as you two, I'd have forgotten my fears and stifled my scruples by now. But it won't be long before you do just that, anyway.

FABRIZIO: Why, madam! You don't know me. Leave me alone – you're mistaking me for someone else.

PASQUELLA: Oh! don't take it the wrong way, dear Fabio. I only said that for your own good.

FABRIZIO: I'm not taking anything the wrong way; but that's not my name and I'm not the man you're looking for.

PASQUELLA: Well, you two will have to do things your own way. But I'll tell you one thing, my lad. There aren't many girls like her – beautiful *and* rich – in the city of Modena. And I wish you'd get on with it, because all this to-ing and fro-ing every day, all this bringing messages and taking messages just makes people talk without doing you any good – and it may do her reputation some harm.

FABRIZIO [*aside*]: This is an extraordinary business, and I can't understand it. Is she mad, or does she really think I'm someone else? I'd like to see where she'll take me, anyway. [*To* PASQUELLA] Let's go, then!

PASQUELLA: But I think I can hear someone indoors there. Wait here a moment, and I'll see if Isabella's alone. If the coast is clear, I'll come back and beckon to you.

FABRIZIO [PASQUELLA *goes indoors*]: I'd like to see what the end of this story will be. Perhaps she's the maidservant of one of the

241

courtesans here and thinks she's going to get a few *scudi* out of me; but she's on the wrong track there. I've been more or less brought up by the Spaniards, and at the end of it all I'd be more likely to have a *scudo* off her than to let her have a penny of my own. Well, someone's going to have a surprise, that's certain. But I'll just step to one side and see what sort of people go in and out of her house, to give myself an idea what sort of woman she is.

[FABRIZIO *moves into wings, Right. Enter* GHERARDO, VIR-GINIO, *Left.* PASQUELLA *re-appears in doorway of* GHERARDO'S *house, and watches them as they approach.* GHERARDO *is wearing unsuitably youthful clothes. He is accompanied by* SPELA.]

GHERARDO: You'll pardon me, I hope, but if that's what's happened, I must give up my claim to your daughter. It isn't just that she couldn't have behaved like that if she wanted me. The thing is that I'm afraid she must have been with someone else.

VIRGINIO: Don't think that, Gherardo! Would I have told you anything about it if that were true? Don't upset the agreement that's been made between us!

GHERARDO: I must ask you not to refer to the matter again.

VIRGINIO: Oh! And you gave me your word!

GHERARDO: I'm entitled to break my word to someone who's betrayed me by his actions. And besides, you don't even know if you're going to get her back yourself. You're trying to sell me a bird in the bush. I heard everything you said when you were talking to Clemenzia.

VIRGINIO: If I can't get her back, I can't give her to you. But if I do get her back, surely you'll be glad to have the wedding as soon as possible?

GHERARDO: Virginio, my wife was the best respected woman who ever lived in this city, and my daughter's a little saint. How can you expect me to take a girl into my family who's run away from her father and goes around from one house to another dressed as a boy, like the wicked women do? Don't you see that I'd never find a husband for my own daughter?

VIRGINIO: In a few days' time it'll all be forgotten. What does it amount to, after all? And there's no one who knows about it but you and myself.

GHERARDO: The whole town will be full of it in no time.

VIRGINIO: No, it won't.

GHERARDO: When did she run away?

VIRGINIO: Last night or this morning.

GHERARDO: Pray God that it may be so! But are you sure that she's in Modena?

VIRGINIO: Yes.

GHERARDO: Well then, you find her and we'll have another word about it later.

VIRGINIO: But do you promise to take her?

GHERARDO: I'll see about that.

VIRGINIO: Say 'yes' now.

GHERARDO: I won't say it now, but . . .

VIRGINIO: Come on! Say it now, with no hedging!

[GHERARDO *notices* PASQUELLA *outside his door.*]

GHERARDO: Steady on a moment . . . What are you out here for, Pasquella? And what's Isabella doing?

PASQUELLA: Why, what do you think? She's on her knees in front of her little altar.

GHERARDO: My blessing on her! My daughter spends all her time in prayer. It's the finest thing in the world.

PASQUELLA: Oh, how right you are! She fasts and keeps vigils more than you'd think possible, and she says her daily prayers like an angel.

GHERARDO: She's just like her poor sainted mother.

PASQUELLA: It's true! It's true! Poor woman! The good works she used to do! She went in for penances and hair shirts like nobody does these days. And when it came to giving alms, there was no one like her. If it hadn't been for the thought of you, she'd have welcomed in every friar or priest or beggar who came to the door and given them all she'd got.

VIRGINIO: Excellent! Excellent!

PASQUELLA: And I'll tell you another thing – a hundred times I've seen her get up a couple of hours before dawn to go to the first mass sung by the friars at San Francesco's, because she didn't want to be seen at her devotions, or be accused of strumpeting her virtues, like a lot of bigoted women I know.

GHERARDO: 'Strumpeting her virtues'? Whatever do you mean by that?

PASQUELLA: Why, strumpeting, like I said! Isn't that right?

VIRGINIO: But 'strumpeting' is a very bad word!

PASQUELLA: Well, I'm sure I often heard her say she didn't want people to think she was strumpeting her virtues abroad.

GHERARDO: Ah, you mean *trumpeting* her virtues abroad – like one of these hypocrites.

PASQUELLA: Maybe. But whatever it is, I'll tell you this – Isabella won't fall short of her mother's example.

GHERARDO: God grant it may be so!

[*Enter* FABRIZIO, *Right. He walks slowly across stage towards them.*]

VIRGINIO: Oh Gherardo, Gherardo! Here comes the wretched girl we were talking about. And she doesn't even hide her face or turn back when she sees her unhappy father! But let's speak to her.

GHERARDO: Mind you don't make a mistake. Perhaps it isn't Lelia after all.

VIRGINIO: What mistake could I make? She's wearing exactly the clothes Sister Novellante described to me.

PASQUELLA [*aside*]: Things are taking an ugly turn. It looks as if I shall be getting what I've asked for.

[*Exit* PASQUELLA. FABRIZIO *begins to walk past* VIRGINIO *and* GHERARDO.]

VIRGINIO: Good morning, my fine young lady! Do you think those clothes are befitting for a girl like you? Is this how you honour your father's family? Is this the way you bring happiness to this poor old gentleman here? I wish I'd died when I begot you! You were born to bring dishonour on me, to bury me alive under mountains of shame. Gherardo! Gherardo! What do you think of your betrothed now? Do you think she does you honour?

GHERARDO: No . . . no . . . Betrothed, eh? I don't know about that.

VIRGINIO: You bad, wicked girl! It would serve you right if he didn't want you any more and you were left on the shelf. But he's going to overlook your follies, and he is going to marry you.

GHERARDO: Steady! . . . Steady!

VIRGINIO: Now go home and get indoors, you miserable creature! There must have been a curse on the milk your mother gave you the day I begot you!

FABRIZIO: Sir, have you no sons in this town, or other relations, or friends, who could take care of you?

VIRGINIO: What an answer! Why do you say that?

FABRIZIO: Because if you have, I can't understand why they let you out of the house when you're in such need of medical assistance. In most places they'd keep you tied up.

VIRGINIO: I ought to keep you tied up! I'd like to cut your throat! Get me a knife, somebody.

FABRIZIO: Sir, you don't know who I am. Maybe you're insulting me because you think I'm a foreigner. But I'm Modenese just as much as you are, and born of just as good a father and just as good a family as yourself.

GHERARDO: She's a fine-looking girl, after all. If there's nothing else wrong beyond what we know about, I'll take her.

VIRGINIO: And why did you leave your father, and run away from the place where I'd arranged for you to be looked after?

FABRIZIO: You never arranged anything for me, that I know of; but I was forced to leave my father.

VIRGINIO: Forced, do you say? Who forced you?

FABRIZIO: The Spaniards.

VIRGINIO: And where have you come from now?

FABRIZIO: From the camp.

VIRGINIO: From the *camp*?

FABRIZIO: Yes, that's right.

GHERARDO: In that case, it's all off!

VIRGINIO: You wretched girl!

FABRIZIO [*jokingly*]: It's all your fault!

VIRGINIO: Gherardo, do me a favour and let me take her into your house. I don't want people to see her like this.

GHERARDO: No, no – take her to your own place.

VIRGINIO: In the name of our old friendship, open up this door for a moment.

GHERARDO: No, I tell you!

VIRGINIO: Listen a moment . . . while we talk, Spela can make sure that she doesn't go anywhere else. [VIRGINIO *and* GHERARDO *go to one side and whisper.*]

FABRIZIO [*aside*]: I've known a lot of lunatics who came from Modena – I won't mention any names just now – But I never saw anyone so mad as this old gentleman who wasn't either tied up or locked up. What a funny bee he's got in his bonnet. As far as I

245

can see, his trouble is that he thinks young men are girls. This is an even better story than the one Molza tells about the Sienese lady who thought she was a wine jar, since after all you don't expect women to have a lot of sense, whereas old men ought to have more than anybody, for various reasons. I wouldn't miss the chance of telling this story on carnival night for a hundred ducats – But here they come again. Let's see what they'll say this time.

GHERARDO: Virginio, I'll be frank with you. In one way I think I will; in another way I think I won't. We could ask her a few more questions, perhaps.

VIRGINIO [*to* FABRIZIO]: Come here!

FABRIZIO: What do you want, sir?

VIRGINIO: You're a very wicked girl!

FABRIZIO: Don't insult me, sir – I won't stand it!

VIRGINIO: You shameless creature!

FABRIZIO: I've warned you, sir!

GHERARDO [*to* FABRIZIO]: Let him speak his mind – can't you see how angry he is? Do what he says!

FABRIZIO: What does he want from me? What have I to do with you or with him?

VIRGINIO: You're still bold enough to talk, I see! Who's your father?

FABRIZIO: Virginio Bellenzini.

VIRGINIO: I'm sorry to hear you say it. You'll make me die before my time!

FABRIZIO: Before your time, sir? An old man of sixty? I wish we could all reckon on reaching that age! Die if you like! You've lived too long already!

VIRGINIO: If I have, it's your fault, you slut.

GHERARDO: Oh, don't let's use that sort of language! [*To* FABRIZIO] Let me talk to you as if you were my daughter or my sister. I'll tell you this much – that's not the way to speak to your father.

FABRIZIO [*aside*]: Birds of a feather, all right! These two have both got the same screw loose. And what a funny one it is, too! Ha! ha! ha!

VIRGINIO: Are you laughing now, on top of everything else?

GHERARDO: It's a bad sign for a child to mock her own father.

FABRIZIO: What's all this about fathers and mothers? I've only one father, and that's Virginio Bellenzini. I only had one mother, and that was Giovanna Bellenzini. You're talking like an idiot. Do you by any chance think that there's no one in Modena who'll back me up?

GHERARDO: Virginio, do you know what's passing through my mind? I think you've driven this poor girl into a melancholy that's ruined her wits.

VIRGINIO: Oh, God! You're right! I felt it from the beginning, when she started addressing me in that impatient, off-hand way.

GHERARDO: No, no – that could just as well arise from something else.

VIRGINIO: What do you mean?

GHERARDO: When a woman loses her honour, she doesn't give a damn for anybody.

VIRGINIO: I think it's some sort of mental trouble.

GHERARDO: Well, it's a funny thing that she remembers her parents' names and yet doesn't seem to know you by sight.

VIRGINIO: Let's put her in your house, as it's so near at hand. I can't take her to my place without half the town seeing us.

FABRIZIO: Those childish old fools look like Melchizedek's elder brothers! What plot are they hatching now?

VIRGINIO: We'll do what we can with fair words until we get her inside the door; then we'll force her into your daughter's room and lock her in with her.

GHERARDO: Very well – I agree.

VIRGINIO: Come on then, daughter! I don't want to go on being angry with you. I'll forgive you everything if you behave properly from now on.

FABRIZIO: Thank you very much!

GHERARDO: That's more like it! That's a good girl!

FABRIZIO: Why, here's the other gay young spark!

GHERARDO: Come on, then! It won't do you any good to be seen standing around in the street in those clothes. Go indoors! [*Calling out to* PASQUELLA *inside his house*] Open the door, Pasquella!

VIRGINIO: Yes, go in, daughter.

FABRIZIO: That's one thing I won't do.

GHERARDO: Why not?

FABRIZIO: Because I don't like going into other people's houses.

GHERARDO: Good! Good! She'll be a virtuous wife – a real Penelope!

VIRGINIO: Didn't I tell you my daughter was a good girl – and a beautiful one too?

GHERARDO [*running an appreciative eye over* FABRIZIO]: Yes ... yes ... in those clothes ...

VIRGINIO [*urging* FABRIZIO *towards the house*]: I just want to say one quick word.

FABRIZIO: Say it out here.

GHERARDO: No, no! That's not right! This is your house – you're going to be my wife.

FABRIZIO: Wife, did you say, you wicked old bu ... bu- ... buffer!

GHERARDO: Your father has promised you to me.

FABRIZIO: Do you take me for one of those creatures who let themselves be ...?

VIRGINIO: Come now! Don't make her angry. Listen, daughter; I won't do anything that you don't want me to do.

FABRIZIO: You old fool! You don't know me very well!

VIRGINIO: Just one word in here! We won't hurt you. Just one!

FABRIZIO: You can have a hundred words with me if you like! Do you think I'm afraid of you?

[FABRIZIO *goes into the house.* GHERARDO *begins to fo!low him.*]

VIRGINIO: Gherardo, now that you've got her indoors, let's see if we can lock her in with your daughter while we send for her clothes.

GHERARDO: Just as you say, Virginio. Pasquella, bring the key of the downstairs room and ask Isabella to come down here.

[GHERARDO *goes indoors, and* VIRGINIO *follows him.*]

# ACT FOUR

*Scene as before.*

[STRAGUALCIA, MESSER PIERO *come out of the* 'FOOL'.]

MESSER PIERO: It would serve you right if he gave you a good thrashing, to teach you to accompany him when he goes out, instead of getting drunk and going to sleep like that, and leaving him to go out by himself.

STRAGUALCIA: And he ought to load you up with brushwood, sulphur, pitch and gunpowder and set fire to you, to teach you not to be what you are!

MESSER PIERO: Drunkard! Drunkard!

STRAGUALCIA: Pedant! Pedant!

MESSER PIERO: Just you wait till I speak to him!

STRAGUALCIA: And you wait till I speak to his father!

MESSER PIERO: What can you tell his father about me?

STRAGUALCIA: And what can you say about me?

MESSER PIERO: I can say that you're a lout, a rogue, a lazy coward, and a drunken lunatic.

STRAGUALCIA: And I can say that you're a thief, a gambler, a slanderer, a cheat, a blackguard, an impostor, a boaster, a dolt, a shameless, ignorant traitor, and a wretched sodomite.

MESSER PIERO [*ironically*]: We know each other pretty well, it seems!

STRAGUALCIA: We do!

MESSER PIERO: Well, that's enough of that. I don't want to put myself on a level with a man like you – it does me no honour.

STRAGUALCIA: Oh, yes, I know! To listen to you, all the noblest blood of the Maremma runs in your veins! But how can you ever be anything but the son of a mule-driver? Don't I come of a better family than you? Once they can say '*cuius masculini*',[21] these wretched fellows think they've a right to trample on everyone else.

21. Stragualcia misquotes an elementary phrase from Latin grammar.

MESSER PIERO: 'Bare-footed walketh poor philosophy!' Whose lips have sullied the fair name of learning now? The lips of an ass!

STRAGUALCIA: The ass will be yourself if you talk like that [*raising imaginary stick*] for I'll load you up with wood.

MESSER PIERO: Now I'll tell you something. *Furor fit laesa saepius sapientia.*[22] One of these days you'll really upset me, Stragualcia. Leave me alone, you wretched stableboy, you waster, you king of wasters!

STRAGUALCIA: Why, you pedant, you king of pedants, pedantissimo, pedant again! Can there be a worse insult than to call a man a pedant? Is there a viler set of fellows, a more blackguardly lot of villains anywhere? Is there a more loathsome trade? And aren't they puffed up with pride when people call them 'Messer This' and 'Messer That', till a man can take off his cap to them at ten paces of distance and they won't even acknowledge it properly. [*Bowing ironically*] At your service, Messer Turd, Messer Squitter, Messer Shit!

MESSER PIERO: *Tractant fabrilia fabri.*[23] You are speaking of what you are.

STRAGUALCIA: I'm speaking of what you love most.

MESSER PIERO: Be off with you! I hate living in the midst of rogues like you.

STRAGUALCIA: You've never been in my midst – though it isn't your fault that you haven't.

MESSER PIERO: Why, in God's name . . .

STRAGUALCIA: 'In God's name', indeed! Look who's cursing and swearing at me now! He knows that I know all about every dirty trick he's ever done, he knows I could get him burnt at the stake, and still he does everything he can to get on the wrong side of me – in more senses than one.

MESSER PIERO: You damned liar! I wouldn't do such a thing.

STRAGUALCIA: And never have, I suppose!

MESSER PIERO: Well, I've decided one thing, Stragualcia. Either you leave our master's service, or I do.

STRAGUALCIA: And how many times have you said that before? Even if you were kicked out, you'd still crawl back.

22. 'Wisdom, if outraged too often, will turn to fury.'
23. 'The workman speaks in the terms of his trade.'

Tell me, now – who else would give you bed and board and share his table and his study with you, except our young master, who's kindness itself?

MESSER PIERO: As though I'd ever lack for a post, if I cared to look around! I've had some good offers, I can tell you.

STRAGUALCIA: Oh, you gorgeous creature! I'd keep quiet, if I were you!

MESSER PIERO: I'm not going to waste any more breath; and nor will you, if you're wise. Go back into the inn and look after our master's property. We can settle accounts with each other later.

STRAGUALCIA: I'll be glad enough to go back to the inn, and I'll make up the account on your behalf – but it'll be up to you to pay. [*He turns back towards the inn, and adds, aside*] If I didn't show my teeth at this wretched fellow from time to time, there'd be no living with him. He's as cowardly as a rabbit. When I turn on him, he doesn't say a word; but if I ever let him get on top of me, he'd tear me to ribbons. That's what his wisdom amounts to! It's a good thing for me that I know him.

[STRAGUALCIA *goes into the inn.*]

MESSER PIERO [*aside*]: The host said Fabrizio would be somewhere over towards the square; so I'd better go this way.

[MESSER PIERO, *about to go off, but catches sight of* VIRGINIO, GHERARDO *emerging from* GHERARDO's *house and waits for them.*]

GHERARDO: As regards the dowry, we'll stick to what we agreed earlier on. I'll give her enough to meet your wishes now, and you add another thousand florins if your son doesn't turn up.

VIRGINIO: That's right!

MESSER PIERO [*aside*]: I've seen that gentleman before, but I can't think where.

VIRGINIO [*to* MESSER PIERO]: What are you staring at, my good sir?

MESSER PIERO [*aside*]: Yes, that's my old master – no doubt about it!

GHERARDO: Let him stare if he wants to. He must be a stranger in Modena. As you know, people in other towns don't take notice of it as we do – they let everyone stare as much as he likes.

MESSER PIERO: If I'm staring, it's not without good reason. [*To* VIRGINIO] Tell me, sir, do you know Messer Virginio Bellenzini of this city?

VIRGINIO: Yes, I do – in fact we couldn't be greater friends. But what do you want from him? If you're thinking of lodging with him, I must tell you that he's very busy and couldn't take care of you properly; so you'd better look elsewhere.

MESSER PIERO: I'm sure that you're Messer Virginio yourself. [*Bowing deeply*] *Salvete, patronorum optime!*[24]

VIRGINIO: Good heavens! Are you Messer Piero de' Pagliaricci, my boy's tutor?

MESSER PIERO: Yes, sir.

VIRGINIO: Oh, my son, my son! Alas! What news of him have you brought? Where did you leave him? How did he die? Why didn't you tell me before? Was he murdered by those traitors, those heathen, those dogs? My son! He was all that I had in the world. Come, good Messer Piero, make short work of it! Tell me everything!

MESSER PIERO: Don't weep, sir, I beg you!

VIRGINIO: Oh, Gherardo, my dear son-in-law! Here's the man who looked after my poor son's education while he was still alive! Dear master! Oh my son, where have they laid you to rest? Don't you even know that? Why don't you tell me? How I long to know everything! Yet how I fear to hear the words I must!

MESSER PIERO: Don't weep, sir! There's nothing to weep about!

VIRGINIO: Why shouldn't I weep for a child so dearly loved? Such a good boy! So promising at his studies! So well mannered! And now those traitors have killed him!

MESSER PIERO: Heaven save you and him from all such disasters! Your son is alive and well.

GHERARDO: That's not so good for me, if it's true. It means I've lost a thousand florins.

VIRGINIO: What do you mean, alive and well? If he were, he'd be with you, surely?

GHERARDO: Virginio, are you certain he's the right man, and not an impostor?

MESSER PIERO: *Parcius ista viris, tamen obiicienda memento.*[25]

VIRGINIO: Tell us more, Messer Piero.

24. 'Greetings, O best of masters!'
25. 'Be more sparing of these insults, which may be thrown back in your teeth later.'

MESSER PIERO: At the sack of Rome, your son was taken prisoner by one Captain Orteca.

GHERARDO: Let's listen – this sounds like a good story!

MESSER PIERO: The captain had two companions. He wanted to trick them out of their share of the ransom, so he sent us secretly to Siena. But a couple of days later it occurred to him that the nobles of that city, who are great upholders of what is right and reasonable, and good friends of Modena, and above all men of honour – it occurred to him, I say, that they might rescue your son and set him free. So the captain took him away from Siena and sent him to a castle belonging to the Lord of Piombino, and made us write off dozens of letters demanding a thousand ducats, which was the ransom he had fixed.

VIRGINIO: My boy! They must have tortured him, surely?

MESSER PIERO: No, no – they treated him like a gentleman.

GHERARDO [aside]: I'm really on tenterhooks now!

MESSER PIERO: We never had any answers to all our letters.

GHERARDO: See what I mean? I knew he'd be leading up to getting some money out of you.

VIRGINIO [to MESSER PIERO]: Go on.

MESSER PIERO: Well, we moved on with the Spanish army to Corregia, and when we arrived there the captain was murdered; and the court took possession of his property and set us free.

VIRGINIO: And where is my son?

MESSER PIERO: Nearer than you think.

VIRGINIO: Is he in Modena?

MESSER PIERO: If you promise me a reward (since the labourer is worthy of his hire), I'll tell you everything.

GHERARDO: So that's it, is it, you crook!

MESSER PIERO: You're being unjust, sir. I a crook? Far be it from me!

VIRGINIO: I'll promise anything you like. Where is he?

MESSER PIERO: At the inn here – the 'Fool'.

GHERARDO: It's all up with those thousand florins, then. But why should I care? As long as I get Lelia, I don't mind. I've got enough money, anyway.

VIRGINIO: Come on, Messer Piero – I can't wait to see him, to embrace him, to kiss him, and dandle him on my knee!

THE DECEIVED

MESSER PIERO: Oh, sir, *quanto mutatur ab illo*![26] He's not a child you can dandle on your knee now! You won't recognize him – he's turned into a fine young man. And I'm sure he won't know you, sir – you've changed too. You've got that beard which you never had before; and if I hadn't heard your voice, I'd never have recognized you myself. And what's the news of my young master's sister?

VIRGINIO: Fine, fine! She's turned into a tall, well-made girl – the image of her mother!

GHERARDO [*mishearing*]: Going to be a mother? You can keep her, in that case – I don't want anything to do with her!

VIRGINIO: No, no – I said she's the image of her mother! Why, Messer Piero, I haven't greeted you properly yet! [*Embraces him.*]

MESSER PIERO: I don't want to boast, sir, but the things I've done for your son . . . I could say a lot if I wanted to. But I've had every encouragement, because whenever I've asked him to do something he's always got on with it.

VIRGINIO: What about his lessons?

MESSER PIERO: He hasn't wasted any time; he's always done the best he could *per varios casus, per tot discrimina rerum.*[27]

VIRGINIO: Call him out here then, without telling him anything. I'd like to see whether he'll recognize me.

MESSER PIERO: He went out not long ago. Let's see whether he's back yet.

[STRAGUALCIA *looks out of the inn door. He is fairly drunk.*]

MESSER PIERO: Stragualcia! Stragualcia! Has our young master come back?

STRAGUALCIA: Not yet.

MESSER PIERO [*aside to* STRAGUALCIA]: Come and speak to Fabrizio's father. This is Messer Virginio.

STRAGUALCIA [*to* MESSER PIERO]: Are you still angry?

MESSER PIERO: You know I never stay angry with you for long.

STRAGUALCIA: Just as well.

MESSER PIERO: Now come and pay your respects to Fabrizio's father.

26. 'What a change there is in him!'
27. 'In so many changes and vicissitudes of life.'

254

STRAGUALCIA [*still addressing* MESSER PIERO]: Wrong way round!
  You should pay respects to me!

MESSER PIERO: I'm not talking about myself, you fool! This gentleman here!

STRAGUALCIA: Is this Fabrizio's father?

MESSER PIERO: Yes!

STRAGUALCIA: O most noble master, you've arrived just in time to
  pay the host! Welcome!

MESSER PIERO: This man was a good servant to your son through all
  his troubles.

STRAGUALCIA [*aggressively*]: Mean to say I'm not one now?

MESSER PIERO: No, no – not at all!

VIRGINIO: My blessing on my dear son! You can be sure I'll repay
  everyone who's borne him company and looked after him.

STRAGUALCIA: You can repay me easily enough!

VIRGINIO: Just tell me what you want.

STRAGUALCIA: Fix me up in the service of this inn, where the host's
  the best company in the world, and the best-equipped and wisest
  man of his trade I ever saw, and the one with most understanding
  of a stranger's needs. I don't believe there's any other paradise but
  this on earth.

GHERARDO: They say he keeps a good table.

VIRGINIO: Have you had anything to eat?

STRAGUALCIA: Yes, a little.

VIRGINIO: What was it?

STRAGUALCIA: Two partridges, six thrushes, a capon, and a bit of
  veal; and only two glasses of wine to go with it.

VIRGINIO: Frulla! Give him whatever he wants, and let me have the
  bill.

MESSER PIERO: And what *do* you want, Stragualcia?

STRAGUALCIA [*to* VIRGINIO]: I kiss your hands . . . That's what I call
  a real master! Now you, Messer Piero, you're too miserable, and
  you want everything for yourself. That's what everyone says about
  you, as you know very well . . . Frulla, bring these gentlemen a
  drink!

  [FRULLA *brings out glasses.* VIRGINIO *takes one.* GHERARDO
  *refuses.*]

MESSER PIERO [*also refusing*]: No, no – not for me!

STRAGUALCIA: I know you'll have a drink in the end. I'll pay, anyway. What shall we have to go with it? A couple of sweet-breads, a slab of sausage ... What do you say, gentlemen? Messer Piero, you must have a drink too.

MESSER PIERO: To make peace with you, I will. [*Does so.*]

STRAGUALCIA: Good! Good! [*To* VIRGINIO] You know, sir, you ought to think a lot of Messer Piero, because he thinks more of your son than he does of his own eyes.

VIRGINIO: And may God reward him for it!

STRAGUALCIA: That's up to you in the first place, sir, and then up to God afterwards. [*To* GHERARDO] But you, sir – won't you have a drink?

GHERARDO: It's not the time for that. [*Accepts glass reluctantly and drinks it quickly.*]

STRAGUALCIA: Be so kind, gentlemen, and come inside till my young master gets back. And as dinner's nearly ready, let's dine here this evening.

MESSER PIERO: That might not be a bad idea.

GHERARDO: I'll leave you now, for I've some things to attend to at home.

VIRGINIO [*aside to* GHERARDO]: Make sure Lelia doesn't get away.

GHERARDO: That's the reason I'm going.

VIRGINIO: She's yours now, and you can do what you like with her – with my blessing.

[VIRGINIO, MESSER PIERO, STRAGUALCIA *go into the inn.*]

GHERARDO [*soliloquizing*]: Ah well, we can't have everything we'd like to have, and patience is a virtue ... But here comes Lelia, unless my eyes are playing a trick on me! She must have got out! That wretched maid of mine must have let her escape.

[*Enter* LELIA, *dressed as a boy, and* CLEMENZIA, *Left. They walk slowly across the stage towards* CLEMENZIA'*s door.*]

LELIA: Well, Clemenzia, don't you think fate's having a fine joke at my expense?

CLEMENZIA: Don't worry, dear – leave it to me, and I'll find some way of making it all right for you. Go and get out of those clothes before anyone else sees you.

GHERARDO [*aside*]: I must talk to her and find out how she escaped. God bless you, Clemenzia, and you too, Lelia, my sweet bride to be.

Who let you out? The maid, I suppose, eh? I'm glad you went straight to your nurse's house; but appearing in public in those clothes is something that doesn't do you any honour, or me either.

LELIA [*aside*]: Oh heavens! He's recognized me! [*To* GHERARDO] Who do you think I am? What Lelia d'you mean? That's not my name!

GHERARDO: Why, you admitted you were Lelia just now, when your father and I locked you up with my daughter! How can you think I don't know you now, my dear little wife? But do go and get out of those clothes.

LELIA: Wife, indeed! I don't want to be a wife any more than you do.

CLEMENZIA: Dear Gherardo, why don't you go back home for the moment? All women do silly things, some in one way and some in another. There probably isn't a single one who doesn't have a little escapade now and then. And the less said about it the better.

GHERARDO: No one will learn anything about this from me . . . But however did she get out of my house, when I'd locked her up in there with Isabella?

CLEMENZIA: Who? Young Lelia here?

GHERARDO: Yes – young Lelia here.

[LELIA *goes into* CLEMENZIA's *house*.]

CLEMENZIA: There must be some mistake. She's been with me the whole time. She put those clothes on for a joke, like girls often do, and she was asking me if they suited her.

GHERARDO: You're trying to muddle me. I tell you we locked her up in my house there, with my daughter Isabella.

CLEMENZIA: Where have you been this morning?

GHERARDO: I've been to the inn here – the 'Fool'. I went there with Virginio.

CLEMENZIA: Have you been drinking?

GHERARDO: Only one glass.

CLEMENZIA: You'd better go and have a sleep – you need it.

GHERARDO: Let me see Lelia again before I go; I've some good news for her.

CLEMENZIA: What is it?

GHERARDO: Her brother's come back safe and sound, and her father's waiting for him at the inn.

CLEMENZIA: Do you mean Fabrizio?

GHERARDO: Yes, that's right.

CLEMENZIA: If I believed that, I'd give you a kiss!

GHERARDO: Thank you! I'd rather it came from Lelia!

CLEMENZIA: I must run and tell her.

GHERARDO: And I must go and give that wretched woman who let her out a piece of my mind.

[CLEMENZIA *runs into her house.* GHERARDO *is about to return to his house, but changes his mind and goes into the inn.* PASQUELLA *comes out of* GHERARDO'S *house, very agitated.*]

PASQUELLA [*soliloquizing*]: Oh dear! Oh dear! I've had such a fright, I had to run out into the street! And really, dear ladies [*addressing female members of the audience*] – if I didn't tell you what happened, you'd never guess. But I'll tell *you* about it, sweet ladies, and not those horrible men, who'd only laugh. Those two old idiots would have it that the young fellow was really a girl, and they locked him up in the downstairs bedroom with my young mistress Isabella, and gave me the key. I thought I'd go in and see what they were doing; and I found them hugging and kissing like mad. That made me want to make sure whether he really was a boy or a girl. Well, my mistress had got him stretched out on the bed, and she called out and asked me to help her while she held his hands; and then he stopped resisting. So I undid him in front; and suddenly something flew up and hit me across the knuckles, and I couldn't tell whether it was a pestle, or a carrot, or one of those other things. But whatever else it might have been, it certainly wasn't undernourished! When I saw what it looked like, I could see this was a case of devil take the hindmost, and away I ran. I'm sure I wouldn't dare to go back into that room myself; but if any of you ladies doesn't believe me and wants to see for yourself, I'll lend her the key. – But here's Giglio. I must see if I can manage things so that I get the rosary and make a fool of him. These Spaniards think they're so clever that they can't believe anyone in the world's a match for them.

[*Enter* GIGLIO.]

GIGLIO [*aside*]: There is Pasquella. I am sure she did think the time go very slowly, because she want so much to be with me. She know already, the baggage, how well the Spaniard can please the woman. How they love us, these Italian sluts!

PASQUELLA [*aside*]: I've got it! I know how to make him cough up! Just leave him to me!

GIGLIO [*aside*]: This wretched washerwoman really think I give her the paternosters. I renounce my oath to the Emperor if I not make her steal enough from her master so that she buy me stockings and doublets and shirts, two at a time. I take my pleasure with her – then I take my rosary without saying anything. But I think she forget it already.

PASQUELLA [*aside*]: If he puts those paternosters in my hands and then gets them back again, he can have the eyes out of my head as well! And if he says anything, I'll get my Spela to frighten him as no Spaniard was ever frightened before!

GIGLIO: Oh blessed be the fortunate mother who beared you and brought you up to be so lovely, so polite, so true! I think you have wait for me.

PASQUELLA: What sweet words these Spaniards have in their mouths! I've been waiting on the doorstep here for more than half an hour, to see if you were passing by, because my master wasn't at home and we could have had a little time together.

GIGLIO: I am sorry, by God, but I have had the things to do. Now let us go in.

PASQUELLA: I'm afraid the master will be back – he's been gone quite a time now. I suppose you forgot the rosary, did you?

GIGLIO: No, no, madam. Here I have it.

PASQUELLA: Let me see . . . Oh! you were going to have it repaired, and you haven't. Why's that?

GIGLIO: I get it done some other time. To tell you the truth, I not remember.

PASQUELLA: It shows how much you care about me, you wretched creature! Oh, I'd like to . . .!

GIGLIO: Do not be angry, madam, not angry with your son; for you know I have no other friend among the ladies.

PASQUELLA: Well! It hasn't taken me long to catch *you* out in a lie! Just now you told me you had two others, and both of them of noble family.

GIGLIO: I have abandon them now, for your sake, because I not want anyone but you . . . You not understand me?

PASQUELLA: That's all right, then. Let me see if that string of beads really is a rosary. It looks very long to me.

GIGLIO: I not know how many beads are there.

PASQUELLA: Then you can't use it much. Do you know your Our Father, I wonder? Give it here for a moment, and I'll count them.

GIGLIO: Take it, then – and now we go indoors.

PASQUELLA: But make sure that no one sees you come in.

GIGLIO: Here is no one.

PASQUELLA: Let's go in, then.

[PASQUELLA *goes in through the door of* GHERARDO's *house, but stops just inside before* GIGLIO *can follow her right in. He stands in the doorway.*]

PASQUELLA: Oh dear! Oh dear! Here are my hens, all around my feet! Stay where you are for a moment, Giglio. If they get out in the street, I'll never have them back before tomorrow morning.

GIGLIO: Be quick, then.

PASQUELLA: Tk! tk! tk! Pretty dears! Pretty dears! Shoo! Shoo! I hope you all break your necks! I'm sure one will get out! Don't let them by, Giglio!

GIGLIO: Where stand these birds? I see neither cocks nor hens!

PASQUELLA: Can't you see them? Here they are! Stand back a little bit, Giglio, and let me shut the door, till I can get them back into their run.

[GIGLIO *stands back.* PASQUELLA *slams the door and bolts it.*]

GIGLIO: But you have shut with the bolt. Why you do that?

PASQUELLA: To make sure the hens don't open it.

GIGLIO: But be quick, before someone come and disturb us.

PASQUELLA: Whoever comes, they won't get in here!

GIGLIO [*aside*]: Damn the old whore! [*To* PASQUELLA] Tell me why you not open!

PASQUELLA: Giglio, darling, do you know something? The first thing I'm going to do is to say my prayers and tell my beads till I get to the end of this rosary. You might as well go home, as far as this evening is concerned. And I was almost forgetting – I've got a special prayer to say, which I hardly ever leave out.

GIGLIO: What tricks are these? What telling beads? What special prayer?

PASQUELLA: Oh, the special prayer! Shall I recite it to you? It recites very nicely!

> Ghostly spirit, ghostly spirit,
>     That wanders night and day!
> With tail upright you came to haunt me,
>     With upright tail you'll go away.
>
> We're birds of a feather,
> You've run into dirty weather;
> You thought you'd snatch me,
> And now you can't catch me.
>                            Amen.

GIGLIO: I not understand your prayer. If you not want to open door, give me back my rosary and I go my way. [*Aside*] By all the holy martyrs, I believe that this miserable old bawd have cheated me! [*Aloud*] Madam Pasquella! Open! Quickly, by your life!
PASQUELLA [*singing*]:

> What ails my love, he doth not come?
>     Another woman's love hath robbed me!
> Alas! Poor Pasquella!

GIGLIO: But what is this? Madam Pasquella, do not keep me waiting here that you should open.
PASQUELLA [*singing*]:

> Sweet lord, I cannot serve you now.
>     Alas!

GIGLIO: Now she make music, curse her. [*Long pause*] She seem not to remember that I stand here. I knock the door down, I swear to God! [*Kicks the door several times.*]
PASQUELLA [*brightly*]: Who's that?
GIGLIO: Your son!
PASQUELLA: What do you want? My master's not at home. Can I take a message for him?
GIGLIO: Give me just one word!
PASQUELLA: You can wait, if you like. He won't be long.
GIGLIO: Open, that I wait inside! [*Aside*] Now she go right indoors!

I renounce the whole world, if I not burn this house down unless she give me back my rosary. [*Kicks door again.*]

PASQUELLA [*appearing at upper window*]: What's the meaning of this? You don't seem to have much sense, if you'll pardon me for saying so! Who are you? Good heavens! Do you want to break the door down?

GIGLIO: I swear by God and by St Litany that I break the door down and burn it too if you not give back my rosary.

PASQUELLA: Eh? What's that? We've no rosemary in the garden here.

GIGLIO: I not say rosemary; I only say my paternosters.

PASQUELLA: And what is it to do with me, if you only say your paternosters? Do you want me to become a heathen blackamoor like yourself, so that I'd have to start learning my Our Father over again from the beginning?

GIGLIO: A curse on the wretched whore! Blackamoor heathen, is it!

PASQUELLA: Listen! If you don't get away from that door, I'll soak you to the skin!

GIGLIO: I not fear water – watch me set fire to this door! [PASQUELLA *empties a bucket over him.*] Damn her to hell! She soak me from head to foot, the old whore, the old wretch, the old bawd, the miserable old woman. The curse of all the Orders of Friars fall on her!

[GHERARDO *comes out of the inn, and stands looking around him for a moment or two.*]

PASQUELLA [*to* GIGLIO]: Did I splash you? I didn't notice you were there. But here's my master now. If you want anything, ask him and don't come bothering me any more.

GIGLIO [*aside*]: If that old man find me here, I get big thrashing. Better run away, I think.

[*Exit* GIGLIO, *hurriedly*, *Right*. GHERARDO *walks over to his own front door.* PASQUELLA *comes down to meet him.*]

GHERARDO: Whatever were you doing with that Spaniard who was at the door? What's he to you, or you to him?

PASQUELLA: He wanted some rosemary, or something. I couldn't make head or tail of it.

GHERARDO: Anyway, why didn't you do what I told you? I'd like to break your neck!

PASQUELLA: Why? What for?

GHERARDO: Why did you let Lelia go out? Didn't I tell you to keep her locked up?

PASQUELLA: But when did she go out? Isn't she still in the room there?

GHERARDO: No, she isn't, damn you!

PASQUELLA: But I know she is!

GHERARDO: And I know she isn't. I've just left her at her nurse's house.

PASQUELLA: But I've just left her in the downstairs room, on her knees, stringing the prayers together as fast as she could go.

GHERARDO: Maybe she got back quicker than I did.

PASQUELLA: But I tell you that she never went out, that I know of. The room's still locked.

GHERARDO: Where's the key?

PASQUELLA: Here it is.

GHERARDO: Give it to me; and if she's not there, I'll break your neck.

PASQUELLA: And if she is, will you buy me a new smock?

GHERARDO: Very well!

PASQUELLA: Let me go and open up for you.

GHERARDO: No; I'll open the door myself. You'll twist things somehow to make an excuse for yourself.

[GHERARDO *takes the key and goes into his house.*]

PASQUELLA [*aside*]: Oh dear! I'm so afraid he'll find them still at it hammer and tongs – though it is quite a time since I left them now.

[*Enter* FLAMMINIO, *Right.*]

FLAMMINIO: Pasquella, how long is it since my boy Fabio was here with you?

PASQUELLA: Why do you want to know?

FLAMMINIO: Because he's a traitor, and I'm going to punish him. And since Isabella has left me for him, she can keep him, which is all she deserves. It's not much of a recommendation for a fine young lady like her, to fall in love with a serving lad.

PASQUELLA: Oh, don't say that! The kindness she shows him is all for your sake.

FLAMMINIO: Tell her she'll be sorry one of these days. When I find him, I've got my knife here with me on purpose, and I'll cut off his lips and his ears and gouge out one of his eyes, and send her the lot on a plate. Then she can have her fill of kissing him.

PASQUELLA [*aside*]: Ah well! The dog barks, while the wolf eats his dinner!

FLAMMINIO: And you'll soon see whether I mean what I say!

[*Exit* FLAMMINIO. *Enter* GHERARDO.]

GHERARDO: Oh God! To be fooled like this! What a trick to be taken in by! Why, poor Gherardo, then! But that traitor Virginio, that damned, dirty traitor! He's put the horns on my head, all right! Oh God! What shall I do?

PASQUELLA: What's wrong, master?

GHERARDO: What's wrong, do you say? Who's that with my daughter? Tell me that!

PASQUELLA: Why, master, I thought *you* knew! Isn't it Virginio Bellenzini's child?

GHERARDO: Child, indeed! My daughter will have to thank that child for the gift of another child by the look of things, more's the pity!

PASQUELLA: Oh! don't say those things! What's wrong? Isn't it Lelia in there?

GHERARDO: It's a man!

PASQUELLA: It can't be! What do you know about it, anyway?

GHERARDO: I saw him with my own eyes.

PASQUELLA: Saw him? Where?

GHERARDO: On top of my daughter, curse it!

PASQUELLA: Well, they must have been having a game.

GHERARDO: They were having a game all right!

PASQUELLA: And did you really see him so as to be sure it was a man?

GHERARDO: Yes, I tell you, yes! I opened the door quickly, and he'd nothing on but his doublet and didn't have time to cover himself.

PASQUELLA: But did you see everything? I bet it was really a girl!

GHERARDO: I tell you he's a man, and there's enough of him to make two men!

PASQUELLA: And what did Isabella say?

GHERARDO: What do you expect her to say? Oh, the shame of it!

PASQUELLA: Why don't you let the young fellow go, now? What are you going to do with him?

GHERARDO: Do with him? I'm going to bring him up before the Governor and have him punished.

PASQUELLA: Perhaps he'll run away.

GHERARDO: I've locked him up in there.

[*Exit* PASQUELLA. VIRGINIO, MESSER PIERO *come out of the inn.*]

GHERARDO: Now here's Virginio, just at the right time!

MESSER PIERO [*to* VIRGINIO]: I'm very surprised that Fabrizio hasn't come back to the inn yet. I don't know what to think.

VIRGINIO: Was he armed?

MESSER PIERO: Yes, I think he was.

VIRGINIO: They'll have arrested him, then. We've got a mayor[28] here who'd arrest a wasp for carrying a sting.

MESSER PIERO: But surely they don't treat foreigners with such discourtesy?

GHERARDO [*coming up to them*]: Good day to you, Virginio! Is this the action of a gentleman? Is this the way to treat a friend? Is this the way to get me into your family? Who do you think you're dealing with? Do you think I'm going to stand for it? I'd like to ...

VIRGINIO: What's your complaint against me, Gherardo? What have I done? I never tried to get you into my family, as you call it. You've been pestering me about that for over a year. If you don't want to go ahead with the match, you needn't.

GHERARDO: Do you still dare to answer me back, as if I were a notorious cuckold? You dirty traitor! Cheat! Fraud! Swindler! The Governor shall hear about this!

VIRGINIO: Gherardo, that's no way for a man like you to talk, and least of all when you're speaking to me.

GHERARDO: The blackguard won't even admit that I've a right to complain, now. You're very full of yourself now that your son's turned up!

VIRGINIO: Blackguard yourself!

GHERARDO: My God! If I were a bit younger, I'd cut you to pieces.

VIRGINIO: Are you going to tell us what you're talking about, or not?

GHERARDO: You shameless rogue!

VIRGINIO: I'm being much too patient with you.

GHERARDO: Thief!

VIRGINIO: Forger!

28. The mayor was also chief of police.

GHERARDO: Liar! Wait till I get at you!

VIRGINIO: I'm waiting. [*Removes his cloak.*]

MESSER PIERO [*restraining* GHERARDO]: Come, come, sir! What madness is this?

GHERARDO: Let me go!

MESSER PIERO [*to* VIRGINIO]: And you, sir – put your cloak on again!

VIRGINIO [*to* GHERARDO]: Who do you think you're talking to! Let me take my daughter home at once!

GHERARDO: I'll cut your throat and hers too!

[GHERARDO *dashes into his own house.*]

MESSER PIERO [*to* VIRGINIO]: What is this gentleman's business with you, sir?

VIRGINIO: I don't know. Earlier on I entrusted my daughter Lelia to him – she's in his house now. He said he wanted to marry her, but you can see how things stand now. I'm afraid he'll do her some injury.

[GHERARDO *rushes out again carrying a halberd.*]

MESSER PIERO [*to* GHERARDO, *restraining him again*]: Steady on, sir! No weapons! No weapons!

GHERARDO: Let me go!

[VIRGINIO *crosses hurriedly to his front door and goes inside.*]

MESSER PIERO [*to* GHERARDO]: What is the nature of your quarrel?

GHERARDO: That traitor's ruined me!

MESSER PIERO: How, sir?

GHERARDO: If I don't cut him to pieces . . . if I don't hew him limb from limb with this halberd . . .

MESSER PIERO: Please be so good as to tell me the reason for your anger!

GHERARDO: We can go into my house, now that traitor's run away, and I'll tell you the whole story. Aren't you his son's tutor – didn't you come to the inn with us?

MESSER PIERO: Yes, that is correct.

GHERARDO: Come on in, then!

MESSER PIERO: I have your promise of safety, have I not?

GHERARDO: Yes, yes! Of course!

[*Exeunt* MESSER PIERO, GHERARDO.]

# ACT FIVE

*Scene as before.*

[VIRGINIO *comes out of his house, carrying a huge rectangular shield, big enough to cover him completely. He is followed by* SCATIZZA *and a couple more of his servants, all armed after a fashion.* VIRGINIO *reviews his troops carefully.*]

VIRGINIO: Now then, all of you, follow me!

[VIRGINIO *leads the way towards* GHERARDO's *house. As they pass the inn,* STRAGUALCIA *looks out.*]

VIRGINIO: You come with us too, Stragualcia.

STRAGUALCIA: With arms, or without? I've no weapons here.

VIRGINIO: Ask the host for some, then!

[STRAGUALCIA *goes into the inn.*]

SCATIZZA: You know, master, with a big shield like that you really ought to have a lance.

VIRGINIO: I don't want a lance. This is all I need.

SCATIZZA: This round shield would be more dashing, as you're wearing a doublet.

VIRGINIO: No, no; this gives more protection. That old sheep seems to think that he's caught me red-handed in some way. I'm afraid he may have murdered my poor girl.

[*Re-enter* STRAGUALCIA, *carrying a huge spit with a joint impaled on it, and a large bottle.*]

STRAGUALCIA: Here's a useful weapon, master. I'll spit the old fellow with this as if he was an ortolan!

SCATIZZA: But what's going to happen to the joint?

STRAGUALCIA: I'm an old campaigner, and I know that the first thing is to make sure of the day's rations.

SCATIZZA: I see. And what about that bottle?

STRAGUALCIA: That's to refresh the troops, if they are driven back after the first engagement.

SCATIZZA: I'm glad you've planned for that, because it's bound to happen.

STRAGUALCIA: Would you like me to spit the lot of them together – father, daughter, servants, house and all like a row of calf livers? I'll drive the spit up the old man's arse and out of his eye, and the others can be spitted sideways like thrushes.

VIRGINIO: The door's open. I expect they're lying in wait for us.

STRAGUALCIA: In wait, eh? I don't like the sound of that. Why should they wait when the spit's ready for them? But here's Messer Piero coming out.

[*Enter* MESSER PIERO *from* GHERARDO's *house.*]

MESSER PIERO [*speaking over his shoulder to* GHERARDO]: Leave it all to me, Messer Gherardo; I'll arrange everything for you.

STRAGUALCIA: Look, master; I believe the tutor's betrayed us and gone over to the enemy! His sort don't often stand firm . . . Shall I give him the honour of first place on my spit?

MESSER PIERO: Messer Virginio, dear master, what are these weapons for?

STRAGUALCIA: Aha! Didn't I tell you?

VIRGINIO: Where's my daughter? Hand her over; I want to take her home. And have you found Fabrizio yet?

MESSER PIERO: Yes, sir, I have.

VIRGINIO: Where is he, then?

MESSER PIERO: In here, Messer Virginio, and he's found himself a beautiful young wife – subject to your approval, of course.

VIRGINIO: A wife, d'you say? Who is she?

STRAGUALCIA: He hasn't wasted much time! Smart lad!

MESSER PIERO: Messer Gherardo's charming and lovely young daughter!

VIRGINIO: Good God! Gherardo? He was trying to murder me a couple of moments ago!

MESSER PIERO: *Rem omnem a principio audies.*[29] Let's go in, and you shall hear the whole story. Messer Gherardo, will you come out now?

[*Enter* GHERARDO.]

GHERARDO: O Virginio, it's the most extraordinary thing you ever heard! Come in!

29. 'You shall hear the whole thing from the beginning.'

STRAGUALCIA: Shall I get him on my spit? I'm afraid he's more of a boiling fowl, really.

GHERARDO: Put down those weapons, all of you. It's time to laugh, not fight.

VIRGINIO: Can I disarm in safety?

MESSER PIERO: In perfect safety – I guarantee it.

VIRGINIO: Right! Go home, you lot, put away the weapons, and bring me my cloak.

[VIRGINIO's *servants go home.* STRAGUALCIA *goes back into the inn.* FABRIZIO *comes out of* GHERARDO's *house.*]

MESSER PIERO: Fabrizio, come and salute your father.

VIRGINIO: But isn't that Lelia?

MESSER PIERO: No, it's Fabrizio.

VIRGINIO [*embracing* FABRIZIO]: My dear son!

FABRIZIO: Dear father, how I've longed to see you!

VIRGINIO: My boy, the tears I've shed for you!

GHERARDO: Come inside, then, Virginio, and you can hear the rest of it. But I'll tell you one thing now – your daughter's safely in her nurse's house.

VIRGINIO: Thank God! Thank God!

[VIRGINIO, FABRIZIO, MESSER PIERO, GHERARDO *go into* GHERARDO's *house. Enter* FLAMMINIO, CRIVELLO, *Left.*]

CRIVELLO: I saw him in Clemenzia's house with these eyes, and heard him there with these ears!

FLAMMINIO: Are you sure it was really Fabio?

CRIVELLO: Do you think I don't know him by sight?

FLAMMINIO: Let's go there now.

[FLAMMINIO, CRIVELLO *begin to walk across to* CLEMENZIA's *house.*]

FLAMMINIO: And if I find him . . .

CRIVELLO: You'll ruin everything, sir. Be patient until he comes out.

FLAMMINIO: God himself couldn't make me patient at this moment.

CRIVELLO: You'll spoil the whole thing!

FLAMMINIO: Very well, I'll spoil it, then.

[FLAMMINIO *knocks at the door.*]

CLEMENZIA [*from above*]: Who's there?

FLAMMINIO: A friend of yours. Come down here for a minute.

CLEMENZIA: Oh! What do you want, Messer Flamminio?

FLAMMINIO: Open up, and I'll tell you.

CLEMENZIA: Wait a moment, and I'll come down.

FLAMMINIO [to CRIVELLO]: As soon as she opens the door, go straight inside and look for him; and if he's there, call out to me.

CRIVELLO: Leave it to me, sir.

CLEMENZIA [speaking through the closed door]: What is it, Signor Flamminio?

FLAMMINIO: What are you doing with my boy in there?

CLEMENZIA [appearing in the doorway]: What boy d'you mean? And where do you think you're going, Crivello? You've got a nerve! Are you trying to force your way into my house? [Pushing him back.]

FLAMMINIO: Clemenzia, I swear by the body of Christ that if you don't give him back to me . . .

CLEMENZIA: Give who back to you?

FLAMMINIO: My boy who's taken refuge in your house.

CLEMENZIA: There's no boy of yours in my house – though there might be a maid!

FLAMMINIO: Clemenzia, it's no time for those tricks. You and I have always been good friends; you've done things for me, and I've done things for you. Now this is something that means more to me than you'd think.

CLEMENZIA: The frenzy of love at work again, I suppose! Come on, now, Signor Flamminio! Give yourself time to cool down!

FLAMMINIO: Hand Fabio over to me!

CLEMENZIA: I will!

FLAMMINIO: That's all I want. Bring him down at once!

CLEMENZIA: Why, take it a bit more calmly! My word, if I were a girl again and happened to take your fancy, I'd be careful not to upset you! What's the news of Isabella?

FLAMMINIO: I'd like to see her dead in a ditch!

CLEMENZIA: Ah! But you don't mean it!

FLAMMINIO: And why shouldn't I mean it? She hasn't left me in much doubt about her feelings towards me!

CLEMENZIA: And why not? You young sparks! Whatever happens to you serves you right, because you're the most ungrateful creatures in the world.

FLAMMINIO: That's not something you should say to me. I might have any other vice proved against me, but not ingratitude. I hate it more than any man alive.

CLEMENZIA: I don't mean you. But there was a girl in this town who noticed that a young knight like yourself was paying attention to her, and she took such a liking to him that she'd eyes for no one else . . .

FLAMMINIO [*interrupting*]: Lucky man! Lucky, lucky man! I'll never be the hero of a story like that!

CLEMENZIA: . . . and then this poor lovelorn child was sent away from Modena by her father. When she had to go, she wept her eyes out, because she was afraid he'd forget her. And the very next thing he did was to go off after another girl, as if he'd never seen the first one in his life.

FLAMMINIO: He can't be a knight! He's a traitor!

CLEMENZIA: Listen; there's worse to come. A few months later the girl came back, and discovered that her man was in love with someone else, who didn't like him very much. And so, to try and help him, she left home, left her father, and put her honour at risk; she dressed up like a manservant and got herself a job in her lover's household.

FLAMMINIO: Did all this happen in Modena?

CLEMENZIA: Yes, it did; and you know both the people concerned.

FLAMMINIO: I'd rather be that lucky fellow than be Duke of Milan.

CLEMENZIA: Listen! This lover of hers didn't recognize her, and used her as a go-between to take messages to his new love. And the poor child did all that he asked, just to give him pleasure.

FLAMMINIO: What a splendid woman! What constancy in love! This is a story that might serve as an example to coming generations! Oh, why can't something like that happen to me?

CLEMENZIA: What would be the use? Even if it did happen to you, you wouldn't leave Isabella.

FLAMMINIO: I'd abandon anybody – I nearly said I'd abandon Christ – for a woman like that. Please, Clemenzia, tell me her name.

CLEMENZIA: Very well. But first of all I'd like you to tell me something. On your word of honour as a gentleman, tell me what you'd do about that poor girl if it *had* happened to you. When you found out what she'd done, would you send her away, would you kill her, or would you think she'd deserved a reward?

FLAMMINIO: I swear this to you by the holy light of the sun you see above us – may I never be able to hold my head up again among gentlemen and knights of my own degree, if it's not true that I'd take that girl for my wife, even if she were poor and ugly and of lowly birth, in preference to the daughter of the Duke of Ferrara.

CLEMENZIA: That's a big thing to swear – and you do swear it, don't you?

FLAMMINIO: I swear it; and I'd do it.

CLEMENZIA [to CRIVELLO]: You can witness that!

CRIVELLO: I heard what he said, and I know he'd do it.

CLEMENZIA: Good – now I can tell you who the girl is, and who the knight is too – Fabio! Fabio! Come down here; your master wants you.

FLAMMINIO: What do you think, Crivello? Do you think I should kill that traitor or not? He *is* a good servant.

CRIVELLO: Oh! I never really believed you'd do it. I knew what would happen. Come on, sir, pardon him! What's the use? That little frip Isabella never really liked you anyway.

FLAMMINIO: That's the truth.

[PASQUELLA *comes out of* GHERARDO's *house. She speaks over her shoulder to someone inside the building.*]

PASQUELLA: Leave it to me – I'll give her your message . . . yes, I understand it all right.

[LELIA, *dressed as a girl, appears in the doorway of* CLEMENZIA's *house.*]

CLEMENZIA: Here's your Fabio, Messer Flamminio! Look carefully – don't you recognize him? You seem very surprised! And can you see that faithful young woman I was telling you about, who was so constant to her love? Have a good look at her, and see whether you know her. Nothing to say now, Flamminio? Why's that? – The man who valued his lady's love at so low a price is yourself! And it's all true. Don't think you've been deceived in any way. You know very well whether I'm speaking the truth – And now keep the promise you made me, or be ready to meet me in trial by battle!

FLAMMINIO: Of all the deceitful tricks . . . this is the finest one that ever was seen! But how could I have been so blind as not to know her?

CRIVELLO [aside]: I've been the blindest of the lot – though I had my doubts, and several times I nearly did something about checking up on them. Damn it! What an ass I've been!

PASQUELLA: Clemenzia, Virginio's in our house, and he wants to see you there at once. His son Fabrizio has come home, and he's given him a wife, and you'll have to go home and put things in order for the reception, as there aren't any other women in his household to attend to it.

CLEMENZIA: Given him a wife? What wife? Who is she?

PASQUELLA: My master's daughter.

FLAMMINIO: What was that? Do you mean Gherardo Foiani's daughter Isabella, or someone else?

PASQUELLA: Someone else, did you say? No, no – it's Isabella herself – Slow and steady ne'er won fair lady, as they say, Signor Flamminio!

FLAMMINIO: But is this certain?

PASQUELLA: As certain as anything in the world. I was there when everything happened. I saw them exchange rings, and embrace, and kiss, and make a great fuss of each other. And before he gave her the ring, my mistress gave him . . . I forget what I was going to say.

FLAMMINIO: But how long ago did this happen?

PASQUELLA: Just now! Just now! And then they sent me running over here to give Clemenzia the news and tell her to come to our house.

CLEMENZIA: I'll be with them in a couple of moments, Pasquella. Run back and tell them so.

[FLAMMINIO *takes* LELIA's *hand.*]

LELIA: Oh God, how many precious blessings you've sent me all together! I could die of happiness!

PASQUELLA: Don't be long! I've got so much to do that it's a real misery. And now I've got to go and buy some things Isabella wants to make her look pretty. Oh! I forgot to mention that they wanted to know if Lelia was here with you. Gherardo's decided to make a match of it.

CLEMENZIA: Well, you can see she's here. But does her father really want to marry her off to that bloodless old spectre? He ought to be ashamed of himself!

PASQUELLA: You can't know my master very well. If you realized how full of life he is, you wouldn't talk like that.

CLEMENZIA: I'll take your word for it! I'm sure you've often tried him out.

PASQUELLA: No more than you have your old master. But I must go.
[*Exit* PASQUELLA.]

FLAMMINIO: Does her father intend to marry her to Gherardo?

CLEMENZIA: Yes, I'm afraid so. See what shocking luck the poor girl has!

FLAMMINIO: He'll never marry Lelia, if he lives to be a hundred, and I won't wish him as long life as that. What I see in this, Clemenzia, is the hand of God, who has shown his mercy to this noble young woman, and had pity on my soul, to save it from perdition. And so, dear Lelia, if this is to your liking, I'll have no other wife but you; and I swear to you, on my honour as a knight, that if I can't have you I'll never look at another woman.

LELIA: You're my master, Flamminio, and you know why I did all that I've done. This is the only thing I've ever wanted.

FLAMMINIO: You've left me in no doubt of that. But forgive me for the pain I gave you when I didn't know who you were – I repent of that most heartily and admit that I was in the wrong.

LELIA: You could never do anything, Signor Flamminio, which wouldn't be right in my eyes.

FLAMMINIO: Clemenzia, I can't bear to put this off to another day, in case some misfortune intervenes to spoil my happiness. I want to marry Lelia here and now, if she's happy to marry me.

LELIA: I am! I am!

CRIVELLO: Thank God that it's all turned out like this! Are you happy now, sir? I'm a notary, as it happens; and if you don't believe me, here's my certificate.

FLAMMINIO: Happy? I'm happier than I've ever been in my whole life!

CRIVELLO: Well, you can get married straight away, and go to bed as soon as you like. [FLAMMINIO *kisses* LELIA.] But I never told you you could do that, did I, sir?

CLEMENZIA: Now do you know what I think would be the best plan? You go into my house – I'll go and tell Virginio the whole story and take the silly smile off Gherardo's face.

FLAMMINIO: Yes, please do that – and don't forget to tell Isabella too.
[CLEMENZIA *crosses stage and goes into* GHERARDO's *house.*

LELIA, FLAMMINIO, CRIVELLO *go into* CLEMENZIA's *house.*
PASQUELLA *comes out of* GHERARDO's *house and looks round, just
as* GIGLIO *enters, Right. He catches sight of her.*]

GIGLIO: By the life of my King, there stand that old wretch Pasquella
who mock me and take my beads by deceit! How glad I am to find
her!

PASQUELLA: Damn that tiresome fellow! He would turn up now! To
hell with him and with all the other Spaniards who ever came over
to Italy! What excuse can I find this time?

GIGLIO: My lady Pasquella!

PASQUELLA: Well, that's something! He's called me a lady!

GIGLIO: Why you mock me, and take my rosary, and not do what
you promise?

PASQUELLA: Sh! Sh! Be quiet! Be quiet!

GIGLIO: Why? Is someone there who listen us?

PASQUELLA: Sh! Sh!

GIGLIO: I not see anyone here. You not deceive me again. What you
have to say?

PASQUELLA: Are you trying to ruin me?

GIGLIO: Are you trying to make fool of me?

PASQUELLA: Be off with you now, and leave me alone! I'll talk to
you some other time.

GIGLIO: You give my rosary and afterwards you talk what you like.
I not want that you can say that you make fool of me!

PASQUELLA: Oh, I'll give it to you later! Do you think I carry it with
me wherever I go? Do you think it means a lot to me, as if I
couldn't have all the paternosters I wanted?

GIGLIO: But why did you shut me outside and make the music and
talk about some ghostly spirit and some prayers and some other
tricks?

PASQUELLA: Talk quietly! Do you want to ruin me? I'll explain
everything. [*Pause.*]

GIGLIO: How you explain? Why you not begin?

PASQUELLA: Come over here so that my mistress won't be able to
see you.

GIGLIO: You try to deceive me again or not?

PASQUELLA: Deceive you, indeed! Do I look like a deceiver?

GIGLIO: Tell me quick what you have to say!

PASQUELLA: Listen, then! While we were talking together, my mistress crept downstairs and was standing round the corner and listening to every word we said. When I started to round up my hens, she went off indoors, but watched through a hole to see what we were doing. I saw what was happening, but I pretended not to know she was there. And I pretended I was cheating you; in fact I showed her the paternosters. And she took them away from me, thinking I'd made a fool of you, and had a good laugh about it, and wound them round her arm. But I'll get them back from her tonight and give them back to you, if you've changed your mind about wanting me to have them.

GIGLIO: But is all this true? Mind you not deceive!

PASQUELLA: Dear Giglio, if it isn't true, I wish I may never see you again! Do you think I don't value your friendship? But there, you Spaniards don't believe in Christ, let alone believing in anyone else!

GIGLIO: But now, why you not do what we had agreed?

PASQUELLA: My mistress got married today, and we're having a party tonight. I've got so much to do that I can't spend any more time with you now. You'll have to wait until another time. [*Aside*] Ugh, what a horrible lot these Spaniards are!

GIGLIO: Tomorrow, then? Tomorrow morning? All right?

PASQUELLA: Leave it to me – I'll remember you when the time comes. [*Aside*] Ugh! Ugh!! Ugh!!!

GIGLIO: I swear to God that I slash your face with the knife if you deceive again!

[*Exit* GIGLIO. PASQUELLA *goes back into* GHERARDO's *house, just as* CLEMENZIA *comes out of it.* CLEMENZIA *crosses to* VIRGINIO's *house, and goes in. Then* CLEMENZIA's *little daughter* CITTINA *comes out of her house, very agitated.*]

CITTINA: There seem to be spirits of some kind haunting that downstairs room! I can hear the bed moving about and rattling as if a ghost or something was shaking it. Oh, it's so frightening! Oh! I can hear one of them talking now. It sounds like a soul in pain, and it's speaking very softly. 'Oh! Oh! Not so hard! Not so hard!' it says. And now there's another voice. 'My life, my darling, sweet hope of my soul, my dearest wife!' it says. But I can't make out the rest of it – I'd like to knock, if I dared. Oh! Now one of them says,

'Wait for me!' I wonder where they're going? And the other says: 'I'll wait, but don't be long!' Oh! Oh! I believe they've broken that bed! It's going faster and faster! *I'm* not waiting for anybody – I'm going to run and tell my mother!

[CITTINA *runs across to* VIRGINIO'*s house in search of* CLEMENZIA *and goes inside.* ISABELLA *and* FABRIZIO *come out of* GHERARDO'*s house.*]

ISABELLA: I thought you were a young man that serves a knight who lives here in Modena. He's so like you that I'm sure he must be your brother.

[FABRIZIO *and* ISABELLA *move across towards* VIRGINIO'*s house.*]

FABRIZIO: Several other people have confused me with him today – even the inn keeper didn't seem sure who I was.

[CLEMENZIA *comes out of* VIRGINIO'*s house and walks across to meet* ISABELLA *and* FABRIZIO.]

ISABELLA: Here comes Clemenzia, your old nurse. She must want to see you.

CLEMENZIA: This must be him – he's so like Lelia! Fabrizio, my dear son, welcome home again! How are you?

FABRIZIO: I'm well, dear nurse. And what news have you of Lelia?

CLEMENZIA: Lelia's well, too. But come indoors – I've got all sorts of things I want to tell you!

[FABRIZIO, ISABELLA *go into* VIRGINIO'*s house.* VIRGINIO *comes out of* GHERARDO'*s front door and calls to* CLEMENZIA *before she can follow them in.*]

VIRGINIO: Clemenzia! [*She waits for him and they walk across towards her front door.*] I'm so pleased that my boy's come home that I don't mind about anything else that's happened.

CLEMENZIA: It must all have been the will of God. And isn't this better than marrying her off to that old broken reed Gherardo? But wait while I go inside and see how things are. When I left the bride and bridegroom just now they were so close that you couldn't have got a blade of grass between them – and they're all on their own in there. [*She goes inside for a few moments and comes out again.*] It's all right, you can come in now!

[CLEMENZIA, VIRGINIO *go into* CLEMENZIA'*s house.* STRAGUALCIA *lurches out of the inn and addresses the audience.*]

STRAGUALCIA: You'd better not wait for them to come out again, because that would make a long story even longer. If you'd like to have some dinner with us, we'll expect you at the 'Fool'. But bring some money with you, because it won't be on the house. If you don't want to come – and I doubt if you will – why, then, stay away and have a good time somewhere else. And now let's hear some applause from the Intronati.

# THE FAITHFUL SHEPHERD

*(Il Pastor Fido)*

*by*

GIAMBATTISTA GUARINI
*(1538–1612)*

# GIAMBATTISTA GUARINI

GIAMBATTISTA GUARINI (1538–1612), like Ariosto, was a courtier who served his prince in a number of different capacities – diplomatic and administrative as well as literary. Ferrara was both his birthplace and the scene of the greater part of his adult career, though he also served in the courts of Florence and Urbino.

The Italian pastoral had reached its highest point of formal perfection in Torquato Tasso's *Aminta* (1573), a lyrical drama of the utmost poetical beauty. Guarini was not such a great poet as Tasso, but when he came to write *The Faithful Shepherd* (1590), he successfully introduced a number of new features into the Arcadian scene – humour, wit, frank sensuality, realistic and sharply drawn characters, and a strongly constructed plot. He also had the luck to acquire the best English translator that any Italian poet has ever had, namely Sir Richard Fanshawe (1608–66).

Fanshawe's spelling and punctuation have been modernized for the present edition, and a total of eleven lines contain emendations designed to remove minor inaccuracies or obscurities. Otherwise the text follows that of the 1647 first edition of Fanshawe's translation.

There are two excellent modern critical editions of Fanshawe's translation of *The Faithful Shepherd* – one by William E. Simeone and Walter F. Staton, Jr, published by the Oxford University Press in 1964, and one by Professor J. H. Whitfield (with the Italian text in parallel), published by Edinburgh University Press in 1976.

# CHARACTERS

in order of appearance

SILVIO, Montano's son, engaged to Amarillis
LINCO, an old servant of Montano
MIRTILLO, in love with Amarillis
ERGASTO, Mirtillo's friend
CORISCA, a wanton nymph, in love with Mirtillo
MONTANO, the chief priest, Silvio's father
TITIRO, father of Amarillis
DAMETA, an old shepherd, employed by Montano
SATYR, in love with Corisca
DORINDA, in love with Silvio
LUPINO, a goatherd, employed by Dorinda
AMARILLIS, Titiro's daughter
NICANDRO, chief assistant to the priest
CORIDON, in love with Corisca
CARINO, Mirtillo's supposed father
URANIO, a friend of Carino
MESSENGER
TIRENIO, a blind prophet

CHORUS of ⎰ Shepherds
⎱ Huntsmen
⎱ Nymphs
⎰ Priests

# ACT ONE

*A woodland pasture in Arcadia. At Left Centre is the entrance to a cave,
by which stands a large boulder. A path leads offstage at Right Centre.
There are several clumps of bushes in the same area.*

[*Enter* SILVIO, LINCO, *Left, with huntsmen.*]

SIL: Go, you that lodged[1] the monster, as you are wont,
    Amongst the neighbouring sheepcotes raise the hunt!
    Rouse eyes and hearts with your shrill voice and horn!
    If ever in Arcadia there were born
    A shepherd who did follow Cynthia's[2] court
    As a true lover of her rural sport,
    Within whose quarry-scorning mind had place
    The pleasure or the glory of the chase,
    Now let him show that courage and that love,
    By following me, where in a little grove
    To valour a large field doth open lie,
    That dreadful boar, I mean, that prodigy
    Of Nature and the woods, that huge, that fell
    And noted'st tyrant that did ever dwell
    And reign in Erimanthus; the fields' mower,
    The mowers' terror. Go you then before,
    And do not only with your early horn
    Anticipate, but wake the drowsy morn!
    [*Exeunt* HUNTSMEN, *Left, sounding their horns.*]
    We, Linco, will to prayers. This perilous chase
    Heaven being our guide we may more boldly trace.
    That work which is begun well is half done,
    And without prayer no work is well begun.

      1. To 'lodge' a beast is to track it to its lair.
      2. Cynthia is another name for Diana, the goddess of hunting.

LIN: Thy worshipping the Gods I well commend,
But not thy troubling them who do attend
The Gods: the priests as yet are all asleep,
To whom day springs yet later, where the steep
Surrounding hills a short horizon make.

SIL: To thee whose heart is hardly yet awake
The whole world sleeps.

LIN:                          Oh, Silvio, Silvio,
Why did frank Nature upon thee bestow
Blossoms of beauty in thy prime, so sweet
And fair, for thee to trample under feet?
Had I thy fresh and blooming cheek, 'Adieu'
I'd say to beasts, and nobler game pursue.
The summer I would spend in feasts and mirth
In the cool shade, the winter by the hearth.

SIL: How's this? Thou art not Linco, sure, for he
Such counsel never used to give to me.

LIN: Counsel must change as the occasion doth;
If I were Silvio, so I'd do in sooth.

SIL: And I, if I were Linco, would do so,
But as I am, I'll do like Silvio.

LIN: Fond youth, for a wild beast so far to roam,
Whom thou must hunt with danger, when at home
One's safely lodged!

SIL:                     Dost thou speak seriously?
How near is it?

LIN:              As thou art now to me.

SIL: Thou art mad.

LIN:               Thou art.

SIL:                        In what wood doth he rest?

LIN: Silvio's the wood, and cruelty the beast.

SIL: Mad I was sure!

LIN:                 To have a nymph so fair
– Rather a goddess of perfections rare –
Fresher and sweeter than a rose new-blown,
Softer and whiter than an old swan's down,
For whom there lives not at this day a swain
So proud 'mongst us but sighs, and sighs in vain:

To have, I say, this matchless paragon
By Gods and men reserved for thee – nay, thrown
Into thy arms without one sigh or tear,
And thou (unworthy!) to disvalue her!
Art thou not then a beast? A savage one?
Rather a senseless clod, a stock, a stone!

SIL: If not to be in love be cruelty,
Then cruelty's a virtue; nor do I
Repent, but boast, I lodge him in my breast
By whom I've conquered love, the greater beast.

LIN: How could'st thou conquer, silly idiot,
Whom thou ne'er triedst?

SIL:                                   In that I tried him not.

LIN: Oh, had'st thou tried him, Silvio, and once found
In mutual lovers what true joys abound,
I know thou'dst say: 'Oh love, the sweetest guest,
Why hast thou been an alien to this breast?'
Leave, leave the woods, leave following beasts, fond boy,
And follow love!

SIL:                        Linco, I take more joy
In one beast caught by my Melampo, far,
Than in the love of all the nymphs that are.
Keep they those joys unto themselves alone
That find a soul in them, for I find none.

LIN: No soul in love, the world's great soul! But, fool,
Too soon (believe't) thou'lt find he is all soul;
Perchance too late, for he'll be sure before
We die to make us all once feel his power.
And take my word, worse torment none can prove
Than in old limbs the youthful itch of love.
All tampering then will but exasperate
The sore. If love a young man wound, he straight
Balms him again; hope holds up sorrow's head,
And smiles revive him, if frowns strike him dead.
But if an aged man those flames endure,
Whose own defects his own repulse procure,
Then, then the wound is insupportable
And mortal; then the anguish is a hell:

285

Then if he pity seek, it is a curse
To go without it, and to gain't a worse.
Ah! hasten not before the appointed day
The curse of days; for if when thou art grey
Thou learn to love, 'twill breed a double sense
Of thy youth's pride, and age's impotence.
Leave, leave the woods, leave following beasts, fond boy,
And follow love!

SIL:              As if there were no joy
But these chimeras in a lover's head
Of strange elysiums, by his fever bred!

LIN: Tell me if in this jolly month of May,
When earth is clad in all her best array,
Instead of bladed fields, brooks uncontrolled,
Green woods and painted meads, thou should'st behold
Bald fields and meads, brooks bound with ice, the pine,
The beech, the ash, the oak, the elm, the vine,
And poplar, like inverted skeletons
Stand desolate, rattling their naked bones –
Would'st thou not say, Nature is out of tune,
The world is sick, and like to die in June?
Now the same horror which thou would'st receive
From such a monstrous novelty, conceive
At thine own self. The all-disposing heaven
To every age hath proper humours given;
And as in old men love absurdly shows,
So young men enemies to love oppose
Nature and Heaven. Look, Silvio, round about,
Examine the whole universe throughout.
All that is fair or good, here or above,
Or is a lover, or the work of love.
The all-seeing heaven, the fruitful earth's a lover,
The sea with love is ready to boil over.
See'st thou yon star[3] of such excelling hue,
The sun's postillion? That's a lover too,
Nor is exempted from her own son's laws,
But feels that passion which her beauties cause.

3. The planet Venus.

286

Perchance this very hour she too did part
From her stol'n sweets and him that keeps her heart.
Mark what a wanton eye she has! In woods
Rough bears, the crook-back dolphin loves in floods,
And sluggish whales. That little bird which sings
So sweetly, and so nimbly plies the wings
Flying from tree to tree, from grove to grove,
If he could speak, would say, I am in love.
But his heart says it, and his tongue doth say't
In language understood by his dear mate.
And, Silvio, hark how from that wilderness
His dear mate answers, And I love no less.
The cows low in the valley; and what's this
But an inviting unto amorous bliss?
The lions roar in solitary groves
Not for their prey, but for their absent loves.
All things that are, but Silvio, are in love;
The burthen's that: here round us and above
No soul but Silvio is a foe to joy.
Leave, leave the woods, leave following beasts, fond boy,
And follow love!

SIL:               Had I my tender years
Committed to the care of thy gray hairs,
That thou shouldst thus effeminate my heart
With love? Knowst thou who I am? who thou art?

LIN: Thou art a man, or shouldst be one, and I
Another; what I teach, humanity.
And if thou scorn that name, which is my pride,
Take heed, instead of being deified,
Thou turn not beast.

SIL:               That monster-taming king,
From whom my lofty pedigree I bring,
Had never grown so valiant, nor so famed,
If first the monster love he had not tamed.

LIN: See, foolish youth, how idly thou talkst now!
Had great Alcides[4] been no lover, how

---

4. Another name for Hercules.

Hadst thou been born? Rather, if he o'ercame
Monsters and men, to love impute the same.
Knowst thou not yet that to comply with fair
Omphale's humour, he not only ware,
Instead of the fierce lion's rugged skin,
Women's soft robes, but taught those hands to spin,
And hold a feeble distaff, which did bear
The knotty club? His interludes were these
Between his acts; and when his ribs were beat
With dear-bought conquests, he would then retreat
Into her lap (the bay of sweet delight)
As in love's port to be new built for fight.
His sighs from his past toils sweet breathings were,
And spirits strengthening him new toils to bear.
For as the iron, of itself too rough,
And of a harsh unmalleable stuff,
Softened with fire and gentler metal, strength
From weakness gathers, and becomes at length
Fit for the noblest use, so hearts untamed,
Which their own stiffness often breaks, enflamed
With generous love, and with his sweets allayed,
Are clearer, apter for great actions made.
If thou art ambitious then to imitate
Great Hercules, and not degenerate
From thy high strain, since woods thou dost affect
Follow the woods, but do not love neglect:
I mean so lawful and so worthy love
As that of Amarillis. I approve
(So far from blaming that as cruelty)
Thy shunning of Dorinda, for in thee
Who standst upon thy blood, 'twere double shame
To scorch thy breast with an unlawful flame,
For injuring thy spouse.

SIL:                 What sayst thou, man?
She is not yet my spouse!

LIN:                 Was there not than
A promise solemnly received and given?
Take heed, proud boy, how thou provokest heaven!

SIL: Man's freedom is heaven's gift, which doth not take
   Us at our word when forcéd vows we make.
LIN: Ay, but (unless our hopes and judgements fail)
   Heaven made this match and promised to entail
   A thousand blessings on't.
SIL:               'Tis like that there
   Is nothing else to do; a proper care
   To vex the calm rest of the Gods above!
   Linco, I like not this, nor t'other love.
   I was a huntsman, not a lover bred;
   Thou who art all for love, go back to bed!
LIN: Thou sprung from Heaven, harsh boy? Nor of divine
   Can I suppose thee, nor of human line.
   Alecto's poison thy cold limbs did fashion;
   Sweet Venus had no hand in thy creation.
   [*Exeunt* SILVIO, LINCO, *Left. Enter* MIRTILLO, ERGASTO, *Right.*]
MIR: O Amarillis, authoress of my flame,
   Within my mouth how sweet now is thy name,
   But in my heart how bitter! Amarillis
   Fairer and whiter than the whitest lilies,
   But crueller than cruel adders far,
   Which having stung (lest they should pity) bar
   Their ears, and fly. If then by speaking I
   Offend thee, I will hold my peace and die.
   I'll hold my peace, but what will that do good
   If hills and dales roar for me, and this wood
   Which thy dear name can ne'er forget, from me
   So often heard, and carved on every tree?
   The winds shall sigh for me, the fountains shed
   Abundant tears, grief mourn and pity plead.
   Or couldst thou bribe whole Nature with a fee
   To silence, lastly Death shall speak for me;
   He'll thunder't out, and to the world proclaim
   I died a martyr in my true love's flame.
ERG: Mirtillo, love is a great pain at best,
   But more, by how much more it is suppressed.
   For as hot steeds run faster at the check,
   Than if you laid the reins upon their neck,

So love restrained augments, and fiercer grows
In a close prison, than when loose he goes.
Why hidst thou thy flame's cause so long from me
When the effect could not concealéd be?
Mirtillo burns, how often have I said,
But inward burns, and will not call for aid.
MIR: Courteous Ergasto, out of my respect
To her, alas, I did myself neglect;
Nor would my festering passion yet unfold,
But that necessity hath made me bold.
I hear a buzzing rumour everywhere,
Which to my heart finds passage through my ear,
That Amarillis shortly weds; nor dare
Ask more, less so I should my love declare,
Or prove my fear too true. Full well I know
(Nor hath love struck me blind) that in my low
And slender fortunes, it were simple pride
To hope a nymph so shaped, so qualified,
So raised in wealth, in spirit and in blood,
– Above all these, so gentle and so good –
Can e'er be mine. No, I have ta'en the height
Of my unhappy star; my sullen fate
Made me for fuel only, born to smother
In fires I cannot kindle in another.
Yet since Fate's pleased I should affect death more
Than life, at least I'd have her know before,
That she's beholding to me for my death,
And deign when I sigh out my latest breath
To cast her fair eyes on me and say: 'Die!'
This reasonable boon obtain would I,
That ere she go to make another blest
In having her, she'd hear me speak at least
But once, my dear Ergasto. Now if love
Or pity of me thy soft entrails move,
Procure me this, this physic only lend,
To make the passage easy to my end!
ERG: From one that loves, a just, from one that dies,
A small request; yet a hard enterprise.

Woe be to her, should her stern father hear
That to stol'n prayers she e'er had lent an ear;
Or if some baser pick-thank should disclose
It to the priest her father-in-law! Who knows
But out of these respects she may eschew
Thy company and yet affect thee too?
For women are more prone to love than men,
But to conceal't have more discretion then.
And if 'twere true that she did love thee, what
Could she do less than shun thee for all that?
She that wants power to help listens in vain,
And flies with pity, when her stay breeds pain.
And I have heard 'tis still the wisest course
To quit that soon which one must quit perforce.

MIR: Oh, were this true, and could I think it so,
Sweet were my pain, and fortunate my woe!
But dear Ergasto – hide it not from me,
So help thee Pan! – who may this bridegroom be,
So loved of all the stars?

ERG:                         Dost thou not know
(I'm sure thou dost) that famous Silvio,
Silvio the rich, the gallant and the fair,
The priest Montano's only son and heir?
'Tis he.

MIR:     Oh happy youth, whose joy appears
So ripe for harvest in his spring of years!
Pardon me, gentle swain, I envy not
Thy happiness, but mourn my own hard lot.

ERG: Indeed there is no reason to envy,
Rather to pity him.

MIR:                 To pity? Why?

ERG: Because he loves her not.

MIR:                           And hath he wit?
Hath he a heart? Is he not blind? And yet
When I consider with what full aspect
Her starry eyes their influence direct
Into my breast, she cannot have a dart
Left in her quiver for another heart.

But why do they a gem so precious throw
To one that knows it not, and scorns it so?
ERG: Because the heavens did through this marriage
  Unto Arcadia long ago presage
  Deliverance. Hast thou not heard that here
  Is paid to the great goddess every year
  Of a nymph's guiltless blood a cruel and
  Unconscionable tribute by this land?
MIR: 'Tis news to me; nor let that strange appear,
  Since I myself am but a stranger here,
  And since I came (by Fate's decree and Love's)
  Almost a constant burgess of the groves.
  But what strange crime deserved so sharp a doom?
  How could such monstrous cruelty find room
  In a celestial mind?
ERG:                Of me then know
  From the first head the torrent of our woe:
  A story that would tears of pity wrest
  From heart of oak, much more from human breast.
  Whilst yet the priesthood was not tied to age,
  A youthful swain of noble parentage,
  Then Dian's priest – Aminta was his name –
  The nymph Lucrina did with love inflame.
  All creatures of her sex exceeded she
  As much in beauty as unconstancy.
  She long requited, or at least to sight
  (If looks and eyes have tongues) she did requite
  The pure affection of the love-sick lad,
  And fed his hopes while he no rival had.
  But when a rustic swain her favour sought,
  (See now a perfect woman!) in a thought
  She left the former, with one sigh was shook,
  With the faint battery of one amorous look.
  Her heart's new guest now takes up all the room,
  Dislodged Aminta ere he knew for whom.
  Hapless Aminta! who from that day forth
  Was so abhorred, held of so little worth,
  By that ungrate whom he did still adore,

That she would neither see nor hear him more.
If this unkindness cut the wretch to the heart,
If he sighed, wept, and raved, to thee who art
Acquainted with love's pangs, I leave to guess.
MIR: Oh, 'twas a torment no man can express!
ERG: When then his tears and prayers he had cast
    After his heart, to Dian turned at last,
    'If ever with pure heart, Goddess,' quoth he,
    'And guiltless hand I kindled flame to thee,
    'Revenge my faith, which a perfidious maid
    'Under safe conduct of her smiles betrayed.'
    The Goddess (gentler than the nymph was) hears
    The faithful lover's and her servant's tears
    And prayers; and pity kindling her just ire,
    By opposition did augment the fire.
    Her powerful bow into her hand she took,
    And in Arcadia's wretched bosom stuck
    Arrows of death and catching pestilence
    Invisible, and therefore without fence.
    Without remorse they execute her rage,
    Without respect on every sex and age.
    Nor antidotes nor medicines here availed,
    Nor flying now; weak art her master failed:
    And oft, whilst he the remedy applied
    Before the patient the physician died.
    The only hope that's left is from the sky,
    So to the nearest oracle they fly,
    Which soon returned an answer clear enough,
    But above measure terrible and rough:
    *That Cynthia was incensed, but that the land*
    *Might be relieved, if by Aminta's hand*
    *That faithless nymph Lucrina, or some one*
    *For her, of the Arcadian nation*
    *Were as an offering to Diana slain.*
    So she, when long she had prayed, long wept in vain,
    And long expected her new lover's aid,
    To the holy altars like a bride arrayed,
    And with what pomp religion could devise,

Was led a miserable sacrifice.
Where at those feet from which hers fled so fast,
The feet of her idolater, at last
Bending her trembling knees, she did attend
From the offended youth a cruel end.
The sacred knife he boldly did unsheathe,
Rage and revenge his nostrils seemed to breathe,
His eyes to sparkle; turning then to her,
Said with a sigh (death's hollow messenger):
'Whom thou hast left, Lucrina, and whom took,
Learn by this blow.' And with that word he struck
Himself, and plunged the knife in his own breast
To the haft: in one both sacrifice and priest
Fell bleeding at her feet, whilst she, amazed
To see that dire unlooked for object, gazed
As one 'twixt life and death, nor yet did know
If grief had stabbed her, or the threatened blow.
But when she found her tongue again, and knew
Distinctly what was acted there, 'O true,
'O brave Aminta,' (bathing in a flood
Of tears) she said, 'O lover, understood
Too late! who by thy death dost give to me
Both life and death. If in forsaking thee
I sinned, lo, I redeem that sin of mine,
Wedding my soul eternally to thine.'
This said, that knife fresh reeking with the gore
Of the now loved in death, and purpled o'er,
She drew from his pale breast, and in her own
Sheathed it again; then willingly sank down
Into Aminta's arms, who yet had breath,
And felt perchance that lightning before death.
Such was this pair of lovers' tragic fall,
'Cause he kept too much faith, she none at all.

MIR: Oh, hapless swain! yet happy in his love,
    Having so rich occasion to approve
    His spotless faith, and dying to revive
    That spark in her he could not being alive!
    But what became then of the poor diseased?
    Did the plague cease? was Cynthia's wrath appeased?

ERG: It did relent, but was not quite put out:
For the same month (the year being wheeled about)
It burst out with more fury, and did make
A dire relapse. This forced us to betake
Ourselves unto the oracle again,
Which uttered now a sadder doom: *That then*
*And yearly, we to night's offended queen*
*A maid or wife should offer, past fifteen*
*And short of twenty; by which means the rage*
*Which swallowed thousands, one death should assuage.*
Moreover a hard law, and weighing well
The nature of that sex, impossible
To keep – a law in bloody letters writ
On wretched women was imposed by it:
*That whatsoever maid or wife should prove*
*In any sort a changeling in her love,*
*Unless some friend would pay the penalty*
*Instead of her, should without mercy die.*
This dire, this national calamity
The good old man hath hope to remedy
By means of this desiréd match; because
The oracle, after some little pause
Being asked again, what end our woe should have,
To our demand this punctual answer gave:
*Your woe shall end when two of race divine*
            *Love shall combine:*
*And for a faithless nymph's apostate state*
*A faithful shepherd supererogate.*[5]
Now there are left in all Arcadia
Of heavenly stock no other slips this day
But Silvio and Amarillis: she
From Pan descended, from Alcides he.
Nor had there ever, to our much regret,
Of those two lines a male and female met,
As now there do: whence the believing father
Great hopes of good not without cause doth gather.

---

5. 'Supererogate' means to make up by excess of merit for the failing of another. (Oxford English Dictionary.)

For though the things foretold by the oracle
Be not fulfilled yet in each particle,
This is the fundamental point; the rest
Is still reserved in Fate's own secret breast,
And of the marriage one day shall ensue.

MIR: And all this do, Mirtillo to undo?
What a long swing is fetched! What armies band
Against one heart half murdered to their hand!
Is't not enough that cruel love's my foe,
Unless fate too conspire my overthrow?

ERG: Alas, Mirtillo, grieving does no good,
Tears quench not love, but are his milk and food.
'Tshall scape me hard, but ere the sun descend
This cruel one shall hear thee. Courage, friend!
These sighs refresh not (as thou dost suppose)
Thy burning heart, but rather are like those
Impetuous winds which in a town on fire
The bellows are to blow and fan it higher:
Love's whirlwinds, bringing to poor lovers ever
Black clouds of grief, which showers of tears deliver.

[*Exeunt* MIRTILLO, ERGASTO, *Right. Enter* CORISCA, *Left.*]

COR: Who ever saw, what heart did ever prove
So strange, fond, impotent a passion? Love,
And cold disdain (a miracle to me
Two contraries should in one subject be
Both in extremes!) I know not how, each other
Destroy and generate, inflame and smother.
When I behold Mirtillo's every grace,
From his neat foot to his bewitching face,
His unaffected carriage, sweet aspect,
Words, actions, looks and manners, they eject
Such flames of love, that every passion
Besides seems to be conquered by this one.
But when I think how dotingly he prizes
Another woman, and for her despises
My almost peerless face (although I say't)
On which a thousand eyes for alms do wait,
Then do I scorn, abhor, and loathe him more

Then ever I did value him before,
And scarce can think it possible that he
Had ever any interest for me.
Oh, if my sweet Mirtillo were mine own,
So that I had him to myself alone
(These are my thoughts sometimes) no mortal wight
More bliss could boast of than Corisca might!
And then I feel such kindly flames, so sweet
A vapour rise, that I could almost meet
His love halfway; yea, follow him, adore
His very steps, and aid from him implore:
Nay, I do love him so, I could expire
His sacrifice in such a pleasing fire.
Then I'm myself again; and 'What!' say I,
'A proud disdainful boy! One that doth fly
From me and love another! that can look
Upon this face of mine, and not be struck,
But guard himself so well as not to die
For love! Shall I, that should behold him lie
Trembling and weeping at these feet of mine
(As many better men have done) incline
Trembling and weeping at *his* feet? Oh, no!
And with this thought into such rage I grow
Against myself, and him, that sounding straight
Unto my eyes and fancy a retreat,
Mirtillo's name worser than death I seem
To hate, and mine own self for loving him;
Whom I would see the miserablest swain,
The most despised thing that doth remain
Upon the earth; and if I had my will,
With my own hands I could the villain kill.
Thus like two seas encountering, hate and love,
Desire and scorn in me dire battle move:
And I (the flame of thousand hearts, the rack
Of thousand souls) languish, and burn, and lack
That pity I denied to others. I
Who have in cities oft been courted by
Gallants and wits, to whom great lords have bent,

And yet withstood volleys of compliment,
Squadrons of lovers, jeered their idle fires,
And with false hopes deluded their desires;
And now enforced to a rustic swain to yield!
In single fight to a fellow that's unskilled!
O thou most wretched of all womankind
Corisca! Where couldst thou diversion find
Hadst thou no other lover? How assuage,
Or by what means deceive thy amorous rage?
Learn women all from me this housewifery:
Make you conserve of lovers to keep by.
Had I no sweetheart but this sullen boy,
Were I not well provided of a joy?
To extreme want how likely to be hurled
Is that ill housewife, who in all the world
But one love only, but one servant hath?
Corisca will be no such fool. What's faith?
What's constancy? Tales which the jealous feign
To awe fond girls – names as absurd as vain.
Faith in a woman (if at least there be
Faith in a woman unrevealed to me)
Is not a virtue, nor a heavenly grace,
But the sad penance of a ruined face,
That's pleased with one, 'cause it can please no more;
A handsome woman sought unto by store
Of gallant youths, if pleased with one alone
No woman is, or is a foolish one.
What's beauty, tell me, if not viewed? or viewed,
If not pursued? or if pursued, pursued
By one alone? Where lovers frequent are,
It is a sign the party loved is rare,
Glorious and bright. A woman's honour is
To have many servants: courtly dames know this,
Who live in towns, and those most practice it
Who have most wealth, most beauty, and most wit.
'Tis clownishness, they say, to reject any,
And folly too, since that's performed by many,
One cannot do: one officer to wait,

A second to present,[6] a third to prate,
A fourth for somewhat else; so it doth fall
Out oft, that favours being general
No favours seem: or jealousy thus thrown
To whet them, all are easier kept than one.
This merry life is by great ladies led
In towns, and 'twas my fortune to be bred
With one of them, by whose example first,
Next by her rules, I in love's art was nurst
Up from my childhood; she would often say:
'Corisca, thou must use another day
'Thy lovers like thy garments – put on one,
'Have many, often shift, and wear out none.
'For daily conversation breeds distaste,
'Distaste contempt, and loathing at the last.
'Then get the start, let not the servant say
'He's turned his mistress, not she him, away.'
And I have kept her rules: I've choice, and strive
To please them all: to this my hand I give,
And wink on him; the handsom'st I admit
Into my bosom; but not one shall get
Into my heart: and yet (I know not how)
Ay me! Mirtillo's crept too near it now.
He made me sigh – not sigh as heretofore,
To give false fire, but true flames to deplore,
Robbing my limbs of rest, my eyes of sleep,
Even I can watch till the grey morning peep
(The discontented lover's truce); even I
(Strange change!) to melancholy walks can fly;
And through the gloomy horrors of this grove
Trace the sweet footsteps of my hated love.
What wilt thou do, Corisca? Sue? My hate
Permits not this, nor stands it with my state.
Wilt thou then fly him? That would show more brains,
But love says no to that. What then remains?
First I will try allurements, and discover
The love to him, but will conceal the lover.

6. Give presents.

I'll use deceits, if that avail me not;
And if those fail me too, my brain shall plot
A brave revenge; Mirtillo shall partake
Hate, if he spurn at love, and I will make
His Amarillis rue that she was e'er
A rival unto me, to him so dear.
Last I will teach you both what 'tis to move
A woman to abhor where she did love.

[*Exit* CORISCA, *Right Centre. Enter* TITIRO, MONTANO,
DAMETA, *Right.*]

TIT: I speak, Montano, what I know is true,
And speak to one who knows more than I do.
Your oracles are still obscurer far
Than we imagine; and their answers are
Like knives, which if they warily be caught
By that safe part which for the hand was wrought,
Are useful; but if rashly they be ta'en
By the edge or point, one may be hurt or slain.
That Amarillis, as thou argu'st should
By heaven be destined for the general good
And safety of Arcadia, who should rather
Desire and joy, than I who am her father?
But when I mark the words of the oracle,
Methinks with those the signs agree not well.
If love must join them, and the one doth fly,
How can that be? How can the strings which tie
The true-love's knot be hatred and disdain?
That cannot be opposed which heavens ordain:
Since then we see such opposition here,
That heavens did not ordain it is most clear.
Had they been pleased that Silvio should have had
My Amarillis, they would him have made
A lover, not a huntsman.

MON:                              Dost not see,
He's young, not yet eighteen? In time e'en he
Will feel the dart of love.

TIT:                              A dog hath got
His love; I know not why a nymph should not.

300

MON: Youths are inclinéd more to recreation.

TIT: And is not love a natural inclination?

MON: Before the time 'tis an unnatural thing.

TIT: Love is a blossom which adorns our spring.

MON: Your forward blossoms seldom come to good.

TIT: They seldom fail where frosts nip not the bud.
But came I hither to dispute with thee,
Montano? I nor can, nor fits it me.
Yet I'm a father too of a most dear
And only child; and (if love do not blear
My eyes) a worthy one; such (under favour)
That many wooed me, and still do, to have her.

MON: Were not this marriage made in heaven by fate,
'Tis made in earth by faith, to violate
Which, Titiro, were rashly to profane
The godhead of great Cynthia, in whose fane
The solemn oath was taken. Now how ready
She is to wrath, and how incensed already
Against this country, thou art not to learn.
But I profess, as far as I discern,
And a priest's mind rapt up above the sky,
Into the eternal councils there can pry,
This knot by the hand of destiny was knit,
And all those signs which should accompany it
(Have thou but faith) will fall out jump and right
In their due time. I'll tell thee more; this night
I in my dream a certain thing have viewed,
Which my old hopes hath more than e'er renewed.

TIT: Dreams are but dreams: but well, what didst thou view?

MON: Thou dost remember, I presume (for who
Amongst us all is such a stupid wight
As to forget?) that lamentable night,
When swelling Ladon, weary of his yoke,
The bank with his rebellious waters broke;
So that where birds were wont to build their nests
Usurping fishes swam; and men and beasts
And flocks and herds, promiscuously ta'en,
The impartial deluge swept into the main.

That very night (O bitter memory!)
I lost my heart, or rather that which I
More dearly prized, a child, a tender one
In swathing bands, and then my only son.
Both then and since (though he be dead) as dear
To me, as if my only son he were.
The cruel torrent ravished him away
Before the people of the house, who lay
In darkness, fear, and sleep buried alive,
With any timely succour could arrive.
We could not find the empty cradle neither,
But, as I guess, that and the child together,
Were swallowed by the flood.

TIT:                                    What else can be
  Supposed? I think I've heard – perchance from thee –
  This loss of thine before; in very truth,
  A miserable one, and full of ruth.
  And I may say, of thy two sons the floods
  Have swallowed one, the other's lost in the woods.

MON: Perhaps kind heavens in the surviving brother
  Will make me rich amends yet for the other:
  'Tis always good to hope. Now list me out:
  'Twas at the dawning of the morn, about
  That mongrel hour which gotten betwixt night
  And day is half an Ethiop and half white,
  When having watched out all the night almost,
  With various fancies of this marriage tost,
  Quite overcome at length with weariness,
  A gentle slumber did mine eyes oppress,
  Which with it such a lively vision brought,
  That though I slept I was awake. Methought
  On famed Alfeo's bank I angling sate
  Under a shady beech. There came up straight
  A grave old man, down to the middle bare,
  His chin all dropping, and his grizzled hair,
  Who with both hands, and countenance benign,
  Put a nak'd weeping infant into mine,
  Saying: 'Lo here thy son, and take good heed

Thou kill him not' – then dived into the reed.
With that, black clouds obscured the heavens round,
And threatening me with a dire tempest, frowned.
I to my bosom clapped the babe for fear,
And cried: 'Shall then one hour both give and bear
Away my joy?' Straight all the welkin turned
Serene, and thunderbolts to ashes burned
Fell hissing in the river, with bows broken
And shafts by thousands, signs which did betoken
Extinguished vengeance; then a shrill voice brake
From the riv'd beech, which in his tongue thus spake:
'*Believe, Montano, and thy hope still nourish,*
*Thy fair Arcadia once again shall flourish.*'
So ever since, in my eyes, mind and breast
The pleasing figure of this dream's impressed,
Standing before me still in every place;
But above all, the courteous mien and face
Of that old man – methinks I see him yet –
Which made me coming now, when thee I met,
Directly to the temple, there with pure
And holy sacrifice my dream to insure.

TIT: Truly, Montano, dreams are histories
Of what is past, rather than prophecies
Of what's to come – mere fragments of some sight
Or thought of the past day, which prints at night
A vain reflection of itself, like those
Which in a cloud the sun opposed shows.

MON: Not always with the senses sleeps the soul;
Rather when she is free from all control
Of cozening forms, which do the senses blind,
Whilst they're asleep, more wakeful is the mind.

TIT: In short, how heavens have destined to dispose
Of our two children, neither of us knows.
But this is clear to both of us: thine flies
And against nature's laws doth love's despise.
And mine, as't proves, is tied; herself yet hath
No benefit of her engagéd faith.
Nor do I know whether she love or no;

That she makes others love, full well I know,
And can I think it probable that she
Should others wound, and go herself still free?
Methinks of late she's altered in her cheer,
Who used all mirth and jollity to appear.
But to put maids in mind of marrying,
And then not marry them, is an ill thing.
As in a curious garden a fair rose,
(Which cloistered up in leaves did late repose,
Under the sable canopy of night,
Upon its mother stalk) with the first light
Raises its head, then opes its tender eye,
Whence whispering bees suck nectar as they fly;
Then to the sun, which on its form doth gaze,
Its purple and perfuméd breast displays;
But if it be not gathered then, and stay
Till it be kissed by the meridian ray,
Before the sun to the other world be fled,
Upon its mourning stalk it hangs the head;
So pale, so shrunk, so without life it shows,
That one can hardly say: 'This was a rose.'
So a young virgin, whilst her mother's care
Shuts and preserves her from the blasting air,
Shuts her own bosom too against desire;
But if she find some amorous youth to eye her,
And hears him sigh, she opes him straight her heart,
And in her tender breast receives love's dart.
Then if by fear, or else by maiden shame,
She be withheld from showing of her flame,
Poor soul! Concealment like a worm in the bud
Lies in her damask cheek sucking the blood:
So all her beauty's gone, if that fire last,
And all her lovers, when her beauty's past.
MON: Take courage, Titiro; do not embase
Thy soul with mortal fears, but nobly place
Thy hopes above. Heaven favours a strong faith,
And a faint prayer ne'er clomb that arduous path.
And if all men should pray to heaven at need,

And pray with hope, much more should heaven's own seed.
Our children's pedigree it is divine,
And heaven, that shines on all, will surely shine
On its own progeny. Come, Titiro,
Together to the temple let us go,
Together offer, thou a he-goat there
To Pan, and I to Hercules a steer.
The gods, who bless the herds, will bless no less
Them who the gods do with those blessings bless.
Trusty Dameta! Go and quickly cull
From my fair herd the best and gentlest bull,
And bring him to me to the temple straight;
Come by the hill – the nearest way is that.

TIT: And, good Dameta, from my herd bring one
Of the best goats.

DAM:            Both shall with speed be done.
May the high gods pleased in their goodness be
To bless, Montano, this thy dream to thee,
Even to thy utmost wish; this memory
Of thy lost son is a good augury.

> [*Exeunt* MONTANO, TITIRO, DAMETA, *Right. Enter* SATYR,
> *Left.*]

SAT: As frosts to plants, to ripened ears a storm,
To flowers the midday sun, to seed the worm,
To stags the toils, to birds the lime-twig, so
Is love to man an everlasting foe.
And he that called it fire pierced well into
Its treacherous nature; for if fire thou view,
How bright and beautiful it is! Approached,
How warm and comfortable! But then touched,
Oh how it burns! The monster-bearing earth
Did never teem such a prodigious birth.
It cuts like razors, like wild beasts devours,
And through a wood like winged lightning scours.
Where e'er it fixes its imperious foot,
Cottage and palace, all must yield unto't.
So love, if thou behold it in a pair
Of starry eyes, in a bright tress of hair,

How temptingly it looks! What kindly flames
It breathes! What peace, what pardons it proclaims!
But in thy bosom if thou do it keep,
So that it gather strength, and 'gin to creep,
No tigress in Hyrcanian mountains nursed,
No Libyan lioness is half so cursed,
Nor frozen snake fostered with human breath.
His flames are hot as hell, bonds strong as death;
He is wrath's hangman, pity's enemy,
And to conclude, love void of love. But why
Accuse I him? Is he the author then
Of all those pranks which mortal wights, not when
They are in love, but out of their wits, do?
Women, perfidious women, 'tis to you
That I impute love's rancour; all that's naught
In him from you is by infection caught.
He of himself is good, meek as the dove
That draws the chariot of the queen of love;
But you have made him wild, for though ye joy
With your own hands to feed the winged boy,
Yet you do shut each pore so of your breast
That in your hearts he cannot build his nest.
And all your care, pride, pleasure ye do place
In the mere outside of a simpering face.
Nor is't your study how to pay true love,
And wager whether shall more constant prove;
To bind two souls in one, and of one heart
To make the other but the counterpart;
But how your silver hair with gold to hatch,
Then purse it up into a net, to catch
Poor souls withal, and like gold valance let
Some curls hang dangling o'er your brows of jet.
How much against my stomach doth it go
To see you paint your cheeks, to cover so
The faults of time and nature! How ye make
Pale feulemort[7] a pure vermilion take,

7. 'Of the colour of a dead or faded leaf, brown or yellowish brown'
according to the *Oxford English Dictionary*.

Fill up the wrinkles, dye black white, a spot
With a spot hide where 'tis, make't where 'tis not.
You tie a thread across, whereof one end
Held in your teeth, the other is sustained
By your left hand, whilst of the running knot
Your right hand makes a noose to ope and shut
Like shaving tongs. This instrument you fit
To your rough downy foreheads, and with it
Shave all the down, and the wild hairs which shoot
Above their fellows, pull up by the root;
And all the while such torment you are in,
That 'tis at once a penance and a sin.
Nor is this all; your qualities are much
After your faces, and your faith is such
As are your works. For what is there in you
That is not counterfeit and painted too?
Do your lips ope? Before ye speak, ye lie
And if ye sigh, ye lie most damnably.
False lights your eyes are, and false weights your ears,
Your hearts false measures, and false pearl your tears;
So look, or talk, or think, or laugh, or cry,
Seem or seem not, walk, stand, or sit, ye lie.
Nay, there's more yet, your cozening those
Most who on you do most repose;
Your loving most those who do least love you,
And choosing to die rather than be true.
These are the arts, these are the ways
That make love hateful in our days.
All his faults then we may most justly lay
On you, or rather on ourselves, for they
Sin that believe you. Then the fault's in me,
Perjured Corisca, who did credit thee,
Come hither only for my bane, I think,
From Argos' wicked streets, of vice the sink.
Yet thou'rt so sly, and play'st so well the scout,
To keep thy deeds and thoughts from tracing out,
That 'mongst the chastest dames thou jett'st it now,
With honesty stamped on thy haughty brow.

What scorns have I received, what discontent
From this ungrateful woman! I repent,
Yea, blush I was so fond. Example take
By me, unskilful lovers, how ye make
An idol of a face – and take't for granted,
There's no such devil as a woman sainted.
She thinks her wit and beauty without peer,
And o'er thy slavish soul doth domineer
Like some great goddess, counting thou wert born
(As a thing mortal) only for her scorn;
Takes all that praise as tribute of her merit
Which is the flattery of thy abject spirit.
Why so much serving? So much admirations?
Such sighs, such tears, such humble supplications?
These are the woman's arms; let us express
Even in our loves valour and manliness.
Time was when I (as lusty as I am)
Thought tears and sighs could woman's heart inflame.
But now I find I erred; for if she bears
A stony heart, in vain are sighs and tears.
We must strike fire out of her breast by dint
Of steel; what fool used bellows to a flint?
Leave, leave thy tears and sighs, if thou would'st make
A conquest of thy dame; and if thou bake
Indeed with unextinguishable fire,
In thy heart's centre smother thy desire
The best thou canst, and watch thy time to do
That which both love and nature prompt thee to.
For modesty's the charter of the woman,
Who will not have her privilege made common;
Nor though she uses it herself with men
Would she have them to use't with her again,
Being a virtue for the admiration
Of them that court her, not their imitation.
This is the plain and natural way of love,
Indeed the only one that I approve.
My coy Corisca shall not find of me
A bashful lover, as I used to be,

But a bold foe, and she shall feel I can
Assault her with the weapons of a man,
As well as with the woman's arms. Twice now
I've caught this eel, and yet I know not how
She hath slipped through my hands; but if she come
A third time near my boat, I'll strike so home
Through both her gills, that I shall mar her flight.
Here comes she forth to pasture every night,
And I like a good hound snuff round about
To find her track. If I do scent her out,
Have at her coat![8] Oh how I mean to be
Revenged upon her! I will make her see
That love sometimes, though he appear stark blind,
Can from his eyes the handkerchief unbind,
And that no woman (though she may awhile)
Can glory long in perjury and guile.

[*Exit* SATYR, *Left. Enter* CHORUS, *Right.*]

CHO: O powerful law, which heaven or nature
    Writ in the heart of every creature!
    Whose amiable violence
    And pleasing rapture of the sense
    Doth bias all things to that good
    Which we desire not understood.
    Nor the exterior bark alone
    Subject to th' sense of everyone,
    Whose frail materials quickly must
    Resolve again into their dust;
    But the hid seeds and inward cause
    Whose substance is eternal, moves and draws.
    And if the ever-teeming world bring forth
    So many things of admirable worth,
    If whatsoever heaven's great eyes
    The sun and moon, or his small spies
    The stars, behold, doth own a soul
    Whose active power informs the whole;
    If thence all human seed have birth,
    All plants and animals; if th'earth

8. Skirt.

Be green, or on her wrinkled brow it snows,
From that immortal and pure spring it flows.
  Nor this alone: on mortal crown
Whatever restless spheres roll down;
Whence all our actions guided are
By a happy or unhappy star;
Whence our frail lives their cue receive
This stage to enter, and to leave;
Whatever thwarts, whatever stills
Our froward and our childish wills
– Which seeming to be fortune's play,
To give, and take our things away,
The world ascribes to her – hath all
From that high virtue its original.

  Soul of the world! if it were thou didst say
Arcadia should have rest and peace one day,
And like a snake renew her youth,
What man dares question so divine a truth?
If what the famous oracle
Of two whom fate should couple did foretell
It spake but as thy mouth – if fixed it be
In the eternal depth of thy decree,
And if the tripods do not falsehoods vent,
Ah! who retards thy will's accomplishment?
Behold, a scornful boy, a foe
To love and beauty: he (although
Extract from heaven) with heaven contends!
Behold another youth offends
In love as much, in vain deserving
To be preferred for humbly serving,
And with his flame thwarts thy decree!
And the less hope he hath to see
His service and his true love's hire,
The clearer burns his faith and fire;
And he now for that beauty dies,
Which t'other (whom 'tis kept for) doth despise.

  Is Jove divided then about his doom?
Hath doubtful fate twins struggling in her womb?

Or doth man's mountain hope, unlevelled yet,
New impious giants in rebellion set
On both sides to assault the tower of Jove,
By loving, and by shunning love?
Have we such strength? and o'er the powers above
Shall two blind powers triumph, disdain and love?
   But thou high mover of the orb, that rid'st
The stars and fate, and with thy wisdom guid'st
Their course, look down upon our tottering state,
And reconcile disdain and love with fate!
That ice, this flame, thaw, quench with heavenly dew,
Make one not fly, another not pursue.
Ah! let not two men's obstinacy stand
Betwixt thy promised mercy and a land!
   And yet, who knows? What we imagine is
Our greatest cross may prove our greatest bliss.
If on the sun no human eye can gaze,
Who then can pierce into Jove's hidden ways?

# ACT TWO

*Scene as before.*

[*Enter* MIRTILLO, *Right,* ERGASTO, *Right Centre.*]

ERG: Oh, what a walk have I had! At the race,
    The mead, hill, river, fountain, wrestling place
    I've been to seek thee; heaven be praised, at last
    I've found thee here.

MIR:                          What news requires such haste?
    Bringst thou me life or death?

ERG:                                  The last's a thing
    Which if I had for thee, I would not bring:
    The former, though I have not for thee yet,
    I hope to bring. But why art thou o'erset
    With thy own sighs? If thou would'st overcome
    Another, overcome thyself at home;
    Take heart, take breath again! – But to proceed
    To that which made me seek thee with such speed;
    The matter's this: Know'st thou – who doth not know? –
    Ormino's sister? Rather tall than low
    She is of stature, cherry-cheeked, her hair
    Inclined to red, and of a sprightly air.

MIR: What is her name?

ERG:                      Corisca.

MIR:                                  Yes, I do
    Know her, and have converséd with her too.

ERG: Know then that she (see the good luck on't! What
    Hath been the means to work it I know not,
    Or on whose score it comes) is grown of late
    With Amarillis very intimate;
    Which I perceiving, a relation made
    Of thy affection unto her, and prayed

Both her assistance and her secrecy
Therein, which she accorded readily.
MIR: O blest a thousand thousand times and more
Than all, Mirtillo, that e'er loved before,
If this be true! But, prithee, did she say
Nothing at all unto thee of the way?
ERG: Nothing as yet, and I will tell thee why:
Corisca said she could not certainly
Determine of the way till she might know
Some circumstances of thy love, that so
She might be better able to discern
The inclination of the nymph, and learn
How to address herself, with subtlety
Or with entreaties – what 'twere best to try,
Or what to leave. This was the cause made me
To come so hastily in search of thee.
Therefore from first to last thou shalt do well
Thy love's whole story unto me to tell.
MIR: I'll do it. But know, friend, to stir again
The bitter memory of love in vain,
Is like the tossing of a torch about
One's head in the air, thinking to shake it out,
When agitation kindles it, and makes
The flame cling faster to the melting wax.
Or like the tugging of a deep-fixt dart,
By which the wound's made greater, and the smart.
Most true it is, I shall a tale relate
Which will demonstrate the unsure estate
Of lovers' hopes, and that howe'er the root
Of love be sweet, it bears a bitter fruit.
    In that fair season when day's wheels outrun
The night's ('twas just a twelvemonth hence) this sun
Of beauty, this fair pilgrim came to bring
With her approach as 'twere a second spring
To my then only rich and happy nest,
Elis and Pisa with her presence blest;
Brought by her mother in those solemn days
When sacrifices and Olympic plays

Through all the world so famous are kept there
In honour of the mighty Thunderer.
Shows worthy sure of those fair eyes; but those
Fair eyes themselves were far the worthiest shows.
Whence I, who till that instant never knew
What flames of love did mean, at the first view
Of those bright lamps, yielded and never fought
One stroke against her; for I felt, methought,
Two fiery balls fly whizzing through my liver,
And beauty (a bold thief) cried 'Stand, deliver
Thy heart, Mirtillo.'

ERG:                              O, love's piercing steel
Which they alone can understand that feel!

MIR: But now to see what cunning love suggests
Even to the youngest and the simplest breasts!
I made a dear young sister of my own,
Who was my cruel nymph's companion
Whilst she in Elis and in Pisa stayed,
Acquainted with my pain. This silly maid
Was all the counsel love allotted me
For managing my amorous business. She
With her own garments decks me in great order
And imps my short hair with a borrowed border,
Then braids it all with flowers, hanging a bow
And quiver by my side, and last doth show
How I should frame my words and countenance, where
No traces of a beard did then appear.
The hour approachéd, she conducted me
Where my nymph used to play; and there found we
Some noble Megarensian maids, whom blood
And love linked to her, as I understood.
'Mongst them was she like royal rose 'mongst low-
Born violets; and when as they had so
For a good space without more pastime stayed,
A Megarensian virgin rose and said:
'What, at a time for pastime so renowned
Shall we without our sports be idle found?
And have not (sisters) we our weapons then

To make mock fights withal as well as men?
By my advice we'll practice our arms now
Against ourselves in jest, as we must do
In earnest one day against men – let's kiss,
And wage a kissing war; and she that gives
The best and savourest one shall have for meed
This curious wreath.' All laughed, and cried; 'Agreed!'
Forthwith, not staying for the word or sign,
These eager Amazons in battle join.
No ranks they kept, no colours knew, nor side,
But all confuséd, and each each defied.
The Megarensian, this perceiving, straight
To the disordered troops sounds a retreat,
And after saith, 'Let her deservedly
The judge of all our kisses be,
Whose mouth is fairest.' With one voice
Of peerless Amarillis they made choice.
She sweetly bending her fair eyes,
Her cheeks in modest blushes dyes,
To shew through her transparent skin
That she is no less fair within
Than she's without; or else her countenance
Envying the honour done her mouth perchance,
Puts on her scarlet robes, as who
Should say, 'And am not I fair too?'
ERG: Blest man to be transformed at such a time,
    As if this accident thou couldst divine!
MIR: The fair judge takes her seat, and now renews
    The amorous fight, according to the use
    Of war; by lots they march up one by one,
    To try their mouths by hers – the paragon
    Of sweetness, or, as I may term it well,
    Of orient pearls a perfumed Indian shell,
    And the two lips a two-leaved coral door
    With honeyed lock, to ope and shut with more
    Facility upon the pearly treasure.
    Oh, my Ergast, that I could tell the pleasure
    Of those sweet kisses! But do thou hence guess it,

That mouth which tasted it, cannot express it.
Extract then all the sweetness which remains
In Hybla-combs, in Cyprian sugar-canes,
It will be nothing to that world of blisses
I sucked from thence.

ERG:           O happy theft! Sweet kisses!

MIR: Sweet, but yet lame; the better half was missing,
The soul which gives perfection to kissing;
For though love gave them, love restored them not.

ERG: But hadst thou not some fear when 'twas thy lot
To kiss?

MIR:      My heart, Ergasto, to say true,
Was at my mouth, and my soul shrunk into
A narrow volume; 'twas one kiss, whence all
My limbs stood tottering like an ill-propped wall.
And when I came under the battery,
And within aim of her sure killing eye,
I feared the majesty of that bright look,
Lest in the very act I should be took
Of theft and guile which I was then about.
But straight her countenance clearing me that doubt
By a serene and unsuspecting smile,
I ventured boldly on. Love stood the while,
Ergasto, like a bee hid in the leaves
Of her lips' roses; and whilst she receives
The kisses of my mouth with hers unmoved
And passive, I the honey only proved.
But when she likewise active grows,
And thrusts out this and t'other rose,
(Whether her gaiety of heart it was,
Or my good luck, for 'twas not love, alas!)
When our two mouths snapped like a bone well set,
And like two tallies that are brothers met,
(Oh my dear sweet and numerous treasure –
Do I outlive so great a pleasure?)
Then, then, I felt the sharp sweet dart,
The amorous sting piercing my heart;
Which was, it seems, restored me then,
That I might have it hurt again.

I then, as soon as I had found
Her lips had given me my death's wound,
Was ready, like some desperate gasping wight,
The weapon which had wounded me to bite:
When suddenly her sweet breath, like the blast
Of an inspiring deity, did cast
A holy damp upon my saucy blood,
Which all immodest and wild heat withstood.
ERG: Oh, modesty, the block and remora[9]
Which ever lies in the true lovers' way!
MIR: Now all of them had had their turns, and come
With thoughts suspended to attend the doom;
When Amarillis, judging mine to exceed
All th' others' kisses, placed the victor's meed
(That curious wreath) with her own snowy hand
Upon my head. But oh! no Libyan sand
Beneath the Sirian[10] dog e'er broiled so much
When he both barks and bites, his rage is such,
As my whole heart was then on fire
Betwixt fruition and desire.
And (being never conquered half so much
As when I was a conqueror) such
My boldness was, that from my head
I reached the wreath to her, and said:
'This is thy due, for thee 'tis meet
Who with thy mouth hast made my kisses sweet.'
And she most courteously accepting it,
For her fair hair made it a coronet,
And crowned mine with another, which before
Upon her own divine temples she wore;
Which is the same I now do bear, and shall
(Heaven willing) to my funeral,
Withered as 'tis, to keep in memory
That happy day; but most to signify
My withered hopes.

9. 'Remora' – the sucker-fish, formerly believed to be able to halt the
progress of any ship to which it attached itself.
10. From Sirius, the Dog-Star, associated with the hottest days of summer.

ERG: Thy case doth pity and not envy claim,
    Mirtillo – or hereafter let thy name
    Be Tantalus; for he that jests with love,
    Or plays with fire, shall pain in earnest prove.
    Poor youth! thou tookst up transitory treasure
    At too much use, and of thy theft the pleasure
    And punishment together didst receive.
    But did she never the deceit perceive?
MIR: I know not that, Ergasto; this I do,
    Whilst she thought Elis worthy of her view,
    She was still bounteous to me of her eye,
    And gracious smiles. But my hard destiny
    Snatching her thence, unwares to me almost,
    I straight came flying hither, where thou knowst
    My father, though he sojourned long abroad,
    Yet still retains his wonted poor abode.
    I came and saw – O sight! – my day, begun
    In such a fair and smiling morn, now run
    To its long west. When I appeared in place,
    The lightning of disdain flashed in her face;
    Then did she bend her eyes, and turn away;
    These meteors bode my death, then did I say.
    Meanwhile, that I should so by stealth depart,
    My tender father took deeply to heart,
    And with the grief on't an infirmity
    So terrible, that he was like to die.
    This forced me back, which proved, alas, in one
    Health to the father, sickness to the son.
    For half a year of a love-caus&eacute;d fever
    I languished, and I think had languished ever,
    If my indulgent father had not sought
    In time the tripod's counsel; whence he brought
    This answer: *that the Arcadian air alone*
    *Could make me well again.* I thereupon
    Returned, Ergasto, to revisit her
    (O fallacy of that grand sophister
    The oracle!) who made my body whole
    To cause eternal sickness in my soul.

ERG: Thou hast related a strange tale in truth,
 Mirtillo, a case worthy of much ruth
 Without all doubt. But oft a desperate state
 Hath proved the cause that cures as desperate
 Have saved the sick. And now 'tis time I go
 To tell Corisca what from thee I know.
 Expect me at the fountain – there will I
 Ere long be with thee.
  [*Exit* ERGASTO, *Right Centre.*]
MIR:                    Go on prosperously,
 And Heaven at need that pity show to thee,
 Courteous Ergasto, which thou showest to me.
  [*Exit* MIRTILLO, *Right. Enter* DORINDA, *leading* SILVIO's *dog,
  and* LUPINO, *Left.*]
DOR: Faithful and fortunate, delight and care
 Of my fair Silvio, and as proud as fair!
 Thrice fortunate Melampo, that I were
 Unto thy cruel master half so dear!
 With that white hand with which he gripes my heart
 He strokes and he feeds thee. He doth not part
 From thee by night, nor part from thee by day;
 Whilst I that so much love him, in vain pray,
 And sigh in vain. And that which worse I bear
 Than all the rest, he gives to thee such dear
 And luscious kisses, one of which would make
 Me rich, and I too kiss thee for his sake
 Happy Melamp; O dog sent from above
 To steer the erring footsteps of blind Love!
 Lead on, sure guide, whither affection me,
 But nature only and instinct draws thee.
 But list a little, doth not a horn blow
 In this near thicket?
SIL [*off stage*]:       So, Melampo, so!
DOR: That is, if love delude me not, the sound
 Of Silvio's voice, who seems to call his hound
 About these woods.
SIL [*off stage*]:       Melampo, so! Ho! Ho!
DOR: It is the very voice of Silvio.

THE FAITHFUL SHEPHERD

Happy Dorinda, to whom heaven hath sent
The selfsame thing in search whereof I went!
I'll hide the dog; with that he holds so dear,
I may chance buy his love. Lupino!

LUP:                                    Here!

DOR: Go take this dog, and hide thee hereabout.
   [LUPINO *shows some alarm at this idea.*]
   Conceiv'st thou me?

LUP:                    I do.

DOR:                          But come not out
   Until I call.

LUP:              I won't.

DOR:                      Nay, quickly, man!

LUP: And do thou quickly take some order than
   That if the dog should have a hungry fit
   He may not swallow me up at a bit.

DOR: A coward? Hence!

   [*Exit* LUPINO *with dog, Right Centre. Enter* SILVIO, *Left.*]

SIL:                          Oh, whither shall I steer
   My wretched steps to follow thee, my dear
   Faithful Melampo? Over hill and plain,
   Till I am tired and foundered, I in vain
   Have hunted for thee. Curséd be the doe
   Thou followedst! But behold, a nymph may know
   Some news of him . . . O vile encounter! This
   Is she, who with her importunities
   Torments me still; but there's no remedy
   Save patience now. Fair nymph, didst thou see my
   Faithful Melampo, whom I slipped while-ere
   After a doe?

DOR:        I, Silvio, fair? I fair?
   Why dost thou call me fair, if that I be
   Not fair in thy eyes?

SIL:                    Fair or foul, didst see
   My dog? Answer me that: if not, I go.

DOR: So harsh to her adores thee, Silvio?
   Who would believe in that sweet shape could nest
   So sour a soul? Thou followst a wild beast

That flies thee, over rocks; and for a cur
Vexest thy body and thy mind; but her
That follows thee, and thy content doth prize
Above the world, thou fliest and dost despise.
Ah! do not follow a wild flying doe,
Let not a tame one, caught already, go.
Do not unbind her.

SIL:               Nymph, I came in search
Of my Melampo, not to hear thee preach.
Adieu.

DOR:     Oh, fly not, cruel Silvio;
I'll tell thee news of thy Melampo.

SIL:                     Go,
Thou mockst, Dorinda.

DOR:              By that love I swear,
That makes me Silvio's servant, I know where
He is. Thou sayst he did a doe pursue?

SIL: He did; and straight I lost them both from view.

DOR: The dog and doe then at this present time
Are in my power.

SIL:            In thy power?

DOR:                   Yes, in mine.
'Twas that I said. Dost thou think much that she
Should love thy dog, ungrateful, who loves thee?

SIL: My dear Dorinda, give 'em to me straight!

DOR: Out, shittle-cock, I'm come to a fine state
When beasts endear me to thee! But indeed,
My heart, thou gets them not without some meed.

SIL: And reason good; I'll give thee – let me see –
[*Aside*] (I'll cozen her!)

DOR:              What wilt thou give to me?

SIL: Two fair queen-apples I will give to thee,
Which my own fairer mother gave to me
The other day.

DOR:         For apples, I want none;
I could give thee two fairer of my own,
And sweeter, too, but that thou carest not
For what I give.

SIL:             Then wouldst thou have a goat?
  Or lambkin? [*Aside*] (But my father will not let
  Me make so bold with what is his as yet.)

DOR: Nor goat, nor lambkin do I care to have;
  Thee only Silvio, and thy love I crave.

SIL: My love? No more? I give 't thee: so
  Give me my dog, dear nymph, now and my doe.

DOR: Ah, that thou knewst the worth of what thou art
  So bounteous of, and spakest now from thy heart!

SIL: Nymph, mark my words: I find thou talkst to me
  Still of a thing called love; what this should be
  I know not: thou wouldst have me love thee, and
  I do, as far as I can understand,
  With all my heart: thou callst me cruel: I
  Am ignorant of what is cruelty.
  How should I please thee?

DOR:              In whom hopest thou, poor
  Dorinda? Whence dost thou expect thy cure?
  From such a beauty as hath felt as yet
  No spark of that which doth all lovers set
  On fire? Art thou my flame, and art not hot?
  Dost thou breathe love, and what it is knowst not?
  That gentle goddess whom the Cyprians honour
  Took a most beauteous human shape upon her
  To bring thee forth: fire-brands thou hast, and dart,
  Witness my flaming and my bleeding heart.
  Add wings, another Cupid thou wilt prove –
  At least want nothing to be Love, but love.

SIL: What is this love?

DOR:            When I behold thy eyes,
  It is the light of Paradise.
  But mine own heart considered well,
  It is the very fire of hell.

SIL: Nymph, what a prating is here with thee!
  Give me my dog and doe, now prithee.

DOR: Give me the love first that I bargained for.

SIL: Have I not given it thee? Fie, what a stir
  There is to please this woman! Take it; do

What thou wilt with it. Who forbids thee? Who
Withholds it? On what trifles dost thou stand?
DOR: Wretched Dorinda, thou dost sow the sand,
　And fondly undertak'st labour in vain.
SIL: What dreamst thou of? Why holdst thou me in pain?
DOR: When thy desire's once granted, thou wilt go
　And leave me straight, perfidious Silvio.
SIL: 　　　　　　　　　　　　　　　No,
　Indeed, fair nymph.
DOR: 　　　　　　Give me a pawn, then.
SIL: 　　　　　　　　　　　　　　Name
　The pawn.
DOR: 　　　Alas, I dare not!
SIL: 　　　　　　　　Why?
DOR: 　　　　　　　　　　For shame.
SIL: But then how can I give it thee?
DOR: 　　　　　　　　　　　I would
　Fain without naming it be understood.
SIL: If thou'rt ashamed to name it, thou maist be
　Ashamed to take it.
DOR: 　　　　　　Promise it to me;
　And I will name it.
SIL: 　　　　　　　I do promise it;
　But thou must name it first.
DOR: 　　　　　　　　　Canst thou not hit
　My thoughts then? I should have conceivéd thee
　If thou hadst said but half so much to me.
SIL: Thou hast more wit than I, Dorinda.
DOR: 　　　　　　　　　　　　　　I
　Have more love, Silvio, and less cruelty.
SIL: Truth is, I am no witch. If thou'dst have me
　To understand thee, speak!
DOR: 　　　　　　　　O misery!
　That which I beg of thee is one of those
　Things thy kind mother upon thee bestows.
SIL: A box o' th'ear?
DOR: 　　　　　　To one that loves thee so?
SIL: Those things my mother doth on me bestow.

DOR: Nay, that's not so; but doth not she give thee
  A kiss sometimes?

SIL:               She neither kisses me,
  Nor would have others kiss me. Is't a kiss
  Thou dost desire of me? It is! it is!
  Thy blush betrays thee. Come, I'll give it thee;
  But first my dog and doe.

DOR:                Dost promise me?

SIL: I promise thee.

DOR:             And with me wilt thou stay?

SIL: Why dost thou vex me thus? Did I not say
  I would?

DOR: Come forth, Lupino! Dost not hear? Lupino!

LUP: Oh! Oh! What a brawling's there!
  Who calls me? Oh, I'm come. It was not I
  That slept, it was the dog slept verily.

DOR: Look, Silvio, there's thy dog, that might to thee
  Have read a lecture of humanity.

SIL: How overjoyed am I!

DOR:              Upon this breast,
  Which thou despisest so, he came to rest.

SIL: Oh, my sweet true Melampo!

DOR:                Setting by[11]
  My sighs and kisses.

SIL:         I will certainly
  Kiss thee a thousand times, poor cur! But hast
  Thou got no harm at all, thou ran'st so fast?

DOR: Fortunate dog, that I might change, alas,
  Estates with thee; I'm come to a fine pass,
  To envy a dog's life. Bend thou thy gait
  Homewards, Lupino; I will follow straight.

LUP: Mistress, I go.

    [*Exit* LUPINO, *Left.*]

SIL [*to dog*]: In fine, thou'st got no harm.

               [*To* DORINDA] Now let me see
  Where is this doe which thou hast promised me?

DOR: Alive or dead would'st have her?

      11. 'Setting by' here means 'holding dear'.

324

SIL:                                    Strange demand!
Alive after the dog hath killed her?
DOR:                         And
If the dog killed her not?
SIL:                       Alive is she?
DOR: Alive!
SIL:        The dearer then the prey to me.
And had my dear Melampo so much art
As not to hurt her?
DOR:                 Only in the heart
She had a little prick.
SIL:                 Either thou'rt mad,
Dorinda, or dost mock me. If she had
A prick i'th' heart, how can she live?
DOR:                The doe
I speak of, I am, cruel Silvio,
Hurt by thee, without being hunted – take me,
I am alive – but dead if thou forsake me.
SIL: Is this that doe? that prey?
DOR:               E'en this; why now
Art thou so discontented? Dost not thou
Love a nymph better than a beast?
SIL:            My hate
Thou art, brute,[12] liar, vile, importunate!
DOR: Is this the guerdon, cruel Silvio,
Is this the meed thou dost on me bestow,
Ungrateful youth? Take thy Melampo free,
And me and all, so thou come back to me;
The rest I do remit. Let me be placed
But in the sunshine thy fair eyes do cast.
Truer than thy Melampo I will trace
Thy steps, and when thou'rt wearied with the chase
I'll wipe thy sweating brow, and on this breast,
Which cannot rest for thee, thy head shall rest;
I'll bear thy arrows, and thy quiver bear,
Through these rough woods; and if there want game there,

12. 'Brute' here represents the Italian word 'brutta', which really means ugly. One of Fanshawe's very few linguistic mistakes.

Shoot at Dorinda's bosom. At this white
Set thy good bow, whene'er it shoots not right.
For I'll be both the prey, if thou think fit,
To keep in ure, and drudge to carry it;
Thy arrows, quiver, and their butt to hit.
But to whom do I talk? alas! to thee
That hear'st me not, and fly'st away from me.
But wheresoe'er thou fly, curst Silvio,
Dorinda will fly after thee, although
To hell itself, if any hell there be
Worse than my love is, and thy cruelty.

[*Exeunt* SILVIO, DORINDA, *Left. Enter* CORISCA, *Right Centre.*]

COR: Fortune beyond my wish hath favoured me;
And fit it is that they should favoured be
Who not with wishes only seek her favour.
Powerful she is, and men with reason have her
In reputation of a goddess. But
We must go meet her then, and wait afoot
To find her humours; and must use our own
Judgement in playing of our game – a drone
Seldom or never doth prove fortunate.
Had not my industry made me the mate
Of her by whom under the name of friend
I have fit means and safe to work my end,
Where had I been? Some fool would now be shy,
And view her rival with a jealous eye,
Bearing the open tokens of ill-will
Writ in her forehead; and she would do ill.
For open foes are easier to evade
Than ambushes that are in friendship laid.
Wise mariners by rocks hid in the sea
Are oft deceived; she knows not how to be
An enemy, that knows not how to seem
A friend. Corisca's skill shall now be seen
In both: nor am I yet so simply dull
To think she doth not love. Well may she gull
Others with this; not me, who am gone out
A mistress in the art. A tender sprout

New peeped out of the bark, within whose breast
There's built for love already a soft nest;
Long wooed, and wooed by so complete a lover,
And – which is worst – kissed too over and over,
And yet hold tight? Believe't (for me) that list.
But my good genius doth me assist;
For look if Amarillis come not here
As sent! I'll walk as if I did not see her.
    [*Enter* AMARILLIS, *Left.*]

AM: Dear happy groves, and you ye solitary
And silent woodlands where true peace doth tarry,
With how much joy do I review you! And
Had my stars pleased to give me the command
Over my self, that I might choose my lot,
And my own way of life, then would I not
For the Elysian groves, about which range
The happy shades, your happy shades exchange.
For what we foolish mortals 'goods' do call,
If rightly understood, are evils all.
He that hath most of them, in truth hath least,
Nor is so much possessor, as possessed;
Not riches, no, but of our freedom snares.
What boots it in the springtime of one's years
To have the attributes of fair and good,
In mortal veins to lock celestial blood,
Graces of body and of mind; here fair
And laughing fields of corn, rich meadows there,
In fruitful pasture-grounds more fruitful flocks,
If with all these the heart contentment lacks?
Happy that shepherdess whom some coarse stuff
Obscurely clothes, yet clean and just enough!
Rich only in herself, and bravely dressed
With nature's ornaments, which are the best;
Who in sweet poverty no want doth know,
Nor the distractions which from riches grow;
Yet whatsoever may suffice the mind
In that estate abundantly doth find;
*Poor, but content!* with nature's gifts retrieves

The gifts of nature, milk with milk revives,
And with the sweet which from the bee she gets
Seasons the honey of her native sweets.
One fountain is her looking-glass, her drink,
Her bath; and if she's pleased, what others think
It matters not; she heeds not blazing stars
That threaten mighty ones: wars or no wars,
It is all one to her; her battlement
And shield is that she's poor: *Poor, but content!*
One only care – 'tis a sweet care – doth keep
Her heart awake: she feeds her master's sheep
With pearléd grass, and with her lovely eyes
Some honest swain, that for her beauty dies –
Not such as men or gods choose to her hand,
But such as love did to her choice commend,
And in some favoured shady myrtle grove
Desires and is desired, nor feels of love
One spark which unto him she doth not show,
Nor shows one spark with which he doth not glow.
*Poor, but content!* True life, which till the breath
Forsakes the body, knowst not what is death.
Would Heaven had made me such a one! But see,
Corisca! Sweet Corisca!

COR:                             Who calls me?
My Amarillis! Dearer than mine own
Eyes or life to me, whither so alone?

AM: No farther than thou seest; nor anywhere
Could I be better, since I meet thee here.

COR: Thou hast met her that never parts from thee,
Sweet Amarillis; and now, credit me,
Was thinking of thee, saying in my heart,
'If I'm her soul, how can she live apart
From me?' When straight I saw thee here – but go,
Thou carest not for Corisca now.

AM:                                    Why so?

COR: Why? Dost thou ask the question? Thou dost wed
Today.

AM:      I wed?

COR:             Yes; and thou keepst it hid
From me.

AM:        How can I tell thee that which I
Am ignorant myself of?

COR:                   Do, deny,
And wear a mask to me.

AM:                         Still jest with me
Corisca?

COR:      I am jested with by thee.

AM: But speakst thou this for truth?

COR:                         I'll swear 'tis so.
And knowst thou nothing of 't indeed?

AM:                            I know
I'm promised; but that I should be a wife
So soon, is news to me upon my life.
But from whom knowst thou it?

COR:                      From my own brother
Ormino; and he says there is no other
Discourse abroad. – Thou seemst perplexed; is this
News to perplex one?

AM:                  Oh, Corisca, 'tis
A hideous gulf; I've heard my mother say
We are then reborn!

COR:               Most true; 'tis our birth day
To a better life – therefore rejoice! Dost fetch
A sigh? Leave sighing to that wretch!

AM:                                What wretch?

COR: Mirtillo, who was present casually
At what my brother told me, and was nigh
Struck dead with grief; yea, doubtless he had died,
If a good cordial I had not applied,
By promising to break this match. Which though
I said only to comfort him, I know,
If need were, how to do it.

AM:                        Canst thou tell
How to break off this match?

COR:                      Yes, very well.

AM: I prithee, how?

329

COR:                    With ease, if thou wert but
  Consenting likewise, and assisting to 't.
AM: Could I suppose this possible, and thou
  Wouldst not reveal it, I would tell thee now
  A secret that hath long burnt in my heart.
COR: Who, I reveal it? Let the earth first part
  And swallow me alive miraculously.
AM: Know then, Corisca, when I think that I
  Must all my life be subject to a boy
  That hates and flies me, and doth take no joy
  But in the woods, preferring hunting far
  Before the love of all the nymphs that are,
  It makes me malcontent – and desperate
  Indeed almost, although I dare not say 't,
  Because my faith I have already given
  Unto my father, and – what's worse – to heaven,
  And break with them I neither will nor may.
  But if thy industry can find a way
  (Always provided that my honesty,
  My faith, my life and my religion be
  Preserved) to untie this knot that galls me so,
  To thee my life and safety I shall owe.
COR: If this it were that caused thy sighing, thou
  Hadst great cause for it, Amarillis. How
  Oft have I said, what pity 'tis to throw
  So rich a thing to one that scorns it so!
  A pearl to a swine! Why speakst not to thy father?
AM: Shame stops my mouth.
COR:                    There's a disease! I'd rather
  For my part have a fistula, or fever.
  But 'twill be cured – o'ercome it once, 'twill never
  Return again.
AM:               That cannot be o'ercome
  That's natural; for if I drive it from
  My heart, it flies into my face.
COR:                         Alas,
  My Amarillis, oft it comes to pass,
  She that through too much wisdom holds her tongue,

Roars out at last like mad, being throughly stung.
Hadst thou before been willing to discover
Thy mind to me, this trouble had been over;
And now thou hast, Corisca's power this day
In all its colours shall itself display.
Into more skilful hands, more faithful than
Mine are, thou never couldst have fallen. But when
From an ill husband thou art free by me,
Shall not an honest suitor welcome be?

AM: We'll think of that at leisure.

COR:                  That good youth
  Mirtillo must not be forgot in sooth.
  For parts, for spotless faith, for shape thou knowst
  Of all men living he deserves thee most:
  And canst thou let him die? O cruelty!
  Nor wilt so much as hear him say, 'I die!'?
  Hear him but once!

AM:                'Twere better he would rest
  In peace, and root a love out of his breast
  That's vain.

COR:         That comfort give him ere he die!

AM: 'Twould rather double his perplexity.

COR: If it do so, the seeking is his own.

AM: And what must I expect, should it be known?

COR: How cowardly thou art!

AM:                 And let me still
  Be cowardly in anything that's ill!

COR: If thou mayst fail me in this small request,
  Then may I fail thee likewise in the rest
  Most justly, Amarillis. So good-bye!

AM: Nay, stay, Corisca, hear!

COR:               Not a word I,
  Unless thou promise me.

AM:              I promise thee
  To hear him speak, provided this may be
  For all.

COR:     It shall.

AM:            And that he may not know

I was acquainted with't.

COR:                    I'll make as though
Ye met by accident.

AM:               And that I may
At my own pleasure freely go away.

COR: Thou shalt, when thou hast heard him.

AM:                       And that he
Shall briefly speak.

COR:           That too is granted thee.

AM: Nor come within my dart's length of me.

COR:                      Fie,
What a stir's here with thy simplicity!
To make it sure he shall not do thee wrong
I'll tie up all his limbs except his tongue.
Wouldst thou have more?

AM:                 'Tis well.

COR:                  And when wilt thou
Do this?

AM:        Whene'er thou wilt – do but allow
Me so much time, as to go home to hear
More certain news about this marriage there.

COR: Go, but with caution, and before thou'rt gone,
Hear a contrivance I have thought upon
As thou wert speaking: in the afternoon
I would have thee without thy nymphs to come
Into this shady walk, where I will be
Before for this occasion, and with me
Nerina, Phillis, Celia, Aglaura,
Eliza, Daphne, Silvia and Laura –
All my no less discreet and witty than
Faithful and secret mates. There thou with them
Shalt play, as thou art wont, at blind-man's-buff,
So that Mirtillo will with ease enough
Be made believe that for thy own pastime
Thou thither cam'st, and not to meet with him.

AM: I like it wondrous well. But dost thou hear?
I would not any of those nymphs were there
The while Mirtillo speaks.

COR:              I do conceive:
  'Twas thought upon with good discretion. Leave
  The getting them away to my endeavour.
  Go! and remember one thing – to love ever
  Thy faithfullest Corisca.

AM:             In her hand
  Since I have put my heart, she may command
  As much love as she pleases.

    [*Exit* AMARILLIS, *Left.*]

COR: Is she not stiff? We must assault this rock
  With greater force. Though she resist my shock,
  Against Mirtillo's she will find no fence,
  I'm sure – I know by self-experience
  The power of lovers' prayers when they invade
  The tender heart of an inclining maid.
  If she do yield, I'll make her so smart for't
  That she shall find her sport was not in sport.
  Through her dark'st words her heart shall be to me
  As visible as in a 'natomy.
  I'll ransack all her veins – that done, and I
  Made mistress of her secret, easily
  I'll wind her so, and lead her by the nose
  To what I'd have, herself shall ne'er suppose,
  Much less shall others, that it was my skill
  That drew her to't, but her unbridled will.

    [SATYR *enters Right Centre behind* CORISCA *and seizes her.*]

COR: Oh, I'm dead!

SAT:           But I was *quick*!
  There's a trick now for your trick.

COR: My Amarillis, I am caught –
  Oh, come back!

SAT:          She hears thee not.
  'Twill now behove thee to be strong.

COR: Oh me, my hair!

SAT:             I have so long
  Stood angling for thee in my boat;
  At last thou'rt struck. 'Tis not thy coat,
  'Tis thy hair, sister, this!

COR:                    To me

This usage, Satyr?

SAT:                    Yes, to thee,

Corisca, or I am mistaken –
That mistress in the art of making
The fine-spun lies, that sells so dear
False words, false hopes and a false leer!
She that so often hath betrayed me,
She that so many fools hath made me
At every turn – the sorceress,
The cheat Corisca!

COR:              I confess

I am Corisca; but not she
Now, that was once so loved by thee
My gentle Satyr.

SAT:              Pray, since when

Am I gentle? I was not then
When me for Coridon thou didst change.

COR: Thee, for another?

SAT:                    See how strange

She makes it now. I warrant then
This is great news to thee. And when
Thou mad'st me Silvia's buskins steal,
The bow of Lilla, Cloris' veil,
And Daphne's gown, that were to be
The price of love – which, promised me,
Thou gav'st another; and when that
Fair wreath I on thy head did plait,
Thou upon Niso didst bestow,
And when thou mad'st me, cold as snow,
Watch many a night out at the fountain,
The cave, the woodside and foot of the mountain,
And for my pains didst laugh at me,
Did I then seem gentle to thee?
Ah, thief! But now as I am here,
I'll make thee pay thy whole arrear.

COR: Oh me! Thou dragst me like a beast!

SAT: I drag thee like thyself then. Wrest

334

Thy neck out of the collar now,
Give me the slip if thou knowst how.
Fox, though thy craft the time before
Did save thee, it shall do't no more.
For this I'm sure thou canst not scape,
Unless thou leave thy head i'th' trap.

COR: Yet give me so much time, I pray,
　As for myself to answer.

SAT:　　　　　　　　Say.

COR: How can I if thou hold me so?

SAT: 'Tis likely I should let thee go!

COR: I'll gage my faith not to go hence.

SAT: What faith? Hast thou the impudence,
Perfidious woman, to name faith
To me? I'll bear thee where there hath
No sun, much less the feet of men
Approached, unto the horrid'st den
Of all this mountain. There (but I
Will act the rest) to mine own joy
And thy dishonour, I will carve
Such vengeance as thy faults deserve.

COR: Canst thou then, cruel! to this hair, which has
Tied fast thy heart, unto this face, which was
Once thy delight, to this Corisca – then
More dear to thee than thine own life was when
Thou swar'st by that, that thou couldst find it sweet
On her behalf even death itself to meet –
Canst thou once think to offer injury,
I say, to her? Oh heavens! Oh destiny!
Whom have I hoped in? Whom can I believe
Again?

SAT:　　　Ah siren! Thinkst thou to deceive
Me still? still rock me with thy flattering charms?

COR: My sweet dear Satyr, do no harm
To her that loves thee. Thou art not a beast,
Nor hast a marble or a flinty breast.
Behold me at thy feet! O pardon me
If ever I (by chance) offended thee,

335

My idol. By those sinewy and more
Than human knees, which clasping I adore,
By that rough manly visage, by that dear
Affection which thou once to me didst bear;.
By the sweet influence of those eyes which thou
Wert wont to call two stars (two fountains now!),
By these salt tears which trickle down so fast,
Pity me now, and let me go.

SAT:                     Thou hast
Moved me, I must confess; and I were gone
If I should hearken to affection.
But, to be short, I do not credit thee;
Thou art too full of wiles and tricks for me,
And he that takes thy word, believes his snares.
Beneath this humble show, beneath these prayers
There's hid Corisca: thou canst never be
Another. Struggling still?

COR:                  My head! O me!
Ah, cruel! Stay a little longer yet,
And grant me but one favour!

SAT:                     What is it?

COR: Hear me a little more!

SAT:                Thou hopest now
With flatteries and squeezed tears to make me bow.

COR: Ah, courteous Satyr! Wilt thou carve in me
Such cruel vengeance?

SAT:              Come, and thou shalt see.

COR: And take no pity of me?

SAT:               None at all.

COR: But art thou firm in this?

SAT:              As a brass wall.
Is this charm ended?

COR:           O thou base, and not
To be exampled rogue! half man, half goat,
And all a beast! Thou carrion that doth stink!
By-blow and blush of nature! If thou think
Corisca loves thee not, thou thinkst the truth.
What should she love in such a comely youth?

That fair stag's head? That chimney-sweeper's broom?
Goat's ears? That grave of rottenness and rheum
Which once had teeth in't?

SAT:                          This to me,
  Thou wicked varlet?

COR:                    E'en to thee!

SAT: To me, thou scold?

COR:                      To thee, thou goat!

SAT [*extending finger and thumb*]: And with these pincers pull I not
  Thy barking tongue out?

COR [*showing teeth*]:        Would thou durst
  Come near't, there's that will scour their rust!

SAT: A paltry woman, and in such
  Condition (being in my clutch)
  To injure[13] me! And dare me too!
  I will . . .

COR:        Base slave, what wilt thou do?

SAT: Eat thee alive, I will!

COR:                       Where be
  The teeth to do it?

SAT:                   Heaven, dost thou see
  And suffer this? But if I do not
  Chastise thee . . . Come along!

COR:                    I wo' not.

SAT: Wo' not, my Mistress Malapert?

COR: Wo' not, in spite of thy foul heart.

SAT: That shall be seen; come or I swear
  This arm I'll from thy shoulder tear!

COR: Tear my head off, I wo' not go
  One foot.

SAT:      Art thou resolvèd so?
  Let's ne'er dispute then any longer,
  But put to trial whether's stronger
  And faster on, thy neck-piece or
  My arm.

  [SATYR *has now let go of* CORISCA's *arm and is pulling her by the*
  *hair.* CORISCA's *hands go up to her head.*]

13. Insult.

337

          Thy hands to help too? Nor
Are these, perverse one, enough guard.
COR: That shall be tried.
SAT:                 It shall.
COR:                 Pull hard!
    [CORISCA's *whole head of hair, or rather wig, comes away in*
    SATYR's *hand. He falls heavily to the ground.*]
COR: Satyr, adieu, get thy neck set!
    [*Exit* CORISCA, *Left.*]
SAT:                 O me!
How I am shattered! oh, my head! my knee!
Oh my back-bone! my thigh! What a vile fall
Was here! To get upon my legs is all
I have the power to do. But can it be
That she should fly, and leave her head with me?
Oh marvellous! ye nymphs and shepherds run,
Flock hither to behold a wonder: one
That runs away without her head, by skill
In magic. Ha! How light it is! How ill
Peopled with brains! How comes it that I see
None of the blood spurt forth? But stay, let me
Peruse it better ... Oh, thou stock, thou stone!
Thou hast no head, if thou think she hath none.
Was ever any man so fooled! See now
If she had not a trick to scape, when thou
Thoughtst her most sure! Thou all made up of wiles,
Wast not enough thy heart, thy face, thy smiles,
Thy looks and speeches falsified were,
But thou must also falsify thy hair?
The glowing amber and the flowing gold
Which you, mad poets, so extol, behold!
Blush, blush now at your error, and recant
Your threadbare theme; instead whereof go paint
The arts of a deformed and impious witch,
Breaking up sepulchres by night, from which
She steals the hair that upon Death's head grows,
To imp her own – which she so neatly does,
That she hath made you praise what ye should more

Than dire Megaera's snaky locks abhor.
These, lovers, are your gyves, I take it, too!
Look on them, idiots; and if, as you
Protest, your hearts are fastened to these hairs,
Now everyone may without sighs or tears
Come by his own. But why do I forbear
To publish her disgrace? Surely that hair
Which stuck with starres adorns the azure sky
Never so famous was as this; and she
Much more that wore it by my tongue shall be
Made infamous to all posterity.

[*Exit* SATYR, *Left. Enter* CHORUS, *Right.*]

CHO: Ah! 'Twas a grievous fault in her (the cause
Of all our sorrows) who, the sacred laws
Of Love offending, by her breach of troth
Kindled against this land the mortal wrath
Of the immortal gods, which not a flood
Of general tears, nor so much guiltless blood
Can quench yet or abate; so high a price
Unspotted faith (expeller of all vice,
And most undoubted argument to prove
A mind descended nobly) bears above.
And such a care to plant love in his creature,
By which we deify our human nature,
Hath the eternal lover. Oh, those blind
Mistaken mortals, who addict their mind
To wealth, for which affection's basely sold,
Watching the carcase of their coffined gold
Like a pale ghost that walks about his grave.
Or why should beauty our free hearts enslave?
These are dead loves; the living and divine
Is where two souls by virtue do combine.
No outward object can with reason move
The heart to love it, 'cause it cannot love:
Only the soul, 'cause that can love again,
Deserves a love, deserves a lover's pain.
    Well may that kiss be sweet that's given to a sleek
And fragrant rose of a vermilion cheek;

And understanding tasters – as are true
And happy lovers – will commend that too.
'Tis a dead kiss, say I, and must be poor,
Which the place kissed hath no means to restore.
But the sweet echoing, and the dove-like billing
Of two encountering mouths, when both are willing,
And when at once both loves advance their bows,
Their shafts drawn home, at once sound at the loose –
How sweet is such revenge! – this is true kissing,
Where there is one for t'other without missing
A minute of the time, or taking more
Than that which in the taking they restore.
Where by an interchange of amorous blisses
At the same time they sow and gather kisses.
Kiss a red swelling lip, then kiss a wrist,
A breast, a forehead or what else thou list,
No part of a fair nymph so just will be
Except the lip, to pay this kiss to thee.
Thither your souls come sallying forth, and they
Kiss too, and by the wandering powers convey
Life into smacking rubies, and transfuse
Into the live and sprightly kiss their use
Of reason, so that ye discourse together
In kisses, which with little noise deliver
Much matter: and sweet secrets, which he spells
Who is a lover – gibberish to all else.

    Like life, like mutual joy they feel, where love
With equal flames as with two wings doth move.
And as where lips kiss lips is the best kiss,
So where one's loved to love best loving is.

# ACT THREE

*Scene as before.*

[*Enter* MIRTILLO, *Right.*]

MIR: Spring, the year's youth, fair mother of new flowers,
New leaves, new loves, drawn by the wingéd hours,
Thou art returned; but the felicity
Thou broughtst me last is not returned with thee.
Thou art returned, but nought returns with thee
Save my lost joy's regretful memory.
Thou art the selfsame thing thou wert before,
As fair and jocund; but I am no more
The thing I was, so gracious in her sight
Who is heaven's masterpiece and earth's delight.
O bitter sweets of love! Far worse it is
To lose, than never to have tasted bliss!
But oh! how sweet were love, if it could not
Be lost, or being lost could be forgot!
Though if my hopes (as mine are wont to be)
Are not of glass, or my love make me see
Them through a multiplying glass – if I
Be not deceived both by myself and by
Another – here I shall that sun behold
Which I adore, impart her beams of gold
To my blest sight, behold her flying feet
Stop at my sad notes; here upon the sweet
Food of that lovely face I shall suffice
After a tedious fast my greedy eyes.
Here, here behold that proud one on me turn
Her sparkling lamps – if not to light, to burn.
And if not fraught with amorous delight,
So kindly cruel as to kill outright.

341

Yet were't but just, that after so much pain
As I have hitherto endured in vain,
Thou, Love, at length shouldst make the sun appear
To this benighted earth serene and clear.
Hither Ergasto did direct me, where
Corisca and my Amarillis were
To play at blind-man's-buff; but I can find
In this place nothing but my love that's blind,
And so deceived, misled by a false guide
To seek that light which is to me denied.
Pray Heaven my hard and envious fate beneath
This sugared pill now have not hid my death.
This tedious stay afflicts me – for to those
That go to meet their loves, each moment shows
An age. Perchance I have arrived too late,
And made for me too long Corisca wait.
Yet I made haste. Now woe is me! If I
Have done this fault, I will lie down and die!

[*Enter* AMARILLIS, *blindfolded,* CHORUS *of* NYMPHS, CORISCA,
*Left.*]

AM: Behold the Buff!
MIR:                    O sight!
AM:                              Come on!
MIR:                                        O voice!
That makes my heart both tremble and rejoice.

[AMARILLIS *puzzled, as the other girls remain silent.*]

AM: What do you do? Lisetta, where art thou
That wert so eager of this sport but now?
And thou, Corisca, whither gone?
MIR:                                I find
Now it is true indeed, that Love is blind.
AM: You there that are appointed for my guides
To hand and to support me on both sides,
Before the rest of our companions come,
Out of these trees conduct me to field-room;
Then leaving me alone amidst the plain,
Amongst our other fellows herd again;
So joining all together, make a ring

About me round, and let the sport begin.
MIR: But what shall I do? Yet I cannot see
    Of what advantage this should be to me
    In my desires; nor see I my north star
    Corisca: succour me, blest heaven!
AM:                         Oh are
    Ye come at last? Ye wantons, did ye mean
    Only to bind my eyes? Begin now, then!
CHO: Love, thou art not blind, I know,
    But dost only appear so
    To blind us: if thy sight's small,
    Thou hast, I'm sure, no faith at all.
    Blind or not, thou triest in vain
    Me into thy net to train.
    And to keep out of thy pound
    Off I get, and traverse ground.
    Blind as thou art, thou couldst see more
    Than Argus' hundred eyes of yore.
    Thou couldst see, blind as thou art,
    Well enough to hit my heart.
    But I were a fool indeed,
    Should I trust thee now I'm freed;
    Sport with thee henceforth that will;
    'Tis a sport with thee to kill.
AM: Aye, but with too much wariness you play:
    Ye should strike first, and after get away.
    Approach me, touch me, and ye shall not fly
    Me then.
MIR:         O ye high Gods! In heaven am I,
    Or earth? O heavens, do your eternal rounds
    Move in such order, warble such sweet sounds?
CHO: Well, blind archer, since thou still
    Urgest me to play, I will.
    Now I clap thy shoulder hard;
    Now I fly unto my guard:
    Strike, and run, and strike again
    And thou wheelst about in vain.
    Now I pinch thee, now remove;

> And have at thee now, blind love!
> Yet thou canst not light on me;
> Why? Because my heart is free.

AM: In faith, Licoris, I had surely thought
> To have caught thee there, and 'twas a tree I caught!
> Ay, dost thou laugh?

MIR:              Would I had been that tree!
> But do I not Corisca hidden see
> Amongst those brakes? And she makes signs as who
> Should say, that something she would have me do.

CHO: A free heart makes a nimble heel.
> Ah traitor! Dost thou tempt me still
> With thy flattering false delight?
> Thus then I renew the fight.
> Slash and fly, and turn and shove,
> And about again, blind love!
> Yet thou canst not light on me;
> Why? Because my heart is free.

AM: Would thou wert pulled up by the root, base tree,
> That I should ever thus be catching thee!
> Deceivéd by the dancing of a bough,
> I did suppose I'd had Eliza now!

MIR: Corisca still is making signs to me,
> And looks as she were angry; perhaps she
> Would have me mix with those nymphs.

AM:              Must I play
> With nothing but with trees then all this day?

COR: I must come forth and speak or he'll not stir.
> To her, white liver! and lay hold on her!
> Why dost thou gape? to have her run into
> Thy mouth? At least, if that thou dar'st not do,
> Let her lay hold of thee. Come, give me here
> This dart, and go to meet her, fool!

MIR:              How near
> To impotence is strong desire! O love!
> That thou shouldst make a man a coward prove!

AM: Play but once more, for now I weary grow.
> Troth, you're to blame for making me run so.

344

CHO: That triumphant God survey
 To whom amorous mortals pay
 Impious tribute! See him snaffled!
 See him laughed at! See him baffled!
 As a hooded hawk, or owl
 With light blinded, when the fowl
 With their armies flock about her,
 Some to beat, and some to flout her;
 She in vain doth rouse and peck
 This and that way with her beak;
 So we baffle and deride
 Thee (blind Love) on every side.
 One doth pinch thy elbow black,
 T'other has thee by the back,
 And thy baiting does no good,
 Nor thy pecking through thy hood,
 Nor thy stretching out thy claws.
 But sweet meats have sour sauce.
 Birds are caught by playing thus:
 So do nymphs grow amorous.

    [*Exit* CHORUS, *Left.* MIRTILLO, *pushed forward by* CORISCA, *is
 caught by the blindfolded* AMARILLIS. CORISCA *withdraws behind
 a bush and watches.*]

AM: In faith, Aglaura, art thou caught at last?
 Thou'dst fain be gone, but I will hold thee fast.

COR [*aside*]: Surely, unless at unawares by main
 Strength I had thrust him on her, I in vain
 Had tired myself to make him thither go.

AM: Thou wilt not speak now – art thou she or no?

COR [*returning for a moment*]: I lay his dart here by him, and unto
 My bush return, to observe what will ensue.

AM: Thou art Corisca, now it is most clear;
 I know thee by thy tallness and short hair.
 'Twas thee I wished to catch, that I might use thee
 Just as I list and thus, and thus abuse thee.
 And thus, and thus. Not yet? But since 'twas thou
 That boundst me, do thou too unbind me now:
 Quickly, my heart, and thou shalt have of me

The sweetest kiss that e'er was given thee.
What dost thou stick at? Thy hand trembles; what,
Art thou so weary? If thy nails will not,
Let thy teeth do't; come, fumbler, let me see –
I can myself untangle without thee.
Fy, how with knots on knots it is perplexed!
The best on't is, thou must be blinded next.
So, now 'tis loosèd . . . Ha! Whom have we here?
Traitor, avaunt! I am unspirited.

MIR:                              Dear
Soul, do not strive to go away.

AM:                              Unhand,
Forcer of nymphs, unhand me, I command.
Ay me! Aglaura and Eliza tarry,
Betrayers of my innocence, where are ye?
Unhand me, villain!

MIR:                    I obey.

AM [*making off*]:              This plot
Corisca laid – now tell her what thou'st got!

MIR: O whither fliest thou, cruel? Ere thou go
Banquet thy eyes yet with my death – for lo,
I pierce my bosom with this dart.

AM [*stopping*]:                Ay me!
What wilt thou do?

MIR:                  That which it troubles thee
Perchance, dire nymph, that any should be said
To have done, but thou!

AM [*aside*]:              Ay me! I'm almost dead!

MIR: And if this action to thy hand be due,
Behold the weapon and the breast!

AM:                              'Tis true;
Thou hast deserved it of me. What could move
Thy heart to such a high presumption?

MIR:                                    Love.

AM: Love never causes rudeness.

MIR:                          Then conclude
I was in love, because I was not rude.
For if within thy arms thou caughtst me first,
I cannot well with rudeness be aspersed,

Since with so fair an opportunity
To be audacious, and to use with thee
The laws of love, I had such power yet over
Myself, I e'en forgot I was a lover.

AM: Upbraid me not with what I blind did do.

MIR: I being in love was blinder of the two.

AM: Prayer and sweet language discreet lovers use
To win their loves – not theft and cheats, to abuse.

MIR: As a wild beast enraged with want of food
Rushes on travellers out of the wood,
So I, that only live on thy fair eyes
– Since that loved food thy cruelty denies,
Or else my fate – if like a ravenous lover
Rushing today upon thee from this cover
Where I had long been famished, I did prove
One stratagem to save my life, which love
Prompted me to, then blame not, cruel maid,
Me but thyself; for if, as thou hast said,
Prayer and sweet language only should be used
By discreet lovers, which thou hast refused
To hear from me, thou by thy cruelty,
Thou by thy flight mad'st me I could not be
A discreet lover.

AM:                      If thou'dst given her over
That fled from thee, thou'dst been a discreet lover.
But know, thou persecutest me in vain;
What wouldst thou have of me?

MIR:                               I'd have thee deign
Once ere I die to hear me.

AM:                          See! As soon
As thou hast asked, thou hast received the boon.
Now then begone!

MIR:                 Ah, nymph! I've scarcely yet
Poured one small drop out to thee of the great
Sea of my tears. If not for pity's sake
Yet for the pleasure thou therein wilt take,
List to a dying man's last accents.

AM:                                    Well,

To shun more trouble, and thy hopes to quell,
To hear thee I'm content. But this before –
Say little, quickly, part and come no more!
MIR: Thou dost command me, cruellest nymph, to bind
In volume too, too small that unconfined
Desire, which scarcely human thought (though it
Be as the soul that holds it infinite)
Hath line to fathom.
That I do love thee more than I do love
My life, if thou doubt'st, cruel, ask this grove,
And that will tell thee; and with it each beast,
Each stupid stock there can the same attest,
Each stone of these high mountains, which so oft
I with the voice of my complaints made soft.
But what need I call any witness else
To prove my love, where so much beauty dwells?
Behold these flowers which make low earth so proud,
Those stars which nail heaven's pavement! All these crowd
Into one ring – a beauty like that same
Is the high cause and forcer of my flame.
For as by Nature water doth descend,
The fire unto the higher regions tend,
The air obliquely spread itself, the ground
Lie still, and heaven about all these turn round,
So naturally do I incline to thee,
As to my chiefest good; so naturally
To those loved beauties (as unto her sole)[14]
With all her winged affections flies my soul.
And he that should imagine he had force
Her from her dearest object to divorce,
Might with as much facility command
The air, the fire, the water and the land,
The heavens too from their accustomed track,
And make the pillars of the world to crack.
But since thou bidst me say but little, I
Shall say but little, saying that I die;

14. 'As unto her sole' means 'as unto her sole good' – referring back to
the word 'good' two lines earlier.

And shall do less in dying, since I see
How much my death is coveted by thee.
Yet I shall do, alas, all that is left
For me to do, of hopes in love bereft.
But, cruel soul, when I am in my grave,
Some pity then upon my sufferings have!
Ah, fair and loved, and that wert once the sweet
Cause of my life, whilst heaven thought it meet,
Turn those bright lamps upon me, as benign
And pitiful as e'er I saw them shine,
Once ere I die, that I may die in peace.
Let those fair amiable eyes release
My life, now bitter, which once sweetened it;
And those bright stars, which my love's torches lit,
Light too my funeral tapers, and forerun
As once my rising, now my setting sun.
But thou, more hard than e'er thou wert before,
Feelst yet no spark of pity, but art more
Stiff with my prayers. Must I then talk alone?
Wretch that I am, discourse I to a stone?
Say 'Die!' at least, if nothing else thou'lt say;
And thou shalt see me die.
    [MIRTILLO *pauses.* AMARILLIS *does not reply.*]
                    O Love! What way
Canst thou not plague me? When this nymph that's nurst
In cruelty, and for my blood did thirst,
Finding my death would now a favour be,
Even that sad favour doth deny to me!
Nor will reply a syllable, nor deign
One stabbing word to put me out of pain?
AM: To answer thee if I had promiséd,
As well as hear thee, this were justly said.
Thou call'st me cruel, hoping that, to shun
That vice, into the contrary I'll run.
But know, my ears are not so tickléd
With that (by me so little merited
And less desiréd) praise thou givst to me
Of beauty, as to hear myself by thee

349

Styled 'cruel' – which to be to any other,
I grant were vice; 'tis virtue to a lover.
And what thou harshness callst and cruelty
Is in a woman perfect honesty.
But say that e'en to a lover 'twere a sin –
Yet tell me, when hath Amarillis bin
Cruel to thee? Was't then when justice bad
To use no pity, yet on thee I had
So much, that I from death delivered thee?
I mean, when 'mongst a noble company
Of modest virgins mingled, thou didst cover
With a maid's habit a libidinous lover;
And, our chaste sports polluting, didst intrude
'Mongst kisses feigned and innocent thy lewd
And wanton kisses – such an act as yet
I blush as oft as I but think on it.
But at that time I knew thee not, heaven knows,
And when I did my indignation rose.
Thy wantonness I from my mind did keep,
And suffered not the amorous plague to creep
To my chaste heart; on my lips' outer skin
The poison stuck, but none of it got in.
  A mouth that's kissed perforce,
If it spit out the kiss, is ne'er the worse.
But what wouldst thou by that bold theft have got,
If I had to those nymphs discovered what
Thou wert? The Thracian women never tore
And murdered Orpheus so on Hebrus' shore,
As they had thee, unless her clemency
Whom thou call'st cruel now had rescued thee.
But she is not so cruel as she ought
To be: for if when she is cruel thought
Thy boldness is so great, what would it be
If she were judgéd pitiful by thee?
That honest pity which I could, I gave;
Other it is in vain for thee to crave,
Or hope: for amorous pity she can ill
Bestow, who gave it all to one that will

Give her none back. If thou my lover be,
Love my good name, my life, my honesty.
Thou seekst impossibles; I am a ward
To Heaven, Earth watches me, and my reward,
If I transgress, is death; but most of all,
Virtue defends me with a brazen wall.
For she that is protected by her honour,
Scorns there should be a safer guard upon her.
Look to thy safety, then, and do not give
Battle to me, Mirtillo; fly, and live
If thou be wise. For out of sense of smart
To abandon life, argues but a faint heart.
And 'tis the part of virtue to abstain
From what we love, if it will prove our bane.

MIR: He that no longer can resist must yield.

AM: Where virtue is, all passions quit the field.

MIR: Love triumphs over virtue.

AM:                                    Let that man
That cannot what he will, will what he can.

MIR: Necessity of loving hath no law.

AM: Love's wounds will heal, which salves of absence draw.

MIR: We fly in vain what we about us carry.

AM: Love drives out love like following billows – marry!

MIR: Strange levity in me thou dost presume.

AM: If all ways fail, time will thy love consume.

MIR: But first my love will have consuméd me.

AM: Is there no cure then for thy malady?

MIR: No cure at all but that which death affords.

AM: Death? let me speak then; and be sure these words
Be as a charm unto thee: though I know
When lovers talk of dying, it doth show
An amorous custom rather of the tongue,
Than a resolve of mind, continuing long,
To do it indeed; yet if thou e'er shouldst take
So strange a frenzy – know, when thou dost make
Away thyself, thou murderst my fame too.
Live then, if thou dost love me, and adieu!
I shall esteem thee henceforth most discreet,

If thou take care we two may never meet.

MIR: Sad doom! without my life how can I live,
Or without death end to my torments give?

AM: Mirtillo, 'tis high time thou wentst away,
Thou hast already made too long a stay:
Begone; and take this cordial along:
Of hopeless lovers there's a numerous throng,
There is no wound but carries with it pain,
And there are others may of love complain.

MIR: I know I'm not the only man hath lost
His love; but only wretched am I tossed
'Twixt life and death, of whom it may be said
That I am neither living, nor yet dead.

AM: Begone, begone!

MIR:                           Oh woeful parting! Oh
End of my days! From thee how can I go
And yet not die? The pangs of death I'm sure
I feel, and all that parting souls endure.
For mine, 'tis passed into my griefs; hence I
Have ceased to live, those live immortally.

   [*Exit* MIRTILLO, *Left.*]

AM: Mirtillo, O Mirtillo, couldst thou see
That heart which thou condemn'st of cruelty
— Soul of my soul! — thou unto it wouldst show
That pity which thou begst from it, I know.
Oh ill-starred lovers! what avails it me
To have thy love! T'have mine, what boots it thee?
Whom love hath joined why dost thou separate,
Malicious fate? And two divorced by fate
Why joinst thou, perverse love? How blest are you
Wild beasts that are in loving tied unto
No laws but those of love! whilst human laws
Inhumanly condemn us for that cause.
Oh why, if this be such a natural
And powerful passion, was it capital?
Nature too frail, that dost with law contend!
Law too severe, that nature dost offend!
But what? they love but little who death fear!

Ah, my Mirtillo, would to heaven that were
The only penalty! Virtue, which art
The binding'st law to an ingenuous heart,
This inclination which in me I feel,
Lanced with the sharp point of thy holy steel,
To thee I sacrifice: and pardon, dear
Mirtillo, her that's only cruel where
She must not pity. Pardon thy fierce foe
In looks and words – but in her heart not so.
Or if addicted to revenge thou be,
What greater vengeance canst thou take on me
Than thine own grief? For if thou be my heart,
As in despite of heaven and earth thou art,
Thy sighs my vital spirits are, the flood
Of tears which follows is my vital blood,
And all these pangs, and all these groans of thine
Are not thy pangs, are not thy groans, but mine.

[CORISCA *emerges from behind her bush.*]

COR: Sister, no more dissembling.

AM:                              Woe is me!
I am discovered!

COR:                I heard all: now see,
Was I a witch? I did believe, my heart,
Thou wert in love; now I am sure thou art.
And wouldst thou keep't from me? Thy closet? Tush,
This is a common evil, never blush!

AM: Corisca, I am conquered, I confess't.

COR: No, now I know't, deny it thou wert best!

AM: Alas! I knew a woman's heart would prove
Too small a vessel for o'erflowing love.

COR: Cruel to thy Mirtillo! – but unto
Thyself much more!

AM:                   'Tis cruelty that grew
From pity.

COR:        Poison ne'er was known to grow
From wholesome root. What difference canst thou show
'Twixt such a cruelty as doth offend
And such a pity as no help will lend?

353

AM: Ay me, Corisca!

COR:                'Tis a vanity,
  Sister, to sigh – an imbecility
  Of mind, and tastes too much of woman.

AM:                            Were't
  Not crueller to nourish in his heart
  A hopeless love? To fly him is a sign
  I have compassion of his case and mine.

COR: But why a hopeless love?

AM:                      Dost thou not know
  I am contracted unto Silvio?
  Dost thou not know besides what the law saith?
  'Tis death in any woman that breaks faith!

COR: O fool! and is this all stands in thy way?
  Whether is ancienter with us, I pray,
  The law of Dian, or of love? This last
  Is born with us, and it grows up as fast
  As we do, Amarillis; 'tis not writ,
  Nor taught by masters – nature printed it
  In human hearts with her own powerful hand.
  Both Gods and men are under love's command.

AM: But if that law my life away should take,
  Can this of love a restitution make?

COR: Thou art too nice: if women all were such,
  And on these scruples should insist so much,
  Good days adieu! I hold them simple souls
  Will live obnoxious to such poor controls.
  Laws are not for the wise: if to be kind
  Should merit death, Jove help the cruel mind![15]
  But if fools fall into those snares, 'tis fit
  They be forbid to steal, who have not wit
  To hide their theft. For honesty is but
  An art, an honest gloss on vice to put.
  Think others as they list; thus I conceive.

15. In this couplet Fanshawe has introduced a completely new idea of his
own. The Italian simply says that if the law were enforced with rigour, there
would be no women left alive in Arcadia at all.

AM: These rotten grounds, Corisca, will deceive.
  What I can't hold 'tis wisdom soon to quit.
COR: And who forbids thee, fool? Our life doth flit
  Too fast away to lose one jot of it;
  And men so squeamish and so curious grown,
  That two of our new lovers make not one
  O' th' old. We are no longer for their tooth
  – Believe't – than while we're new. Bate us our youth,
  Bate us our beauty, and, like hollow trees
  Which had been stuffed with honey by the bees,
  If that by lickerish hands away be ta'en,
  Dry and despiséd trunks we shall remain.
  Therefore let them have leave to babble what
  They please, as those who know nor reckon not
  What the poor woman Amarillis bears.
  Our case alas is differing much from theirs.
  Men in perfection as in age increase,
  Wisdom supplies the lack of handsomeness:
  But when our youth and beauty, which alone
  Conquer the strength and wit of men, are gone,
  All's gone with us; nor canst thou possibly
  Say a worse thing, or to be pardoned thee
  More hardly, than 'old woman'. Then before
  Thou split on that unevitable shore,
  Know thine own worth, and do not be so mad,
  As when thou mayst live merry, to live sad.
  What would the lion's strength boot him, or wit
  Avail a man, unless he uséd it?
  Our beauty is to us that which to men
  Wit is, or strength unto the lion. Then
  Let us use it while we may,
  Snatch those joys that haste away.
  Earth her winter-coat may cast,
  And renew her beauty past;
  But, our winter come, in vain
  We solicit spring again:
  And when our furrows snow shall cover,
  Love may return, but never lover.

AM: Thou sayst all this only to try me, sure,
    Not that thy thoughts are such. But rest secure,
    Unless the way thou unto me shalt show
    Be a plain way, and warrantable too,
    To break this match, I am resolved to die
    A thousand deaths ere stain my honesty.
COR: More wilful woman I did never know;
    But since thou'rt so resolvéd, be it so!
    Tell me, good Amarillis, seriously:
    Dost thou suppose thy Silvio sets by
    His faith as much as thou thy honesty?
AM: Thou mak'st me laugh at this; wherein should he
    Express a faith, who is to love a foe?
COR: Love's foe? Oh fool! Thou knowst not Silvio!
    He is the still sow,[16] he. Oh, these coy souls!
    Believe them not: the deep stream silent rolls.
    No theft in love so subtle, so secure,
    As to hide sin by seeming to be pure.
    In short, thy Silvio loves – but 'tis not thee,
    Sister, he loves.
AM:           What goddess may she be?
    For certainly she is no mortal dame
    That could the heart of Silvio inflame.
COR: Nor goddess, nor yet nymph.
AM:                 What hast thou said?
COR: Dost thou know my Lisetta?
AM:               Who? the maid
    That tends thy flocks?
COR:         The same.
AM:               It cannot be
    She, I am sure, Corisca?
COR:          Very she,
    I can assure thee, she is all his joy.
AM: A proper choice for one that was so coy!
COR: But wilt thou know how he doth pine away
    And languish for this jewel? Every day
    He feigns to go a-hunting.

    16. 'The still sow eateth all the draff,' according to an old proverb.

AM:                          Every morn,
  Soon as it dawns, I hear his curséd horn.
COR: And just at noon, when others are i' th' heat
  Of all the sport, he doth by stealth retreat
  From his companions, and comes all alone
  Unto my garden by a way unknown;
  Where underneath a hawthorn hedge's shade,
  Which doth the garden fence about, the maid
  Hears his hot sighs, and amorous prayers, which she
  Comes laughing afterwards and tells to me.
  Now hear what I to serve thee've thought upon;
  Or rather, what I have already done.
  I think thou knowst, that the same law which hath
  Enjoined the woman to observe her faith
  To her betrothéd, likewise doth enact
  That if the woman catch him in the fact
  Of falsehood, spite of friends[17] she may deny
  To have him, and without disloyalty
  Marry another.
AM:                    This I know full well;
  And thereof some examples too could tell,
  Of my own knowledge: Egle having found
  Licotas false, remained herself unbound.
  Armilla did from false Turingo so,
  And Phillida from Ligurino go.
COR: Now list to me: my maid (by me set on)
  Hath bid her credulous lover meet anon
  In yonder cave with her – whence he remains
  The most contented of all living swains,
  And waits but the hour. There shalt thou catch him, where
  I too will be, witness of all to bear;
  For without this our plot would be in vain.
  So without any hazard, or least stain
  To thine or to thy father's honour, thou
  Shalt free thyself from this distasteful vow.

17. 'Friends' here means 'relations', as often in seventeenth-century English.
'Spite of friends' means 'whatever your family may say'.

AM: I like it rarely; but the way, the way,
Corisca?

COR:       Marry, thus – observe me, pray!
In the middle of the cave, which narrow is,
And very long, upon the right hand lies
Another lesser grot, I know not whether
By nature, or by art, or both together
Made in the hollow stone, whose slimy wall
Is hid with clinging ivy, and a small
Hole in the roof lets light in from above,
Fit receptacle for the thefts of love,
Yet cheerful too enough. There shalt thou hide
Thyself, and hidden in that place abide
Till the two lovers come. I mean to send
Lisetta first and after her her friend,
Following his steps myself aloof; and when
I shall perceive him stepped into the den,
Rush after him will I. But lest he should
Escape from me, when I have laid fast hold
Upon him, I will use Lisetta's aid,
And joining both (for so the plot is laid
Between us two) together we will make
A cry, at which thou too shalt come, and take
The penalty o' th' law 'gainst Silvio.
Then my Lisetta and we two will go
Before the priest; and so shalt thou untie
The nuptial knot.

AM:       Before his father?

COR:       Why,
What matters that? Thinkst thou Montano's blood
Will stand in balance with his country's good?
Or that his sacred function he'll neglect
For any carnal or profane respect?

AM: Go to then, setting all disputes aside,
I wink, and follow thee my faithful guide.

COR: Then linger not, my heart, enter into
The cave.

AM:       Unto the temple first I'll go

To adore the gods; for unless heaven give
Success, no mortal enterprise can thrive.

COR: To devout hearts all places temples are:
It will lose too much time.

AM:                                    In using prayer
To them that made time, time cannot be lost.
    [*Exit* AMARILLIS, *Right.*]

COR: Go then and return quickly – So almost
I'm past the bad way; only this delay
Gives me some cause of trouble; yet this may
Be of use too. Something there would be done
To abuse my honest lover Coridon.
I'll say, I'll meet him in the cave, and so
Will make him after Amarillis go.
This done, by a back way I'll thither send
The priest of Dian her to apprehend.
Guilty she will be found, and sentencéd
To death without all doubt. My rival dead,
Mirtillo is mine own, his cruelty
To me being caused by 's love to her. But see
The man! I'll sound him till she comes. Now rise,
Rise all my love into my tongue and eyes.
    [*Enter* MIRTILLO, *Left.*]

MIR: Hear, ye damned spirits that in hell lament,
Hear a new sort of pain and punishment!
See in a turtle's look a tiger's mind!
She, crueller than death, 'cause she did find
One death would not suffice her bloody will,
And that to live was to be dying still,
Enjoins me not to make myself away,
That I might die a thousand times a day.

COR [*aside*]: (I'll make as though I saw him not.) – I hear
A doleful voice pierce my relenting ear;
Who should it be? Mirtillo, is it thou?

MIR: I would it were my ghost.

COR:                                    Well, well; but how
(And tell me true) thyself now dost thou find
Since to thy dearest nymph thou brak'st thy mind?

MIR: As one who in a fever cast,
Forbidden liquor longed to taste,
If gotten sets it to his mouth,
And quenches life, but cannot drouth:
So I, with amorous fever long
Consuméd, from her eyes and tongue
Sweet poison sucked, which leaves me more
Enflaméd than I was before.

COR: Love upon us no power can have
But what ourselves, Mirtillo, gave.
As a bear doth with her tongue
Polish her misshapen young[18]
Which had else in vain been born:
So an amorist giving form
To a rude and faint desire
That would otherwise expire,
Hatches love; which is at first
Weak and raw, but when 'tis nursed,
Fierce and cruel. Take't upon
My word, an old affection
Tyrannizes in a breast,
And grows a master from a guest.
For, when the soul shall once be brought
To be fettered to one thought,
And that not have the power to move
A minute from its object, love
(Made for delight) will turn to sadness,
And (which is worse) to death or madness.
Therefore my advice shall be
To part thy love to two or three.

MIR: Let death or madness me betide,
Rather than my flame divide.
Amarillis, though she be
Cruel and unkind to me,
Is my life and reason too,
And to her I will be true.

18. It was believed that a bear cub was born as a formless mass of flesh,
which had to be literally licked into shape by its mother.

COR: Foolish swain! that canst not tell
    How to make a bargain well.
    What? change love for hatred? I
    Rather now than do't would die.
MIR: Cruelty doth faith refine,
    As the fire the golden mine.
    Where were the loyalty of love,
    If women should not tyrants prove?
    In my many sufferings this
    All my joy and comfort is;
    Sorrows, tortures, exile, gall,
    Here's a cause will sweeten all.
    Let me languish, let me burn,
    Let me anything but turn.
COR: O brave lover! Valiant breast!
    More impetuous than a beast,
    And yet tamer than a rock,
    Which endures the ocean's shock!
    In lover's hearts there cannot be
    A worse disease than constancy.
    O most unhappy those in whom
    This foolish idol finds a room,
    Which shackles us, when we might prove
    The sweet variety of love.
    With this dull virtue constancy,
    Tell me, simple lover, why
    Amarillis? For her face,
    Whom another must embrace?
    Or dost thou affect her mind,
    Which to thee is not inclined?
    All then thou canst dote upon
    Is thine own destruction.
    And wilt thou be still so mad
    To covet that cannot be had?
    Up, Mirtillo, know thy parts:
    Canst thou want a thousand hearts?
    Others I dare swear there be
    That would sue as much to thee.

MIR: To be Amarillis' thrall
  Is more than to command them all.
  And if she my suit deny,
  All that's pleasure I defy.
  I to make another choice?
  In another I rejoice?
  Neither could I if I would,
  Neither would I if I could:
  But if possible to me
  Such a will or power be,
  Heaven and love before that hour
  Strip me of all will and power!

COR: Thou art enchanted: otherwise
  Couldst thou too thyself despise?

MIR: I must, when I'm despised by her,
  Corisca.

COR:        Come, Mirtillo, ne'er
  Deceive thyself; perhaps thou dost suppose
  She loves thee in her heart, although she shows
  An outward scorn. If thou but knew what she
  Talks oftentimes to me concerning thee!

MIR: All these are trophies of my constant love,
  With which I'll triumph o'er the powers above,
  And men below, my torments, and her hate,
  O'er fortune and the world, o'er death and fate.

COR [aside]: (Wonder of constancy! If this man knew
  How much he's loved by her, what would he do?)
  Mirtillo, how it pities me to hear
  These frantic speeches! Tell me, wert thou e'er
  In love before?

MIR:             Fair Amarillis was
  My first, and shall be my last love.

COR:                                Alas!
  It should seem then that thou didst never prove
  Any but cruel, but disdainful love.
  O that 't had been thy chance but once to be
  In love with one that's gentle, courteous, free!
  Try that a little: try it, and thou'lt find

How sweet it is to meet with one that's kind,
That loves and honours thee as much as thou
Thy sour and cruel Amarillis; how
Delightful 'tis to have a joy as great
As is thy love, a happiness complete
As thy own wish – to have thy mistress twine
About thy neck, and her sighs echo thine;
And after say: 'My joy, all that I have,
All that I am, and thy desires can crave,
As thy devotion is: if I am fair,
For thee I'm fair; for thee I deck this hair,
This face, this bosom; from this breast of mine
I turned out my own heart to harbour thine.'
But this is a small river to that vast
Sweet sea of pleasure which love makes us taste,
And they alone that taste can well relate.

MIR: A thousand thousand times most fortunate
Is he that's born under so blest a star!

COR: Hear me Mirtillo – [*Aside*] (ere I was aware
I'd almost called him mine) a nymph as fair
As the proud'st she that curls or spreads to the air
Her golden tresses, worthy of thy love
As thou of hers, the honour of this grove,
Love of all hearts, by every worthier swain
In vain solicited, adored in vain,
Doth love thee only, and thee only prize
More than her life, and more than her own eyes.
Mirtillo, scorn her not, if wise thou be;
For as the shadow doth the body, she
Will follow thee through all the world: she will
At thy least word and beck be ready still
As thy obedient handmaid; night and day
With thee she'll pass the tedious hours away.
Ah! do not waive, Mirtillo, do not waive
So rare a bliss: the perfect'st joys we have
Are those which neither sighs nor tears do cost,
Nor danger, and on which least time is lost.
Here thou hast pastime at thy door, a feast

Upon the table always ready dressed,
To please thy taste. Ay me! canst thou receive
A greater gift than this? Mirtillo, leave
Leave this cold hunting after flying feet,
And her that runs to thy embraces, meet.
Nor do I feed thee with vain hopes; command
Her come, and she that loves thee is at hand –
Now, if thou say the word.

MIR:                  I prithee rest
Content, my palate is not for a feast.

COR: Try but what joy is made of once, and then
Return unto thy wonted grief again,
That thou mayst say thou hadst a taste of both.

MIR: Distempered palates all sweet things do loathe.

COR: Yet do't in pity unto her that dies,
Unless she enjoy the sun of thy fair eyes.
Uncharitable youth, art thou not poor,
And canst thou beat a beggar from thy door?
Ah! what thou wouldst another should extend
To thee, do thou now to another lend.

MIR: What alms can beggars give? In short, I swore
Allegiance to that nymph whom I adore,
Whether she tyrant proved or merciful.

COR: Oh, truly blind, and – most unhappy – dull
Mirtillo! Who is't thou art constant to?
I am unwilling to add woe to woe;
But thou art too much wronged in faith, and I
That love thee am not able to stand by
And see thee so betrayed. If thou suppose
This cruelty of Amarillis grows
From zeal to virtue or religion,
Thou'rt gulled: another doth possess the throne
And thou, poor wretch, whilst he doth laugh, must cry.
What, stricken dumb?

MIR:                 I'm in an ecstasy,
'Twixt life and death suspended, till I know
Whether I should believe thee now or no.

COR: Dost not believe me then?

MIR:                           If I did, I
  Had not survived it sure: and I will die
  Yet, if it be a truth.
COR:                   Live, caitiff, live
  To be revenged!
MIR:                 But I cannot believe
  It is a truth.
COR:           Wilt thou not yet believe
  But force me to tell that which it will grieve
  Thy soul to hear? Dost thou see yonder cave?
  That is thy mistress' faith's and honour's grave:
  There laughs she at thee, there makes of thy annoy
  A poignant sauce to thy tired rival's joy.
  In short, there oft a base-born shepherd warms
  Thy virtuous Amarillis in his arms.
  Now go and sigh, and whine, and constant prove
  Unto a nymph that thus rewards thy love!
MIR: Ay me, Corisca, dost thou tell me true,
  And is it fit I should believe thee too?
COR: The more thou searchest, 'twill the worser be.
MIR: But didst thou see't, Corisca? Woe is me!
COR: Truth is, I did not see it, but thou mayst,
  And presently, for she her word hath passed
  To meet him there this very hour. But hide
  Thyself beneath that shady hedge's side,
  And thou thyself shalt see her straight descend
  Into the cave, and after her, her friend.
MIR: So quickly must I die?
COR:                       See! I have spied
  Her coming down already by the side
  O' th' temple – mark how guiltily she moves!
  Her stealing pace betraying their stolen loves.
  To mark the sequel, do thou here remain,
  And afterwards we two will meet again.
    [*Exit* CORISCA, *Left.*]
MIR: Since the discovery of the truth's so near,
  With my belief I will my death defer.
    [MIRTILLO *takes cover. Enter* AMARILLIS, *Right. She comes to a*

*halt at a point some way from* MIRTILLO's *hiding-place and he does*
*not hear the opening lines of her soliloquy.*]

AM: No mortal work successfully is done
Which with the immortal gods is not begun.
Full of distractions, and with heavy heart
I did from hence unto the temple part:
Whence – heaven be praised – I come as light as air,
And strangely comforted; for at my prayer
Pure and devout, I felt from thence, methought,
Another soul into my body shot,
Which whispered: 'Fear not, Amarillis, go
Securely on.' Aye, and I will do so,

[AMARILLIS *crosses to a point near* MIRTILLO's *hiding-place.*
*He hears what follows.*]

Heaven guiding. – Fair mother of love, befriend
Her that on thee for succour doth depend;
Thou that as queen in the third orb dost shine,
If e'er thou feltst thy son's flames, pity mine.
Bring, courteous goddess, by a secret path
Quickly that youth to whom I've pawned my faith.
And thou, dear cave, till I have done my work,
Suffer this slave of love in thee to lurk.
But, Amarillis, all the coast is clear,
None nigh to see thee, and none nigh to hear.
Securely enter! O Mirtillo, O
Mirtillo, if thou dream'dst wherefore I go!

[AMARILLIS *goes into the cave.* MIRTILLO *comes out of his hiding-*
*place.*]

MIR: I wake, and see what I could wish to have been
Born without eyes, that I might not have seen;
Or rather not to have been born. Curst fate!
Why hast thou thus prolongéd my life's date,
To bring me to this killing spectacle?
Mirtillo, more tormented than in hell
The blackest soul is – not to doubt thy grief?
Not to be able to suspend belief?
Thou, thou hast heard and seen't: thy mistress is
Another man's – and, which is worse, not his

Whose by the world's laws she was bound to be,
But by love's laws snatched both from him and thee.
O cruel Amarillis! to undo
This wretched man, and then to mock him too
With that unconstant mouth which once did meet,
And once did call Mirtillo's kisses sweet,
But now his loathéd name (which haply rose
Like bitter drink that 'gainst the stomach goes)
Because it should not bitterness impart
To thy delight, hath spued out of thy heart?
Since therefore she who gave thee life hath ta'en
That life away, and given it again
T'another, why dost thou thy life survive,
Wretched Mirtillo? Why art thou alive?
   Die, die Mirtillo unto grief and smart,
As unto joy already dead thou art!
Die, dead Mirtillo; since thy life is so,
Let thy pangs likewise be concluded. Go
Out of the anguish of this death, which still
Keeps thee alive, that it may longer kill.
But shall I die then unrevengéd? Sure
I'll slay him first that did my death procure.
I will dispense with my dire love of death
Till I have justly ta'en away his breath
Who slew my heart unjustly. Yield, stout grief
To anger, death to life, till in my life
I have avenged my death.
Let not this steel be drunken with the flood
Of its own master's unrevengéd blood;
Nor this right hand be pity's till it hath
First made itself the minister of wrath.
Thou that enjoyst my spoils, whate'er thou be,
Since I must fall, I'll pull thee after me.
In the same brake I'll plant myself again,
And when I spy him coming to the den,
Will rush upon him with this piercing dart
At unawares, and strike him through the heart.
But is't not base to strike him out of sight?

It is – defy him then to single fight,
Where valour may my justice prove! But no,
This place is unto all so known, and so
Frequented, that some swains may interpose:
Or, which is worse, enquire of me whence grows
Our quarrel; which if I deny, 'tis naught
They'll think; if feign a cause, I may be caught
Then in a lie; if tell't, her name will be
Blasted with everlasting infamy:
In whom, although I never can approve
That which I see, yet I must ever love
That which I fancied and did hope t' have seen,
And that which ought, I'm sure, in her t' have been.
Die basely then the base adulterer,
Who hath slain me and hath dishonoured her!
Aye, but the blood may (if I kill him here)
The murder show, and that the murderer?
What do I care? Aye, but the murderer known
Bewrays the cause for which the murder's done.
So this ungrateful woman runs the same
Hazard this way of shipwreck in her fame.
Enter the cave then, and assault him there!
Good, good! Tread softly, softly, lest she hear;
That she's at the other end her words implied.
Now hid with branches in the rock's left side
There is a hollow at the steep stair's foot;
There without any noise I'll wait to put
In execution my design. My foe
Despatched, his bleeding carcass I will throw
To my she-foe, to be revenged on two
At once. The selfsame steel I'll then imbrue
In mine own blood; so three shall die in brief,
Two by my weapon, and the third of grief.
A sad and miserable tragedy
Of both her lovers shall this tigress see,
Of him she loves and him she scorns. And this
Cave which was meant the chamber of their bliss,
To her and to her minion shall become

And (which I more desire) t' her shame, a tomb.
  [*Enter* SATYR, *Left.*]
But you, dear footsteps, which I long have traced
In vain – unerring path, lead me at last
To where my love is hid. To you I bow;
Your print I follow. O Corisca, now
I do believe thee – now thou'st told me true!
  [*Exit* MIRTILLO, *into cave.*]
SAT: Does he believe Corisca, and pursue
  Her steps to Erycina's cave? A beast
  Hath wit enough to apprehend the rest.
  But if thou dost believe her, thou hadst need
  Have from her good security indeed,
  And hold her by a stronger tie than I
  Had lately of her hair. But stronger tie
  On her there cannot be than gifts. This bold
  Strumpet herself to this young swain hath sold,
  And here by the false light now of this vault
  Delivers the bad ware which he hath bought.
  Or rather, 'tis heaven's justice which hath sent
  Her hither to receive her punishment
  From my revenging hands. His words did seem
  To imply she made some promise unto him,
  Which he believed: and by his spying here
  Her print, that she is in the cave 'tis clear.
  Do a brave thing, then! Stop the mouth o' th' cave
  With that great hanging stone, that they may have
  No means of scaping; to the priest then go
  And bring by the back way (which few do know)
  His ministers to apprehend, and by
  The law deservedly to make her die.
  For 'tis not unto me long since unknown
  That she contracted is to Coridon,
  However he (because he stands in fear
  Of me) to lay his claim to her forbear.
  But now I'll give him leave at once to be
  Revenged on her both for himself and me.
  But I lose time in talk. From this young grove

I'll pull a tree up by the root, to move
The stone withal. So, this I think will do.
How heavy 'tis! The stone hath a root too.
What if I mined it with this trunk, and so
As with a lever heaved it from below?
Good, good! now to the other side as much
How fast it sticks! I did not think it such
A difficult attempt as it hath proved.
The centre of the earth were easier moved.
Nor strength nor skill will do this work, I see;
Or does that vigour which was once in me
Now fail me at my need? What do ye do,
My perverse stars? I will, in spite of you,
I will remove it yet! The devil haul
Corisca, I had almost said, and all
The sex of them! O Pan Lyceus, hear,
And to move this be movéd by my prayer!
Pan, thou that all things canst and all things art,
Thou once thyself didst woo a stubborn heart;
Revenge on false Corisca now thine own,
And my despiséd love. I move the stone
Thus by the virtue of thy sacred name!
Thus rolls it by the virtue of the same.
So, now the fox is trapped, and finely shut
Where she had earthed herself. I'll now go put
Fire to the hole, where I could wish to find
The rest of women, to destroy the kind.

[*Exit* SATYR, *Right Centre. Enter* CHORUS, *Right.*]
CHO: O love, how potent and how great thou art!
Wonder of nature and the world! What heart
So dull, as not to feel thy power? What wit
So deep and piercing, as to fathom it?
Who knows thy hot lascivious fires will say:
'Infernal spirit, thou dost live and sway
'In the corporeal part.' But whoso knows
How thou dost men to virtuous things dispose,
And how the dying flame of loose desires
Looks pale, and trembles at thy chaster fires,

Will say: 'Immortal god, i' th' soul alone
Thou hast establishéd thy sacred throne.'
Rare monster! wonderfully got betwixt
Desire and reason; an affection mixed
Of sense and intellect; with knowing, wild;
With seeing, blind; a god, and yet a child;
And, such, thou swayst the earth – and heaven too,
On which thou treadst as we on t'other do.
Yet (by thy leave!) a greater miracle,
A mightier thing than thou art I can tell.
For all thou dost, that may our wonder claim,
Thou dost by virtue of a woman's name.

   Woman! the gift of heaven – or of him rather
Who made thee fairer, being of both the father –
Wherein is heaven so beautiful as thou,
That rolls one goggle eye in its vast brow
Like a grim Cyclop? – not a lamp of light,
But cause of blindness and Cimmerian night
To the bold gazer! If that speak, it is
A thundering voice; and if it sigh, the hiss
Of earth-engendered winds. Thou, with the fair
Angel-like prospect of two suns, which are
Serene and visible, dost still the winds
And calm the billows of tempestuous minds.
And sound, light, motion, beauty, majesty,
Make in thy face so sweet a harmony,
That heaven (I mean this outward heaven) must needs
Confess thy form the form of that exceeds;
Since beauty that is dead less noble is,
Than that which lives and is a place of bliss.
With reason therefore man – that gallant creature
That lords it over all the works of nature –
To thee as lady paramount pays duty,
Acknowledging in thine thy maker's beauty.
And if he triumphs gain, and thrones inherit,
It is not because thou hast less of merit,
But for thy glory; since a greater thing
It is to conquer than to be a king.

But that thy conquering beauty doth subdue
Not only man, but e'en his reason too,
If any doubt, he in Mirtillo hath
A miracle that may constrain his faith.
This wanted, woman, to thy power before,
To make us love where we can hope no more.

# ACT FOUR

*Scene as before.*

    [*Enter* CORISCA, *Left.*]

COR: My heart and thoughts till now were so much set
    To train that foolish nymph into my net,
    That my dear hair, which by that rogue was ta'en
    From me, and how to get it back again
    I quite forgot. Oh, how it troubled me
    To pay that ransom for my liberty!
    But 't had been worse to have been a prisoner
    To such a beast, who though he doth not bear
    A mouse's heart, might have moused me. For I
    Have, to say truth, fooled him sufficiently,
    And like a horse-leech did him suck and drain
    As long as he had blood in any vein.
    And now he's moved I love him not; and moved
    He well might be, if him I e'er had loved.
    How can one love a creature that doth want
    All that is lovely? As a stinking plant
    Which the physician gathered for the use
    He had of it, when he hath strained the juice
    And virtue out, is on the dunghill thrown,
    So having squeezed him, I with him have done.
    Now will I see if Coridon into
    The cave's descended. Ha! What do I view?
    Wake I? or sleep I? Or am drunk? But now
    This cave's mouth open was, I'm sure; then how
    Comes it now shut? and with a ponderous
    And massy stone rolled down upon it thus?
    Earthquake I'm sure to unhinge it there was none.
    Would I knew certainly that Coridon

And Amarillis were within; and then
I cared not how it came. He's in the den,
If, as Lisetta said, he parted were
From home so long ago. Both may be there,
And by Mirtillo shut together. Love,
Pricked with disdain, hath strength enough to move
The world, much more a stone. Should it be true,
Mirtillo could not have devised to do
Aught more according to my heart than this,
Though he Corisca had enthroned in his
Instead of Amarillis; I will go
The back way in, that I the truth may know.

    [*Exit* CORISCA, *Right Centre. Enter* DORINDA, *dressed in a wolf's
    skin cloak, and* LINCO, *Left.*]

DOR: But Linco, didst not thou know me indeed?
LIN: Who could have known thee in this savage weed
  For meek Dorinda? But if I had been
  A ravenous hound, as I am Linco, then
  I to thy cost had known thee for a beast.
  What do I see? What do I see?
DOR:                   Thou seest
  A sad effect of love; a sad and strange
  Effect of loving, Linco!
LIN:               Wondrous change!
  Thou a young maid, so soft, so delicate,
  That wert, methinks, an infant but of late,
  Whom in my arms I bore, as I may say,
  A very little child but yesterday,
  And steering thy weak steps, taught thee to name
  (When I thy father served) daddy and mam,
  Who like a tim'rous doe (before thy heart
  Was made a prey to insulting love) didst start
  At everything that on the sudden stirred,
  At every wind, at every little bird
  That shook a bough, each lizard that but ran
  Out of a bush, made thee look pale and wan,
  Now all alone o'er hills, through woods dost pass
  Fearless of hounds or savage beasts.

DOR:                              Alas!
She whom love wounds no other wound doth fear.
LIN: Indeed, fair nymph, love showed his godhead here,
From woman to a man transforming thee,
Or rather to a wolf.
DOR:                    If thou couldst see
Into my breast, O Linco, then thou'dst say,
A living wolf upon my heart doth prey
As on a harmless lamb.
LIN:                        Is Silvio
That wolf?
DOR:         Alas, who else can be 't?
LIN:                           And so,
'Cause he's a wolf, thou a she-wolf wouldst be,
To try, since on thy human visage he
Was not enamoured, if he would at least
Affect thee in the likeness of a beast,
As being of his kind. But prithee, where
Gotst thou these robes?
DOR:                       I'll tell thee: I did hear
Silvio would chase today the noble boar
At Erimanthus' foot; and there before
The morning peeped was I, from wood to wood
Hunting the hunter; by a crystal flood
From which our flocks did climb the hills, I found
Melampo, the most beauteous Silvio's hound,
Who having quenched his thirst there, as I guess,
Lay to repose him on the neighbouring grass.
I, who love anything that's Silvio's,
Even the very ground on which he goes,
And shadow which his beauteous limbs do cast,
Much more the dog on which his love is placed,
Stooping, laid sudden hold on him, who came
Along with me as gentle as a lamb.
And whilst 'twas in my thoughts to lead him back
Unto his lord and mine, hoping to make
A friend of him with what he held so dear,
He came himself to seek him, and stopt here.

Dear Linco, I'll not lose thee so much time,
As to tell all that's passed 'twixt me and him:
This only, to be brief – after a long
Preface of oaths on one another strung,
And treacherous promises, this cruel swain
Flung from me full of anger and disdain,
Both with his own Melampo (to his lord
So true) and with my dear and sweet reward.

LIN: O cruel Silvio! ruthless swain! But what
Didst thou do then, Dorinda? Didst thou not
Hate him for this?

DOR:               Rather (as if the fire
Of his disdain love's fire had been) his ire
Increased my former flame. His steps I trace,
And thus pursuing him towards the chase,
I met hard by with my Lupino, whom
Before a little I had parted from;
When straight it came into my head that I
In his attire, and in the company
Of shepherds might be thought a shepherd too,
And undiscovered my fair Silvio view.

LIN: In a wolf's likeness among hounds, and none
Bite thee? 'Tis much, Dorinda, thou hast done!

DOR: This, Linco, was no miracle, for they
Durst not touch her who was their master's prey.
There I, out of the tents, amidst the crew
Of neighbouring shepherds that were met to view
The famous pastime, stood admiring more
To see the huntsman than the hunted boar.
At every motion of the furious beast
My cold heart shivered in my breast;
At every action of the brave young man
My soul with all her touched affections ran
In to his aid. But my extreme delight
Again was poisoned with the horrid sight
Of the fierce boar, whose strength and vast
Proportion all proportion passed.
As an impetuous whirlwind in a great

And sudden storm, which all that it doth meet
– Houses, and trees, and stones – before it bears,
All it can get within its circle tears
To pieces in an instant: so the boar
Wheeling about, his tusks all foam and gore,
Piled in one heap dogs slain, spears knapped, men wounded.
How oft did I desire to have compounded
For Silvio's life with the enragéd swine,
And for his blood to have given the monster mine!
How oft was I about to run between
And with my body his fair body screen!
Spare, cruel boar! how often did I cry,
Spare my fair Silvio's breast of ivory!
Thus to myself I spake, and sighed, and prayed,
When his fierce dog, armed with a breastplate made
Of hard and scaly barks of trees, he slipped
After the beast, now prouder being dipped
Throughly in blood, and lifted from the ground
On slaughtered trunks. The valour of that hound,
Linco, exceeds belief, and Silvio
Not without reason surely loves him so.
As a chafed lion, which now meets, now turns
From an untaméd bull's well brandished horns,
If once he come with his strong paw to seize
Upon his shoulder, masters him with ease:
So bold Melampo, shunning with fine sleights
The boar's short turns, and rapid motion, lights
At length upon his ear; which having bit
Quite through, and lugged him twice or thrice by it,
He with his teeth so nailed him to the ground
That at his vast bulk now a mortal wound
Might levelled be with greater certainty
– Before but slightly hurt – then suddenly
My lovely Silvio, calling on the name
Of Dian, 'Goddess, do thou give me aim,'
Quoth he, 'the horrid head is thine!' This said,
His golden quiver's swiftest shaft to the head
He drew, which flying to that very point

Where the left shoulder knits with the neck joint,
There wounded the fierce boar – so down he fell.
Then I took breath, seeing my Silvio well,
And out of danger. Happy beast! to die
So sweet a death, as by that hand, which I
Would beg my end from.

LIN:                 But what then became
Of the slain beast?

DOR:             I know not, for I came
Away, for fear of being known; but I
Suppose the head to the temple solemnly
They'll bear, according to my Silvio's vow.

LIN: But wilt thou not get out of these weeds now?

DOR: Yes, but my garments with my other gear
Lupino has, who promised to stay here
With them, but fails. Dear Linco, if thou love
Me, seek him for me up and down this grove;
Far off he cannot be. Meanwhile I'll take
A little rest (dost see there?) in that brake.
There I'll expect thee; for I am o'ercome
With weariness and sleep, and will not home
Accoutred thus.

LIN:              I go – but stir not then
Out of that place till I return again.

> [DORINDA *retires behind a bush,* Right Centre, *and lies down. Exit*
> LINCO, *Right Centre.*]

> [*Enter* CHORUS *of* SHEPHERDS, Right. *Their* LEADER *addresses*
> *them.*]

LEADER: Have ye heard, shepherds, that our demi-god
(Montano's and Alcides' worthy blood)
This day hath freed us from that dreadful beast
Which all Arcadia lately did infest,
And that he is preparing himself now
I'th' temple for it to perform his vow?
If for so great a benefit we'd show
Our gratitude, to meet him let us go,
And join our tongues and hearts together there
To honour him as our deliverer.

Which honour, though it be reward too small
For such a fair and valiant soul, 'tis all
Virtue can have on earth.

[*Enter* ERGASTO, *Right Centre.*]

ERG:                           O sad disaster!
O bitter chance! O wound that hath no plaster!
O day to be for ever steeped in tears!

CHO: What doleful voice is this that strikes our ears?

ERG: Stars, that are enemies to man always,
Why do you mock our faith? Why do you raise
Our hope on high, that when it falls again
The precipice may be with greater pain?

LEADER: Ergasto, by his voice! – and it is he.

ERG: But why do I accuse heaven wrongfully?
Accuse thyself, Ergasto – thou alone,
Thou, thou against the steel didst knock the stone;
Thou laidst the match unto the tinder, whence
A flame unquenchable is kindled since.
But heaven doth know, I for the best did do it,
And pity only did induce me to it.
O ill-starred lovers! wretched Titiro!
Poor Amarillis! Childless Father! O
Mourning Montano! O Arcadia gone
In a consumption far, and we undone!
In short, most sad, all I have seen or see!
Or speak, or hear, or think!

LEADER:                          What may this be,
Alas, that in one accident alone
Includes a general desolation?
This way he bends his course; let us go meet
Him, swains!

ERG:            Eternal Gods! is it not yet
Time to abate your wrath?

CHO:                          Unfold to us,
Courteous Ergasto, what afflicts thee thus.
Why dost thou moan?

ERG:                   Your ruin and mine own,
The ruin of Arcadia I moan.

CHO: Alas! Why so?

ERG:                    The very staff, the stay
  Of all our hope, is broke, is pulled away!

CHO: Speak plainer.

ERG:                    Titiro's daughter, that sole prop
  Of her old house, and father, the sole hope
  Of our deliverance, promised here below,
  Above decreed to marry Silvio,
  As the only means that should Arcadia save,
  That heavenly maid, so sober and so grave,
  That precedent of honour, crowned with lilies
  Of chastity, that peerless Amarillis –
  She, she . . . Alas! I have no heart, no breath
  To tell it you.

CHO:          Is dead?

ERG:                    Is near her death

CHO: Alas! what have we heard?

ERG:                    Nothing, as yet . . .
  She dies a malefactress – that, that's it!

CHO: A malefactress, Amarillis? How,
  Ergasto?

ERG:     Caught with an adulterer now;
  And if ye stay a little longer here
  Led pinioned to the temple ye shall see her.

CHO: O female structures, glorious and most fair,
  But weak withal! O chastity, how rare
  Art thou! – and shall it then be truly taxed,
  No woman's chaste but she that ne'er was aksed?

ERG: Indeed, when she that's virtue's self doth fall,
  We well may doubt the virtue of them all.

CHO: Pray, if it will not too much trouble be,
  Tell the whole story to these swains and me.

ERG: I will. – The priest early today, ye know,
  Did with this wretched nymph's sad father go
  Unto the sacred temple: with one care
  Both movéd, to facilitate with prayer
  Their children's desired marriage. For this end
  At once their incense did to heaven ascend,

At once their offerings bled, their sacrifice
At once was done with due solemnities,
And such glad auspice, that no entrails e'er
Were fairer seen, no flame was more sincere,
And less eclipsed with smoke: moved with such signs,
Thus the blind prophet speaks, and thus divines: –
'This day, Montano, shall thy Silvio love;
'Thy daughter, Titiro, a wife shall prove.
'Go and prepare the marriage.' O absurd
And vain depending on an augur's word!
And thou as blind in soul as in thy eyes,
If thou hadst said, 'Prepare her obsequies',
Then a true prophet thou hadst proved indeed.
Yet all the standers-by were comforted,
And the old fathers wept for joy apace,
And Titiro was parted from the place,
When in the temple suddenly were heard
Sinister omens, and dire signs appeared
Boding heaven's wrath. At which, alas, if each
Stood there astonished and bereft of speech
After so fair beginnings, friends, judge you!
Meanwhile the priests themselves alone withdrew
Into an inner room: and whilst they there,
And we without, intent in praying were,
Devout and weeping, puffing through the press
The cursèd Satyr, lo! demands access
Unto the priests. I, porter of that place,
Admit him. He then (oh, he has a face
To bring ill news!) cried: 'Fathers, if your prayer
Find not the Gods, your vows and incense are
Not acceptable and your sacrifice;
If from your altars an impure flame rise,
Think it not strange! That likewise is impure
Which is committing now hard by your door,
In Ericina's cave – a false nymph there
Is breaking with a base adulterer
Your laws, and her own faith. Send with me now
Your ministers, and I will show them how

I'th' act to take them. Then – O human mind!
When thy fate's near, how dull thou art, how blind! –
The good priests breathed, supposing 'twas no more
But remove them, and heaven would as before
Look on their sacrifice benignly. There-
Upon they order their chief minister
Nicandro presently to take that guide,
And bring both lovers to the temple tied.
With all his under-ministers he goes,
Pursuing that vile Satyr through a close
And crooked way into the cave. The maid,
Struck with their torches' sudden light, assayed
From where she was to run out of the door,
Which that base dog had stopped, it seems, before.

CHO: And what did he the while?

ERG:                   He went his ways
When he had led Nicandro to the place.
But, friends, I cannot tell the general
Astonishment that fell upon us all,
When it the daughter proved of Titiro:
Who taken, in a trice (I do not know
Out of what place) forth bold Mirtillo flew,
And a sharp dart which he was armed with threw
Like lightning at Nicandro; which, if it
The place that it was aiméd at had hit,
Had sent him to the shades. But, whether I
May call it fortune or agility,
At the same instant the one aimed his blow,
The other stepped a little backward; so
The mortal steel passed by, leaving his breast
Untouched, and in his coat of skins did rest;
Into the which, I know not how, 'twas wove
So intricately, that Mirtillo strove
In vain to pull it out; and so he too
Was taken.

CHO:        And with him what did they do?

ERG: He to the temple by himself was brought.

CHO: For what?

ERG:                To try if he'd discover aught
  Touching the fact in question. Perhaps too
  The affront he in their minister did do
  Unto the priestly majesty might some
  Penance deserve. Would yet I might have come
  To comfort my poor friend!

CHO:                                What hindered thee?

ERG: The waiters at the altar may not be
  Admitted to delinquents. Therefore I,
  Sequestered from the other company,
  Go by myself unto the temple, where
  With many a prayer and devouter tear
  I'll beg of heaven that it would chase away
  This sullen storm that overclouds our day.
  Dear shepherds, rest in peace, and join with ours
  Your prayers, to batter the celestial towers.

CHO: We will, when we have paid to Silvio
  That duty first we to his goodness owe.
  O ye great Gods! now, now, if ever, prove
  Your anger less eternal than your love.

  [*Exeunt* SHEPHERDS, *Left*, and ERGASTO, *Right. Enter* CORISCA,
  *Right Centre.*]

COR: Empale ye triumph-decking laurel boughs,
  Empale my glorious and victorious brows!
  Into Love's lists (hedged round about with flame)
  This day 'I came, I saw, I overcame'!
  This day hath heaven and earth, nature and art,
  Fortune and fate, friend and foe ta'en my part.
  Even that base Satyr who abhors me so
  Hath helped me too, as if he too did go
  Some share with me. How much more happily
  Did fortune bring Mirtillo in than I
  Contrived to have brought Coridon! to make
  Her crime more show of likelihood to take.
  And though Mirtillo's apprehended too,
  That matters not; they soon will let him go.
  The adultress only pays the penalty.
  O famous triumph! Solemn victory!

If lying may deserve a trophy, I
Deserve a trophy for my amorous lie;
Which from this tongue and bosom hath done more
For me than love with all his charms before.
But this is not a time to talk – withdraw
Thyself, Corisca, till the doom of law
Fall on thy rival's head, for fear that she,
To excuse herself, should lay the blame on thee.
Or that the priest himself should wish to know
What thou canst say, before he gives the blow.
When a mine springs, 'tis good to stand aloof;
A lying tongue requires a flying hoof.
I'll hide me in those woods, and there will make
Some stay, till it be time to come and take
Possession of my joys. Oh! it hath hit
Beyond all thought. Success hath crowned my wit.

[*Exit* CORISCA, *Left. Enter* NICANDRO, AMARILLIS, *Right Centre.*]

NIC: A heart of flint, or rather none had he,
Nor human sense, that could not pity thee,
Unhappy nymph, and for thy sorrow grieve
The more, by how much less they can believe
This should befall thee, who have known thee best.
For were it but to see a maid distressed
Of venerable countenance, and that showed
So virtuous and so excellently good;
One that for heavenly beauty merited
Temples and sacrifices, to be led
Unto the temple as a sacrifice,
Who could behold it without melting eyes?
But he that should consider further, how,
And for what purpose thou wert born – that thou
Art daughter unto Titiro, and should
Have married been unto Montano's blood
(Two the most loved and honoured, shall I say,
Shepherds or fathers of Arcadia).
And that, being such, so great, so famous, and
So beautiful a nymph, and that did stand

384

By nature so remote from thy death's brink,
Thou shouldst now be condemned. He that doth think
On this and weeps not, wails not thy mishap,
Is not a man, but wolf in human shape.

AM: If my mishap had come through mine own fault,
And the effect had been of an ill thought
As of a deed that seems ill, it had been
Less grievous to me to have death pay sin.
And very just it were I should have spilt
My blood to wash my impure soul from guilt,
To quench heaven's wrath; and since man too had wrong,
Pay what to human justice did belong.
So might I still a crying conscience,
And mortified with a due inward sense
Of deserved death, render myself more fit
To die, and through that purgatory get
Perchance to paradise. But now in all
My pride of youth and fortune thus to fall,
Thus innocent, is a sad case, a sad,
Nicandro.

NIC:        Nymph, would to heaven men had
Sinned against thee, rather than thou 'gainst heaven.
For satisfaction might be easier given
To thee for thy wronged fame, than unto it
For its wronged deities. Nor know I yet
Who wronged thee but thyself. Wert thou not caught
Alone with the adulterer in a vault?
To Silvio precontracted wert not thou?
And so thy nuptial faith hast broken – how
Then innocent?

AM:        For all this have not I
Transgressed the law: and innocently die.

NIC: Not nature's law perchance – 'Love where thou wilt!' –
But that of men and heaven – 'Love without guilt!'

AM: Both men and heaven (if all our fortune be
Derived from thence) transgressed have against me.
For what but an ill destiny could bid
That I should die for what another did?

NIC: What was that, nymph? Bridle thy tongue, with high-
    Flown grief transported e'en to blasphemy.
    The ills we suffer our own wrongs pull down;
    Heaven pardons many wrongs, but it doth none.
AM: I blame in heaven only my own star –
    But one that hath deceived me, more by far.
NIC: Then blame thyself; thyself thou didst deceive.
AM: I did when I a cozener did believe.
NIC: They who desire to be deceived are not.
AM: Dost think me naught?
NIC:                       Nay, ask thy actions that!
AM: Actions are oft false comments on our hearts.
NIC: Yet those we see, and not the inward parts.
AM: The heart may be seen too with the eyes of the mind.
NIC: Without the senses' help those eyes are blind.
AM: The senses must submit to reason's sway.
NIC: Reason in point of fact must sense obey.
AM: Well, I am sure an honest heart I have.
NIC: Prithee who brought thee then into the cave?
AM: My folly and too much credulity.
NIC: Thou trustedst with a friend thy honesty?
AM: I trusted a friend's honesty.
NIC:                       Thy blood?
    Was that the friend thou wouldst have understood?
AM: Ormino's sister, who betrayed me thither.
NIC: 'Tis sweet when lovers are betrayed together.
AM: Mirtillo entered without my consent.
NIC: How enter'dst thou then, and for what intent?
AM: Let this suffice, 'twas not for him I came.
NIC: It cannot, if no other cause thou name.
AM: Examine him about my innocence!
NIC: Him who hath been the cause of thy offence?
AM: Call her to witness who betrayed me hath!
NIC: Why should we hear a witness without faith?
AM: By chaste Diana's dreadful name I swear!
NIC: Thou by thy deeds art perjured unto her.
    Nymph, I am plain, I cannot flatter thee
    Into a hope which in extremity

Will leave thee more confounded. These are dreams.
A troubled fountain cannot yield pure streams,
Nor a bad heart good words; and where the deed
Is evident, defence offence doth breed.
What dost thou talk? Thou shouldst have guarded more
Than thy life now, thy chastity before.
Why dost thou cheat thyself?

AM:                              O misery!
    Must I then die, Nicandro? Must I die?
    None left to hear? None to defend me left?
    Of all abandoned? Of all hope bereft?
    Only of such a mocking pity made
    The wretched object as affords no aid?

NIC: Be patient, nymph, and give me cause to tell,
    Though thou didst ill, yet that thou suff'rédst well.
    Look up to heaven, since thence thou drawst thy birth.
    All good or ill we meet with upon earth
    From thence as from a fountain doth distil,
    And as no good is here unmixed with ill,
    So punishment, that's ill to flesh and blood,
    As to the account we must make there is good.
    And if my words have cut thee, 'tis but like
    A faithful surgeon, who a vein doth strike,
    Or thrusts his instrument into the wound
    Where it is mortallest and most profound;
    In being cruel, merciful. Then be
    Content with what is writ in heaven for thee.

AM: Oh, 'tis a cruel sentence, whether it
    In heaven for me, or in earth be writ!
    Yet writ in heaven I'm certain it is not,
    For there my innocence is known. But what
    Doth that avail me, if that die I must?
    That's the strait narrow passage! To be dust,
    Nicandro, that's the bitter cup! But oh!
    By that compassion thou to me dost show,
    Lead me not to the temple yet – stay! stay!

NIC: Who fears to die, dies every hour o' th' day.
    Why hangst thou back, and drawst a painful breath?

Death hath no ill in't but the fear of death.
And he that dies when he hath heard his doom,
Flies from his death.

AM:                              Perchance some help may come.
Father, dear father, dost thou leave me too?
An only daughter's father, wilt thou do
Nothing to save me? Yet before I die
A parting kiss to me do not deny.
Two bosoms shall be piercéd with one blow,
And from thy daughter's wound thy blood must flow.
O father! (once so sweet and dear a name,
Which I was never wont to invoke in vain)
Thy belov'd daughter's wedding callst thou this?
Today a bride; today a sacrifice!

NIC: Good nymph, no more! why dost thou bootlessly
Stay thus tormenting both thyself and me?
The time calls on: I must convey thee hence,
Nor with my duty longer may dispense.

AM: Dear woods adieu, then; my dear woods, adieu!
Receive these sighs (my last ones) into you,
Till my cold shade, forced from her seat by dire
And unjust steel, to your loved shades retire.
For sink to hell it can't, being innocent;
Nor soar to heaven, laden with discontent.
Mirtillo, O Mirtillo! most accurst
The day I saw, the day I pleased thee first!
Since I, whom thou above thy life didst love,
Became thy life, that thou my death mightst prove.
She dies condemned for kindness now to thee,
Whom thou hast still condemned of cruelty.
I might have broke my faith as cheap! Ay me!
Now without fault or fruit I die – or thee,
My dear Mirtill . . . [Faints].

NIC:                              Alas! she dies indeed.
Poor wretch! Come hither, shepherds, with all speed;
Help me to hold her up. O piteous case!
She finished in Mirtillo's name her race.
Unhappy maid! – She breathes yet, and I feel

Some signs of life pant in her bosom still.
To the next fountain let us carry her;
Perchance cold water may recover there
Her fleeting spirits. – Stay, will not relief
Be cruelty to her, who dies of grief
To prevent dying by the axe? Howe'er,
Yet let us not our charity forbear.
Men ought to lend their aid in present woe;
What is to come, none but the Gods foreknow.

[*Exeunt* NICANDRO, AMARILLIS, *Right. Enter* CHORUS *of*
HUNTSMEN *and* SHEPHERDS, *with* SILVIO, *Left.*]

HUNTSMEN: O glorious youth! true child of Hercules,
That kill'st so soon such monstrous beasts as these!

SHEPHERDS: O glorious youth! by whom lies slain and quelled
This Erymanthian monster – living, held
Invincible! Behold the horrid head,
Which seems to breathe death when itself is dead!
This is the famous trophy, noble toil
Of him whom we our demi-god do style.
Extol his great name, shepherds, and this day
Keep ever solemn, ever holiday.

HUNTSMEN: O glorious youth! true child of Hercules,
That kill'st so soon such monstrous beasts as these!

SHEPHERDS: O glorious youth! that dost despise thine own
For other safeties. Virtue climbs her throne
By these steep stairs; and the high Gods have set
Before her palace gates labour and sweat.
He that would land at joy must wade through woes;
Nor by unprofitable base repose,
Abhorring labour, but from gallant deeds
And virtuous labour true repose proceeds.

HUNTSMEN: O glorious youth! true child of Hercules,
That kill'st so soon such monstrous beasts as these!

SHEPHERDS: O glorious youth! by whom these plains deprived
Of tillage and of tillers long, retrieved
Their fruitful honours have. The ploughman now
Securely goes after the lazy plough,
Sows his plump seed, and from earth's pregnant womb

Expects the wished fruits when the season's come.
No more shall churlish tusk, or churlish foot
Trample them down, or tear them up by th' root.
Nor shall they prosper so as to sustain
A beast to be their own and others' bane.

HUNTSMEN: O glorious youth! true child of Hercules,
That kill'st so soon such monstrous beasts as these!

SHEPHERDS: O glorious youth! as if presaging thine,
The heaven today doth in full glory shine.
Such peradventure was that famous boar
Alcides[19] slew – yet so thy act is more,
It being, Silvio, thy first labour, as
Of thy great ancestor the third it was.
But with wild beasts thy infant valour plays,
To kill worse monsters in thy riper days.

HUNTSMEN: O glorious youth! true child of Hercules,
That kill'st so soon such monstrous beasts as these!

SHEPHERDS: O glorious youth! how well are joined in thee
Valour and piety! See, Cynthia, see
Thy devout Silvio's vow! Behold with white
And crooked tusk, as if in thy despite,
The proud head arm'd on this side and on that,
Seeming thy silver horns to emulate!
If then, O powerful goddess, thou didst guide
The young man's shaft, he is in justice tied
To dedicate the trophy unto thee
By whom he did obtain the victory.

HUNTSMEN: O glorious youth! true child of Hercules,
That kill'st so soon such monstrous beasts as these!

[*Exeunt* CHORUS, SILVIO, *Right. Enter* CORIDON, *Left.*]

CORIDON: I have forborne till now to credit what
The Satyr told me of Corisca late,
Fearing it might be some malicious lie
Devised by him to shake my constancy.
For most improbable it seemed that she,
In the same place where she expected me
(Unless the message which Lisetta brought

19. Hercules.

To me from her were false), should straight be caught
With an adulterer. And yet – the truth
To say – here's a shrewd token, and it doth
Perplex me much to see the mouth o' th' den
Just in that manner he related then
Shut and dammed up with such a massy stone.
Ah, false Corisca! too well by mine own
Experience of thy ungracious deeds
I know thee now: stumbling so oft, thou needs
Must fall at last. So many frauds, so many
Lies and vow-breaches might have warnéd any
Whom folly or affection did not blear
That some such fearful tumbling cast was near.
'Twas well for me I tarried by the way;
A happy chance my father made me stay,
Though I did then suppose him foolishly
To 've been a tedious remora. Had I
Come at Lisetta's hour, I might have seen
Something which poison to my eyes had been.
But what shall I do now? Armed with disdain,
Shall I revenge and mischief entertain?
No! I have loved her, and this act doth crave
My pity, not my anger – Shall I have
Pity on one deceived me? – *Me!* – She hath
Deceived herself, leaving a man of faith
To give herself a prey into the hand
Of an ignoble swain, a stranger and
A vagabond, that will tomorrow be
More wavering, more without faith than she.
Shall I take pains then to revenge a wrong
That carries with it the revenge along,
And quenches all my indignation so
'Tis turned to pity? – She hath scorned me, though!
She's honoured me; for she who thus could choose
Highly commends the man she doth refuse.
*She* scorned me, who the way did never know
How she should love receive, or how bestow;
Who liked at random still, or had this curse

If two were offered her, to take the worse.
But tell me, Coridon, how can this be?
Though scorn of being scornéd move not thee
To take revenge, surely to have been crossed
By such a loss should do 't? – I have not lost
Her whom I never had: myself I have
Regained, whom I unto another gave.
Nor can it a loss be terméd to remain
Without a woman so unsure and vain.
In fine, what have I lost? Beauty without
Virtue: a head with all the brains picked out:
A breast that hath no heart: a heart that hath
No soul in it; a soul that hath no faith.
A shade, a ghost, a carcass of affection,
Which will tomorrow turn to putrefaction.
Is this a loss? I will be bold to say 't
'Tis a great purchase and a fortunate.
Is there no woman in the world but she?
Can Coridon want nymphs as fair as she,
And far more true? But she may well want one
Will love her with such faith as Coridon,
Whom she deserved not. Now if I should do
That which the Satyr did advise me to,
Accusing her of vow-breach, in my breath
I know it lies to have her put to death.
But I have not a heart so aspine, I,
That with the wind of woman's levity
It should be moved. Too great a happiness
And honour 'twere to their perfidiousness,
If with the trouble of a manly breast,
And breaking of the happy peace and rest
Of an ingenuous soul, I were to be
Revenged upon Corisca now. For me,
Then let her live; or, to express it better,
By me not die, live for my rival let her!
Her life's revenge for me sufficient.
Live let her to dishonour – to repent.
I know not how to envy him, or loathe

Her, but with all my heart do pity both.
   [*Exit* CORIDON, *Left. Enter* SILVIO, *Right*.]
SIL: O goddess of the slothful, blind, and vain,
  Who with foul hearts, rites foolish and profane,
  Altars and temples hallow to thy name!

Temples – or sanctuaries vile, said I,
To protect lewdness and impiety,
Under the robe of thy divinity?

And thou, base goddess, that thy wickedness,
When others do as bad, may seem the less,
Giv'st them the reins to all lasciviousness.

Rotter of soul and body, enemy
Of reason, plotter of sweet thievery,
The little and great world's calamity!

Reputed worthily the ocean's daughter –
That treacherous monster, which with even water
First soothes, but ruffles into storms soon after.

Such winds of sighs, such cataracts of tears,
Such breaking waves of hopes, such gulfs of fears,
Thou mak'st in men, such rocks of cold despairs;

Tides of desire so headstrong, as would move
The world to change thy name, when thou shalt prove
Mother of rage and tempests, not of love.

Behold what sorrow now and discontent
On a poor pair of lovers thou hast sent!
Go thou, that vaunt'st thyself omnipotent,

Go faithless goddess, save that nymph whom thou
Has poisoned with thy sweets (if thou know'st how)
From her swift death's pursuing footsteps now.

Oh, what a happy day was that for me,
When my chaste soul I did devote to thee,
Cynthia, my great and only deity!

True goddess! unto whose particular shrine
The fairest souls in all the earth incline,
As thou in heaven dost all the stars outshine.

How much more laudable and free from pain
The sports are which thy servants entertain
Than those of faithless Ericina's train!

Wild boars are killéd by thy worshippers;
By wild boars miserably killed are hers.
O bow, my strength and joy! My conquerors

My arrows! Let that bugbear love come try
And match with you his soft artillery!
They whom you wound do in good earnest die.

But too much honour hence to thee would come,
Vile and unwarlike boy, to chastise whom
(I speak 't aloud) a rod's enough!

ECHO [*answering from within*]:     *Enough!*
SIL: What art thou that repliest? Echo, or Love?
  That so dost imitate the same?
ECHO:                 *The same!*
SIL: Most wished! but tell me true: art thou he?
ECHO:                     *He!*
SIL: The son of her that for Adonis once
  So miserably pined away?
ECHO:             *Away!*
SIL: Well – of that goddess who was found in bed
  With Mars, when the stars shot to see her shame,
  And the chaste moon blushed at her folly?
ECHO:                 *O lie!*
SIL: What madness 'tis to whistle to the wind!
  Come, if thou dar'st, to the wide air!

ECHO: *I dare!*

SIL: And I defy thee. But art thou her son
Legitimate, or else a by-blow?

ECHO: *I glow!*

SIL: Oh! The smith's son that's called a god?

ECHO: *A God!*

SIL: Of what? The follies of the world?

ECHO: *The world.*

SIL: The bawd thou art. Art thou that terrible boy
That tak'st such sharp revenge upon those wights
Who thy absurd commands digest not?

ECHO: *Jest not!*

SIL: What punishments dost thou inflict on those
Who in rebellion persevere?

ECHO: *Severe!*

SIL: And how shall I be punished, whose hard heart
Hath always been at odds with love?

ECHO: *With love!*

SIL: When, sot, if my chaste breast be to those flames
More opposite than night to day?

ECHO: *Today!*

SIL: So quickly shall I be in that strait?

ECHO: *Straight!*

SIL: What's she that can bring me to adoring?

ECHO: *Dorin.*

SIL: Dorinda, is it not, my little child,
Thou wouldst say in thy lithping gibberish?

ECHO: *Ish!*

SIL: She whom I hate more than the lamb the wolf?
And who to this shall force my will?

ECHO: *I will!*

SIL: And how? and with what arms? and with what bow?
Shall it be happily with thine?

ECHO: *With thine!*

SIL: Thou mean'st, perchance, when by thy wantonness
It is unbent, and the nerve broken?

ECHO: *Broken!*

SIL: Shall my own bow, after 'tis broken too,

    Make war on me? And who shall break it? Thou?

ECHO:                                           *Thou!*

SIL: 'Tis plain now thou art drunk. Go sleep! But say
    Where shall these miracles be wrought? Here?

ECHO:                                           *Here!*

SIL: O fool! and I am going now from hence.
    See if thou hast not proved thyself today
    A prophet with the wine inspired.

ECHO:                                    *Inspired!*

SIL: But stay, I see, unless I much mistake,
    A greyish thing at couch in yonder brake;
    'Tis like a wolf – and certainly 'tis one!
    Oh, what a huge one 'tis! how overgrown!
    Oh, day of prey to me! What favours are
    These, courteous goddess! In one day a pair
    Of such wild beasts to triumph o'er! But why
    Do I delay this work, my deity?
    The swiftest and the keenest shaft that is
    In all my quiver – let me see, 'tis this –
    I do select: to thee I recommend it,
    O archeress eternal – do thou send it
    By fortune's hand, and by thy power divine
    Guide it into the beast. His skin is thine,
    And in thy name I shoot. – O lucky hit!
    Just where the eye and hand designéd it.
    Would now I had my javelin here, to make
    An end of him at once, before he take
    The wood for shelter; but the place shall yield
    Me weapons. – Not a stone in all the field!
    But why do I seek weapons, having these?
    This second arrow lays him at his ease.
    – Alas! what do I see? What hast thou done,
    Unhappy Silvio? What hast thou run
    Thyself into? Thou hast a shepherd slain
    In a wolf's skin! O action to remain
    For ever overwhelmed with grief! to lie
    Under salt water everlastingly!
    The wretch too I should know, and he that so

Doth lead and prop him up is Linco. O
Vile arrow! viler vow! but vilest *thou*
That didst direct that arrow, hear that vow!
I guilty of another's blood? I kill
Another? I that was so free to spill
My blood for others, and my life to give?
Throw down thy weapons, and inglorious live,
Shooter of men, hunter of men. But lo
The wretched swain! than thee less wretched though!
[*Enter* LINCO, *Right Centre, leading in* DORINDA.]

LIN: Lean, daughter, on my arm with all thy weight,
    Wretched Dorinda, do!

SIL:               Dorinda's that?
    I'm a dead man!

DOR:         O Linco, Linco! O
    My second father!

SIL:            'Tis Dorinda: woe,
    Woe on thee, Silvio!

DOR:           Linco, thou wert sure
    Ordained by fate to be a stay to poor
    Dorinda. Thou receivédst my first cry
    When I was born; thou wilt, now I'm to die,
    My latest groan; and these thy arms which were
    My cradle then, shall now become my bier.

LIN: Ah daughter! or more dear than if thou wert
    My daughter, speak now to thee for my heart
    I can't; grief melts each word into a tear.

DOR: Not so fast, Linco, if thou lov'st me – dear
    Linco, nor go, nor weep so fast; one rakes
    My wound too bad, t'other a new wound makes.

SIL [*aside*]: Poor nymph! how ill I have repaid thy love!

LIN: Be of good comfort, daughter; this will prove
    No mortal wound.

DOR:            It may be so; but I
    That am a mortal, of this wound shall die.
    Would I knew yet who hurt me!

LIN:                Get thee sound,
    And let that pass. Revenge ne'er cured a wound.

SIL [*aside*]: Why dost thou stay? What mak'st thou in this place?
   Wouldst thou be seen by her? Hast thou the face,
   Hast thou the heart to endure it? Silvio, fly
   From the sharp dart of her revenging eye!
   Fly from her tongue's just sword! I cannot go
   From hence; and what it is I do not know,
   But something holds me, and would make me run
   To her whom I of all the world did shun.
DOR: Must I then die and not my murderer know?
LIN: 'Twas Silvio.
DOR:             How dost know 'twas Silvio?
LIN: I know his shaft.
DOR:                Then welcome death, if I
   Shall owe thee to so sweet an enemy!
LIN: Look where he stands! We need demand no further;
   His posture and his face confess the murther
   Alone. – Now heaven be praiséd, Silvio,
   Thy all-destroying arrows and thy bow
   Thou'st plied so well about these woods, that now
   Thou'rt gone out thy arts-master! Tell me, thou
   That 'dost like Silvio, not like Linco', who
   Made this brave shot, Linco or Silvio?
   This 'tis for boys to be so over-wise;
   Would thou hadst taken this old fool's advice!
   Answer, thou wretch: what lingering misery,
   What horror shalt thou live in if she die?
   I know thou'lt say, thou err'dst, and thought'st to strike
   A wolf; as if 'twere nothing (schoolboy-like)
   To shoot at all adventures, and not see,
   Nor care whether a man or beast it be.
   What goatherd, or what ploughman doth not go
   Clad in such skins? Oh, Silvio, Silvio!
   Soon ripe, soon rotten! If thou think, fond child,
   This 'chance' by chance befell thee, thou'rt beguiled.
   These monstrous things without divine decree
   Hap not to men. Dost thou not plainly see
   How this thy unsupportable disdain
   Of love, the world and all that is humane,

Displeases Heaven? High Gods cannot abide
A rival upon earth, and hate such pride,
Although in virtue ... Now thou'rt mute, that wert
Before this hap unsufferably pert.

DOR: Silvio, give Linco leave to talk, for he
Knows not what power Love gave thee over me
Of life and death. If thou hadst struck my heart,
Thou'dst struck what's thine – mark proper for thy dart!
Those hands to wound me thy fair eyes have taught.
See, Silvio, her thou hat'st so! See her brought
To that extremity where thou wouldst see her!
Thou sought'st to wound her; see her wounded here!
To prey upon her; lo, she is thy prey!
Thou sought'st her death, and lo she's dying! Say,
Would'st thou aught else of her? What further joy
Can poor Dorinda yield thee? Cruel boy,
And void of bowels! Thou wouldst ne'er believe
That wound which from thy eyes I did receive;
This which thy hands have given canst thou deny?
Those crystal showers which issued from my eye,
Thou couldst not be persuaded were my blood;
What dost thou think now of this crimson flood
Which my side weeps? But if o'erwhelmed with scorn
That bravery be not wherewith thou wert born,
Deny me not (thou cruel soul, yet brave),
Deny me not ('tis all the boon I crave),
When I shall sigh into thee my last breath,
One sigh of thine. O happy, happy death!
If thou vouchsafe to sweeten it with these
Kind words and pious: 'Soul, depart in peace!'

SIL: Dorinda, my Dorinda, shall I say,
Alas, when I must lose thee the same day,
Thou'rt mine? Now mine, when death to thee I give,
That wert not mine when I could make thee live?
Yes, mine I'll call thee; and thou mine shalt be
In spite of my opposing destiny!
For if thy death our meeting souls disjoin,
My death shall reunite us. – All that's mine,

Haste to revenge her! I have murdered thee
With these curst arrows; with them murder me!
I have been cruel unto thee; and I
Desire from thee nothing but cruelty.
I scorn'd thee in my pride; look! with my knee
Low louting to the earth, I worship thee;
And pardon of thee, but not life, demand.
Take shafts and bow; but do not strike my hand
Or eye (bad ministers, 'tis true, yet still
But ministers of an unguilty will)
– Strike me this breast, this monster hence remove,
Sworn enemy of pity and of love.
Strike me this heart, to thee so cruel. Lo,
My baréd breast!

DOR:                    *I* strike it, Silvio?
I strike that breast? Sure, if thou didst not mock,
Thou wouldst not show 't me naked. O white rock!
Already by the winds and briny main
Of my rough sighs and tears oft struck in vain!
But dost thou breathe? nor art to pity barred?
Art thou a tender breast, or marble hard?
I would not idolize fair alabaster
(Led by the human likeness), as thy master,
And mine, when on the outside he did look,
A harmless woman for a beast mistook.
*I* strike thee? Strike thee Love! Nor can I wish
For my revenge a greater plague than this.
Yet must I bless the day that I took fire,
My tears and martyrdom. All I desire
Is that thou praise my faith, my zeal: but no
Revenging me. But, courteous Silvio,
That to thy servant kneelst – why this to me?
Or if Dorinda must thy mistress be,
Obey her then: the first command I give,
Is that thou rise; the second, that thou live.
Heaven's will be done with me – I shall survive
In thee, and cannot die whilst thou'rt alive.
But if thou thinkst unjust I should be found

Without all satisfaction for my wound,
Be that which did it punished. 'Twas that bow:
Let that be broke – I'm well revengéd so.

LIN [*aside*]: A very heavy doom!

SIL:                                    Come then, thou mad,
   Thou bloody actor of a deed so sad;
   That thou mayst ne'er break thread of life again,
   Thus do I break thee and thy thread in twain,
   And send thee a useless trunk back to the wood.
   Nor you [*addressing his arrows*] ill-sanguined with an innocent's
      blood,
   Which my dear mistress' side so rudely rent,
   Brothers in ill, shall 'scape your punishment.
   Not shafts, nor flights, but sticks – since ye shall want
   Those wings and heads which garnished you – avaunt
   Plumed and disarméd arms. How well, O Love,
   Didst thou foretell me this from yonder grove,
   In a prophetic echo. O thou high
   Conqueror of gods and men, once enemy,
   Now lord of all my thoughts! If 'tis thy glory
   To tame a heart that's proud and refractory,
   Divert death's impious shaft, which with one blow,
   Slaying Dorinda will slay Silvio
   (Now thine). So cruel death, if it remove
   Her hence, will triumph o'er triumphant love.

LIN: Now both are wounded: but the one in vain,
   Unless the other's wound be healed again.
   About it then!

DOR:              Ah Linco! do not, pray,
   Carry me home disguised in this array.

SIL: Why should Dorinda go to any house
   But Silvio's? Surely she shall be my spouse
   Ere it be night, either alive, or dead.
   And Silvio in life or death will wed
   Dorinda.

LIN:        Now she may become thy wife,
   Since Amarillis is to marriage, life,
   And virtue lost. Blest pair! Ye gods that do

Wonders, with one cure now give life to two!

DOR: O Silvio! I shall faint, my wounded thigh
Feebly supporting me.

SIL:               Good remedy
For that! Take heart! Thou'rt mine and Linco's care,
And I and Linco thy two crutches are.
Linco, thy hand!

LIN:          There 'tis.

SIL:               Hold fast – a chair
Let's make for her of our two arms. Rest here,
Dorinda, suffering thy right hand to embrace
The neck of Linco, thy left mine – now place
Thy body tenderly, that the hurt part
May not be strained.

DOR:          O cruel pricking dart!

SIL: Sit at more ease, my love.

DOR:              It is well now.

SIL: Dear Linco, do not stagger.

LIN:            Nor do thou
Swag with thine arm, but steady go and wary;
It will concern thee. Ah! we do not carry
A boar's head now in triumph.

SIL:               Say, my dear,
How is it now?

DOR:        In pain; but leaning here,
My heart, to be in pain is pleased to be;
To languish, health; to die, eternity.

    [*Exeunt* SILVIO, DORINDA, LINCO, *Left. Enter* CHORUS, *Right.*]

CHO: Fair golden age! when milk was the only food,
And cradle of the infant world the wood
(Rocked by the winds); and th'untouched flocks did bear
Their dear young for themselves. None yet did fear
The sword or poison; no black thoughts begun
To eclipse the light of the eternal sun;
Nor wandering pines unto a foreign shore
Or war, or riches (a worse mischief) bore.
That pompous sound, idol of vanity,
Made up of title, pride, and flattery,

Which they call honour whom ambition blinds,
Was not as yet the tyrant of our minds;
But to buy real goods with honest toil
Amongst the woods and flocks, to use no guile,
Was honour to those sober souls that knew
No happiness but what from virtue grew.
Then sports and carols amongst brooks and plains
Kindled a lawful flame in nymphs and swains.
Their hearts and tongues concurred – the kiss and joy
Which were most sweet, and yet which least did cloy
Hymen bestowed on them. To one alone
The lively roses of delight were blown;
The thievish lover found them shut on trial,
And fenced with prickles of a sharp denial.
Were it in cave or wood, or purling spring,
Husband and lover signified one thing.
　　Base present age, which dost with thy impure
Delights the beauty of the soul obscure,
Teaching to nurse a dropsy in the veins,
Bridling the look – but giv'st desire the reins.
Thus, like a net that spread and covered lies
With leaves and tempting flowers, thou dost disguise
With coy and holy arts a wanton heart;
Mak'st like a stage-play, virtue but a part,
Nor think'st it any fault love's sweets to steal,
So from the world thou canst the theft conceal.
　　But thou that art the king of kings, create
In us true honour! Virtue's all the state
Great souls should keep. Unto these cells return
Which were thy court, but now thy absence mourn.
From their dead sleep with thy sharp goad awake
Them who, to follow their base wills, forsake
Thee, and the glory of the ancient world!
Let's hope: our ills have truce till we are hurled
From that. Let's hope; the sun that's set may rise,
And with new light salute our longing eyes.

# ACT FIVE

*Scene as before.*

[*Enter* CARINO, URANIO, *Left.*]

URA: All places are our country where we're well:
   Which to the wise is wheresoe'er they dwell.
CAR: It is most true, Uranio; and no man
   By proof can say it better than I can,[20]
   Who leaving long ago my father's house
   (Being very young, and then ambitious
   Of something more than holding of the plough,
   Or keeping sheep) travelled abroad; and now
   To the same point where I began, return,
   When my gilt locks are to the silver worn.
   Yet a sweet thing, it needs must be confessed,
   To any that hath sense, is his first nest.
   For nature gave to all men at their birth
   Something of secret love unto that earth
   Where they were born, which never old doth grow
   In us, but follows wheresoe'er we go.
   The loadstone which the wary mariner
   Doth as director of his travels bear
   Now to the rising sun, now to his set,
   Doth never lose that hidden virtue yet,
   Which makes it to the north retort its look:
   So he that hath his native soil forsook,
   Though he may wander far, much compass take,
   Aye, and his nest in foreign countries make,
   Yet that same natural love doth still retain
   Which makes him wish his native soil again.

20. Carino represents Guarini himself, and the speeches that follow refer to
events in his life as a courtier and court poet, with the names of places and
people changed.

O fair Arcadia! the sweetest part
Of all the world – at least to me thou art –
Which my feet tread on, but my thoughts adore!
Had I been landed blindfold on thy shore,
Yet then should I have known thee, such a flood
Of sudden joy runs races with my blood:
Such a magnetic powerful sympathy
And unaccustomed tenderness feel I.
Thou then, that my companion hast been
In travels and in sorrows, shalt be in
At my joys too; 'tis reason thou shouldst go
My half in happiness as well as woe.

URA: Companion of thy travels I have been,
Not of the fruit thereof; for thou art in
Thy native soil, where thou repose mayst find
For thy tir'd body and more tiréd mind:
But I that am a stranger, and am come
So many leagues from my poor house, and from
My poorer and distresséd family,
Trailing my wearied limbs along with thee,
For my afflicted body well may find
Repose, but not for my afflicted mind;
Thinking what pledges do behind remain,
And how much rugged way I must again
Tread over ere I rest. Nor do I know
Who else could have prevailed on me to go
From Elis in my grey unwieldy age,
Not knowing why, so long a pilgrimage.

CAR: Thou knowst my sweet Mirtillo, who was given
As a son to me by propitious heaven,
Some two months since came hither to be well
By my advice – or of the oracle,
To speak more true, which said the Arcadian air
Was the only means that could his health repair.
Now I, that find it an exceeding pain
Without so dear a pledge long to remain,
Consulting the same oracle, enquired
When he'd return whom I so much desired.

The answer was the same I tell thee now:
'*Unto thy ancient country return thou:*
'*Where with thy sweet Mirtillo thou shalt be*
'*Happy; for in that place by heaven he*
'*Is marked out for great things: but till thou come*
'*Into Arcadia, touching this be dumb.*'
Thou then, my faithfullest companion,
My loved Uranio, who hast ever gone
A share in all my fortunes hitherto,
Repose thy body, and thou shalt have too
Cause to repose thy mind: 'twixt me and thee,
If heaven perform what it hath promised me,
All shall be common: no success can glad
Carino, if he see Uranio sad.
URA: My dear Carino, what I do for thee
Rewards itself, if it accepted be.
But what at first could make thee to forgo
Thy native country, if thou lov'st it so?
CAR: A love to poetry, and to the loud
Music of fame resounding in a crowd.
For I myself (greedy of foreign praise)
Disdained Arcadia only should my lays
Hear and applaud, as if my native soil
Were narrow limits to my growing style.
I went to Elis and to Pisa then,
Famous themselves, and giving fame to men;
There saw I that loved Egon, first with bays,
With purple then, with virtue decked always,
That he on earth Apollo's self did seem.
Therefore my heart and harp I unto him
Did consecrate, devoted to his name.
And in his house, which was the house of fame,
I should have set up my perpetual rest,
There to admire and imitate the best,
If as heaven made me happy here below,
So it had given me too the grace to know
And keep my happiness. How I forsook
Elis and Pisa after, and betook

Myself to Argos and Mycene, where
An earthly god I worshipped, with what there
I suffered in that hard captivity,
Would be too long for thee to hear, for me
Too sad to utter. Only this much know:
I lost my labour, and in sand did sow.
I writ, wept, sung, hot and cold fits I had,
I rid, I stood, I bore, now sad, now glad,
Now high, now low, now in esteem, now scorned;
And as the Delphic iron, which is turned
Now to heroic, now mechanic use,
I feared no danger, did no pains refuse,
Was all things, and was nothing – changed my hair,
Condition, custom, thoughts, and life, but ne'er
Could change my fortune. Then I knew at last
And panted after my sweet freedom past.
So, flying smoky Argos and the great
Storms that attend on greatness, my retreat
I made to Pisa, my thought's quiet port,
Where – praise be given to the Eternal for't –
Upon my dear Mirtillo I did light,
Which all past sorrows fully did requite.
URA: A thousand thousand times that man is blest
Can clip the wings of his aspiring breast,
Nor for the shadow of great happiness
Doth throw away the substance of the less!
CAR: But who'd have dreamed midst plenty to grow poor,
Or to be less by toiling to be more?
I thought by how much more in princes' courts
Men did excel in titles and supports,
So much the more obliging they would be –
The best enamel of nobility.
But now the contrary by proof I've seen:
Courtiers in name, and courteous in their mien
They are; but in their actions I could spy
Not the least spark or dram of courtesy.
People in show smooth as the calméd waves,
Yet cruel as the ocean when it raves.

Men in appearance only I did find;
Love in the face, but malice in the mind.
With a straight look a squinting heart, and least
Fidelity where greatest was professed.
That which elsewhere is virtue is vice there;
Plain troth, square dealing, love unfeigned, sincere
Compassion, faith inviolable, and
An innocence both of the heart and hand
They count the folly of a soul that's vile
And poor, a vanity worthy their smile.
To cheat, to lie, deceit and theft to use,
And under show of pity to abuse,
To rise upon the ruins of their brothers,
And seek their own by robbing praise from others,
The virtues are of that perfidious race.
No worth, no valour, no respect of place,
Of age, or law, bridle of modesty,
No tie of love, or blood, nor memory
Of good received; no thing's so venerable,
Sacred or just, that is inviolable
By that vast thirst of riches, and desire
Unquenchable of still ascending higher.
Now I – not fearing since I meant not ill,
And in court-craft not having any skill,
Wearing my thoughts charàctered in my brow,
And a glass-window in my breast – judge thou
How open and how fair a mark my heart
Lay to their envy's unsuspected dart.

URA: Who now can boast of earth's felicity,
   When envy treads on virtue's heels?

CAR:                     O my
   Uranio, if since my muse and I
   From Elis passed to Argos, I had found
   Such cause to sing as I had ample ground
   To weep, perchance in such a lofty key
   I'd sung my master's glorious arms, that he
   Should have no cause for the felicity
   Of his Maeonian trumpet to envy

Achilles: and my country (which doth bring
Such hapless poets forth as swan-like sing
Their own sad fates) should by my means have now
A second laurel to impale her brow.
But in this age – inhuman age the while! –
The art of poetry is made too vile.
Swans must have pleasant nests, high feeding, fair
Weather to sing; and with a load of care
Men cannot climb Parnassus' cliff: for he
Who is still wrangling with his destiny
And his malignant fortune, becomes hoarse,
And loses both his singing and discourse.
But now 'tis time to seek Mirtillo out;
Although I find the places hereabout
So changed and altered from their ancient wont,
I for Arcadia in Arcadia hunt.
But come, Uranio, gladly for all this;
A traveller with language cannot miss
His way – or since thou'rt weary, thou wert best
To stay at the next inn to take some rest.

[*Exeunt* CARINO, URANIO, *Right. Enter* TITIRO, *Right.*]

TIT: Which first, my daughter, shall I mourn in thee?
Thy loss of life, or of thy chastity?
I'll mourn thy chastity: for thou wert born
Of mortal parents, but not bad. I'll mourn
Not thy life lost, but mine preserved to see
Thy loss of life and of thy chastity.
– Thou, with thine oracle's mysterious cloud
Wrongly conceived, Montano, and thy proud
Despiser both of love and of my daughter,
Unto this miserable end hast brought her.
Ay me! How much more certain at this time
My oracles have showed themselves than thine!
For honesty in a young heart doth prove
But a weak sconce against assaulting love;
And 'tis most true, a woman that's alone
Hath a most dangerous companion.

[*Enter* MESSENGER, *Right Centre.*]

MESS: Were he not underground, or flown through the air,
　I should have found him, sure. But soft, he's there,
　I think, where least I thought. Thou'rt met by me
　Too late, old father, but too soon for thee;
　I've news.

TIT:　　　　　What bring'st thou in thy mouth? The knife
　That hath bereft my daughter of her life?

MESS: Not that; yet little less. But how, I pray,
　Gotst thou this news so soon another way?

TIT: Doth she then live?

MESS:　　　　　　　　　She lives, and in her choice
　It is to live or die.

TIT:　　　　　　　　Blest be that voice!
　Why is she then not safe, if she may give
　Her 'no' to death?

MESS:　　　　　　　　Because she will not live.

TIT: *Will* not? What madness makes her life despise?

MESS: Another's death. And – if that thy advice
　Remove her not – she is thereon so bent
　That all the world cannot her death prevent.

TIT: Why stand we talking here then? Let us go.

MESS: Stay – yet the temple's shut. Dost thou not know
　That none but holy feet on holy earth
　May tread, till from the vestry they bring forth
　The destined sacrifice in all its trim?

TIT: But before that . . .

MESS:　　　　　　　　She's watched.

TIT:　　　　　　　　　　　　　In the interim
　Relate then all that's past, and to me show
　The truth unveiled.

MESS:　　　　　　　Thy wretched daughter – oh
　Sad spectacle! – being brought before the priest,
　Did not alone from the beholders wrest
　Salt tears; but, trust me, made the marble melt,
　And the hard flint the dint of pity felt.
　She was accused, convict, and sentence passed
　All in a trice.

TIT:　　　　　　Poor girl! And why such haste?

MESS: Because the evidence was clear as day;
  Besides, a certain nymph – who she did say
  Could witness she was guiltless – was not there,
  Nor could by any search be brought to appear.
  Then the dire omens of some threatened ill,
  And horrid visions which the temple fill,
  Brook no delay, to us more frightful far
  By how much more unusual they are,
  Nor ever seen, since the vext powers above
  Revenged the wrong of scorned Aminta's love
  Who was their priest – whence all our woes had birth.
  The goddess sweats cold drops of blood, the earth
  Is palsy-shook; the sacred cavern howls
  With such unwonted sounds as tortured souls
  Send out of graves, and belches up a smell
  From its foul jaws, scarce to be matched in hell.
  His sad procession now the priest began
  To lead to a bloody death thy daughter, when
  Mirtillo seeing her – behold a strange
  Proof of affection! – proffered to exchange
  His life for hers, crying aloud: 'Her hands
  'Untie (Ah! how unworthy of such bands!)
  'And in her stead, who is designed to be
  'A sacrifice to Dian, offer me
  'A sacrifice to Amarillis!'
TIT:                                  There
  Spake a true lover, and above base fear!
MESS: The wonder follows – she that was afraid
  Before of dying, on the sudden made
  Now valiant by Mirtillo's words, replied
  Thus, with a heart at death unterrified:
  'But dost thou think, Mirtillo, then to give
  'Life by thy death to her, who in thee doth live?
  'It cannot, must not be: come, priests, away
  'With me to the altar now without delay!'
  'Ah,' cried the swain, 'such love I did not lack!
  'Back, cruel Amarillis, oh come back!
  'Now art thou more unkind than e'er thou wert:

411

''Tis I should die!' Quoth she: 'Thou act'st my part.'
And here between them grew so fierce a strife
As if that life were death and death were life.
O noble souls! O pair eternally
To be renowned, whether ye live or die!
O glorious lovers! If I had tongues more
Than heaven hath eyes, or sands are on the shore,
Their voices would be drownéd in the main
Sea of your endless praises. Glorious dame,
Daughter of Jove, eternal as thy father,
That mortals' deeds immortalizest, gather
Thou the fair story, and in diamond pages
With golden letters write to after ages
The bravery of both lovers.

TIT:                                    But who won
The conquest in that strife of death?

MESS:                                    The man.
Strange war, which to the victor death did give,
And where the vanquished was condemned to live.
For thus unto thy daughter spake the priest:
'Nymph, let us alone, and set thy heart at rest;
'Changed for another none can be again,
'Who for another in exchange was ta'en:
'This is our law.' Then a strict charge he gave,
Upon the maid such careful watch to have
As that she might not lay a violent hand
Upon herself through sorrow. Thus did stand
The state of matters, when in search of thee
Montano sent me.

TIT:                                    'Tis most true, I see,
Well-watered meads may be without sweet flowers
In spring, without their verdant honour bowers,
And without chirping birds a pleasant grove,
Ere a fair maid and young without her love.
But if we loiter here, how shall we know
The hour when to the temple we should go?

MESS: Here better than elsewhere, for here it is
The honest swain must be a sacrifice.

TIT: And why not in the temple?

MESS:                              Because in
  The place 'twas done our law doth punish sin.
TIT: Then why not in the cave? The sin was there.
MESS: Because it must be in the open air.
TIT: By whom hast thou these mysteries been told?
MESS: By the chief minister, and he by old
  Tirenio, who the false Lucrina knew
  So sacrificéd, and Aminta true.
  But now 'tis time to go indeed: for see,
  The sacred pomp descends the hill. Yet we
  May for thy daughter to the temple go
  Before they come. Devotion marches slow.

    [*Exeunt* TITIRO, MESSENGER, *Right. Enter* MONTANO, MIR-
    TILLO, NICANDRO, CHORUS *of* SHEPHERDS, CHORUS *of*
    PRIESTS, *Right.*]

SHEPHERDS: Sol's sister, daughter of great Jupiter,
  That shin'st a second sun in the first sphere
                    To the blind world!
PRIESTS: Thou whose life-giving and more temperate ray
  Thy brother's burning fury doth allay,
  Whence bounteous nature here produces after
  All her blest offsprings, and air, earth and water
  Enriches and augments with vegetals,
  With creatures sensitive, with rationals:
  Ah, pity thy Arcadia, and that rage
  Thou dost in others, in thyself assuage!
SHEPHERDS: Sol's sister, daughter of great Jupiter,
  That shin'st a second sun in the first sphere
                    To the blind world!
MON: Now, sacred ministers, the altars dress:
  You likewise, swains, that show yourselves no less
  Devout than they, your voices all unite,
  And once again invoke the queen of night!
SHEPHERDS: Sol's sister, daughter of great Jupiter,
  That shin'st a second sun in the first sphere
                    To the blind world!
MON: Now shepherds and my servants all,
  Withdraw yourselves, and come not till I call.

    [SHEPHERDS *withdraw to side of stage.*]

Valiant young man, who to bestow upon
Another, life, abandonest thine own,
Die with this comfort: for a puff of breath,
Which by the abject spirit is called death,
Thou buy'st eternity; and when the tooth
Of envious time, consuming the world's youth,
Millions of lesser names devouréd hath,
Then thou shalt live the pattern of true faith.
But (for the law commands that thou shouldst die
A silent sacrifice), before thou ply
Thy knee to earth, if thou wouldst ought deliver,
Speak – and hereafter hold thy peace for ever.

MIR: Father – for though thou kill me, yet I must
Give thee that name – my body to the dust,
Whereof 'twas made and kneaded up, I give;
My soul, to her in whom alone I live.
But if she die, as she hath vowed, of me
What part, alas, will then surviving be?
How sweet will death be unto me, if I
In mine own person, not in hers, may die!
And if he merit pity at his death
Who for mere pity now resigns his breath,
Take care, dear father, of her life, that I
Wing'd with that hope to a better life may fly.
Let my fate rest at my destruction,
Stop at my ruin; but, when I am gone,
Let my divorcéd soul in her survive
Although from her I was divorc'd alive.

MON [aside]: Scarcely can I refrain from weeping now;
O our mortality, how frail art thou!
[to MIRTILLO] Son, be of comfort, for I promise thee
I will perform all thou desir'st of me.
Here's my hand on't, and solemnly I swear,
Even by this mitred head.

MIR:                          Then vanish, fear!
And now for the most faithful soul make room,
For, Amarillis, unto thee I come!
With the sweet name of Amarillis, I

414

Close up my mouth, and silent kneel to die.

MON: Now, sacred ministers, the rites begin.
With liquid odoriferous gums keep in
The flame, and strewing frankincense and myrrh
Whole clouds of perfume to the gods prefer.

SHEPHERDS: Sol's sister, daughter of great Jupiter,
That shin'st a second sun in the first sphere
                                    To the blind world!

[*Enter* CARINO, *Right.*]

CAR: Did ever man so many houses view,
And the inhabitants thereof so few?
But see the cause! If I mistake me not,
They're gotten all together here. Oh what
A troop! how rich! how solemn! It is sure
Some sacrifice.

MON:            Give me the golden ewer
With the red wine, Nicandro.

NIC:                        There.

MON:                              So may
Soft pity in thy breast revive today
By this unguilty blood, goddess divine,
As by the sprinkling of these drops of wine
This pale and dying flame revives. – Set up
The golden ewer; reach me the silver cup.
– So may the burning wrath be quenched, which in
Thy breast was kindled by a false maid's sin,
As with this water – poured out like our tears –
I quench this flame.

CAR:                A sacrifice! but where's
The offering?

MON:          Now all's prepared; there lacks
Only the fatal stroke. Lend me the axe.

CAR: I see a thing, unless my eyes mistake,
Like a man kneeling, this way with his back.
Is he the offering? 'Tis so: ah, wretch!
And o'er his head the priest his hand doth stretch.
Oh my poor country! after all these years
Is not heaven's wrath yet quenched with blood and tears?

SHEPHERDS: Sol's sister, daughter of great Jupiter,
   That shin'st a second sun in the first sphere
                To the blind world!
MON: Revengeful goddess, who a private fault
   With public rod dost punish – thou hast thought
   Fit so to do, and so in the abyss
   Of providence eternal fixed it is –
   Since faithless Lucrin's tainted blood was thought
   For thy nice justice too impure a draught,
   Carouse the guiltless blood then of this swain,
   By me now at thy altar to be slain
   A willing sacrifice, and to his lass
   As true a lover as Aminta was.
SHEPHERDS: Sol's sister, daughter of great Jupiter,
   That shin'st a second sun in the first sphere
                To the blind world!
MON: Ah, how my breast with pity now relents!
   What sudden numbness fetters every sense!
   I ne'er was so before. To lift this axe
   My hands lack strength, and my heart courage lacks.
CAR: I'll see the wretch's face, and so be gone;
   For such dire sights I cannot look upon.
MON: Perhaps the sun, though setting, will not look
   On human sacrifice, and I am struck
   Therefore with horror. Shepherd, change thy place,
   And to the mountain turn thy dying face.
   So, now 'tis well.
CAR:           Alas, what gaze I at?
   Is't not my son? Is't not Mirtillo, that?
MON: Now I can do't.
CAR:           'Tis he!
MON:               And aim my blow . . .
CAR [*coming forward*]: Hold, sacred minister, what dost thou do?
MON: Nay, thou profane rash man, how dar'st thou thus
   Impose a sacrilegious hand on us?
CAR: O all my joy, Mirtillo! I ne'er thought . . .
MON: Avaunt, old man, that dot'st, or art distraught!
CAR: To embrace thee in this sort.

MON:                                    Avaunt, I say!
  It is not lawful impure hands to lay
  Upon things sacred to the gods.
CAR:                                    'Twas they
  That sent me to this place.
    [NICANDRO *seizes* CARINO, *but* MONTANO *checks him.*]
MON:                          Nicandro, stay.
  We'll hear him, and then let him go his way.
CAR: Ah, courteous minister! Before thy hand
  Upon the life of this young man descend,
  Tell me but why he dies. This I implore
  By that divinity thou dost adore.
MON: By such a goddess thou conjur'st me, that
  I should be impious to deny. But what
  Concerns it thee?
CAR:                More than thou dost suppose.
MON: Because to die he for another chose.
CAR: Then I will die for him. Oh, take instead
  Of his, this old already tottering head!
MON: Thou rav'st, friend!
CAR:                    Why am I denied that now
  Which unto him was granted?
MON:                          Because thou
  A stranger art.
CAR:            And if I should prove none,
  What then?
MON:        Although thou shouldst, it were all one,
  Because he cannot be exchanged again
  Who for another in exchange was ta'en.
  But who art thou, if thou no stranger be?
  Thy habit speaks thee not of Arcady.
CAR: Yet am I an Arcadian.
MON:                      I did ne'er
  See thee before, to my remembrance, here.
CAR: My name's Carino. I was born hard by:
  This wretch's father, who is now to die.
MON: Hence! hence! lest through thy fond paternal love
  Our sacrifice should vain and fruitless prove.

417

CAR: Oh, if thou wert a father!

MON:                         I am one;
  Aye, and the father of an only son.
  A tender father, too; yet if this were
  My Silvio's head – by Silvio's head I swear –
  I would as forward be to do to his
  What I must do to this. For no man is
  Worthy this sacred robe but he that can
  For public good put off the private man.

CAR: Yet let me kiss him ere he die!

MON [stopping him]:                   Nor touch!

CAR: O mine own flesh and blood! Art thou so much
  A tyrant to me too, as to afford
  To thy afflicted parent not one word?

MIR: Dear father, peace!

MON:                     Alas! we are all spoiled!
  The sacrifice – O heavens! – is defiled!

MIR: That blood, that life which thou didst give to me,
  Spent for a better cause can never be.

MON: Did I not say his vow of silence he
  Would break, when he his father's tears should see?

MIR: That such a gross mistake I should commit!
  My vow of silence I did quite forget.

MON: But, ministers, why do ye gazing stay?
  Him to the temple quickly reconvey!
  There in the holy cloister again take
  The voluntary oath of him: then back
  Returning him with pomp, along with you
  For a new sacrifice bring all things new –
  New fire, and new water, and new wine.
  Quickly, for Phoebus doth apace decline.

  [Exeunt NICANDRO and PRIESTS, Right, with MIRTILLO.]

MON: Now, thou old doting fool: thank heaven thou art
  His father, for, by heaven, unless thou wert,
  Today I'd make thee feel my fury, since
  Thou hast so much abused my patience.
  Knowst thou who I am? Knowst thou that this wand
  Doth both divine and human things command?

418

CAR: Let not the priest of heaven offended be
 For begging mercy.
MON:     I have suffered thee
 Too long, and that hath made thee insolent.
 Dost thou not know, when anger wanteth vent
 In a just bosom, it is gathering strength
 Within, and bursts out with more force at length?
CAR: Anger was never in a noble mind
 A furious tempest, but a gentle wind
 Of passion only, which but stirs the soul,
 Where reason still doth keep her due control,
 Lest it should grow a standing pool, unfit
 For virtuous action. If I cannot get
 Thee to extend that mercy which I crave,
 Afford me justice – this I ought to have
 From thee. For they who laws to others give,
 Ought not themselves without all law to live.
 And he that is advanced to greatest sway,
 Him that requireth justice must obey.
 And witness I require it now of thee!
 Do't for thyself, if thou wilt not for me.
 Thou art unjust if thou Mirtillo slay.
MON: I prithee, how?
CAR:     To me didst thou not say,
 Thou mightst not offer here a stranger's blood?
MON: I did; and said what heaven commanded.
CAR:         Good:
 This is a stranger then.
MON:    A stranger? What?
 Is he not then thy son?
CAR:    All's one for that.
MON: Is't 'cause thou gotst him in a foreign land?
CAR: The more thou seek'st, the less thou'lt understand.
MON: It skills not here, *where*, but by *whom* he's got.
CAR: I call him stranger, 'cause I got him not.
MON: Is he thy son then, and not got by thee?
CAR: I said he was my son – not born of me.
MON: Thy grief hath made thee mad.

CAR:                              I would it had!
  I should not feel my grief, if I were mad.
MON: Thou art or mad, or impious, choose thou whether.
CAR: For telling the truth to thee I am neither.
MON: How can both these – 'son' and 'not son' – be true?
CAR: Son of my love, not of my loins.
MON:                              Go to!
  He is no stranger, if he be thy son:
  If he be not, no harm to thee is done.
  So father or not father, thou'rt confuted.
CAR: Truth is truth still, though it be ill disputed.
MON: That man that utters contradictions must
  Speak one untruth.
CAR:                Thy action is unjust,
  I say again.
MON:        Let all this action's guilt
  Light on my head, and on my son's.
CAR:                              Thou wilt
  Repent it.
MON:      Thou shalt, if thou wilt not take
  Thy hands from off me.
CAR:                    My appeal I make
  To men and gods.
MON:              To gods despised by thee?
CAR: And if thou wilt not hear, hearken to me
  O heaven and earth! and thou great goddess here
  Adored! Mirtillo is a foreigner,
  No son of mine. The holy sacrifice
  Thou dost profane.
MON:              Bless me good heavens from this
  Strange man! Say then, if he be not thy son,
  Who is his father?
CAR:              'Tis to me unknown.
MON: Is he thy kinsman?
CAR:                Neither.
MON:                    Why dost thou then
  Call him thy son?
CAR:              'Cause from the moment when

I had him first, I bred him as mine own
Still with a fatherly affection.
MON: Didst buy him? steal him? from whence hadst him?
CAR:                                             From
Elis – the gift of a strange man.
MON:                      From whom
Had that strange man him?
CAR:                   That strange man? Why, he
Had him of me before.
MON:              Thou mov'st in me
At the same time both laughter and disdain.
What thou gav'st him, did he give thee again?
CAR: I gave to him what was his own; then he
Returned it as his courteous gift to me.
MON: And whence hadst thou (since thou wilt make me mad
For company) that which from thee he had?
CAR: Within a thicket of sweet myrtle, I
Had newly found him accidentally,
Near to Alfeo's mouth, and called him thence
Mirtillo.
MON:      With what likely circumstance
Thou dost thy lie embroider! Are there any
Wild beasts within that forest?
CAR:                   Very many.
MON: Why did they not devour him?
CAR:                      A strong flood
Had carried him into that tuft of wood,
And left him in the lap of a small isle
Defended round with water.
MON:                   Thou dost file
One lie upon another well. And was
The flood so pitiful to let him pass
Undrowned? Such nurses in thy country are
The brooks, to foster infants with such care?
CAR: He lay within a cradle, which with mud
And other matter gathered by the flood
Caulked to keep out the water, like a boat
Had to that thicket carried him afloat.

MON: Within a cradle lay he?

CAR:                                    Yes.

MON:                                              A child

In swathing bands?

CAR [*nodding*]:        A sweet one – and it smiled.

MON: How long ago might this be?

CAR:                                            'Tis soon cast:

Since the great flood some twenty years are passed,

And then it was.

MON [*aside*]:        What horror do I feel

Creep through my veins!

CAR:                                        He's silenced, and yet will

Be obstinate. Oh, the strange pride of those

In place, who, conquered, yield not, but suppose

Because that they have all the wealth, with it

They must be masters too of all the wit!

Sure, he's convinced; and it doth vex him too,

As by his muttering he doth plainly show;

And one may see some colour he would find

To hide the error of a haughty mind.

MON: But that strange man of whom thou tellst me – what

Was he unto the child? his father?

CAR:                                                    That

I do not know.

MON:                    Nor didst thou ever know

More of the man than thou hast told me?

CAR:                                                          No.

Why all these questions?

MON:                                    If thou sawst him now,

Shouldst know him?

CAR:                              Yes: he had a beetle-brow,

A down-look, middle stature, with black hair.

His beard and eyebrows did with bristles stare.

MON: Shepherds and servants mine, approach!

  [SHEPHERDS, *led by* DAMETA, *return to centre of stage.*]

DAM:                                                        We're here.

MON: Which of these shepherds who do now appear

To him thou talk'st of likest seems to thee?

422

CAR: Not only like him, but the same is he
 Whom thou talk'st with; and still the man doth show
 The same he did some twenty years ago,
 For he hath changed no hair, though I am gray.

MON: Withdraw, and let Dameta only stay.
 [*To* DAMETA] Tell me, dost thou know *him*?

DAM:           I think I do;
 But where, or how, I know not.

CAR:        I'll renew
 Thy memory by tokens.

MON:      Let me talk
 First with him if thou please, and do thou walk
 Aside awhile.

CAR [*going*]:  Most willingly what thou
 Command'st I'll do.

MON:      Tell me, Dameta, now,
 And do not lie.

DAM [*aside*]:  O gods, what storm comes here!

MON: When thou cam'st back – 'tis since some twenty year –
 From seeking of my child, which the swol'n brook
 Away together with its cradle took,
 Didst thou not tell me thou hadst sought with pain
 All that Alfeo bathes, and all in vain?

DAM: Why dost thou ask it me?

MON:       Answer me this:
 Didst thou not say thou couldst not find him?

DAM:           Yes.

MON: What was that little infant then which thou
 In Elis gav'st to him that knows thee now?

DAM: 'Twas twenty years ago; and wouldst thou have
 An old man now remember what he gave?

MON: He is old too, and yet remembers it.

DAM: Rather is come into his doting fit.

MON: That we shall quickly see. Where art thou, stranger?

CAR: Here.

DAM [*aside*]: Would thou wert interred, and I from danger!

MON: Is this the shepherd that bestowed on thee
 The present, art thou sure?

CAR:                              I'm sure 'tis he.

DAM: What present?

CAR:                      Dost thou not remember when
  In Jove Olympic's fane,[21] thou having then
  Newly received the oracle's reply
  And being just on thy departure, I
  Encountered thee, and asking then of thee
  The signs of what thou'dst lost, thou toldst them me;
  Then I did take thee to my house, and there
  Showed thee thy child laid in a cradle; where
  Thou gav'st him me.

DAM:                      What is inferred from hence?

CAR: The child thou gav'st me then, and whom I since
  Have brought up, as a tender father doth
  An only son, is this unhappy youth
  Who on this altar now is doomed to die
  A sacrifice.

DAM:          O force of destiny!

MON: Art studying for more lies? Hath this man said
  The truth or not?

DAM:                      Would I were but as dead
  As all is true!

MON:              That thou shalt quickly be
  If the whole truth thou dost not tell to me.
  Why didst thou give unto another what
  Was not thine own?

DAM:                      Dear master, ask not that!
  For heaven's sake do not; too much thou dost know
  Already.

MON:        This makes me more eager grow.
  Wilt not speak yet? Still keepst thou me in pain?
  Thou'rt dead if I demand it once again!

DAM: Because the oracle foretold me there,
  That if the child then found returnéd e'er
  To his own home, he should be like to die
  By 's father's hand.

CAR:                      'Tis true, myself was by.

21. In the temple of Olympic Jove.

MON: Ay me! now all is clear. This act of mine
  The dream and oracle did well divine.
CAR: What wouldst thou more? Can aught behind remain?
  Is it not plain enough?
MON:               'Tis but too plain.
    [*Turning to* DAMETA.]
  I know, and thou hast said, too much. I would
  I had searched less, or thou less understood.[22]
    [*Turning back to* CARINO.]
  How, O Carino, have I ta'en from thee
  At once thy son and thy calamity!
  How are thy passions become mine! This is
  My son – O too unhappy son, of this
  Unhappy man! O son preserved and kept
  More cruelly than thou from hence wert swept
  By the wild flood, to fall by thy sire's hand,
  And stain the altars of thy native land!
CAR: Thou father to Mirtillo? Wondrous! How
  Didst lose him?
MON:         By that horrid flood which thou
  Hast mentioned. O dear pledge! Thou wert safe then
  When thou wert lost; and now I lose thee when
  I find thee.
CAR:      O eternal providence!
  For what deep end have all these accidents
  Lain hid so long, and now break forth together?
  Some mighty thing thou hast conceivéd, either
  For good or evil. Some unwontéd birth
  Thou art big with, which must be brought on earth.
MON: This was the thing my dream foretold me; too
  Prophetic in the bad, but most untrue
  In the good part. This 'twas which made me melt
  So strangely; this that horror which I felt
  Creep through my bones, when I heaved up my hand.
  For nature's self seemed to recoil, or stand
  Astonishéd, to see a father go
  To give that horrid and forbidden blow.

22. This means 'I would that I had asked less or that you had known less'.

425

CAR: Thou art resolvéd then not to go on
  With this dire sacrifice?
MON:                    No other man
  May do it here.
CAR:                  Shall the son then be slain
  By his own sire?
MON:                   'Tis law; and who dare strain
  His charity to save another man,
  When true Aminta with himself began?
CAR: Oh my sad fate! what am I brought to see?
MON: Two fathers' overacted piety
  Murther their son: thine to Mirtillo, mine
  To heaven. Thou by denying he was thine
  Thought'st to preserve him, and hast lost him; I,
  Searching with too much curiosity,
  Whilst I was to have sacrificed thy son,
  As I supposed, find and must slay my own.
CAR: Behold the horrid monster fate hath teemed!
  O cruel! O Mirtillo, more esteemed
  By me than life! Was this it which to me
  The oracle foretold concerning thee?
  Thus dost thou make me *in my country blest*?
  Oh my dear son, whilom the hope and rest
  But now the grief and bane of these gray hairs!
MON: Prithee, Carino, lend to me those tears;
  I weep for my own blood. Ah, why, if I
  Must spill it, is it mine? Poor son! But why
  Did I beget thee? – Why was I got rather?
  The pitying deluge saved thee, and thy father
  Will cruelly destroy thee. Holy powers
  Immortal! Without some command of yours,
  Not the least wave stirs in the sea, breath in
  The air, nor leaf on earth. What monstrous sin
  Hath been by me committed 'gainst your law,
  This heavy judgement on my head to draw?
  Or if *I* have transgressed so much – wherein
  Sinned my poor son? Wilt thou not pardon him,
  And then with one blast of thy anger kill
  Me, thundering Jove? But if thy bolts lie still,

My blade shall not; I will repeat the sad
Example of Aminta, and the lad
Shall see his father through his own heart run
His reeking blade, rather than kill his son.
Die, then, Montano! Age should lead the way,
And willingly I do't. Powers – shall I say
Of heaven or hell? – that do with anguish drive
Men to despair: behold, I do conceive
(Since you will have it so) your fury! I
Desire no greater blessing than to die.
A kind of dire love to my natural goal
Doth lash me on, and hallow to my soul,
'To death, to death!'

CAR:             'Las, poor old man! In troth
I pity thee; for, though we need it both,
Yet as by day the stars forbear to shine,
My grief is nothing, if compared with thine.

[*Enter* TIRENIO, *the blind old prophet, Right, guided by a* BOY.]

TIR: Make haste, my son; yet tread secure, that I
May without stumbling trace thee through this wry
And craggy way, with my old feet and blind.
Thou art their eyes, as I am to thy mind.
And when thou comest where the priest is, there
Arrest thy pace.

MON:           Ha! Whom do I see here?
Is't not our reverend Tirenio? he
Whose eyes are sealed up earthward, but heaven see?
Some great thing draws him from his sacred cell,
Whence to behold him is a miracle.

CAR: May the good gods pleased in their bounty be
To make his coming prosperous to thee!

MON: Father Tirenio, what miracle
Is this? What mak'st thou from thy holy cell?
Whom dost thou seek? What news?

TIR:               I come to speak
With thee; and news I bring, and news I seek.

MON: But why comes not the holy order back
With the purged offering and what doth lack
Besides to the interrupted sacrifice?

TIR: Oh how much often doth the want of eyes
    Add to the inward sight! For then the soul
    Not gadding forth, but recollected whole
    Into itself, is wont to recompense
    With the mind's eyes the blindness of the sense.
    It is not good to pass so slightly over
    Some great events unlooked for which discover
    In human businesses a hand divine,
    Which through a cloud of seeming chance doth shine.
    For heaven with earth will not familiar be,
    Nor face to face talk with mortality.
    But those great wondrous things which us amaze,
    And on blind chance the more blind vulgar lays,
    Are but heaven's voice: the deathless gods affect
    To speak to mortals in that dialect.
    It is their language, mute unto our ears,
    But loud to him whose understanding hears.
    A thousand times most happy is that wight
    That hath an understanding pitched so right!
    The good Nicandro, as thou gav'st command,
    Was ready now to bring the sacred band,
    Whom I withheld by reason of a change
    That fell out in the temple; which so strange
    Event comparing with what happened here
    At the same time to thee, 'twixt hope and fear
    I know not how, struck and amazed I stand.
    Whereof by how much less I understand
    The cause, so much the more I hope and fear
    Some happiness, or some great danger near.
MON: That which thou understandest not, I do
    Too well, and to my sorrow feel it too.
    But is there aught in hidden fate can shun
    Thy all-divining spirit?
TIR:                Oh my son!
    If the divine use of prophetic light
    Were arbitrary,[23] it would then be hight

23. This means 'If a seer could call on the power of prophecy whenever
he liked, it would be a natural talent instead of a gift from heaven.'

The gift of nature, not of heaven. I find,
'Tis true, within my undigested mind
That there is something hidden in the deep
Bosom of fate, which she from me doth keep,
And this hath moved me now to come to thee
To be informed more clearly who is he
That's found to be the father of the youth
To die now, if Nicandro told us truth.

MON: Thou knowst him but too well, Tirenio.
How wilt thou wish anon that thou didst know
Or love him less?

TIR:              I praise thee, O my son,
For taking pity and compassion
On the afflicted – 'tis humanity.
Howe'er, let me speak with him.

MON:                 Now I see
Heaven hath suspended in thee all that skill
In prophecy which it was wont to instil.
That father whom thou seek'st to speak withal
Am I!

TIR:    Art thou his father, that should fall
To Dian now an immolation?

MON: The wretched father of that wretched son!

TIR: Of that same *faithful shepherd*, who to give
Life to another, would himself not live?

MON: Of him who dies his murderess' life to save,
And murders me, who unto him life gave.

TIR: But is this true?

MON:           Behold the witness!

CAR:                That
Which he hath told thee is most true.

TIR:               And what
Art thou that speakst?

CAR:           Carino, thought to be
Till now the young man's father.

TIR:              Was that he
The flood took from thee long ago?

MON:                Yes, yes,

Tirenio!

TIR:       And dost thou style for this
Thyself a wretched father? Oh how blind
Is an unhallowed and terrestrial mind!
In what thick mists of error, how profound
A night of ignorance are our souls drowned
Till thou enlighten them, from whom the sun
Receives his lustre, as from him the moon!
Vain men, how can you boast of knowledge so?
That part of us by which we see and know
Is not our virtue, but derived from heaven,
That gives it, and can take what it hath given.
O in thy mind, Montano, blinder far
Than I am in mine eyes! What juggler,
What dazzling devil will not let thee see
That if this noble youth was born of thee,
Thou art the happiest father, and most dear
To the immortal deities, that e'er
Begot son in the world? Behold the deep
Secret, which fate did from my knowledge keep!
Behold the happy day, with such a flood
Expected of our tears and of our blood!
Behold the blesséd end of all our pain!
Where art thou, man? Come to thyself again!
How is it that thou only dost forget
That famous happy oracle that's writ
In all Arcadian hearts? How can it be
That with thy dear son's lightning upon thee
This day, thy sense is not prepared and clear
The thunder of that heavenly voice to hear:
'*Your woe shall end when two of race divine*
                      '*Love shall combine;*
(Tears of delight in such abundance flow
Out of my heart, I cannot speak.) '*Your woe . . .*
'*Your woe shall end when two of race divine*
                      '*Love shall combine;*
'*And for a faithless nymph's apostate state*
'*A faithful shepherd supererogate.*'

Now tell me, thou: this shepherd here of whom
We speak, and that should die, is he not come
Of divine race, Montano, if he's thine,
And Amarillis too of race divine?
Then who I pray but love hath them combined?
Silvio by parents and by force was joined
To Amarillis, and is yet as far
From loving her as love and hatred are.
Then scan the rest, and 'twill be evident
The fatal voice none but Mirtillo meant.
For who indeed since slain Aminta hath
Expressed such love as he, such constant faith?
Who but Mirtillo for his mistress would,
Since true Aminta, spend his dearest blood?
This is that work of supererogation:
This is that faithful shepherd's expiation
For the apostate false Lucrina's fact.
By this admired and most stupendious act
More than with human blood the wrath of heaven
Is pacified, and satisfaction given
Unto eternal justice for the offence
Committed 'gainst it by a woman. Hence
It was, that he no sooner came to pay
Devotions in the temple, but straightway
All monstrous omens ceased: no longer stood
The eternal image in a sweat of blood,
The earth no longer shook, the holy cave
No longer stank, and shrieks no longer gave,
But such sweet harmony and redolence
As heaven affords – if heaven affect the sense.
O providence eternal! O ye powers
That look upon us from yon azure towers!
If all my words were souls, and every soul
Were sacrificed upon your altars whole,
It were too poor a hecatomb to pay
So great a blessing with; but as I may,
Behold, I tender thanks, and with my knee
Touching the earth in all humility

Look up on you that sit enthroned in heaven.
How much I am your debtor, that have given
Me leave to live till now! I have run o'er
Of my life's race a hundred years and more,
Yet never lived till now, could never deem
My life worth keeping till this instant time.
Now I begin my life, am born today.
But why in words do I consume away
That time that should be spent in works? Help, son,
To lift me up; thou art the motion
Of my decayéd limbs.

MON:                               Tirenio,
I have a lightness in my bosom so
Locked in, and petrified with wonder, that
I find I'm glad, yet scarcely know at what.
My greedy soul unto herself alone
Keeps all her joy, and lets my sense have none.
O miracle of heaven! far, far beyond
All we have seen, or e'er did understand!
O unexampled bounty! O the great,
Great mercy of the gods! O fortunate
Arcadia! O earth, of all that e'er
The sun beheld or warmed, most blest, most dear
To heaven! Thy weal's so dear to me, mine own
I cannot feel, nor think upon my son
(Twice lost and found) nor of myself buoyed up
Out of the depth of sorrow to the top
Of bliss when I consider thee. But all
My private joy, set by the general,
Is like a little drop in a great stream
Shuffled and lost. O happy dream! (No dream,
But a celestial vision.) *Now again*
*Shall my Arcadia* (as thou saidst) *be in*
A flourishing estate!

TIR:                               But why dost thou
Stay here, Montano? Heaven expects not now
More human sacrifice from us. No more
They are times of wrath and vengeance, as before:

But times of grace and love. Glad nuptial bands,
Not horrid sacrifices at our hands
Our goddess now requires.
TIR:                              How long to night?
MON: An hour, or little more.
TIR:                              We burn daylight.
Back to the holy temple let us go.
There let the daughter of old Titiro
And thy son interchange their marriage vow
To become man and wife, of lovers now.
Then let him bring her to his father's straight,
Where 'tis heaven's pleasure that these fortunate
Descendants of two gods should henceforth run
United in one stream. – Lead me back, son;
And thou, Montano, follow me.
MON:                              But stay:
That faith which formerly she gave away
To Silvio, she cannot now withdraw
And give Mirtillo, without breach of law.
CAR: 'Tis Silvio still, Mirtillo was called so
At first, thy man told me, and 'Silvio'
By me changed to 'Mirtillo', to which he
Consented.
MON:        True – now I remember me.
And the same name I gave unto the other,
To keep alive the memory of his brother.
TIR: 'Twas an important doubt. Follow me now.
MON: Carino, to the temple too come thou!
Henceforth Mirtillo shall two fathers own;
Thou hast a brother found, and I a son.
CAR: To thee a brother in his love, a father
To him, a servant (in respect) to either,
Carino will be always; and since I
Find thee to me so full of courtesy,
I will the boldness take to recommend
Unto thy love my second self, my friend.
MON: Share me between you.
CAR:                              O eternal gods,

Between our prayers' slow-winding paths, what odds
There is (by which we climb to heaven) and those
Directer lines by which to us heaven bows!

[*Exit* TIRENIO, *Right, followed by others. Enter* CORISCA, *Left,*
LINCO, *Right Centre.*]

COR: So it seems, Linco, that coy Silvio,
When least expected, did a lover grow.
But what became of her?

LIN:                    We carried her
To Silvio's dwelling, where with many a tear
(Whether of joy or grief I cannot tell)
His mother welcomed her. It pleased her well
To see her son now married, and a lover;
But for the nymph great grief she did discover.
Poor mother-in-law! ill-sped, though doubly sped:
One daughter-in-law being hurt, the other dead.

COR: Is Amarillis dead?

LIN:                 'Tis rumoured so.
That's now the cause I to the temple go,
To comfort old Montano with this news,
One daughter-in-law he gains, if one he lose.

COR: Is not Dorinda dead, then?

LIN:                       Dead? Would thou
Wert half so live and jocund as she's now!

COR: Was't not a mortal wound?

LIN:                      Had she been slain
With Silvio's pity she had lived again.

COR: What art so soon could cure her?

LIN:                        I will tell
Thee all the cure. Listen to a miracle.
With trembling hearts, and hands prepared to aid,
Women and men stood round the wounded maid.
But she would suffer none to touch her save
Her Silvio: for the same hand which gave,
She said, should cure the wound. So all withdrew
Except myself, he and his mother: two
To advise, the third to act. Then Silvio,
Removing first from her blood-dappled snow,

434

Gently the cleaving garments, strove to pluck
The arrow out, which in her deep wound stuck.
But the false wood, forth coming, gave the slip
To the iron head, and left it in her hip.
Here, here the lamentable cries began:
It was not possible by hand of man,
Or iron instrument, or aught beside,
To get it out. Perchance to have opened wide
The wound by a greater wound, and so have made
One iron dive after another, had
Effected the great cure. But Silvio's hand,
Too pitiful, too much with love unmanned
The surgeon was, so cruelly to heal.
Love searches not with instruments of steel
The wounds he makes. As for the lovesick maid,
In Silvio's hands her wounds grew sweet, she said.
And Silvio said (not yet discouragéd):
'Thou shalt out too, thou shalt, curst arrowhead;
'And with less pain than is believed – the same
'Who thrust thee in can pull thee out again.
'By using hunting I have learned to cure
'This mischief which my hunting did procure.
'A plant there is much used by the wild goat
'When there's a shaft into her body shot.
'She showed it us, and nature showed it her:
'Remembered happily! Nor is it far
'From hence.' Straight went he to the neighbouring hill,
And there a flasket with this plant did fill,
Then came again to us; thence squeezing out
The juice, and mingling it with centaury root
And plaintain leaf, thereof a poultice made.
O wonderful! As soon as that was laid
Upon the sore, the blood was stanchéd straight,
And the pain ceaséd; and soon after that,
The iron coming without pain away,
Did the first summons of the hand obey.
The maid was now as vigorous and sound
As if she never had received the wound.

Nor mortal was't; for the arrow having flown,
As happed, betwixt the muscles and the bone,
Pierced but the fleshy part.

COR:                              Thou hast displayed
Much virtue in a plant, more in a maid.

LIN: What afterwards between them happenéd
May better be imaginéd than said.
This I am sure, Dorinda's well again,
And now can stir her body without pain;
Though thou believ'st, Corisca, I suppose,
He hath given her since more wounds than that; but those,
As they are made by a different weapon, so
Themselves are of a different nature too.
And such a trick this cruel archer has
Of hitting all he shoots at, since he was
A huntsman, that to show he's still the same,
Now he's a lover too he hits the game.

COR: Old Linco still!

LIN:                          Faith, my Corisca, still,
If not in strength, I'm Linco in my will.
Nor yet, though my leaf's withered, am I dead;
But all my sap into the root is fled.

[*Exit* LINCO, *Left.*]

COR [*aside*]: My rival thus despatched, I'll now go see
If I can get my dear Mirtillo free.

[*Enter* ERGASTO, *Right.*]

ERG: O day with wonders fraught! O day of mirth!
All love! and blessings all! O happy earth!
O bounteous heaven!

COR:                          But see! Ergasto's here;
How opportunely doth he now appear!

ERG: At such a time let every living thing,
Heaven, earth, air, fire, the whole world laugh and sing!
To hell itself let our full joys extend,
And there the torments of the damned suspend.

COR: What rapture's this?

ERG:                          Blest woods! whose murmuring voice
When we lamented did lament – rejoice

436

At our joys too, and wag as many tongues
As you have leaves now dancing to the songs
Of the pleased birds, and music of the air
Which rings with our delight! Sing of a pair
Of noble lovers the felicity
Unparalleled!

COR:    He doth speak certainly
Of Silvio and Dorinda. Everything,
I see, would live. How soon the shallow spring
Of tears dries up with us! But the swol'n river
Of gladness tarries with the longer liver.
Of Amarillis, who is dead, there's now
No more discourse; the only care is how
To laugh with them that laugh – and 'tis well done.
Each man hath too much sorrow of his own.
Whither so glad Ergasto dost thou go?
Unto a wedding happily?

ERG:      I do
Indeed. Hast heard, Corisca, then, the wonder
O'th' two blest lovers? Was't not strange?

COR:      I under-
Stood it of Linco now with joy of heart,
Which my great grief doth mitigate in part
For the sad death of Amarillis.

ERG:     How!
Whom dost thou speak of, or speak I, thinkst thou?

COR: Why, of Dorinda and of Silvio.

ERG: What Silvio? What Dorinda? Dost not know
Then what hath passed? My joy its lineage draws
From a more high, stupendous, noble cause.
Of Amarillis and Mirtillo I
Discourse, the happiest pair that this day fry
Under the torrid zone of love.

COR:     Is not
Then Amarillis dead, Ergasto?

ERG:     What
Death? She's alive, glad, beauteous, and a wife.

COR: Thou mockst me, shepherd.

ERG:                                        No, upon my life.
COR: Was she not then condemned?
ERG:                                        She was, 'tis true;
   But presently she was acquitted too.
COR: Do I dream this? or dost thou dreams relate?
ERG: Stay here a little; thou shalt see her straight
   Come with her faithful and most fortunate
   Mirtillo from the temple (where they're now,
   And interchangéd have their nuptial vow)
   Towards Montano's, of the bitter root
   Of their long loves to gather the sweet fruit.
   O hadst thou seen men's joys spring in their eyes!
   If thou hadst heard the music of their cries!
   The temple's still as full as it can hold
   Of numbers numberless; men, women, old,
   Young, prelates, laymen, are confounded there
   Together, and distracted cannot bear
   Their joy. With wonder everyone doth run
   To see the happy couple, everyone
   Adores them, everyone embraces them.
   Their pity one extols, another's theme
   Their constant faith is, or those graces given
   To them by nature, or infused from heaven.
   The lawn, the dale, the mountain, and the plain
   Resound the *faithful shepherd*'s glorious name;
   Oh happy, happy lover, to become
   From a poor swain almost a god so soon.
   From death to life (while I speak this) to pass,
   And change a winding-sheet, which ready was,
   For a remote, despaired-of nuptial,
   Though it be much, Corisca, is not all.
   But to enjoy her, who he seemed to enjoy
   In dying for her – her who would destroy
   Herself, not to excuse, but share his fate –
   His mate in life, and not in death his mate:
   This is such joy, such ravishing joy is this
   As doth exceed all we can fancy bliss.
   And dost not thou rejoice, and apprehend

A joy for Amarillis, that's thy friend,
As great as that which I do for my true
Mirtillo?

COR:      Yes, dost thou not see I do?
ERG: Oh, if thou hadst present been
    Amarillis to have seen,
    As the pledge of faith when she
    Gave her hand to him, and he
    As the pledge of love did either
    Give or receive – I know not whether –
    A sweet inestimable kiss,
    Surely thou hadst died of bliss!
    There was scarlet, there were roses,
    All the colours, all the posies
    Art or nature e'er did mix
    Were excelled by her pure cheeks,
    Covered with a waving shield
    By her blushing beauty held,
    Stained with blood, which did provoke
    From the striker a new stroke.
    And she coy and nice in show,
    Seemed to shun, that she might so
    With more pleasure meet the blow;
    Leaving it in doubt, if that
    Kiss were ravishéd or not.
    With such admirable art
    'Twas in part bestowed, in part
    Snatched from her. And that disdain
    Which she did so sweetly feign,
    Was a willing 'No', an act
    Mixed of conquest and compact.
    Such a coming in her flying
    As showed yielding in denying.
    Such sweet anger at the abuse
    In forcing her, as forced him use
    That force again; such art to crave
    The thing she would not, yet would have,
    As drew him the faster on

To snatch that which would be gone.
O heavenly kiss! Corisca, I
Can no longer hold: Goodbye!
I'll marry too – the powers above
Give no true joy to men but love.
  [*Exit* ERGASTO, *hurriedly, Left.*]
COR: If he, Corisca, have told truth, this day
  Quite cures thy wits, or takes them quite away.
  [*Enter wedding procession, Right, headed by* MIRTILLO *and* AMAR-
  ILLIS. CHORUS *of* SHEPHERDS.]
CHO: Holy Hymen hear our prayer,
  And our song! The earth hath not
  A more happy loving pair,
  Both of them divinely got:
  Pull, holy Hymen, pull the destined knot!
COR: Ay me! Ergasto told me true, I see!
  This is the fruits, wretch, of thy vanity!
  O thoughts! O wishes! as injust, as vain
  And fond. Would I an innocent have slain
  To compass my unbridled will? So blind,
  So cruel was I? Who doth now unbind
  Mine eyes? Ah wretch! What do I see? – My sin
  With the mask off just as 'tis here within!
CHO: Holy Hymen hear our prayer,
  And our song! The earth hath not
  A more happy loving pair,
  Both of them divinely got:
  Pull, holy Hymen, pull the destined knot!
  See, thou *faithful shepherd*, where
  After many a briny tear,
  After many a stormy blast,
  Thou art landed now at last.
  Is not this – behold her! – she
  Heaven and earth denied to thee?
  And thy cruel destiny?
  And her icy chastity?
  And thy degree so far beneath?
  And her contract? and thy death?

Yet, Mirtillo, lo! she's thine.
That sweet face, those eyes divine,
Breast and hands, and all that thou
Seest and hearst, and touchest now,
And so often hast in vain
Sighed for, now thou dost obtain,
As thy constant love's reward:
Yet thy lips hath silence barred?
MIR: 'Cannot speak; I do not know
Whether I'm alive or no,
Or if these things real be
Which I seem to hear and see.
Sweetest Amarillis mine
(For my soul is lodged in thine)
I from thee would gladly know –
Tell me, love, are these things so?
CHO: Holy Hymen hear our prayer,
And our song! The earth hath not
A more happy loving pair,
Both of them divinely got:
Pull, holy Hymen, pull the destined knot!
[CORISCA *hesitates, and begins to shed some of her finery.*]
COR: But why do you, you still about me stay,
Arts to deceive the world, arts to betray?
The body's robes, but the soul's rags! For one,
I'm sure she's cozened by you, and undone.
[*Strewing silks before the bride's feet.*]
Pack hence; and as from worms ye had your birth,
Return to worms, and strew your grandame earth.
Once ye were weapons of lascivious love:
But now the trophies of fair virtue prove!
CHO: Holy Hymen hear our prayer,
And our song! The earth hath not
A more happy loving pair,
Both of them divinely got:
Pull, holy hymen, pull the destined knot!
COR: What sticks thou at, Corisca? 'Tis a day
Of pardons, this: then ask without dismay!

What dost thou dread? No punishment whate'er
Can fall so heavy as thy fault lies here.
Fair and happy pair – the love
Of us here and those above –
If all earthly power this day
To your conquering fates give way,
Let her likewise homage do
To your conquering fates, and you,
Who all earthly power employed
To have made their ordinance void.
Amarillis! true it is,
He had mine, who had thy heart;
But thou only hast gained his,
'Cause thou only worthy art.
Thou enjoy'st the loyal'st lad
Living; and, Mirtillo, thou
The best nymph the world e'er had
From the birth of time till now.
I the touchstone was to both:
Tried her chastity, his troth.
But, thou courteous nymph, before
Thou on me thy anger pour,
Look but on thy bridegroom's face:
Something thou wilt spy therein
That will force thee to show grace,
As it forcéd me to sin.
For so sweet a lover's sake
Upon love no vengeance take:
But, since thou the flames dost prove,
Pardon thou the fault of love!
AM: I do not only pardon, but respect
    Thee as my friend, regarding the effect,
    And not the cause. For poisons, if they make
    Us well, the name of sovereign medicines take;
    And painful lancings for that cause are dear.
    So whether friend or foe, or whatsoe'er
    Thou wert to me in purpose and intent,
    Yet my fate used thee as her instrument

To work my bliss, and that's enough. For me
'Twas a good treason, a blest fallacy
I'm sure. And if thou please to grace our feast,
And to rejoice with us, thou art my guest.

COR: Thy pardon is to me a better feast;
A greater joy, my conscience now at rest.

MIR: And I all faults 'gainst me can pardon well
But this long stop.

COR:                    Joys on you both! Farewell!

[*Exit* CORISCA, *Left.*]

CHO: Holy Hymen hear our prayer,
And our song! The earth hath not
A more happy loving pair,
Both of them divinely got:
Pull, holy Hymen, pull the destined knot!

MIR: Am I so wedded then to grief and anguish
That in the midst of joy too I must languish?
Was not this tedious pomp enough delay,
But I must meet too my old remora
Corisca?

AM:      Thou art wondrous hasty.

MIR:                              Oh
My treasure, yet I am not sure, but go
In fear of robbing still, till as my spouse
I do possess thee in my father's house.
To tell thee true, methinks I fare like one
Who dreams of wealth, and ever and anon
Fears that his golden sleep will break, and he
Be waked a beggar. I would gladly be
Resolved by some more pregnant proof, that this
Sweet waking now is not a dream of bliss.

CHO: Holy Hymen hear our prayer,
And our song! The earth hath not
A more happy loving pair,
Both of them divinely got:
Pull, holy Hymen, pull the destined knot!

[*Wedding procession continues across stage and exit Left.*]

CHO: O happy couple, that hath sown in tears,

443

And reaps in comfort! What a foil your fears
Prove to your joys! Blind mortals, learn from hence,
Learn, ye effeminate, the difference
Betwixt true goods and false. All is not joy
That tickles us; nor is all that annoy
That goes down bitter. True joy is a thing
That springs from virtue after suffering.

# FOR THE BEST IN PAPERBACKS, LOOK FOR THE

In every corner of the world, on every subject under the sun, Penguin represents quality and variety – the very best in publishing today.

For complete information about books available from Penguin – including Pelicans, Puffins, Peregrines and Penguin Classics – and how to order them, write to us at the appropriate address below. Please note that for copyright reasons the selection of books varies from country to country.

**In the United Kingdom:** Please write to *Dept E.P., Penguin Books Ltd, Harmondsworth, Middlesex, UB7 0DA*

If you have any difficulty in obtaining a title, please send your order with the correct money, plus ten per cent for postage and packaging, to *PO Box No 11, West Drayton, Middlesex*

**In the United States:** Please write to *Dept BA, Penguin, 299 Murray Hill Parkway, East Rutherford, New Jersey 07073*

**In Canada:** Please write to *Penguin Books Canada Ltd, 2801 John Street, Markham, Ontario L3R 1B4*

**In Australia:** Please write to the *Marketing Department, Penguin Books Australia Ltd, P.O. Box 257, Ringwood, Victoria 3134*

**In New Zealand:** Please write to the *Marketing Department, Penguin Books (NZ) Ltd, Private Bag, Takapuna, Auckland 9*

**In India:** Please write to *Penguin Overseas Ltd, 706 Eros Apartments, 56 Nehru Place, New Delhi, 110019*

**In Holland:** Please write to *Penguin Books Nederland B.V., Postbus 195, NL–1380AD Weesp, Netherlands*

**In Germany:** Please write to *Penguin Books Ltd, Friedrichstrasse 10–12, D–6000 Frankfurt Main 1, Federal Republic of Germany*

**In Spain:** Please write to *Longman Penguin España, Calle San Nicolas 15, E–28013 Madrid, Spain*

**In France:** Please write to *Penguin Books Ltd, 39 Rue de Montmorency, F-75003, Paris, France*

**In Japan:** Please write to *Longman Penguin Japan Co Ltd, Yamaguchi Building, 2–12–9 Kanda Jimbocho, Chiyoda-Ku, Tokyo 101, Japan*

### Netochka Nezvanova   Fyodor Dostoyevsky

Dostoyevsky's first book tells the story of 'Nameless Nobody' and introduces many of the themes and issues which dominate his great masterpieces.

### Selections from the Carmina Burana   A verse translation by David Parlett

The famous songs from the *Carmina Burana* (made into an oratorio by Carl Orff) tell of lecherous monks and corrupt clerics, drinkers and gamblers, and the fleeting pleasures of youth.

### Fear and Trembling   Søren Kierkegaard

A profound meditation on the nature of faith and submission to God's will which examines with startling originality the story of Abraham and Isaac.

### Selected Prose   Charles Lamb

Lamb's famous essays (under the strange pseudonym of Elia) on anything and everything have long been celebrated for their apparently innocent charm; this major new edition allows readers to discover the darker and more interesting aspects of Lamb.

### The Picture of Dorian Gray   Oscar Wilde

Wilde's superb and macabre novella, one of his supreme works, is reprinted here with a masterly Introduction and valuable notes by Peter Ackroyd.

### A Treatise of Human Nature   David Hume

A universally acknowledged masterpiece by 'the greatest of all British Philosophers' – A. J. Ayer

# FOR THE BEST IN PAPERBACKS, LOOK FOR THE 🐧

## PENGUIN CLASSICS

**A Passage to India**   E. M. Forster

Centred on the unresolved mystery in the Marabar Caves, Forster's great work provides the definitive evocation of the British Raj.

**The Republic**   Plato

The best-known of Plato's dialogues, *The Republic* is also one of the supreme masterpieces of Western philosophy whose influence cannot be overestimated.

**The Life of Johnson**   James Boswell

Perhaps the finest 'life' ever written, Boswell's *Johnson* captures for all time one of the most colourful and talented figures in English literary history.

**Metamorphoses**   Ovid

A golden treasury of myths and legends which has proved a major influence on Western literature.

**A Nietzsche Reader**   Friedrich Nietzsche

A superb selection from all the major works of one of the greatest thinkers and writers in world literature, translated into clear, modern English.

**Madame Bovary**   Gustave Flaubert

With *Madame Bovary* Flaubert established the realistic novel in France; while his central character of Emma Bovary, the bored wife of a provincial doctor, remains one of the great creations of modern literature.